Confucian Liberalism

SUNY series in Chinese Philosophy and Culture

Roger T. Ames, editor

Confucian Liberalism
Mou Zongsan and Hegelian Liberalism

ROY TSENG

Published by State University of New York Press, Albany

© 2023 State University of New York

All rights reserved

Printed in the United States of America

No part of this book may be used or reproduced in any manner whatsoever without written permission. No part of this book may be stored in a retrieval system or transmitted in any form or by any means including electronic, electrostatic, magnetic tape, mechanical, photocopying, recording, or otherwise without the prior permission in writing of the publisher.

For information, contact State University of New York Press, Albany, NY
www.sunypress.edu

Library of Congress Cataloging-in-Publication Data

Name: Tseng, Roy, author.
Title: Confucian liberalism : Mou Zongsan and Hegelian liberalism / Roy Tseng.
Description: Albany : State University of New York Press, [2023] | Series: SUNY series in Chinese philosophy and culture | Includes bibliographical references and index.
Identifiers: LCCN 2022013287 | ISBN 9781438491110 (hardcover : alk. paper) | ISBN 9781438491134 (ebook) | ISBN 9781438491127 (pbk. : alk paper)
Subjects: LCSH: Mou, Zongsan. | Confucianism. | Liberalism. | Hegel, Georg Wilhelm Friedrich, 1770–1831.
Classification: LCC B5234.M674 T74 2022 | DDC 181/.112—dc23/eng/20220826
LC record available at https://lccn.loc.gov/2022013287

10 9 8 7 6 5 4 3 2 1

To my wife, Nadia (殷齊)
my son, Elliot (俋理), and my daughter, Claire (恪理)

Contents

Acknowledgments ix

Abbreviations xi

Introduction: Confucianism Meets Liberalism 1

Part I: Confucian Ethics

Chapter 1 Confucianism in Comparative Perspective 27

Chapter 2 Returning to Moral Religion 59

Chapter 3 The Endless Pursuit of Self-Perfection 89

Part II: Civil Liberalism

Chapter 4 Democracy and the Politics of Innovation 115

Chapter 5 Civility and the Renovation of Tradition 143

Chapter 6 The Confucian Political Ideal Revisited 183

Part III: Perfectionist Liberalism

Chapter 7 Confucian *Res Publica*: Citizens and the State 211

Chapter 8 Freedom and Rights	245
Conclusion	275
Notes	281
Bibliography	347
Index	367

Acknowledgments

This book was initially conceived when I held a visiting scholarship post (2013–2014) at Cardiff University, UK, where I learned incalculable amounts from the thought-provoking talks I had with Professor David Boucher and Professor Andrew Vincent. As celebrated experts of British idealism, they greatly inspired my Hegelian reading of New Confucianism. Their kindness and care, too, remain an abiding memory of my stay.

I would like to extend my appreciation to the Ministry of Science and Technology, Taiwan, for its generous support of this book project through the *Renwen Xingyuan* Scholarly Monograph Grant (人文行遠專書寫作計畫). I am more than pleased to express my overwhelming thanks to Professor Stephen C. Angle, Professor Ming-Huei Lee (李明輝), Professor Norman Y. Teng (鄧育仁), Professor Kuan-Min Huang (黃冠閔), Professor Yuan-Tse Lin (林遠澤), Professor Chia-Ming Chen (陳嘉銘), Professor Alvin Chen (陳禹仲), Professor Sungmoon Kim (金聖文), Professor David Elstein, and Professor Max Lin (林子立), who have contributed extraordinary academic insights and comments throughout my writing process. I am, as well, thankful to Professor Chin-Shing Huang (黃進興), Professor Carl Shaw (蕭高彥), Professor Joseph Chan (陳祖為), and Professor Wing-Cheuk Chan (陳榮灼), for their conversations. All of them are exemplary academics in their own right, and I have been immeasurably fortunate to learn from them. My deep gratitude also goes to my colleagues at the Research Center for Humanities and Social Sciences, Academia Sinica, especially the director of the Center for Political Thought, Professor I-Chung Chen (陳宜中). I am extremely indebted to the brilliant group of political theorists in Taiwan; many of them have steered my philosophical thinking further than I could imagine.

Hsiao-Chun Wang (汪曉君), Claire Wang (王慧瑀), I-Fu Chao (趙翊夫), and Stella Chan (詹乃潔) have been loyal readers, and I honestly appreciate their keen editorial assistance. I truly thank editor Kent M. Suárez for his major help. Special thanks to my students, Chia-Hao Hsu (許家豪), Brian Chen (陳建綱), James Liu (劉佳昊), Adan Shen (沈明璁), and Wayne Lee (李煒) for their sincere friendship. I also would like to show my heartfelt thanks to SUNY editor of Chinese Philosophy and Culture Series, Professor Roger Ames, and SUNY Press codirector James Peltz, who work with artistry and commitment and whose guidance has been indispensable. For their supportive feedback and advice, I am grateful to the two anonymous reviewers of the manuscript.

Most importantly, without the unfailing support from my family, this book never could have been written. In gratitude and love, I dedicate this book to my wife, Nadia (殷齊), and to my son and daughter, Elliot (伲理) and Claire (恪理). Much more should be said here.

In closing, I may have accumulated more debts than it is possible to enumerate in a short note, and I hope for a chance to thank everyone in person.

Many thanks as well for permission to republish revisions of previous publications:

An earlier version of chapter 2 appeared as "Revisiting Mou Tsung-san's Idea of Moral Religion: A Dialogue with Hegel and T. H. Green," in *Intellectual History* 4 (2015): 168–223.

An earlier version of chapter 3 appeared as "The Endless Pursuit of Self-Perfection: A Hidden Dialogue between Mou Zongsan and F. H. Bradley," in *Philosophy East and West* 69, no. 3 (2019): 828–48.

An earlier version of chapter 6 appeared as "Political Meritocracy versus Ethical Democracy: The Confucian Political Ideal Revisited," in *Philosophy and Social Criticism* 46, no. 9 (2020): 1033–52.

Substantial changes have been made to an earlier version of chapter 8, which appeared as "The Idea of Freedom in Comparative Perspective: Critical Comparisons between the Discourses of Liberalism and Neo-Confucianism," in *Philosophy East and West* 66, no. 2 (2016): 539–58.

Abbreviations

Works by Mou Zongsan [Mou Tsung-San] 牟宗三

CW   *Mou Zongsan xiansheng quanji* 牟宗三先生全集 (Complete Works of Mou Zongsan) (Taipei: Linking Publishing Co., 2003), 33 vols.

MYX   *Mingjia yu Xunzi* 名家與荀子 (School of Names and Xunzi) (Taipei: Xuesheng shuju, 1979); collected in *CW* II-(1).

XYX   *Xinti yu xingti* 心體與性體 (Mind-Reality and Xing-Reality) (Taipei: Zhengzhong shuju, 1968–1969), 3 vols.; collected in *CW* V, VI, and VII.

DLX   *Daode de lixiangzhuyi* 道德的理想主義 (Moral Idealism) (Taipei: Xuesheng shuju, 1959); collected in *CW* IX-(1).

LSZ   *Lishi zhexue* 歷史哲學 (Philosophy of History) (Taipei: Xuesheng shuju, 1988); collected in *CW* IX-(2).

ZYZ   *Zhengdao yu zhidao* 政道與治道 (The Way of Politics and the Way of Governance) (Taipei: Xuesheng shuju, 1961); collected in *CW* X.

ZDZ   *Zhi de zhijue yu Zhongguo zhexue* 智的直覺與中國哲學 (Intellectual Intuition and Chinese Philosophy) (Taipei: Commercial Press, 1971); collected in *CW* XX.

XYW   *Xianxiang yu wuzishen* 現象與物自身 (Phenomena and Noumena) (Taipei: Xuesheng shuju, 1975); collected in *CW* XXI.

YSL   *Yuanshan lun* 圓善論 (On the Summum Bonum) (Taipei: Xuesheng shuju, 1985); collected in *CW* XXII.

SYG	*Shidai yu ganshou* 時代與感受 (Impression of the Times) (Taipei: Ehu chubanshe, 1995); collected in CW XXIII.
SYGX	*Shidai yu ganshou xupian* 時代與感受續編 (The Sequel to Impression of the Times); collected in CW XXIV.
ZAO	*Zaoqi wenji* 早期文集 (Early Writings); collected in CW XXV and XXVI.
RJL	*Renwen jiangxi lu* 人文講習錄 (Lectures on Humanity) (Taipei: Xuesheng shuju, 1996); collected in CW XXVIII-(1).
ZZT	*Zhongguo zhexue de tezhi* 中國哲學的特質 (The Features of Chinese Philosophy) (Taipei: Xuesheng shuju, 1963); collected in CW XXVIII-(2).
SJJ	*Zhongguo zhexue shijiu jiang* 中國哲學十九講 (Nineteen Lectures on Chinese Philosophy) (Taipei: Xuesheng shuju, 1983); collected in CW XXIX.
SM	*Shengming de xuewen* 生命的學問 (The Learning of Life) (Taipei: Sanmin shuju, 1970). This is the only book that is not included in the Complete Works of Mou Zongsan, owing to a copyright issue.
SSJ	*Zhongxi zhexue zhi huitong shisi jiang* 中西哲學之會通十四講 (Fourteen Lectures on the Merging of Chinese and Western Philosophy) (Taipei: Xuesheng shuju, 1990); collected in CW XXX-(1).
WZ	*Wushi zishu* 五十自述 (Autobiography at the Age of Fifty) (Taipei: Ehu chubanshe, 1989); collected in CW XXXII-(1).
SM	*Shengming de xuewen* 生命的學問 (The Learning of Life) (Taipei: Sanmin shuju, 1970). This is the only book not included in Complete Works of Mou Zongsan, owing to a copyright issue.

Translations

NL	*Nineteen Lectures on Chinese Philosophy: A Brief Outline of Chinese Philosophy and the Issues It Entails*, trans. Esther C. Su (San Jose: The Foundation for the Study of Chinese Philosophy and Culture, 2015).
LW	*Late Works of Mou Zongsan: Selected Essays on Chinese Philosophy*, ed. and trans. Jason Clower (Leiden and Boston: Brill, 2014).

Introduction

Confucianism Meets Liberalism

The Main Purposes of the Book

The rationale of this book is to examine the possibility and plausibility of what I shall call "Confucian liberalism" from a comparative viewpoint. To this end, I shall focus on the reverberations and intersections between the discourses of Chinese Confucianism and European liberalism, primarily through a concentration on the thought of Mou Zongsan [Mou Tsung-San] (牟宗三 1909–1995), the most original and probably the most conspicuous thinker in the New Confucianism (*Xinrujia* 新儒家) of Taiwan and Hong Kong. Taken as a whole, the materials presented in this book will comprise a cross-cultural panorama of theorizing on morality, civility, and politics in the Chinese-speaking world, paving the way toward a fusion of the horizons of Confucian legacy and Hegelian liberalism. As such, not only is it aimed at presenting a "rooted global philosophy,"[1] to use Stephen Angle's phrase, but it is also intended to extend a renewed reconstruction of Mou Zongsan's philosophy along the lines of reexamining the reception of liberal expressions in the Chinese context.

CROSS-CULTURAL DIALOGUE

As far as cross-cultural dialogue is concerned, my study will involve three major strands of inquiry. First, in light of the *ideological debate* regarding cultural encounter, Confucian liberalism is conceived in objection to the two extreme poles identified as the Western-centric and the Sino-centric, or more exactly, anti-Confucian liberalism and antiliberal Confucianism, still hovering over Chinese political discourse. Indeed, in the realm of Chinese political discussion, the stereotype often has it that where liberalism accommodates the values of individuality, democracy, freedom, and rights, Confucianism appreciates instead those of community, meritocracy, "inner sagehood" (*neisheng* 內聖), and duty. Against this context, Mou Zongsan serves as a good starting point for seeking moral resonance, civil essence, and political reverberation across cultures because his ideas are formulated within an immediate comparative scheme, in search of a reconciliation between Confucianism and Western democracy (and science). In the main, aspiring to overcome the moral crisis of mainstream liberalism and the political pitfalls of traditional Confucianism all at once, Mou has established, as I hope to make clear, a Hegelian form of ethical liberalism rooted in the spirit of *ren* 仁 (humaneness). That said, far from seeing New Confucianism as a philosophical school pervaded by nostalgia for a past age, what concerns me here is the manner in which it brings out a "politics of innovation" within the "Confucian forms of life."

Second, as regards the pursuit of *mutual understanding* between different cultures,[2] it seems to me that the "standard viewpoint" fostered by scholars of both extreme poles consists of a partial appreciation of liberal values in particular and Western modernity in general. As a result, a substantial part of this book is designed to make explicit the crucial but often overlooked relevance of British idealism (as a Hegelian liberalism) in making sense of the ethical import of liberal vocabulary appearing in the writings of New Confucianism.[3] Put in other terms, on top of Kant and Hegel, my work will bring together for the first time New Confucianism and British idealism so as to arrive at a renovated appreciation of liberal values in Confucian terms. Accordingly, in spite of staying sensitive to cultural differences,[4] my main objective is to build the conceptual bonds between a particular stream of Confucianism and a certain form of liberalism. My key claim is that despite the divergences, there are significant commonalities to be discovered between these apparently distinct philosophical traditions, particularly in the way in which they construct their core arguments for an "ethics of self-realization," a "deep concern for civility," and a "perfectionist reading of politics," which in turn reveal to us the shared value of human dignity across cultures.

Third, in terms of reassessing *liberal vocabulary* from a cross-cultural perspective, central to this book is an endeavor to explore the formulation of a specific set of "idealist" expressions of subjectivity, individuality, democracy, citizenship, open society, the state, freedom, rights, and so on, in the Chinese-speaking world. Overall, I am trying to make a case that, as with the British idealists, Mou in his Hegel-inspired political writings has embarked on a revolutionary bid to merge the spirit of *ren* with a cluster of Hegelian political expressions into an anticipation of Confucian liberalism. In other words, through the lens of British idealists, it is hoped that the mapping of liberalism in the Chinese context can be recast in a significant way.

The Study of Mou Zongsan

Consistent with the three layers of questions concerning cross-cultural dialogue, the general picture of Mou's philosophy delineated in the book will be remarkably *distinctive* in three basic senses, in that it will emphasize the "spirit of reconciliation," engagement with contemporary Confucian political theory, and a turn to Hegel and beyond.

First, despite Mou's enormous achievement in theorizing on the prospect of Confucian liberalism, his Hegelian presentation of the "blossoming of democracy" (*minzhu kaichu* 民主開出) has been severely criticized by both anti-Confucian liberalism and antiliberal Confucianism. Insofar as my proposal for Confucian liberalism is at odds with the "standard viewpoint," an underlying theme of this book is to bring the "spirit of reconciliation" out of Mou's work with the purpose of defying the widespread tendency to assert an uncompromising incongruence between Western democratic politics and Confucian "humane government" (*renzheng* 仁政). In this manner, the ultimate goal of Mou's political philosophy can be seen as an attempt to offer a synthesis of the several pairs of ideas that are usually believed to be in opposition to each other, including the antagonism between the individual and community, the conflict between citizens and the state, the contrast between negative and positive freedom, the asymmetry between right and good, and so forth.

Second, the landscape of contemporary Confucian political theory has been dramatically altered for the past two decades or so, but the names of Mou and other leading New Confucians are only mentioned in passing.[5] To make the most of the legacy of New Confucianism, I plan to place Mou into the context of the updated debate between "Confucian democracy" and "Confucian meritocracy." In so doing, it will be reaffirmed that Mou's political thinking, if properly reconstructed in a

Hegelian vein, will give us renovated ground to relocate democracy and liberal values into the *Confucian lived forms of life.*

Third, the attack on Hegel's political philosophy, made by cold war liberals such as Isaiah Berlin and Karl Popper,[6] had a lasting impact on the reception of liberalism in the Chinese context; even Mou's disciples have afterward turned to recast Confucian democracy by reference to Kantian liberalism. In contrast to major scholarship on Mou's studies *solely* focusing on the importance of Kant, my exploration will bring back the bearing of Hegel and the British idealists in reconsidering the historic achievement of New Confucianism. To be sure, one of my primary objectives in this book is to reconstruct a theoretical outlook of Confucian liberalism via a series of dialogues between Mou, Kant, Hegel, and the British idealists. By this means, we are expected to arrive at a deeper understanding of the diversity of liberalisms and a profounder reassessment of the affinities between New Confucianism and Hegelian liberalism in respect of an ethics of self-realization and a set of liberal expressions at stake.

New Confucianism and Hegelian Liberalism

Before placing Mou's work into the context of contemporary Confucian political theory, let me first say something about the specific current of Confucianism that concerns me in this book, followed by a description of the general meaning of liberalism and the noteworthy relevance of British idealism.

The Significance of New Confucianism

I must confess from the beginning that a full examination of the historical background from which New Confucianism emerges is beyond the scope of the book.[7] To make obvious the significance of New Confucianism, as John Makeham remarks, a preliminary differentiation has to be made between "Confucian revivalism"—a "conservative cultural phenomenon" that has taken various forms in modern China—and New Confucianism as a "distinctive philosophical movement" that was *retrospectively* identified in the early 1980s.[8] In retrospection, as we are normally told, there have been, by and large, three generations of New Confucianism:[9] the first generation embraces the eminent thinkers such as Xiong Shili [Hsiung

Shih-Li] (熊十力 1885–1968), Liang Shuming [Liang Shu-Ming] (梁漱溟 1893–1988), Feng Youlan [Fung Yu-Lan] (馮友蘭 1895–1990), and He Lin (賀麟 1902–1993); the second one mainly comprises the four leading philosophers who signed the milestone "Declaration on Behalf of Chinese Culture Respectively Announced to the People of the World" (*Wei Zhongguo wenhua jinggao shijie renshi xuanyan* 為中國文化敬告世界人士宣言 1958), namely, Zhang Junmai [Carsun Chang] (張君勱 1887–1969), Xu Fuguan [Hsu Fu-Kuan] (徐復觀 1904–1982), Tang Junyi [Tang Chun-I] (唐君毅 1909–1978), and Mou Zongsan; finally, the well-known scholars affiliated with the third generation in promoting Confucianism globally include Liu Shuxian [Liu Shu-Hsien] (劉述先 1934–2016), Cheng Zhongying [Cheng Chung-Ying] (成中英), Jin Yaoji [Ambrose Yeo-Chi King] (金耀基), and Tu Weiming [Tu Wei-Ming] (杜維明).

Among the New Confucians, Mou's philosophical accomplishment is most impressive to many commentators; in my view, Mou can be justifiably regarded as the most important Chinese philosopher in the twentieth century. Considering the themes of this book, my usage of the term "New Confucianism" will largely be confined to the "most specific" meaning in Yu Yingshi's [Yu Ying-Shih] (余英時 1930–2021) definition, namely, "those people who belong to Xiong Shili's 'school' (*pai* 派),"[10] chiefly taking account of Mou Zongsan, Tang Junyi, and Xu Fuguan. To be sure, in Mou's own classification, following the first period of the pre-Qin founders of authentic Confucianism, viz., Confucius and Mencius, and the second period of Song-Ming Neo-Confucianism, the ultimate goal of the third period of New Confucianism is to make possible "three unities" (*santong* 三統): to re-erect the "orthodoxy of Confucianism" (*daotong* 道統), to accept the "knowledge of science" (*xuetong* 學統), and to develop the "politics of democracy" (*zhengtong* 政統).[11] In this book, nonetheless, I shall focus on the topics of *daotong* and *zhengtong* in respect of Mou's moral and political philosophy, largely putting aside Mou's discussion of *xuetong* in respect of epistemology.

As regards morality, it is notable to observe that Mou, Tang, and Xu were all greatly influenced by Xiong Shili, "the first philosopher after Wang Yangming [Wang Yang-Ming] (王陽明 1472–1529) to inherit and promote moral spirituality in general, and moral metaphysics in particular."[12] For this reason, the most representative cultural mission of the Declaration stated above consists of a robust commitment to the "learning of the heart-mind and *Xing*-nature (human nature)" (*xin xing zhi xue* 心性之學), that is, a philosophical reexamination of the moral perfectibility of humanity with regard to a comprehensive theory of moral metaphysics. As we shall see, Mou spent most of his intellectual life re-erecting the new *daotong* in support of the "learning of the heart-mind and *Xing*-nature."[13]

In terms of politics, the philosophical endeavor to combine the Confucian tradition with political modernity was, among others, initiated by Xiong Shili's transfiguration of democracy as the new crux of "outer kingliness" (*waiwang* 外王). Greatly inspired by Xiong, Mou, Tang, and Xu were eager to establish, in their own way, Confucian democracy as the hub of the "new outer kingliness" (*xin waiwang* 新外王), that is, what Mou refers to as *zhengtong*. Contrary to the "standard viewpoint" in question, it seems plain that the cultural hybridity identified as Confucian democracy in their writings is all but hostile to both the extreme poles of anti-Confucian liberalism and antiliberal Confucianism.

More precisely, the New Confucians generally agree that there are two related but distinguishable aspects of democracy, namely, moral and political (also referred to as rational and institutional). And thus, it is likely that the moral spirit of Confucianism may provide solid ground for the functioning of democratic institutions, as long as the "moral rationality"—to use Tang Junyi's phrase—spelling out the character of Confucianism in respect of dignity and respect is to be reunited with liberal democracy through practice.[14]

In no way, then, do the New Confucians deny that the pursuit of "rule by *de*" (*dezhi* 德治) in the Confucian tradition might have hindered the development of democracy in ancient China. But this gives us no sufficient reason to infer that the moral spirit of Confucianism, if properly rebuilt, will do more harm than good to democracy. For the most part, it is against this context that Xu Fuguan sets out to embark on a ground-breaking examination of the disparity between "cultivating oneself" (*xiuji* 修己) and "governing the people" (*zhiren* 治人) in Confucianism, resulting in a potential differentia between the personal and the public.[15]

Put clearly, the New Confucians actually realize that the institutions of democracy cannot develop out of Confucianism *itself* directly, for to develop democracy *in real terms* involves the will to power, the conflict of interest, class struggle, and so forth. But *in philosophical terms*, a disclosure of the anticipation of democracy in Chinese societies will definitely be insufficient, if we refuse to ask this vital question: *How can democracy work at all in a cultural setting traditionally fostered by Confucian civilization?* Consequently, for the New Confucians, the starting point for examining the possibility and plausibility of merging liberal democracy with Confucian culture is a bid to develop a "significantly different political philosophy."[16] All things considered, one of the main tasks of Confucian political philosophy at present is to connect the basis of democracy, not with the morality of Confucianism as a whole—this is apparently the business of a "moral metaphysics"—but with a restatement of the moral principles of "governing the people," or to put it another way, the moral codes of the Confucian political ideal.

THE NEW OUTER KINGLINESS

For this reason, Mou thus progresses to make a famous distinction between the "way of politics" (*zhengdao* 政道) associated with the institutions and values of democratic politics and the "way of governance" (*zhidao* 治道) related to moral cores of "humane government," that is, the Confucian political ideal in Mou's restatement. Ostensibly, a significant part of Mou's political philosophy is designed to provide an in-depth analysis of the disparity between the "way of politics" and the "way of governance" in relation to a series of contrasting terms.

In a basic sense, the "way of politics" is taken to mean the "objective form" of "constitutional democracy," which could serve as the most credible justification for the "legitimacy of political authority" at the end of the day, whereas the "way of governance" presents the "essential elements" of "humane government," spelling out the "virtue of the ruler" in traditional Confucianism. These concepts, in Mou's scrutiny, are basically in line with the two distinguishable presentations of human reason. In a nutshell, the "way of politics" is grounded in the "constructive presentation of reason" (*lixing zhi jiagou biaoxian* 理性之架構表現), which is aimed at developing the situation of "Sub-Ordination" (*duilie zhi ju* 對列之局) under the name of Understanding (*zhixing* 知性), whereas the "way of governance" is associated with the "functional presentation of reason" (*lixing zhi yunyong biaoxian* 理性之運用表現), which is intended to retain the relationship of "Co-Ordination" (*lishu quanxi* 隸屬關係) in favor of a harmonious moral order. Or alternatively, as Mou puts it elsewhere, the "way of politics" and the "way of governance" also can be appreciated as two different dimensions of democracy, namely, the "extensional meaning of democracy" (*minzhu zhi waiyan de yiyi* 民主

之外延的意義) concerning "political power" (*zhengquan* 政權) and the "intensional meaning of democracy" (*minzhu zhi neirong de yiyi* 民主之內容的意義) regarding "governing power" (*zhiquan* 治權).

In the course of this book, we shall have opportunities to make clear the significance of these technical terms where appropriate. For now, it is more urgent to single out that unlike the most scholarship on Mou's political thinking, concentrating on the novelty of the "way of politics" alone, I contend that to fully grasp Mou's discussion of the subtlest model of Confucian democracy, the "way of politics" and the "way governance" are of equal importance. That said, in accordance with my endeavor to employ a Hegelian reinterpretation of Mou's political thought, the focus of attention will be evenly directed to Mou's decisive invention of the "way of politics," as well as his critical recovery of the moral elements of the "way of governance" as the key ingredients of what I shall call "Confucian democratic civility," or alternatively, a set of "Confucian public virtues" constituting Confucian *res publica*. In this manner, the voice of Mou's democratic theory presented in this book is unique, in that to adopt a saying of Feng Youlan, the author is devoted to "continuing" (*jiezhu* 接著) rather than "repeating" (*zhaozhu* 照著) what Mou has said about the prospect of the "new outer kingliness,"[17] leading to a fuller understanding of Confucian liberalism.

To be more precise, it is my central argument that while the "way of politics" denotes a "politics of innovation" in the face of the newly emergent *historical condition* identified as the age of democracy, Mou's discussion of the core characteristics of the "way of governance" actually gives rise to a democratic rebuilding of "Confucian civility," or so to speak, "Confucian democratic civility," whose function resembles the "etiquette of democracy," to use Stephen Carter's expression,[18] in an open society. Or, to put it another way, Mou's Confucian liberalism is all but a "Confucian" way of re-evaluating liberal values in the sense that the moral foundation of democracy is, after all, based on Confucian *res publica*, that is, a Confucian notion of the common good surrounded by a set of Confucian governing and civic virtues.

As such, despite the fact that Mou repudiates antiliberal Confucianism for the benefit of democracy, he insists at the same time that democracy cannot be separated from morality for good as anti-Confucian liberalism claims, mainly because good operation of democracy in the Chinese cultural setting must rest on a well-ordered civil society grounded in Confucian *res publica*, consistent with the elements of "humane government." In short, Mou's presentation of Confucian liberalism, far from sliding into the extremes of Western-centrism and Sino-centrism, makes a Hegelian synthesis of the "way of politics" and the "way of governance."

THE FAMILY OF LIBERALISMS

Instead of treating liberalism as a single form, I take it that there never has been "*a liberalism*" but "only a family of liberalisms."[19] In contemporary political theory we have, for example, with Richard Rorty, Kantian liberalism versus Hegelian liberalism;[20] with Charles Taylor, procedural liberalism versus communitarian liberalism or rights-based liberalism versus republican liberalism;[21] and with John Gray, rationalistic liberalism versus agonistic liberalism.[22] Considering the aims of this book, there are, accordingly, three main aspects of liberalism that need to be pointed out.

First, I agree with Alan Ryan that in light of *political creeds*, the history of liberalism is a "history of opposition to assorted tyrannies"[23] in favor of a group of liberal values, such as individual freedom, human rights, moral equality, democracy, tolerance, open society, pluralism, and so forth. Not surprisingly, different liberals may have different views about the different scopes and priorities of liberal values. In search of Confucian liberalism, nonetheless, it suffices to stress that at the heart of the practice of liberalism lies an attempt to seek the moral equality of all human beings by resisting the use of arbitrary and unaccountable power.[24]

In this regard, it is worth mentioning that for Mou, a careful reexamination of "humane government" actually unveils the ideas of individual freedom and moral equality in objection to oppression and domination, but it simply lacks the "way of politics" related to a set of liberal institutions, such as the rule of law, constitutionalism, and democracy, for making happen the spirit of *ren* in the political sphere. Hence, as stated, Mou argues that the modern transformation of Confucianism hinges on a "politics of innovation" that envisions a free society that can accommodate Confucian civilization and liberal values all together. Overall, it is against this context that I come to identify Mou's anticipation of Confucian liberalism as a Hegelian form of "ethical liberalism."

Second, it has been said that Western liberalism recognized as *a historical product of the civilizing process* is the "offspring of the Enlightenment,"[25] prone to treat reason and progress as the kernel of modernity. In the Chinese context, however, it is the crisis of civilization caused by Western imperialism since the late nineteenth century that gave rise to the "paradigm shift" of political language. For this reason, it seems appropriate to remark that from the very beginning, the endeavor to merge Confucian culture and liberal values has its roots in the long-standing question of whether Confucianism is compatible with modernity.

On this matter, my general view is that just like liberalism, there has been a "family of enlightenments," as J. G. A. Pocock claims, and that the gist of Confucian liberalism is, by definition, more analogous to *a* "moderate" enlightenment than to *a* "radical" one.[26] That is to say, unlike both the "radicalism" of anti-Confucian (or antitraditional) liberalism and the "traditionalism" of antiliberal (or anti-Westernized) Confucianism, Confucian liberalism attempts to combine the traditional practice of Confucian civility with the progressive avowal of liberal values. In the case of Mou, his anxiety for preserving what I have otherwise called "Confucian democratic civility" with regard to the "way of governance" consists of a bid to reassess the public good in Confucianism from the standpoint of liberalism. Insofar as Confucian liberalism seeks to bring together Confucian civility (civilization and public norms) and liberal politics, it can be further itemized as a form of "civil liberalism."

Third, as far as *the justification of liberalism* is concerned, there are certainly a variety of liberal theories, including the natural rights tradition, the brand of social contract theory (be it Hobbesian or Kantian, contractarian or contractualist), and the consequentialist approach.[27] Despite the differences, the consensus of mainstream liberalism is, by and large, in support of "state neutrality" and "rights as trumps." To be sure, the leading liberal philosophers in our time, including Bruce Ackerman, Ronald Dworkin, Charles Larmore, Will Kymlicka, John Rawls, and so on, all would grant that the principle of neutrality is a defining feature of liberalism, acting as "a means of showing respect to persons who, as rational purposive beings, often select and act on controversial conceptions of the good."[28] In other words, rights-based liberalism urges that "rights are best understood as trumps over some background justification for political decisions that states a goal for the community as a whole."[29]

By way of contrast, Confucian liberalism in association with "humane government" is devoted to undertaking a perfectionist reading of politics grounded in the ethics of self-realization underpinning this book. Put in other terms, since the business of government in Confucianism, as Mou clearly puts it, is to "attain accomplishment according to the individual's nature" (*jiu geti er shuncheng* 就個體而順成), the "way of governance" mentioned above simultaneously contains a certain conception of the common good, or so to speak, Confucian *res publica* containing a set of Confucian governing and civic virtues. In this regard, what is central to Mou's project of Confucian liberalism is not so much about a "politics of rights" but about a "politics of the common good," alluding to some sort of "perfectionist liberalism."

This, of course, does not mean that "perfectionist liberalism" belittles the individual, freedom, and rights; to be fair, what really sets these two versions of politics apart is the debate over the methodology in political theory. Instead of giving a detailed account of this debate, it is sufficient to only note here that while Confucian liberalism understood as a Hegelian form of "ethical liberalism" emblematizes both "civil liberalism" and "perfectionist liberalism," the overall features of Confucian liberalism at large bear striking similarities to the wing of Hegelian liberalism encouraged by the British idealists. Accordingly, regardless of the widespread belief that there is a serious tension between Confucianism and rights-based liberalism,[30] there is still a possibility of merging Confucian ethics, Confucian civility, and Confucian *res publica* with liberal values by reference to the legacy of British idealism.

The Relevance of British Idealism

That being said, we are now in a better position to single out the relevance of British idealism in reassessing the liberal outlook of New Confucianism from a comparative viewpoint. For the most part, it is my observation that the leading British idealists, including T. H. Green (1836–1882), F. H. Bradley (1846–1924), Bernard Bosanquet (1848–1923), R. G. Collingwood (1889–1943), and in some qualified sense, Michael Oakeshott (1901–1990), are driven to resolve—albeit in distinctive ways—the ideological disputes over the contrasts between modernity and tradition, politics and civility, individuality and sociability, citizens and the state, negative freedom and positive freedom, and the like.

More exactly, as regards the characteristics of moral thinking, there do exist some salient affinities between New Confucianism and British idealism. For example, like Mou Zongsan and Tang Junyi, the British idealists have common roots in German thought, especially in Kant and Hegel, apart from the influence of Plato and Aristotle.[31] Again, similar to Confucianism in general, the British idealists hold that the self and the social are inseparable, that the ultimate end in morality is to fulfill a "morally worthwhile life" in a society, and that "human beings' ideas of what is good and of what constitutes a morally worthwhile life are continually developing."[32] On the whole, echoing the moral spirituality of Confucianism, the themes of British idealism consist of "an emphasis on moral practice and life in community, the recognition of the values of culture and social institutions, the centrality of self-realization and human flourishing, and an openness to new experience."[33]

And thus, in spite of Mou's insistence that Chinese and Western philosophy can be conceivably connected only via the lens of Kant, it remains the case that in terms of moral practice, New Confucianism and British idealism share a similar view of what may be referred to as the ethics of self-realization. In fact, it is largely thanks to the British idealists that the term "self-realization" became widely recognized in the English-speaking world.[34] Above all, for the British idealists, self-realization means the perfection of human personality or human character, namely, the full actualization of one's moral capacities and ends toward a higher self. By the same token, the core of Confucian ethics, as Stephen C. Angle puts it, "should be centered around the ideal of all individuals developing their capacities—ultimately aiming at sagehood—through their relationship with one another and with their environment."[35]

In terms of political theory, the British idealists are greatly indebted to Hegel, on the account that they gravitate toward examining the meaning of politics with regard to history, culture, and civilization. In this manner, Oakeshott's profound discussion of the relationship between individuality and tradition, and Collingwood's attempt to relate the purpose of a body politic to the ideals of civility, are advantageous for illuminating the political theory of New Confucianism. For, in line with Oakeshott and Collingwood, Mou and his companions are all motivated to find potential resolutions for relocating newly emergent political values into the lived forms of life in a given community. In other words, Oakeshott's and Collingwood's civility-based *ways of theorizing* are interestingly comparable to Mou's political thought, in that the sharp contrasts between progressivism and traditionalism, between modernity and tradition, etc., can be effectively reconciled.

What is more, there is a great deal of agreement about political philosophy among the British idealists in the name of perfectionist liberalism (except for Oakeshott). Although "Hegelian to different degrees,"[36] the British idealists can be identified as post-Kantian writers who admire a large measure of liberal values and try to redefend them in a Hegelian way. The upshot is that the British idealists' endorsement of human fulfillment or self-realization not only plays a crucial part in their Hegel-inspired defense of democracy, freedom, and rights without sliding into authoritarianism, but it also serves as an internal critique of mainstream liberalism, which initiates the ethical turn to liberalism. Put differently, it is to the credit of the British idealists, notably Green, that the cultivation of individuality rooted in an ethics of self-realization is further established as a liberal conception of the common good, functioning as a yardstick against which the ethical character of the citizen and the crucial values of freedom and rights are justified in accordance with the moral ideals of an open society. In this regard, conducting a profound dialogue between Mou and Green would help shed light on the liberal aspect of Confucian *res publica* in the Chinese context.

Contemporary Confucian Political Theory

To illuminate the uniqueness of Confucian liberalism in a fuller sense, let me move to shed some light on the taxonomy of contemporary Confucian political theory.

Anti-Confucian Liberalism versus Antiliberal Confucianism

On the whole, the anti-Confucian liberals such as Yin Haiguang [Yin Hai-Kuang] (殷海光 1919–1969) and Zhang Foquan [Chang Fo-Chuan] (張佛泉 1907–1994)[37] maintain that the endeavor to combine Confucianism with liberal values not only commits an error of neglecting the cultural incompatibility between the Chinese and Western worlds,[38] but also falls victim to a categorical confusion between morality and politics, allowing leeway for the conceptual abuse of the notions of positive freedom and common good, resulting in a more authoritative character of the state. In contrast, the antiliberal Confucians declare that the credulous acceptance of liberal values is uncritical of Western-centrism, neglects both the moral crisis of liberal democracy and the political problems confronting China and undervalues the political tradition of Confucianism. In this book I plan to engage with arguments from both camps in detail. But here, I just want to round off the category of antiliberal Confucianism in a way that leads to various versions of contemporary Confucian political theory.

To begin with, as opposed to Mou's "spiritual Confucianism" (*xinxing Ruxue* 心性儒學) based on a "rooted global philosophy" of *ren*, the recently emerged discourse of "political Confucianism" (*zhengzhi Ruxue* 政治儒學) advocated by Jiang Qing (蔣慶), among others, is keen to establish a state-supported "Confucian religion"[39] in place of Mou's philosophical examination of moral religion. Poles apart from Jiang, Chen Lai (陳來) rests his own version of "socialist Confucianism" on an *ontological* explanation of *ren*,[40] taking "benevolence as substance and harmony as means";[41] yet, in order to eradicate the domination of Western values, he is apt to set forth a "Sinified" standard on universal values. Encouraged by the rapid growth of cultural self-confidence, a young scholar affiliated with "contemporary Confucianism" lately depicted the preponderance of Western culture in China as "a turtledove taking over the nest of a magpie" (*jiu zhan que chao* 鳩佔鵲巢), meaning that the Western pursuit of democracy and freedom has for so long occupied the central place belonging to Chinese culture that it is time now for Confucians to "eliminate the heresy."[42]

Against this context, we are not surprised that there appears a propensity to reflect on China's current state of affairs from a Confucian viewpoint, including Fan Ruiping's (范瑞平) "reconstructionist Confucianism,"[43] Kang Xiaoguang's (康曉光) "politics of benevolence,"[44] Jiang Qing's "Confucian constitutionalism,"[45] "the China model" of Daniel A. Bell,[46] and so forth. In general, while Fan and Kang are disposed to file an entire objection to liberal values, Jiang and Bell aim to incorporate the elements of both Confucian meritocracy and liberal democracy into a "mixed" regime. In this book, the latter writers are still considered to be antiliberal, despite that some of their work aims to transcend the predicament of abstract individualism and the pitfalls of mainstream liberalism, since they ultimately refuse to implement the *full* picture of democracy and liberal values associated with the "way of politics" in the Chinese context.

Therefore, another feature related to antiliberal Confucianism is to go back over the advantages of Confucian political tradition, giving rise to an ongoing movement toward Confucian meritocracy. Apart from the writings of Jiang and Bell, the idea of Confucian meritocracy also can be found in Bai Tongdong's (白彤東) "new mission of an old state,"[47] Li Chenyang's (李晨陽) "Confucian elitism,"[48] and Joseph Chan's (陳祖為) "Confucian political perfectionism."[49] Despite criticizing liberal democracy, as indicated, these writers are determined to merge the meritocratic distribution of political power according to personal virtues and talents with a *limited* adaptation of elections and participation. It is to their credit that the Confucian values of harmony, deference, and hierarchy have reentered the discussion of contemporary political theory, and the proper relation between morality and politics has been reconsidered in Confucian terms. Despite the different versions of Confucian meritocracy,[50] Mou's Confucian liberalism in the long run departs from all of them in demanding that the ultimate end of the Confucian political ideal that he aspires to, namely, "fulfilling self-realization" with regard to *others* in an ethical life, could only be actualized through nothing but the venue of democracy.

Confucian Democracy or Confucian Meritocracy

In this fashion, contemporary Confucian political theory can be further divided into two main groups: Against Confucian meritocracy or "Confucian meritocratic perfectionism," the followers of Confucian democracy or "Confucian democratic perfectionism"[51] are surrounded by the "Confucian pragmatism" of David Hall, Roger Ames, and Tan Sor-Hoon (陳素芬);[52] Stephen Angle's project for "progressive Confucianism";[53] and Sungmoon Kim's version of "public reason Confucianism,"[54] to name only a few.

Confucian liberalism has both similarities with and differences from the main approaches to Confucian democracy. In general, it parts company with them in stressing the importance of self-development and the sociality of human beings, in affirming the relationship between democracy and moral development, and in welcoming political freedom and participation. Nonetheless, unlike "pragmatist Confucianism," which rests on the authority of John Dewey, Confucian liberalism takes British idealism as the closest Western correlate to elucidate Confucian democracy.[55] Contrary to the Deweyan rejection of a metaphysics of ethics, I contend that Mou's lifelong devotion to rebuilding a "Confucian moral metaphysics" deserves serious discussion in its own right.

The spirit of Confucian liberalism largely amounts to "progressive Confucianism," standing up for the "core Confucian commitment to individual and collective moral progress."[56] In brief, Confucian liberalism is like "progressive Confucianism" in believing that the essence of Confucianism lies in an ethics of self-realization involving an "endless process" of seeking the full development of the virtues of humaneness, righteousness, propriety, wisdom, and faithfulness, but it needs the venue of "new outer kingliness" to make happen its own core commitment. Consequently, I also agree with Angle on affirming a "certain degree of convergence between Confucianism and the liberal tradition," on distinguishing political virtue from personal virtue, and on making evident the boundaries of the political.[57] Surely, Angle's pursuit of "virtue-ritual-politics" is, by default, a bid to harmonize these three dimensions of value. By contrast, this work focuses on Mou's transformation of Confucian civility into "Confucian democratic civility," which consists of a set of Confucian governing and civic virtues consistent with liberal elements.

Speaking of Confucian ritual proprieties, Kim is correct in observing that East Asian societies were not historically illustrated by value pluralism and lacked the Rawlsian notion of democratic political culture embedded in civil society, and thus, to regulate moral disagreements, Kim proposes "public reason Confucianism" to urge citizens to "cultivate reason" that they employ in democratic deliberation and political participation—hence "public reasons"—by reference to Confucian cultural values—hence "Confucian public reasons." In fact, Kim's appeal to "public reason Confucianism" to mediate between communal values and democratic citizenship, and especially between moral perfectionism and liberal concerns,[58] is saliently reminiscent of the New Liberalism of British idealism. In this regard, my own search for Confucian *res publica* in terms of "ethical citizenship" and a "nondominant idea of the common good" may make a significant addition to "Confucian democratic perfectionism"[59] from a fresh new perspective.

As a final point, the fact that Confucian liberalism prefers Confucian democracy over Confucian meritocracy does not imply that it entirely gives away the pursuit of a harmonious order, which is essential to Confucianism throughout time. Rather, the truth is that Confucian liberalism, identified as a "rooted global philosophy," engages in critical dialogue with relevant ideas from other philosophical traditions to temper the progress of the rootedness of Confucianism—hence its spirit of *ren*—in a global context—hence the pursuit of *common humanity*. In this manner, the "spirit of reconciliation" at work can be deemed an attempt to prevent our collective hope for social harmony from turning into authoritarianism and to restrain the deferential sentiments and hierarchical relationships existing in Confucian societies from domination and oppression in public opinion. In short, not only does Confucian liberalism uphold the ethical view that participation "in shaping public goals and endeavors [is] of great importance to one's moral development,"[60] but it also maintains the liberal emphasis on preventing potential damages to humanity caused by political evils.

From Kantian to Hegelian

Given the importance of Mou, we are not surprised by the fact that there have been a number of important commentaries on Mou's legacy appearing in the past two decades or so.[61] Compared to the current literature concerning the study of Mou, the two vital ways of extending Mou's Confucian liberalism, namely, Kantian and Hegelian, are what particularly concern me here. While it is true that Mou's disciples and followers form a group of "Kantian New Confucians," within which the work of Li Minghui [Lee Ming-Huei] (李明輝)[62] provides a benchmark, this book is intended to shift the focus of attention from Kant to Hegel and beyond.

As we shall see in detail, Mou surely believes that Kant's philosophy, representing the highest peak of Western philosophy, could be very beneficial, on several grounds, in shedding light on traits of Chinese philosophy. My point of departure, however, is predicated on the premise that although Mou highly appreciates Kant's great achievement in moral philosophy, he takes issue with Kant largely for the reason that Kant clearly denies the existence of "intellectual intuition" (*zhi de zhijue* 智的直覺) in grasping the thing-in-itself, but a common thread running throughout Chinese philosophy, including Confucianism, Daoism, and Buddhism, is the total affirmation of "intellectual intuition."

If focusing on Confucianism, there thus appear, for Mou, serious limitations in Kant's treatment of free will as a "postulate" of practical reason, in the "bifurcated" world of nature and morals, or phenomena and noumena that Kant left for us, and in the "Christian" backdrop that Kant takes for granted when addressing the moral ideal of the highest good (the *summum bonum*). In short, in view of the fact that Kant's metaphysics of morals is tightly associated with an attitude toward the "finitude in human beings," it falls short of establishing a deep-rooted moral metaphysics, particularly with regard to concerns about the actualization of the ideal self in pursuit of the ultimate meaning of human life.

Against this context, I have several reasons for drawing on Hegel's insights when pondering the possibility and plausibility of Confucian liberalism as Mou did. First, Mou's philosophical project of connecting the "way of politics" with the "way of governance," or alternatively, reuniting the political *form* of liberal democracy with the ethical *content* of Confucian civility, as I see it, conforms to a dialectical pattern that takes after Hegel.

Second, despite the fact that Mou also picks holes in Hegel, he greatly recognizes the value of Hegel's idea of "concrete philosophy" in respect of real subjectivity, actualization, embodiment, individuality, the concrete universal, and so forth. All in all, in the post-Kantian setting, Hegel can be deemed an internal critique of Kant, who has never discarded the gist of the moral subject that Mou conveys to establish the spirituality of Confucianism.

Third, Mou's political writings were critically influenced by Hegel and full of Hegelian terminology, such as "subjective freedom," "objective spirit," the "self-awareness of the individual" (*geti de zijue* 個體的自覺), "self-negation" (*ziwo kanxian* 自我坎陷), and so forth. Besides, Mou's diagnosis of the crisis of modernity and the dilemma of liberalism was to a great extent inspired by Hegel. For example, Mou remarks that liberalism today has lost its "moral ideals," or "moral spirituality," in the sense that "the presentation of [its] freedom is negative and incautious."[63] And here, by "moral spirituality" of liberalism, Mou means the "unity of subjectivity and objectivity in rationality," which is true "freedom (in Hegel's definition)."[64] The upshot here is that the historical reception of liberalism, together with political modernity, in the Chinese context is rather limited. As such, it has been largely neglected that Hegel, as John Rawls correctly claims, "stands in the liberal tradition" and that Hegel is a "moderately progressive reform-minded liberal" as well as a "defender of the modern constitutional state."[65]

In addition to the above considerations, there are three other reasons that can help clarify the credibility of extending our attention from Hegel to the Hegelian liberalism of the British idealists. For one, it should be remembered that there is textual evidence indicating that Mou was familiar with the work of British idealism. In brief, as Mou confessed, it was through Tang Junyi that he learned about Bradley's "reconciliatory dialectic" (*xiaorong bianzhengfa* 消融辯證法) and came to realize the gist of dialectical thinking and the importance of Hegel's philosophy.[66]

For another, while Mou bitterly blamed Hegel for treating the Absolute as a "bare concept" without moral import from the very beginning, he openly admitted that Bradley's "reconciliatory dialectic" successfully resolved this shortcoming rooted in Hegel's philosophy. For this reason, Mou sympathized with Tang's opinion that Bradley's "reconciliatory dialectic" can to a large extent help elucidate Chinese philosophy in general and the spirit of *ren* in particular.[67]

Third, as a matter of fact, the liberal traits of Hegel's political thinking have long ago been captured by Bonsanquet, when he says that "the whole political philosophy of Kant, Hegel, and Fichte is founded on the idea of freedom as the essence of man" first announced by Rousseau.[68] On the whole, it is to the credit of the British idealists that the mapping of liberalism has been significantly extended by incorporating a cluster of important issues that equally concern the New Confucians, the issues touching on history, civility, tradition, community, the common good, self-realization, and the like.

The Structure of the Chapters

Before turning to accomplish in full the main purposes of the book stated above, let me quickly say a few words about the structure of its chapters.

THE MORAL OUTLOOK OF CONFUCIANISM

I shall begin chapter 1 with an examination of the moral outlook of Confucianism from a comparative perspective, by bringing together Mou, Kant, Hegel, and the British idealists in dialogue. Based on this scheme, I am equipped to explain more fully the reasons for incorporating Hegel and the British idealists into a reconstruction of Mou's Confucian liberalism in the following two chapters.

In terms of moral religion, I argue in chapter 2 that Hegel's "immanent theology," aiming to settle the division between God and man in Catholicism, actually provides Mou with an essential framework for spelling out the "religiousness" of the attainment of "inner sagehood" in Confucianism with regard to the principle of the "conformity of Heaven and man in union" (*tianren heyi* 天人合一). Considering the purposes of this book, it is instructive to further compare Mou with the work of T. H. Green. There are, by and large, three main aspects that Green contributes to amplify the idea of moral religion in the thought of Hegel: the disapproval of the orthodox Christian view that God exists externally, a reinterpretation of the attributes of God through internalization, and the moral ideal of self-realization as the fulfillment of one's moral ability through communicating with the way in which God works in history.

To elaborate on the ethics of self-realization, another dialogue between Mou and Bradley will be undertaken in chapter 3. There are several observations that I wish to make. First, like New Confucianism, there is also a tendency to emphasize the social dimension of the moral self in British idealism. Second, as for moral practice, Bradley also criticizes Kant for treating freedom as a postulate from a Hegelian perspective. As such, Bradley's analysis of the dialectical movement from "pleasure for pleasure's sake," via "duty for duty's sake," to "my station and its duties" can help bring to light the concrete actualization of *ren*. Third, regarding moral reality, both Mou's and Bradley's main opinions border on Hegel's "concrete universal"; therefore, similar to Mou's claim that "although man is finite, he can be infinite,"[69] Bradley points out that to take self-realization as the moral end is to "realize yourself as an infinite whole," which refers to being "specified in yourself, but not specified by anything foreign to yourself."[70]

Having untangled the knotty conceptual links between New Confucianism and British idealism in respect of an ethics of self-realization, in subsequent chapters, I am turning to sustain Mou's effort in applying a Hegelian reading of liberal vocabulary, such as democracy, civility, individuality, the political subject (citizenship), public good, the state, freedom, and rights, in association with the moral spirit of "fulfilling self-realization" in Confucianism. In so doing, I am simultaneously determined to explain away the misconceptions about the merging of Confucianism and liberalism launched by both anti-Confucian liberalism and antiliberal Confucianism.

In Pursuit of Civil Liberalism

To make my case, I contend in chapter 4 that as for democracy, Mou actually raised three main questions: (1) Why did ancient Confucianism not develop democracy? (2) How can Confucianism develop democracy? And, as I shall make efforts to explain in the rest of the book, (3) what is the subtlest model of Confucian democracy? Seen in light of the Hegelian scheme, Mou's answer to the first question points to the fact that traditional Confucianism failed to formulate the bare concept of "subjective freedom" that unveils the regeneration of democracy in the modern epoch, that is, an "independent political subject" having the sense of freedom and rights. To develop democracy out of Confucianism, as a result, Mou employs Hegel's philosophy of history to remark that the moral subject must endure a process of "self-negation" such that the political subject in question can be separated from itself. The crucial point here, however, is that for Mou, the separation between morality and politics is only transient and that the challenge to reconcile "subjective freedom" with "common meanings" must be regarded as the next stage of the progress of Confucian spirituality in a modern society. In this sense, as Mou continues, the subtlest model of Confucian democracy lies in an attempt to "reconnect" the "way of politics" (in respect of Western *political reasoning*) with the "way of governance" (in respect of Confucian *moral reasoning*) in an "indirect" and "limited" way.

To see more clearly the Hegelian scheme at work, I begin chapter 5 by arguing that a significant aspect of the political philosophy of New Confucianism in general is to arrive at a fusion of cultural conservatism and political progressivism, with the purpose of reuniting the habitual practices of Confucian civility with the enlightened values of liberal democracy. By engaging in a comprehensive study of the very concept of "civility," not only does this chapter aspire to clarify the misconceptions about the relationships between civilization and barbarism, between modernity and tradition, and between individuality and community in the writings of anti-Confucian liberalism and antiliberal Confucianism, but also, and for this reason, it will be able to open the door to rebuilding Confucian liberalism from a "civil" perspective. More exactly, given that the family of expressions related to "civility" such as civil society, public spirit, civic virtue, and citizenship are of great importance in shaping the multiple faces of modernity and complicated meanings of liberalism, Confucian liberalism is suitable to be presented as a form of civil liberalism, which aims to reunite the "way of politics" related to liberal democracy with the "way of governance" incorporating what I have called "Confucian democratic civility," namely, a set of governing and civic virtues embedded in the Confucian forms of life.

To enunciate this central argument, I am obligated to say more about Mou's retreatment of "humane government" in chapter 6. To my knowledge, the mottos and dictums that Mou reattributes to "humane government" are not only consistent with the moral grounding of democracy in the primary sense of "treating humanity as an end," but they also denote the habitual embodiments of *ren* in Chinese political culture. Moreover, Mou's viewpoint largely reflects the distinction between "cultivating oneself" and "governing the people" that Xu Fuguan has famously made. And thus, as opposed to "Confucian meritocracy" promoted by antiliberal Confucianism, central to Mou's version of the Confucian political ideal is an attempt not so much to focus on a process of selecting the talented leader but to mark out the duties that the virtuous leader should impose upon himself when exercising the art of governing and cultivating.

All in all, Mou's democratic retreatment of Confucian civility—hence, "Confucian democratic civility"—falls into three categories: the legitimacy of authority, the purpose of government, and the limits on the abuse of power. While developing democracy is Mou's resolution to the longstanding predicament of political legitimacy in Confucianism, it is notable that Mou's discussion of the key elements of "humane government" entirely sticks to the principle of "self-restriction" (*ziwoxianzhi* 自我限制) and that, in line with the ethics of self-realization, he takes "attaining accomplishment according to the individual's nature" as the ultimate end characterizing the common good in Confucianism—hence, Confucian *res publica*. One serious problem at once arises: How, then, is it possible to relate the political form of liberal democracy to the ethical import of the common good anchored in an ethics of self-realization without bringing about social domination and exploitation by the state? In response to this query, I contend that conducting a far-reaching dialogue between New Confucianism and British idealism will help demonstrate the extent to which Confucian *res publica* can be expanded as a nondominant and nonexploitative theory of the common good. To this end, I need to clarify the meaning of perfectionist liberalism by reconsidering both the *political* and *ethical* connotations of the related liberal expressions, such as citizens, open society, the state, freedom, and rights.

Toward Perfectionist Liberalism

My presentation of Confucian *res publica* in chapter 7 takes as the point of departure the view that the governing virtues associated with "humane government," as a consequence of the "blossoming of democracy" and the appearance of the political subject, can be transformed into a set of civic virtues. That said, as Mou suggests, not only are the cores of "humane government" consistent with the social version of an open society characterized by the liberal values of autonomy, plurality, and openness, but the "way of *zhongshu*" (*zhongshu zhi dao* 忠恕之道) underpinning the spirit of *ren* is also in harmony with the moral ideals of liberalism in favor of individuality, human dignity, tolerance, and equal respect. To be sure, my Hegelian reinterpretation of Mou's Confucian liberalism is devoted to broadening the horizons of liberal commitments at large in that it tries to offer a more adequate explanation about the moral consideration of *others*.

What is more, via a comprehensive dialogue between Mou and Green, I shall make two further points: in light of the state, Mou would agree with Green that the purpose of government should be restricted to providing every individual with equal opportunity to "pursue his own good life" (contributing to the flourishing of humankind) within a "fair system of rights," by removing "obstacles to self-realization"; in light of citizenship, both thinkers subscribe to an ethical conception of citizens, demonstrating the significance of Hegel's ethical life in shaping the mutual relationship between citizens with regard to the lived forms of life. By and large, there are three main categories of civic virtue exemplifying Mou's Confucian appreciation of the common good that echo Green's concerns, namely, "ethical mutuality," "helping others do good," and "caring about the better-being of all the rest." As such, Mou's Confucian liberalism is at the same time free from the charges of anti-individualism, monism, and panmoralism (*fan daodezhuyi* 泛道德主義) made by anti-Confucian liberalism and able to transcend the moral weakness of mainstream liberalism in respect of atomism, nihilism, and egoism bolstered by antiliberal Confucianism.

The purpose of chapter 8 is to continue to figure out the relevance of a common good in making sense of freedom and in offering an alternative justification for rights, vis-à-vis the scheme of perfectionist liberalism. As regards freedom, I am drawing my attention to an asymmetry that emerges in conceptualizing negative and positive freedom in the Chinese context, suggesting that whereas liberalism is closely associated with negative freedom, that is, rights, the adoption of positive freedom only leads to an oppressive society. It is against this context that anti-Confucian liberalism argues that Confucianism is unavoidably at odds with liberalism as the pursuit of "humane government" is predicated upon a perfectionist reading of humanity, tending to recognize *ren* as true freedom. At this point, I suggest that an exploration of Green's theory of freedom is advantageous to shedding new light on the plausibility of Confucianism liberalism, if only because Green's engagement with a Hegelian synthesis of negative and positive freedom in respect of a common good, far from sliding into totalitarianism or authoritarianism, has anticipated much of the *internal* critique of liberal values launched by the contemporary promoters of communitarianism and republicanism such as Charles Taylor.

On the other hand, once we focus on the expression of rights, the main objections presented by antiliberal Confucianism will appear as follows: rights discourse utterly neglects the fact that there is no such thing as rights in Confucianism, that Confucianism is more liable to proclaim the priority of community and tradition over the individual and rights, and that liberal democracy has its own serious pitfalls. To draw my work to a close, I declare that Hegelian liberalism is, in fact, more beneficial than Kantian liberalism in responding to the objections at stake, largely because the Kantian approach, at least in contemporary political theory, is considered to be *culturally insensitive*,[71] thanks to its endorsement of a theory of natural rights, formalism, and atomistic individualism. By contrast, from what has been said thus far, it can be reasonably inferred that Mou's political thought accommodates a Hegelian "recognition theory of rights," which, as advocated by Green again, strives to justify rights with regard to a common good. In the case of Confucian liberalism, this means that Confucian *res publica* on the agenda may help us to deliberate the reasons why we should "have rights" by reference to the existing forms of life and manners of thinking in the Chinese context.

Part I
Confucian Ethics

Chapter 1

Confucianism in Comparative Perspective

Introduction

Mou Zongsan is a good starting point for examining the communications between Chinese and Western philosophy because his ideas are, by and large, formulated from an immediate comparative viewpoint. To be sure, Mou is best known today for reframing the philosophical outlook of Confucianism, together with Buddhism and Daoism, vis-à-vis the Kantian frame. In Mou's words, "if we wish to relate Confucianism to Western philosophy, we must make that connection through Kantian philosophy."[1] A significant part of this chapter, accordingly, is designed to go along Mou's Kantian path to illuminate the moral features of Confucianism and the uniqueness of Confucian moral metaphysics.[2] Despite Mou's achievement in linking the Confucian moral subject with Kantian autonomy, it remains the case that there are salient differences between Mou and Kant and that some crucial insights yielded within Mou's far-reaching philosophical venture are greatly indebted to Hegel's concrete philosophy.[3] As such, another crucial thread running throughout this chapter is to elucidate how and in what sense "Mou can be compared to Hegel and considered a great successor of Kantian philosophy."[4]

To make my case, this chapter will be divided into three main sections. In the first, I am going to give a brief outline of Kant's philosophical mission, followed by the three key features that Mou finds in the canons of orthodox Confucianism through the Kantian lens, namely, "inner morality" (*neizai daodexing* 內在道德性), a "vertical expression of the vertical system" or a "vertically expressed vertical system" (*zongguan zongjiang* 縱貫縱講), and the endless pursuit of the "perfect good" (*yuanshan* 圓善).

Be that as it may, Mou's broader motivation for rebuilding a "moral metaphysics" is to surpass the limits of Kant's "moral theology." In response to Heidegger's unveiling of the "finitude in human beings" embedded in Kant's first *Critique*, Mou realizes that what emphatically marks out Chinese philosophy is that, for Kant, human beings cannot have "intellectual intuition" (*zhi de zhijue* 智的直覺) in knowing noumena, but the mainstreams of Chinese philosophy all affirm this faculty for human beings, resulting in the ontological stance that "although man is finite, he can be infinite."[5] In this regard, the three main components highlighting Confucian moral metaphysics are the identification of the "infinite heart-mind" (*wuxianxin* 無限心) as a principle of moral creation, the proposal of a "two-level ontology," namely, a level of "attachment" (*zhi* 執) suitable for understanding phenomena and a level of "nonattachment" (*wuzhi* 無執) attempting to grasp noumena as a "value concept" in the strong sense, and finally, the proclamation of Confucianism as "teaching" in the perfect sense, that is, the "perfect teaching" (*yuanjiao* 圓教).

Having touched on Mou's departure from Kant, in the third section I am turning to look back on Mou's engagement with Hegel. The upshot is that even if Confucian "moral metaphysics" is superior to Kant's "metaphysics of morals," there is, ironically, a critical flaw in this superiority, namely, that the sincere and ceaseless pursuit of the "perfect good" in the past meant that the overall direction of Confucianism always looked inward in search of the "moral subject" and never looked outward to develop the particular "knowing subject" and the independent "political subject," upon which science and democracy are based. To develop science and democracy for the prospect of Chinese culture, Mou suggests that Confucianism has to endure a process of "self-negation" (*ziwo kanxian* 自我坎陷) in the Hegelian sense. Rather than demonstrating directly the significance of Hegel's insights in shaping Mou's anticipation of Confucian liberalism, here I only intend to begin bringing in Hegel's concrete philosophy by examining his criticisms of Kant in terms of real subjectivity, the full meaning of reality, and the idea of the concrete universal.

The Intrinsic Character of Confucianism

Mou's quest for a restatement of the "intrinsic and unique character"[6] of Chinese philosophy in general and Confucianism in particular is based on his critical examination of Kant's works.[7] For the sake of clarity, it seems appropriate to begin my study with a short introduction to the Kantian frame as we shall make reference to it time and again.

THE KANTIAN FRAME: NATURE AND FREEDOM

On the whole, the fact that Kant is a key figure for Mou's project has mostly to do with Kant's "Copernican revolution," which makes human *subjectivity* the first priority in modern philosophy. In a nutshell, for Kant, the thinking subject possesses a natural ability to synthesize the given data in a certain way; real knowledge is possible only when experience is added to an *a priori* objective reference: Man sorts out the manifold sensations, first in "time and space," and then according to the principles of pure understanding, that is, categories.[8] In this scheme, traditional metaphysics at once turns out to be a vain attempt to acquire knowledge of God, the soul, and the self because all the things to be legitimately known are phenomena that manifest themselves as *objects* in time and space according to the categories, whereas God, the soul, and the self are neither spatial nor temporal, and they are thus merely "things-in-themselves," or alternatively, noumena, which are inaccessible to subjectivity.

That said, Kant only accepts the lawful role of "sensible intuition" or "empirical intuition" in giving the content of experience to subjectivity, but he clearly declines to bestow upon men the kind of faculty that only God has, that is, the faculty of "intellectual intuition" capable of creating and realizing "things-in-themselves." This is the reason why Kant tries to show that traditional metaphysics, susceptible to "transcendental illusions" by misusing the power of reason, only leads to insoluble "antinomies" instead of progress, unlike in physical science.[9] All this reaffirms that "the critique of pure reason can be regarded as the true tribunal of all disputes of pure reason," and it is "directed to the determining and estimating of the rights of reason in general, in accordance with the principles of their first institution."[10] Thus, Kant's motive for holding that human beings cannot have "intellectual intuition," far from depreciating human agency, is to set the phenomenal boundaries of intelligible discourse so as to place human knowledge, as well as the purpose and hope of human life, on brand-new philosophical ground.

For this reason, when practical reason is at stake, the aim of Kant's moral philosophy is not to search for a new morality, nor to deny moral discourse, but to ascertain the possibility of moral certainty by discovering *a priori* principles or postulates underlying the whole body of discourse and rendering this discourse intelligible, and thereby making our moral life on a purely rational basis possible.[11] Put succinctly, Kant's key point is that "there is no possibility of thinking of anything at all in the world, or even out of it, which can be regarded as good without qualification, except a good *will*,"[12] which in turn points to the fact that we, fully rational beings, are in essence free agents who can autonomously judge our own moral status by the use of reason. Hence, Kant simply regards his moral theory as an attempt to discover a "supreme law of freedom,"[13] that is, rational principles for the intelligent direction of the activities of free agents. In other words, for Kant, morality is a system of laws of freedom, indicating what ends the fully rational beings ought to choose for themselves and how they ought to act with regard to these ends.

The laws of freedom or morality set forth by reason are articulated by Kant in terms of various formulations of "categorical imperative," which culminate in the "kingdom of ends." There are, by and large, three propositions that underline the "categorical imperative."[14] First, moral conduct is to act "from duty" by the guidance of reason irrespective of any desire or inclination. Second, moral activity is to act "on the principle of the moral law," and so the moral self in Kant's philosophy is a "disengaged self" consisting of a set of abstract rules. Third, "duty is the necessity of an action done out of respect for the law"; here what concerns Kant regarding the principle of morality is its character as a command. In short, for Kant, being moral is finalized by moral law rather than eternal objects; morality requires the autonomy of free will which allows the moral subject to "act from duty, on maxim and out of the respect for the law."

Therefore, what Kant leaves us with is a bifurcated world: the physical world and the world of freedom, nature and morality, phenomena (things as they appear to us), and noumena (things as they are in themselves). We surely cannot ascertain the world of freedom through scientific reason, but in a like manner, our scientific reasoning does not prove that the physical world is the only possible world. And if one's understanding of the physical world depends on theoretical reasoning, then the moral life, the consciousness of obligation, depends on practical reason, and opens to a sphere of reality which man affirms by "rational faith"[15] as a demand of the moral law. That said, since human beings cannot have "intellectual intuition" of noumena, we are unable to *know*, although we are eager to *hope*, that we are free, that God exists, and that the soul can be immortal. To end with Kant's words, if "the philosopher is not an artificer in the field of reason, but himself the lawgiver of human reason," then it may be concluded:

> The legislation of human reason (philosophy) has two objects, nature and freedom, and therefore contains not only the law of nature, but also the moral law, presenting them at first in two distinct systems, but ultimately in one single philosophical system. The philosophy of nature deals with all *that is*, the philosophy of morals with that which *ought to be*.[16]

Inner Morality

We shall soon have an opportunity to look over Mou's criticisms of Kant. Here, my primary task is to describe the special character of Chinese philosophy with the help of the Kantian frame. To begin with, Mou declares that Kant's project can be reformulated into two parts, namely, "empirical realism" and "transcendental idealism."[17] If what "empirical realism" really affirms is the accomplishment of Western philosophy in respect of empirical science (and the institutionalization of democracy), the center of attention in Chinese philosophy has largely been on the different track of "transcendental idealism," hunting for a fuller comprehension of humanity and morality. For this reason, Mou makes it clear that "the focus of Chinese philosophy was life. Because of this emphasis on life, Chinese culture and philosophy valued virtue."[18]

Although the purpose of Kant's first *Critique* is to lay a foundation for objective knowledge within the realm of "empirical realism," this does not affect the fact that the core of Kant's moral philosophy, that is, the idea of "inner morality" or autonomy, can be used to rebuild the principal outlook of Chinese moral thinking in a modern way. Thus, apart from the instances of "transcendental realism" and "empirical realism," and the like, several sets of contrasting idioms related to Kant's "inward turn" to subjectivity[19] are equally important to Mou's setting the ground for a moral metaphysics. The idioms include "subjectivity" and "objectivity," "intensional" and "extensional," "inward" and "outward," and so on.

In one sense, these idioms are also of use for marking the categorical distinction between Chinese and Western culture. For instance, in Mou's expression, while "the focus of Christians is always outward and upward," the Confucians are turning inward, looking downward;[20] while science is concerned with "extensional truth," and its "objectivity" is verified by Russell's "principle of extensionality" and "principle of atomicity," the real meaning of morality deals with the "intensional truth," which lies nowhere but in our own "subjectivity." In summation, Mou writes:

> Extensive truths are related to mathematical and physical quantities, whereas intensive truths are not. Intensive truths are related to life, and only life has intensiveness. Intensiveness pertains to life and to the Subject. Only life as the Subject can exhibit intensiveness.[21]

In another, deeper sense, however, it is to Kant's credit that his idea of moral autonomy can help bring out to a great extent a lucid image of Chinese philosophy in the sense of putting emphasis on the Subject and "opening the subjective gate."[22] As Mou puts it, along the lines of Kant's "inward turn" to the autonomy of free will,

> The focus of Chinese philosophy lies in "subjectivity" and "inner morality." While the three mainstreams of Chinese thought, namely, Confucianism, Buddhism, and Daoism, all call attention to subjectivity, only Confucianism, the mainstream of all mainstreams, goes further to give prescriptions to subjectivity, turning it into "inner morality," the result of which is moral subjectivity.[23]

Put in other terms, among the three traditions of Chinese philosophy: "regarding being perceptive in the minute changes of events, Daoism is unsurpassed"; "in examining the karma-consciousness, Buddhism is unsurpassed"; "in opening up the sources of moral values, and in building up the moral Subject, Confucianism is unsurpassed."[24] Indeed, as Confucius's *ren* 仁 (humaneness) or Mencius's *Xing*-nature 性 (human nature) discloses, good is always "internal to the Subject" and can never be truly understood from external objects in the Confucian tradition.[25]

Thus, it comes as no surprise that for Mou, in the West a real understanding of the essence of morality only began with Kant. This is not only because Kant turned down the Platonic tradition of using a "cognitive attitude to define and understand value,"[26] but also because Kant came to regard practical reason as a self-regulating activity, which, by treating the person as an end and not as a means, goes to restore the person as the Subject. In brief, Kant has successfully changed the landscape of Western moral philosophy by shifting the focus of attention from the "heteronomy of the will" to the "autonomy of the will";[27] this emphasis on autonomy is precisely the reason why "Kant can connect with Confucianism."[28]

A Vertical Expression of the Vertical System

To see the commonality between Confucianism and Kant in a fuller sense, however, it is important to turn to another formulation coined by Mou, that is, a "vertical expression of the vertical system." For Mou, as for other New Confucians, Confucianism as a moral theory basically consists of two essential parts, namely, moral practice and moral metaphysics. Confucian moral practice, for the most part, involves a process of moral transformation, moral development, or moral progression, in terms of which "a small person can transcend himself to become a gentleman, and a gentleman can transcend himself to become a sage, however rarely this last goal is reached."[29] In this regard, the expression of "immanent transcendence" (*neizai chaoyue* 內在超越) is meant to imply that "the transcendence of the self is a moral transformation toward a better or ideal self within the world rather than a translation of the self to or beyond the boundaries of the world."[30] As such, seen in light of moral metaphysics, it appears that Confucian moral practice is closely related to a profound study of the moral potentiality of the ideal self, that is, "attaining sagehood" (*chengsheng* 成聖). On this account, the phrase of "immanent transcendence" also denotes that the stress on moral practice in Confucianism has been fostered by a philosophical examination of the ultimate meaning of human life.

What Mou means by "vertical system" is, by and large, the philosophical system that is surrounded with "ultimate concern" on account of pursuing the "final, ultimate level [of philosophical understanding]," the "ultimate source of all things,"[31] which, in the field of moral philosophy, is equal to the highest good (the *summum bonum*) in Kant's Western background.[32] Thus read, the "vertical system" is likely to be associated with Kant's search of "transcendental principle." Against this context, Confucius's *ren*, to take an obvious example, is the "transcendental principle" of "rites and music" (*liyue* 禮樂)[33] that constitute the basic norms of a community.[34] In a similar manner, the postulate of free will in Kant's moral philosophy can be regarded as the ultimate source of practical reason as well. By way of contrast, the appearance of logical positivism, for example, stands perfectly for a "horizontal system," in that the ultimate concern is replaced by an empirical verification of scientific knowledge.[35]

Although, so understood, it appears that some other traditions of Western moral philosophy are prone to adopt the "vertical system," the crucial difference is that only the Kantian frame, which Confucianism parallels, is a "thoroughgoing vertical system that is also vertically expressed."[36] This is because, even if Kant sees free will merely as a postulate, it still touches on the ultimate realm of reality. That said, what underscores a "vertical expression" or a "vertical theory" is the philosophical attempt to affirm the ultimate meaning of human life through moral practice on a substantial foundation of *existence*. On the other hand, a "horizontal expression" alludes to the endeavor to resolve the ultimate concern by means of an epistemological approach or for the sake of pursuing objective knowledge.

In this manner, the "vertical system" of Confucianism is "vertically expressed" all at once, because either Confucius's *ren* or Mencius's *Xing*-nature, or what Wang Yangming [Wang Yang-Ming] (王陽明 1472–1529) refers to as *liangzhi* 良知 ("original knowing," or more exactly, the "knowing-reality of enlightened awareness"), not only functions as the "transcendental ground" of moral actions, but also regards the "ontological origin" of all things, namely, the *existence* of the ultimate realm of reality. In other words, unlike Kant, Confucianism actually grants that man is capable of having "intellectual intuition," which is able to create its own *object* as well as make happen moral *activity*. This means that *liangzhi* identified as "intellectual intuition" is not limited to human actions; rather, it must be related to the emergence of things. "Accordingly, moral activity is at the same time cosmological creation. In terms of the moral creativity, nature and morals can be united."[37] To quote Mou:

> Using an old Chinese expression, it is the "unceasing pureness of virtue" (*dexing zhi chun yi buyi* 德行之純亦不已). Analytically speaking, the reason that virtue can be lastingly pure is because there is a transcendental ground; this transcendental ground is what Mencius calls *Xing*-nature as in the "goodness of *Xing*-nature" (*xingshan* 性善). This *Xing*-nature is moral creativity.[38] With this moral creativity as our *Xing*-nature, we can

continuously and unceasingly initiate the everlasting pureness of virtue. The unceasing pureness of virtue comes from the creativity of Xing-reality (xingti 性體), and is not preexisting. To cause the disappearance of what is there and the appearance of what is not there is creativity. The most pertinent meaning of creativity is in moral creativity, which is also what Kant calls the "causality of the will." The causality we discuss in knowledge is natural causality. Kant's "causality of the will" is special causality. This is the principle of creativity, and it is represented as "Xing-nature" in Confucianism.[39]

It follows that the term "Xing-reality" famously invented by Mou is consistent with the "causality of the will" as a special causality in Kant's discussion, meaning the creativity of the moral ability built into the Subject. To quote Mou again,

The meaning [of xingti] is, in fact, simply the "moral ability" or "moral spontaneity" that men have to conduct moral practice self-consciously, that is, "moral ability" or "moral spontaneity" understood as "inner morality." The autonomy of the heart-mind, or what Kant refers to as "autonomy of the will," is precisely this "Xing-nature" (xing 性). Whereas when it is taken to mean "reality" (ti 體), it stands for "moral creative reality."[40]

THE PERFECT GOOD

I shall return to reveal the differences between Mou's reconstruction of Confucian moral metaphysics and Kant's metaphysics of morals in respect of "intellectual intuition" shortly. For now, I just want to point out that the third aspect of Kant's moral thinking advantageous for making sense of Confucianism in modern times points to the pursuit of the "perfect good," that is, the highest good or the *summum bonum*, "which, for its part, is to be looked upon as embodying the totality of the end pursued by practical reason."[41] Put succinctly, although it is the moral law that serves as the ground determining the will upon which the *summum bonum* is to be promoted, by no means does Kant exclude happiness, the "satisfaction of all our desires,"[42] from being an end in itself. "Morality," as Kant claims, "is, strictly speaking, not the doctrine telling us how to *make* ourselves happy, but the doctrine telling us what we must do to be *worthy* of happiness."[43] In this regard, the practical law takes two forms: That which is associated with happiness is called "pragmatic" (rule of prudence), whereas that "which has no other motive than *worthiness of being happy*" is called "moral" (law of morality).[44] The search for the *summum bonum* is, in the end, concerned with the "exact correspondence of morality (or virtue) and happiness" (*defu yixhi* 德福一致).[45]

The caveat, however, is that in ordinary life there is no necessary connection between *worthiness of being happy* and the actual attainment of happiness, in that following the moral law does not always result in the satisfaction of desires, and *vice versa*. Or, to put it another way, the former belongs to the kingdom of ends, whereas the latter belongs to that of nature; as such, the highest good is not within the reach of our sensible intuition. Kant's answer to this challenge, as shown, is to hold rational faith in the existence of God, along with the hope that our soul can be immortal and that we are free; as Kant famously puts it, "I had therefore to remove *knowledge* in order to make way for *belief*."[46] Put clearly, even though the postulates at stake are beyond the reach of one's understanding, in practical meaning they should remain *matters of faith*. This is to say that in moral activity one should act *as if* God existed, *as if* the soul were immortal, and *as if* one's will were free. Along these lines of reasoning, in the second *Critique* as well as *Religion within the Limits of Reason Alone*, Kant thus embarks on a renovated study of moral theology, aiming to recast the religious aspect of moral practice in a fresh new light: "It is morally necessary to assume the existence of God."[47] In short, the pursuit of the highest good is not so much related to the understanding of God but to our rational faith in God, who represents the "idea of moral perfection" at the end of the day. To quote Kant:

> Even the Holy One of the Gospels must first be compared with our ideal of moral perfection before he is cognized as such; even he says of himself: "Why do you call me (whom you see) good? None is good (the archetype of good) but God only (whom you do not see)" [*New Testament*, Matthew 19: 17]. But whence have we the concept of God as the highest good? Solely from the *idea* of moral perfection that reason frames *a priori* and connects inseparably with the concept of a free will.[48]

Kant's appreciation of the highest good echoes, once again, the moral outlook of Confucianism for two main reasons. At the start, Confucianism is in line with Kant's vital argument that "of the two layers of legislation, practical reason is prior to speculative reason."[49] Put briefly, although in ancient China the Kantian dichotomy between nature and morality did not really exist, it was not unusual to divide "knowing" (*zhi* 知) in Confucianism into two parts, which, in Mencius's words, can be recognized as the "sense of hear-and-see" regarding external things, and the "thinking activity" of the Subject previously described as "inner morality." In fact, Mencius's view paved the way for a more significant division between "hear-and-see knowing" (*jian wen zhi zhi* 見聞之知) and "virtuous knowing" (*dexing zhi zhi* 德行之知) throughout the development of Song-Ming Neo-Confucianism.[50] And here, it is plain that Confucian learning as a rule gives priority to "virtuous knowing" (practical reason) over "hear-and-see knowing" (theoretical reason).

What is more, just as the *summum bonum* is the final end of a philosophical system in Kant's context, the ideal of Confucianism is to "attain sagehood" by practicing the "teaching" of the sage. As Mou states,

> The real philosophical question, as etymology shows, is the "love of wisdom," that is, what Kant understands to be the practical knowledge of wisdom. What is wisdom? Only that which can be directed to the highest good is wisdom. While the impulse to aspire to the highest good is the "love of wisdom," this is possible only under the guidance of the concept of reason. Therefore, the "love of wisdom" implies the "love of realizing"; this is what the sage in ancient China called "teaching." What is teaching? Whichever is capable of inspiring human reason and of purifying human life to reach out to the sagehood of the highest good through the path of practice is teaching. All this is obviously about noumena; to give it an academic name, it belongs to "transcendent metaphysics (*chaojue de xingshangxue* 超絕的形上學)."[51]

All this indicates that strictly speaking, the meaning of "transcendent" is categorically different from that of "transcendental," in that unlike Kant's "transcendental idealism," Confucianism recognized as a form of "transcendent metaphysics" is devoted to appreciating noumena with the affirmation of "intellectual intuition." For the sake of clarity, in the following discussion wherein Mou's treatment of this specific feature of Confucianism is involved, I shall replace "transcendental" with "transcendent."

ORTHODOX CONFUCIANISM

To round off his argument, Mou maintains that from Confucius and Mencius of the pre-Qin period (before 255 BC), to the emergence of Neo-Confucianism in the Song (960–1280) and Ming (1368–1644) dynasties, the Confucians held in common the essential character of erecting the moral subject on the basis of "transcendent ground" in support of the "perfect good"; indeed, this is the major reason for putting them together as a great tradition of seeking "inner sagehood" (*neisheng* 內聖). In this manner, the key features of Confucianism disclosed above are reflected in the main themes of the Five Canons of the Confucian tradition, comprising the *Analects* (*Lunyu* 論語), the *Mencius* (*Mengzi* 孟子), the *Great Learning* (*Daxue* 大學), the *Doctrine of the Mean* (*Zhongyong* 中庸), and the *Yi Commentaries* (*Yi Zhuan* 易傳). In other words, even though Confucius and Mencius are separated by more than one hundred years, separated from the *Doctrine of the Mean* and the *Yi Commentaries* by two or three hundred years, and separated from Song-Ming Neo-Confucianism by over one thousand years, "the life and wisdom in each of the classics echo each other to form a sequence of ideas."[52]

To make a long story short: Confucius's discussion of *ren* paves the way for the moral subject, because *ren* is primarily understood as a state of our own heart-mind, and how we deal with our own affairs. As Confucius says, "if I desire *ren*, then *ren* will be there"; "if one day men can restore 'ritual propriety' (*li* 禮), then that day the empire will return to *ren*."[53] On some occasions, *ren* is even treated as the degrees of ease that our heart-mind feels about things in everyday life.[54] Even if it is true that "one does not hear the Master talk about the nature and the *Dao* of Heaven,"[55] it remains the case that the idea of Heaven, emerging from the Three Dynasties of Xia (夏), Shang (商), and Zhou (周), retains ontological meaningfulness in Confucius's moral thinking. In fact, thanks to the connection between Heaven and the "inner morality" of the human heart-mind initiated by Confucius, a mutually resonant and vitally interrelated school of thought known as Confucianism takes shape in Chinese history.

As for Mencius, recent scholarship (including Mou's major work on the "perfect good") has attempted to take Mencius as a crucial turning point for the Kantian reconstruction of Confucianism. This is mainly because, in Mencius's articulation, the heart-mind of compassion, the heart-mind of shame, the heart-mind of courtesy and modesty, and the heart-mind of right and wrong that make up the "four germs" of cardinal virtues, identified respectively as *ren* 仁 (humaneness), *yi* 義 (righteousness), *li* 禮 (ritual proprieties), and *zhi* 智 (wisdom), "are not welded on to me from the outside; they are in me originally."[56] That is to say, Mencius's employment of "heart-mind" (*xin* 心) to explain "*Xing*-nature" (*xing* 性), together with his famous expression of the "goodness of *Xing*-nature" (*xingshan* 性善), is analogous to Kant's maxim that one should act only according to good will. With Mencius, the "transcendent ground" of moral activity therefore points nowhere but to what Heaven has endowed with our "authentic heart-mind" (*benxin* 本心). Thus, "a different view is simply due to want of reflection. Hence it is said, 'Seek and you will find them. Neglect and you will lose them.'"[57]

The *Great Learning* also fits perfectly into the "vertically expressed vertical system" because the work's heuristic expression, "the *Dao* of the Great Learning is to illuminate luminous virtue," actually confirms two things. In one sense, there is the "transcendent ground" presented by the "*Dao* of the Great Learning" itself; in the other sense, the *Dao* becomes approachable to the subject by "illuminating luminous virtue" already implanted in the human heart-mind. On the whole, the *Great Learning* teaches that whenever the illumination is to be presented, the moral subject is to be restored in a way that leads to the pursuit of the highest good.

Again, the first sentence of the *Doctrine of the Mean* restates the relationship between *Xing*-Nature and *Dao* by articulating that: "What is endowed from Heaven is *Xing*-nature, what is in accordance with *Xing*-nature is *Dao*, and what facilitates the fulfillment of *Dao* are teachings."[58] In this fashion, the fundamental idea of "vigilance in solitude" (*shendu* 慎獨) in the *Doctrine of the Mean*, in line with Zengzi's [Tseng Tzu] (曾子) famous saying that I am committed to "examining myself in three areas every day,"[59] equally "emphasizes the Subject, and establishes the Subject through practice (*gongfu* 功夫)."[60]

Finally, even if the topic of the *Yi Commentaries* has a lot to do with cosmology, as it urges us to "thoroughly comprehend the capabilities of the divine Spirit in order to know the process of transformation," its exposition of the "*Dao* of Heaven" is in no way separated from the *Xing*-nature inherent in the Subject. Instead, the divine in question is wholly determined by the virtue of sincerity, which is "manifested through the Subject" and "belongs in the realm of morality."[61] Thus, with the *Doctrine of the Mean* and the *Yi Commentaries*, it becomes more obvious that the cosmological order is principally identical with the moral order in the orthodox Confucian tradition.

As regards Song-Ming Neo-Confucianism, Mou declares that there are, for the most part, three major systems: (1) that of Lu Xiangshan [Lu Hsiang-Shan] (陸象山 1139–1193) and Wang Yangming; (2) that of Hu Wufeng [Hu Wu-Feng] (胡五峰 1105–1161) and Liu Jishan [Liu Chi-Shan] (劉蕺山 1578–1645); and (3) that of Cheng Yichuan [Cheng I-Chuan] (程伊川 1033–1107) and Zhu Xi [Chu Hsi] (朱熹 1130–1200). In a nutshell,

> The first system starts subjectively from a philosophical-anthropological thesis on the human heart-mind, whereas the second one starts objectively from ontological assertions about *Tian* 天 (Heaven). In any event, Mou regards these systems together in the mainstream of Confucianism. In contrast, the third system is excluded from the mainstream, although through his comprehensive philosophical system, Zhu Xi has exerted tremendous influence on the subsequent development of Confucianism.[62]

According to Mou, then, the most influential Song Neo-Confucian, Zhu Xi, is somewhat outside of the orthodox tradition in that by taking a "horizontal expression of the vertical system," his notion of being is "merely being but not at the same time activity."[63] Given that Zhu Xi has had such a great impact on the later development of Confucianism, Mou thus dubs him a "secondary son installed as clan master" (*biezi weizong* 別子為宗).[64] A key thread running throughout Mou's rebuilding of Confucian moral metaphysics, as I shall carry on to illustrate, lies in the idea of *being as activity*.

Confucian Moral Metaphysics

That being said, I now plan to give a general picture of the Confucian moral metaphysics via Mou's ontological criticisms of Kant.

Philosophical Anthropology: Intellectual Intuition

Mou's scrutiny on the ontological aspect of Kant's philosophy is mainly due to the stimulus that he has received from Heidegger's *Kant and the Problems of Metaphysics*,[65] in which Heidegger claims: If we follow Kant in contemplating all interest of human reason in terms of the following three critical questions: "(1) What can I know? (2) What should I do? (3) What may I hope?"[66] then "because these three questions ask about this one [problem], finitude, they are allowed themselves to be related to the fourth: What is a human being?"[67]

More exactly, as we have seen, Kant contends that human beings only have "sensible intuition" of *presenting* the "object" of knowing within a spatiotemporal world, shorn of "intellectual intuition" of *creating* the "object" of knowing, namely, the "transcendental object of sensible intuition," or what Kant otherwise calls "something=X."[68] For this reason, Heidegger deems Kant's first *Critique* a "fundamental ontology," dealing for the first time with "the problem of the necessity of the question concerning *the finitude in human beings* for the purpose of a laying of the ground for metaphysics"; in other words, what Kant provides us with is an "ontological analytic of *the finite essence of human beings* which is to prepare the foundation for the metaphysics which belongs to human nature."[69]

While motivated by Heidegger's verdict of Kant's philosophy, Mou does not agree with Heidegger's approach to establish a "pre-Plato classic ontology," spiraling down toward the empirical world.[70] Instead, given that practical reason is prior to theoretical theory, Mou is more likely to see the first *Critique* as laying a foundation for the "metaphysics of morals."[71] And so, in order to display the general picture of "moral metaphysics" in Confucianism, he is driven to read Kant upside down by reversing the interest of human reason in the following way:[72] (1) What ought I to do? (2) What may I hope? (3) What can I know? (4) What is a human being? For the most part, unlike Kant's reading of finitude into humanity, Chinese philosophy gives a more unrestrained account of the ultimate meaning of human life as its search for *the ontological foundation of morals* is predicated upon the affirmation of "intellectual intuition." That said, the Confucian *liangzhi*, the Buddhist *prajna* 般若 (wisdom), and the Daoist *xiongzhi* 玄智 (mystical seeing) can all be seen as a conviction of "intellectual intuition." In Mou's words,

> If I look back on Chinese philosophy through the lens of Kant's terminology, then I find out that no matter whether

Confucianism, Buddhism or Daoism, all seem to have asserted that we are capable of enjoying intellectual intuition. Otherwise, it would be impossible to become a sage, a Buddha, or even an authentic man. Thus, we cannot ascribe intellectual intuition to God alone; [within Chinese tradition], although man is finite, he can be infinite. In Western tradition, by contrast, whatever is finite is finite, whatever is infinite is infinite. Within such a tradition, man can never enjoy intellectual intuition. . . . But [within Chinese tradition] if human beings are really short of intellectual intuition, then all of Chinese philosophy would collapse completely, and thousands of years of effort would become in vain, turning out to be an illusion.[73]

In what follows, accordingly, I am about to shed light on the three related features of Mou's usage of "intellectual intuition," namely, "creating its own object of intuiting," being "capable of instituting thing-in-itself," and "knowing the whole."[74] By this means, it is hoped that we may arrive at a better understanding of Mou's reconstruction of the Confucian "moral metaphysics," which, as opposed to Kant's "metaphysics of morals," is characterized by the "infinite heart-mind," the "ontology of non-attachment," and the "perfect teaching." As stated, in contrast to Kant's "transcendental metaphysics," what Mou has tried to arrive at is a form of "transcendent metaphysics" grounded in the key concept of "intellectual intuition."

The Infinite Heart-Mind: The Principle of Moral Creativity

In the beginning, the groundwork of Kant's moral philosophy will be shaky as a result of denying the infinite essence of human begins. For, "if human minds are not infinite in this sense, then they cannot issue imperatives with no limitation, and the categorical imperative as the basis of morality is impossible."[75] Thus seen, that which Kant's philosophy is in short supply of is the idea of the "infinite heart-mind," which stands for "the transcendental foundation of moral action and is itself absolutely and infinitely universal."[76] To be sure, either Confucius's *ren* or Mencius's *Xing*-nature amounts to the "infinite heart-mind" so understood, capable of participating in the highest moral order through moral practice. Again, that is why *liangzhi* can be translated as the "knowing-reality of enlightened awareness," meaning that its constant activity is not linked to the limited heart-mind in the "hear-and-see world" but to the endless pursuit of "virtuous knowing," concerning the *luminous illumination* of the "unceasing pureness of virtue."

Put in other terms, thanks to denying "intellectual intuition" to human beings, Kant is silent about the "causality of the will" in relation to the "principle of ontological [creative] actualization."[77]

> Confucianism, however, begins the discussion of this principle not from "will," but from *ren*, or from *Xing*-nature as in the "goodness of *Xing*-nature." "*Xing*-nature" is not an empty concept; rather, a heart-mind of sympathy, a heart-mind of shame and aversion, a heart-mind of right and wrong, and a heart-mind of humility are all included. It also includes Confucius's *ren*. It is creativity and fully implies the very meaning of creativity. Understanding is not the principle of creativity. Only the will is the principle of creativity. The kind of creativity based on the principle of will is moral creativity.[78]

Instead of following Kant in seeing the discussion of noumena as a matter of "mysticism" or "fanaticism,"[79] then, the "infinite heart-mind" is *at the same time* equivalent to *Xing*-reality from the subjective side and to *Dao*-reality from the objective side. As Mou contends,

> In the case of intellectual intuition, things are developed internally in an unrestrained manner. Thus, heart-mind absorbs things into itself. Things are not open to heart-mind, but are the exhibition of the infinite heart-mind, that is, the manifestation and openness of the infinite heart-mind: things are where the infinite heart-mind is working, and the infinite heart-mind works where things are. Thus, they are one and the same. For this reason, things are in no sense objects [as experienced in time and space and according to the categories].[80]

Another way of making the same point is to say that the "heart-mind of *ren*" (*renxin* 仁心) and the "*Dao* of Heaven," or "*Xing*-reality" and "*Dao*-reality," are interrelated in such a way that they are just like two sides of the same coin: "When manifested as the creativity that objectively creates all things, it is *Dao*-reality. When settled in human beings, it is *Xing*-reality."[81] In short, as I shall further explore from the perspective of moral religion in the next chapter, Confucianism undoubtedly contains "existential resonance," asserting that the unceasing reality is one and the same.

The Ontology of Nonattachment: Noumena as a Value Concept

The second line of reasoning that Mou conveys to argue against Kant's rejection of "intellectual intuition" has to do with the distinction between phenomena and noumena. In a basic sense, the distinction at stake reflects Kant's Christian background: the separation of the finite essence of human beings from the infinite character of God; thus, as Heidegger indicates, in Kant's system the subject is divided into the viewpoint of God and that of human beings. In other words, phenomena and noumena do not refer to two different things; instead, they just stand for two different *perspectives* of seeing the same thing. As for God, whose mind is infinite, what is seen is always thing-in-itself; for human beings, whose minds are finite, what is seen is confined to phenomena.

In Mou's understanding, however, this distinction is unsustainable unless human beings can have "intellectual intuition." For one, in keeping with the bifurcated world Kant left, thing-in-itself is not only the "transcendental object of sensible intuition" from the perspective of knowledge, but also, and more importantly, it is the "transcendental object of intellectual intuition" from the perspective of morality. As such, thing-in-itself cannot *just* be "something=X"; rather, it has to be a "value concept" in the strong sense.[82] Consequently, denying "intellectual intuition" to human beings will result in a depreciation of the potentiality of moral development as the pursuit of the highest good, which as Kant claims, is "a problem of transcendence, not a matter of degree."[83] Besides, if human beings are left without "intellectual intuition," the world of morals related to noumena will be nothing but empty. In order to grasp the "concrete and true meaning of noumena clearly and distinctly," and thus, to understand morals in a fuller sense, we should not "locate the infinite mind in God alone."[84]

Against this context, another crucial difference between Chinese and Western philosophy can be repeated with regard to two types of ontology. On the one side, Kant's restricted view of experiencing things through time and space, and by reference to categories and apperceptions, can be seen as a form of "attachment" in human knowing in the Chinese context. That is why the activity of knowing can be understood as the "knowing of the attaching mind" (*sixin zhi zhi* 思心之知) and the type of ontology related to it, the "ontology of attachment" (*zhi de cunyoulun* 執的存有論). On the other, what Kant refers to as thing-in-itself, the infinite mind of God or the "intellectual intuition" that only belongs to God, signifies "nonattachment" in Chinese. Without the "attachment" of the knowing mind, the kind of ontology it advocates can be named the "ontology of nonattachment" (*wuzhi de cunyoulun* 無執的存有論). The point is that whereas in the "ontology of nonattachment" the emphasis is "on the liberation from attachment so as to enhance the meaning of our existence," in the "ontology of attachment," the stress is "on the pursuit of knowledge and the establishment of institutions."[85]

Put differently, the "infinite heart-mind" filled with "intellectual intuition" is nonattached, inasmuch as it is capable of knowing and realizing *Dao*-reality in a way that allows no arbitrary divisions between heart-mind and things, subjectivity and objectivity, and the like. Thus, while Kant includes the existence of God as one of the three postulates, in Confucianism,

> *Dao*-reality can be a substitute for God. Since heart-mind-reality and *Dao*-reality are one and the same, there is only one postulate, and this can be God if one wishes to invoke God; it can be freedom if one wishes to invoke freedom, and it can be the immortality of the soul if one wishes to invoke the immortality of the soul. Chinese do not specify individual souls, but see "heart-mind" as the absolute, universal, and everlasting unity.[86]

In the language of Confucianism, this is to say that "there is nothing beyond heart-mind, nothing beyond *Dao*, and nothing beyond *Xing*-nature,"[87] in accordance with the "conformity of Heaven and man in union" (*tianren heyi* 天人合一). For this reason, Zhang Zai [Chang Tsai] (張載 1020–1077), for example, urges us to develop "the knowledge of heart-mind" so as to grasp and participate in "Heaven's ceaseless generation" in the "Great Void" (*taixu* 太虛), and Wang Yangming arrives at a perfect understanding of the moral ideal of Confucianism by saying that "the great man thinks of Heaven, earth, and the myriad things as oneness."[88]

In no way, however, does Mou intend to abandon the distinction between phenomena and noumena altogether. The truth is rather that he is eager to develop a "two-level ontology,"[89] settling the ontological status of both scientific knowledge and moral thinking. In brief, given that "virtuous knowing" is prior to "hear-and-see knowing," the epistemic mind associated with the knowing subject actually stems from the "infinite heart-mind" related to the moral subject. To make his point, Mou draws on the Buddhist idea of "one heart-mind opening two gates" (*yixin kai liangmen* 一心開兩門) in substantiating the possibility of switching from the "ontology of nonattachment" to the "ontology of attachment." Mou's accommodation of a Kant-like epistemology for Chinese philosophy is beyond the scope of this study. Here, I just want to reiterate in passing that for Mou, to develop a knowing subject on which science rests and to develop a political subject on which democracy rests are similar, in that they both involve a process of "self-negation" in the Hegelian sense. For the sake of structure, I shall not deal with the topic of "self-negation" until chapter 4.

The Perfect Teaching: The Unity between Morals and Nature

Finally, as regards the *summum bonum*, that is, the "exact correspondence of morality and happiness," we have seen that Kant's solution is to assume the existence of God. The main issue that Mou raises to Kant, however, is this: If it is the case that in reality a man's pursuit of "virtue" in the moral world is not always in just proportion to the "happiness" he enjoys in the natural world, then it is difficult to comprehend "how a divine intelligence or divine volition (*shensi shenyi* 神思神意), which is absolutely different from that of a human being, can make them [viz., morals and nature] harmonious transcendentally and externally," or alternatively, "how those which are not coordinate may at once become coordinate simply because there is a God who creates them."[90] As opposed to Kant, Mou makes it clear that what Confucianism has actually accomplished is a vital form of "perfect teaching," that it is only in terms of Confucian "perfect teaching" that the possibility of the "exact correspondence of morality and happiness" can be exhibited, and that the gist of Confucian "perfect teaching" has been perfectly expressed in the principle of the "conformity of Heaven and man in union," and the like.

Unlike Kant, Confucianism firmly believes that everyone has the ability to become a sage through moral practice, regardless of the invocation of God. Besides, it will be remembered that in the Confucian tradition "whatever the sages speak are teachings." More accurately, as indicated, "a teaching is anything which suffices to educate people's reason and guides people to purify human life-force through practical effort (*shijian* 實踐) to the fullest extent possible (*zhi qi ji* 至其極)."[91] Hence, the doctrine of the *summum bonum* in Confucianism can be dubbed the "perfect teaching" as it is concerned with the wisdom of teaching in the perfect sense, that is, the *Dao* of the sage in making possible the "completeness of the entire life" (*quanbu rensheng zhi jizhi* 全部人生之極致).[92] Also, it is instructive to note that Mou's treatment of the "perfect teaching" in Confucianism, despite receiving aspirations from Tiantai Buddhism,[93] differs from both Buddhism and Daoism[94] in that only Confucianism endorses a "vertical backbone of moral creativity,"[95] presenting the "vertically expressed vertical system" in the utmost sense.

What is more, while the idea of *renxin*, *benxin* or *liangzhi* is akin to Kant's free will in the sense of guiding our moral consciousness to act rationally in accordance with the moral law, moving toward the state of the *summum bonum*, against Kant, there is a robust tendency to affirm "intellectual intuition" and to see the "infinite heart-mind," be it *renxin*, *benxin*, or *liangzhi*, as a principle of moral creativity in association with the "unceasing pureness of virtue" in Confucianism. That said, in the case of a Confucian sage, the ultimate meaning of human life, the highest value of noumena, is not so much recognized as God's knowledge but created and exhibited by the "infinite heart-mind" or the "infinite intellectual heart-mind" (*wuxian zhixin* 無限智心),[96] which "takes everything as a whole." To quote the *Doctrine of the Mean*, it is concurrently "taking part in the creation of the world and assisting in change and cultivation" (*cantiandi zanhuayu* 參天地贊化育).[97] Thus seen, not only does the "infinite heart-mind" constantly expresses "teachings" via the moral practice of the sage, but it also "replenishes and creates all beings" (*runze er chuangsheng yiqie cunzai* 潤澤而創生一切存在). To quote Mou,

> The [noumenal] mind-intent-knowledge (*xin yi zhi* 心意知) replenishes and creates all beings. At the same time, it also contains the "unceasing pureness of virtue" pursued by our conduct which abides by the autonomous heavenly principle

> (*zilu tianli* 自律天理) within mind-intent-knowledge, and all beings replenished and created by the mind-intent-knowledge necessarily change with it. This is happiness—that the conditions of all beings change with [mind-intent-knowledge], everything being satisfactory, with no dissatisfaction to speak of it, is happiness. In this way, virtue and being mutually entail, and through this dialectical entailment, virtue and happiness merge into one single whole.[98]

All this indicates that regarding the "infinite heart-mind," it is impossible to tell apart virtue and existence. Thanks to the presence of "intellectual intuition," the Confucian "perfecting teaching" therefore makes a distinguished case about the possibility of an "exact correspondence of morality and happiness," in which morals and nature are united as a concrete universal.

In this scheme, Confucius's saying of "practicing *ren* and knowing Heaven" (*jiangren zhitian* 踐仁知天) also may help greatly bring to light the authentic meaning of the "perfect teaching" as it accords entirely with the "conformity of Heaven and man in union." Again, this way of thinking is thoroughly revealed in Mencius's belief that the moral practice of "giving full realization to heart-mind" (*jinxin* 盡心) is deeply rooted in the ontological matters of "knowing *Xing*-nature" (*zhixing* 知性) and "knowing Heaven" (*zhitian* 知天). Undeniably, counter to the Kantian gap between morality and happiness, Mencius's notion of the "perfect teaching" immediately establishes a connection between "Heavenly dignity" (*tianjue* 天爵) and "human nobility" (*renjue* 人爵) or between "what is prescribed" by *Xing*-nature (*suoxing* 所性) and "what is pleased" by human desire (*suole* 所樂).[99] From Confucius and Mencius to Song-Ming Neo-Confucianism, the "perfect teaching" of the vertical backbone has finally been captured in Hu Wufeng's extremely thoughtful statement, indicating that "Heavenly principle and human desire are different functions of the same reality."[100]

Moral Metaphysics versus Metaphysics of Morals

To complete this section, let me now try to summarize the contrast between Mou's "moral metaphysics" and Kant's "metaphysics of morals." In general, Mou agrees with Kant's distinction between "theological ethics" and "moral theology." For the most part, the former "contains moral laws, which presuppose the existence of a supreme ruler of the world," whereas the latter consists of a "conviction of the existence of a supreme being—a conviction which bases itself on moral laws."[101] More precisely, while the search for "metaphysical ethics" or "theological ethics" can be seen as a bid to establish morality on the ground of metaphysics or theology, "modifying 'metaphysics' and 'theology' with the adjective 'moral,'" as Mou argues, is meant to imply that "metaphysics and theology are based on morality."[102] In a stricter sense, however, what Kant has at last achieved is something like a "metaphysics of morals," and for this reason, Mou's restatement of the Confucian "moral metaphysics" still varies from Kant's system in some pivotal ways.

First and foremost, at the heart of Mou's project lies the affirmation of "intellectual intuition," whereas Kant holds that only God can have this knowledge. Accordingly, in Mou's "moral metaphysics," ontology and morality are so closely related that "the objects of our knowledge, including the selves that we know, have moral value"; rather, for Kant at his most rigorous, "phenomena are known and noumena have value."[103] Instead of repeating the features of "intellectual intuition" underpinning Mou's idea of "moral metaphysics," we only need to bear in mind that for Mou, the most distinctive character of Confucianism on this matter is that it identifies *ren* and *Xing*-nature as the "infinite heart-mind" that enjoys the ability of moral creativity. And thus, as I shall elucidate in the subsequent chapters, Mou constantly refuses to see freedom merely as a postulate: "if freedom is only a postulate not a *presentation* (*chengxian* 呈現), (for it is not within the reach of empirical knowledge), then moral laws, the categorical imperative, and so on, must be in vain";[104] this is the key point that Kant cannot get hold of. From this, it also follows that Mou and Kant have strikingly different views about the role of human feeling in morality.[105]

Focusing on the central problem of the subject or the self, it can be added that in addition to the "empirical self" described in Kant's anthropology, Kant sets the "knowing self" apart from the "moral self": the "knowing self" unifies experience through the "unity of apperception," while the "moral self" is linked to the autonomy of free will. In other words, owing to the assumption of the bifurcated world, Kant is reluctant to synthesize the various forms of the self into a "higher self," and he thinks that to explore the existence of the self is beyond the realm of cognitive knowledge. Even if the knowing subject is able to think of his *body* as an object of outer sense and to experience the contents of his *consciousness* as objects of inner sense, he cannot have "intellectual intuition" of intuiting *himself* as an object.[106]

Although Mou strongly agrees with Kant on separating the essence of moral reasoning from that of scientific reasoning, he fears that the insufficiency of Kant's "transcendental idealism" will bring about a cultural crisis of scientism and technocracy. It is largely on this account that Mou writes:

> He (Kant) opened the door to higher levels of thought. The reason we engage Kantian philosophy is to provide an uplifting path [beyond knowledge]; only by moving upward can philosophy be firmly sustained. If it is not sustained with uplifting concerns [beyond knowledge], it descends into positivism. In a certain sense, Kant is the most encompassing logical positivist.[107]

Without a doubt, a more profound involvement of Mou's philosophy is aimed at making a Confucian response to the predicaments of Western modernity rooted in Kant's bifurcated world. Inasmuch as Confucianism is, after all, concerned with the erection of the moral subject and the full actualization of humanity, it is not surprising that Mou attempts to employ post-Kantian philosophical resources to make more conspicuous the characteristics of Confucianism. As we shall see shortly, for example, Mou greatly appreciates Hegel's archetypal critique of Kant's treatment of free will as a postulate, along the lines of the principle of actualization, embodied individualism, and the endless process of moral development toward the higher self, or real subjectivity.

In a like manner, despite the fact that Mou's "two-level ontology" does not necessarily abandon the distinction between phenomena (science) and noumena (morality), he takes issues with Kant's account of the ultimate realm of reality. According to Mou,

> If Western philosophy makes Kant its center, it must develop and move ahead further. Otherwise it will continue the present downward slide. Those German philosophers who came after Kant, such as Fichte, Schelling, and Hegel, all saw this. . . . [I]n Hegel there was a propensity to digest the three postulates into one. . . . In this manner we have moved a step forward:

turning from what Kant calls "moral theology" into Confucian "moral metaphysics."[108]

This clearly implies that counter to Kant's divisions of the three postulates mentioned above, Mou takes the reality to be *one and the same*. That said, on the ontological level, *Xing*-reality and *Dao*-reality are so identified that the full meaning of reality, as Hegel contends, rejects any divisions between mind and things, subjectivity and objectivity, man and God, and the like.

Finally, in spite of ascribing "intellectual intuition" to God, Kant maintains that we can never determine whether God possesses this faculty; indeed, for Kant, the existence of God is a hope rather than true knowledge. It follows that as far as Kant's "metaphysics of morals" is concerned, morality is divorced from theology and metaphysics at the end of the day. In contrast, the Confucian "moral metaphysics" in Mou's denotation aims to seek an "identification of morals and religiousness," a "unification of morals and metaphysics."[109]

This is to say that the focus of attention in Mou's "moral metaphysics" is the "universe in its metaphysical dimension." Thus, morals are at once pointing to "the practical approach toward the actualization in our lives and through our deeds (including emotions and intentions) of the ultimate (metaphysical, cosmological, ontological) reality shared by both the universe and by our nature."[110] Therefore, despite the differences, Mou has every so often referred to *ren* and *Xing*-nature as the "concrete universal" in the Hegelian vein.

Confucianism as a Concrete Philosophy

The above discussion, as I see it, clearly makes room for opening dialogue between Mou and Hegel and the British idealists.

THE IMPORTANCE AND LIMITATIONS OF HEGEL

Just as Mou was an admirer of Kant, it is equally known to his readers that Mou held Hegel in very high esteem, not to mention that Mou's earlier writings on political philosophy were essentially dependent on Hegel's philosophy of history and that Mou's usage of "self-negation" was replete with Hegelian insights. To be sure, Mou's political philosophy is still far from being well studied, partly because an adequate account of its Hegelian sources has not been provided due to a lack of awareness of Hegel's contributions to liberalism in the Chinese context. In acknowledging his debts to Hegel in general, Mou remarks:

> Thus, strictly speaking, Hegel is not a philosopher in the orthodox tradition of Western philosophy . . . [because] the problems discussed by Hegel are not representative thought, nor conceptual analysis. What he discussed was concrete philosophy, whereas what Western philosophy has emphasized has been abstract analysis. What is concrete philosophy? For example, discussion of morality, religion, art, and history all belong to concrete philosophy. Hegel always discussed these things. . . . *And it is very easy for Chinese people to understand the sort of things he discussed. People dislike Hegel because he did not express himself in a felicitous manner. We are not going to adopt his way of expression, but as to the truths he discussed, we will often refer to them.* [emphasis mine][111]

What, then, are the "truths Hegel discussed?" To this, Mou responds elsewhere that

> Hegel's talking about the philosophy of spirit is far better [than Kant]. I have often borrowed his terms for the sake of expressions, such as "real subjectivity," "in itself," "for itself," the "concrete universal." Nonetheless, this merely means that I borrow his method, rather than that his philosophical implications are identical with the teaching of virtue-accomplishment in Confucianism.[112]

Before going any further to examine how the Hegelian insights are at work in Mou's philosophical project, however, I want to declare at the outset that in addition to complaining about Hegel's style of presentation, Mou has several reservations about Hegel. For one thing, in spite of giving praise to Fichte for "having the best understanding of Kant's practical reason among post-Kantian Western philosophers," Mou also criticizes Fichte, Hegel, and Schelling "for affirming intellectual intuition without offering arguments against Kant's denial of it."[113]

In Mou's viewpoint, this is mainly because neither of these thinkers relates "intellectual intuition" to a notion of the "infinite heart-mind" in association with the principle of moral creativity. In the end, against the context of Christianity, Hegel still holds that it is God who creates humanity, the meaning of history, and the law of nature.

Also, Mou is not content with Hegel's usage of dialectic in his Logic, in that the Absolute is treated as a bare concept *without moral import* from the very beginning. In Mou's words,

> Hegel's great Logic was erected without a basis. He cut off the background of the "display of spirit in human praxis" and without any basis adopted a bare "Absolute" as the starting point of his dialectical development, and this dialectical development began with the "Absolute itself" in the medium of pure thought and pure reason and unfolded paradoxically to the end. In this way, he deduced all the categories. This is actually a paradox of thought itself and is an unnecessary grand trick.[114]

Finally, probably influenced by cold war liberalism, Mou concedes that Hegel's theory of the state, in default of careful examination, would be sliding into totalitarianism with the rise of Marxism.[115] "Some say that Hegelian philosophy helps breed totalitarianism, but very seldom do people say the same of Confucianism, Buddhism, or Daoism."[116]

Be all this as it may, in opening cross-cultural moral dialogue between Mou and post-Kantian Western philosophy, Hegel matters a lot. Because, seen in light of the history of philosophy, Hegel was one of the most significant *internal* critics of Kant. In this regard, it is worth reiterating that Hegel actually developed his "concrete philosophy" without throwing away the moral features of Confucianism that Mou has tried hard to spell out via the Kantian frame, namely, the moral subject, the ultimate meaning of human life, and the pursuit of the highest good.

REAL SUBJECTIVITY

Let me now resume the main Hegelian terminology at stake. The first thing that concerns me in this study is the idea of real subjectivity. More exactly, in Kant's transcendental analysis, as shown, morality derives neither from traditions and communities, nor from the law of nature, nor from the inclination of the nature of men, but from pure reason alone. Seen from the Hegelian perspective, however, there are prices that Kant has to pay for this purity, namely, to commit to procedural formalism irrespective of the true *actualization* of human freedom and to espouse abstract individualism irrespective of the full *potentiality* of human reason. On the one hand, in terms of formalism, Mou comments with a Hegelian tone that for Kant,

> Free will, the immortality of the soul, and the existence of God are of significance and of veracity only when they are seen from the standpoint of practical reason. However, the lack of the idea of *Xing*-reality, and the treatment of freedom as a postulate, have made the notion of free will almost in vain, and practical reason itself almost remote from practice. And thus, his plan of metaphysics of morals (whose contents are free will, thing-in-itself, the unification of morality and nature) is unclear and vague, unable to demonstrate, to accomplish itself in a complete sense.[117]

On the other hand, in terms of individualism, it appears equally true that Kant's definition of human reason as lawgiver is applied to a limited concept of human reason and says little about the unlimited potentiality of human reason in realizing the *Dao*-reality, the highest good, through concrete practice in context. In his earlier writings, Mou clearly writes in a Hegelian sense that *ren* or *Xing*-nature recognized as the fullest presentation of human reason amounts to the "universal reason regulated by humanity in harmony with divinity."[118]

Furthermore, complementing the slogan that "although man is finite, he can be infinite," Mou articulates elsewhere that "even if the world has an end, human wishes are endless."[119] This affirms that Confucianism takes not a biological but a practical viewpoint in examining the meaning of what it is to be a human being. Thus, it is expected that through endless efforts, *Xing*-reality, which by nature is not an abstract idea but the concrete universal of the authentic heart-mind, understood as *ren*, *Xing*-nature, or *liangzhi*, will be actualized to the highest level possible in specific situations.

Taken as a whole, while the Kantian idea of moral practice is associated with "disengaged subjectivity," meaning that moral conduct is to act "from duty" through the guidance of "reason" irrespective of any desire and inclination and regardless of any culture and history, the Hegelian pursuit of self-realization, according to Charles Taylor, provides "one of the most profound and far-reaching attempts to work out a vision of embodied subjectivity, of thought and freedom emerging from the stream of life, finding expression in the forms of social existence, and discovering themselves in relation to nature and history."[120] In other words, "the moral subject in Kant lacks the power of *self-realization*, which means there is a narrowing of the 'autonomy' of the moral subject as its moral *self-legislation*" (emphasis mine).[121] In short, what Taylor means by "embodied subjectivity" is just another expression of "real subjectivity," the "higher self" or the "true self" in Mou's critical appreciation of Kant through the lens of Hegel.

THE FULL MEANING OF REALITY

What is closely related to embodied subjectivity is Hegel's discussion of reality in relation to absolute idealism. As one scholar correctly expresses,

> For Hegel, reality (*Wirklichkeit*) in its full sense requires the cooperation of two principles, namely the universal principle of the idea and the particular principle of individuality or subjectivity. Without the latter, no progress is possible, because only the individual subject can provide the kind of opposite (*Gegensatz*) without which there is no vehicle for the idea to become real. Freedom, for instance, is one of Hegel's more concrete names for the idea that evolves in history, but without human beings who strive to be free and who establish institutions meant to secure their freedom, the idea of freedom lacks reality and remains abstract. The principle of individuality manifests itself as the particular will of human beings who make freedom their purpose and set out to put it into practice.[122]

As we shall see in chapter 4, it is largely based on the full meaning of reality as such, together with the Hegelian philosophy of history, that Mou comes to elucidate what he famously says about the "blossoming of democracy" (*minzhu kaichu* 民主開出) through a process of "self-negation." For now, I just want to remark that in Mou's understanding, while Chinese culture contains "subjective spirit" and "absolute spirit," democracy, as well as the modern state, law, and sovereignty, involves "objective spirit."[123] In order to develop democracy out of Confucianism, as a result, the spirit of *ren*, simultaneously acting as the idea of freedom, must endure a dialectical *shift* in terms of which the Chinese people who "strive to be free" may be able to "establish institutions meant to secure their freedom."

Concrete Universality

As a final point, the distinction between the "extensional truth" of science and the "intensional truth" of morality mentioned above is, in point of fact, consistent with the two different kinds of truth, namely, "abstract universality" penetrating the mainstream tradition in the West and the "concrete universality" promoted by Hegel, among others. Hegel's idea of the "concrete universal" is meaningful to Chinese philosophy, simply because "*ren* is not an abstract idea and it can be concretely manifested in real life."[124] In the course of this book, there will appear a number of occasions for the author to shed light on this important issue. For the present, it suffices to remark that according to Mou,

> Confucian *ren* has infinitely many manifestations.... The manifestations of *ren* occur in response to different situations, such as in response to parents, friends, and siblings. *Ren* manifests itself in the different situations as a process with elasticity.[125]

By no means, however, does this mean that abstract universality is unimportant for the future development of Chinese culture as it is on extensional truth that science and democracy rest. Rather, if it is true that the gist of cross-cultural dialogue is, after all, centered on mutual understanding, then only when we realize truths that are universal in all cultures can the communications between, say, Chinese and Western philosophy, become meaningful. Taking as the point of departure the premise that the crisis of Chinese culture lies in the lack of science and democracy developing out of Western culture whereas Western culture lacks the profound wisdom of life found in Chinese culture, Mou's ultimate purpose of undertaking philosophical dialogue is to make the case that "adjustment" is required on both sides: While intensional truth may help people in the extensional-truth-learning Western culture "adjust their attitudes toward life," Chinese culture is in need of extensional truth to develop science and democracy.[126]

Beyond Hegel

Up to this point, we have seen the affinities and disparities between Mou, Kant, and Hegel. In my interpretation of Mou's plan, although it is only through the Kantian scheme that both the intrinsic character of Confucianism as a moral theory and the uniqueness of Confucian moral metaphysics can be made obvious, this does not affect the fact that Hegelianism is of great significance in enhancing Confucian practical reason, especially in respect of actualization, embodiment, and manifestation, from a comparative perspective. Here as elsewhere in this study, it is my central argument that as Mou is a post-Kantian thinker, his intellectual resources rely on both Kant and Hegel.

This at once brings our attention back to British idealism once again. I have previously given a succinct account of the reasons indicating the relevance of this school of thought. To intensify my stance, it can be added here that the British idealists, despite being influenced by Hegel, do not forsake Kantian autonomy.[127] Considering the post-Kantian setting, it seems that Mou's line of reasoning is remarkably akin to T. H. Green, who claims that while the ultimate end in morality is Kantian autonomy, this Kantianism is blended with a Hegelianism (and indeed, an Aristotelianism), "so that the self is seen to be mediated through others, that the community (*qua* kingdom of ends) is necessary to the realization of the self, and that this kingdom of ends is reflected in existing institutions."[128]

In the main, for the British idealists, self-realization means the perfection of human personality or human character, namely, the full actualization of one's moral capacities and ends toward a higher self. That said, the Hegelian ideas of embodied subjectivity, the ideal self, the full meaning of reality, objective spirit, the actualization of freedom, the concrete universal, and so on, also play a crucial part in shaping the formula of self-realization. As we shall see in chapter 2, in terms of real subjectivity, Mou's earlier statement on moral religion is not dissimilar to Hegel's and Green's viewpoints.

What is more, just like Confucianism, there is also a tendency to emphasize the social dimension of the moral self in the works of the British idealists. In fact, as I shall elaborate in chapter 3, bearing a striking resemblance to Mou's claim that "although man is finite, he can be infinite," F. H. Bradley, for instance, points out that to take self-realization as the moral end is to argue that "what one desires is self as a whole," that "the self is to be realized as an infinite whole," and that "the only way a man can do that, given his finitude, is to know and will himself as a member in an infinite whole."[129] Also, Mou actually thinks that Bradley's employment of "reconciliatory dialectic" (*xiaorong bianzhengfa* 消融辯證法) in ethical studies can be seen as a vital revision of Hegel's dialectical logic, which renders the Absolute a "bare concept without moral import from the very beginning." More to the point, Bradley's attempt to transcend the partialities of both Kantian deontology (in favor of the moral law) and utilitarianism (in favor of pleasure), or put differently, to reconnect morality with nature, is advantageous to illuminating the idea of moral perfection in Confucianism from a comparative perspective.

In political terms, it should be remembered that the political theory of British idealism is believed to have made substantial contributions to a Hegelian form of "ethical liberalism" by clarifying some of the ambiguous meanings in Hegel's political philosophy, such as the attack on the abstract individualistic assumption of mainstream liberalism and procedural democracy, the actualization of true freedom in both personal and political contexts, the central place of the common good in collective life, the rights recognition thesis, and so forth. Provided that there are salient affinities between New Confucianism and British idealism in terms of the ethics of self-realization, it is my conviction that to uncover a far-reaching hidden dialogue between them would not only help "liberalize" the political thought of Confucianism in an ethical way, but also "enrich" our general understanding of humanity as a whole across cultures.

In short, given that the philosophical outlook of British idealism not only owes much to both Kant and Hegel, but as a political movement also makes substantial contributions to a Hegelian form of ethical liberalism, a potential interlocution between New Confucianism and British idealism can help bring to light what I have referred to as Confucian liberalism.

Chapter 2

Returning to Moral Religion

Introduction

One of the major themes underpinning the rebirth of New Confucianism in the modern epoch has been an attempt to reformulate the religious aspect of Chinese culture.[1] For instance, the centrality of moral religion in Confucianism was greatly emphasized in the famous "Declaration on Behalf of Chinese Culture Respectively Announced to the People of the World" (*Wei Zhongguo wenhua jinggao shijie renshi xuanyan* 為中國文化敬告世界人士宣言 1958), the authors of which, on top of Mou Zongsan, also included Tang Junyi [Tang Chun-I] (唐君毅 1909–1978), Zhang Junmai [Carsun Chang] (張君勱 1887–1969), and Xu Fuguan [Hsu Fu-Kuan] (徐復觀 1904–1982):

> While investigating China's practice of moral or ethical principles, we will also discover the religiously transcendental feeling embedded within them. In Chinese Humanism, there can be no denial or negligence of the concept of "conformity of virtue between Heaven and man," or "unity of Heaven and man." This may be interpreted as "Nature and human nature are two in one," or "Heaven and man are in comprehensive harmony." "Heaven" so-called may, of course, portray various meanings. In one sense, it is the visible sky. However, the concept of Heaven in ancient China plainly refers to God as having human personality. Although a variety of interpretations appeared in the thoughts of Confucius, Mencius,

Lao Tzu [Laozi] (老子) and Chuang Tzu [Zhuangzi] (莊子), they all attributed to the concept of Heaven a transcendental meaning as distinguished from the realistic man himself or from the realistic relation between man and man.[2]

To begin with, three points should be clarified to facilitate a proper understanding of the Confucian notion of moral religion. First, according to Confucianism, there is no arbitrary division between morality and religion; in the deepest sense moral consciousness is dependent on religious consciousness, which offers an objective moral source and the highest moral ideal for human action. That said, seen from the perspective of moral religion, the ethical course of learning to be fully human is predicated on the "idea of homo *religiosus*," which conveys an "ontological assertion about human nature."[3] In sharp contrast to modern secular systems of morality, such as rights-based liberalism, existentialism, and postmodernism, the constellation of moral religion in Confucian thought contains a cluster of comprehensive metaphysical viewpoints about the creation of the world, the first principles of morals, the nature of man, and, perhaps, the meaning of human history.

Second, the *religiousness* of Confucianism does not point to the rituals, institutions, and authorities of a conventional religion; rather, "religiousness" here means the pathway for man to fulfill his spiritual life. That is to say, Confucianism as a moral religion is a "religion without Church";[4] what makes it a "religion" is not "ecclesiastical" aspects that would concern a "theologian," but the true meaning of being a man, which concerns a "philosopher." In this regard, it is not surprising that a pivotally important principle in Confucianism is the "conformity of Heaven and man in union" (*tianren heyi* 天人合一), the "conformity of virtue between Heaven and man" (*tianren hede* 天人合德), or the "same substance of Heaven and man" (*tianren tongti* 天人同體), which entails the anthropocosmic view that "to fully express our humanity, we must engage in a dialogue with Heaven because human nature, as conferred by Heaven, realizes itself not by departing from its source but by returning to it."[5] In short, an internalized conception of Heaven, and its ultimate meaning for completing humanity, lies at the heart of Confucian moral religion.

Third, given the ultimate guiding force of *tianren heyi*, it follows that the moral ideal that characterizes Confucianism is closely related to a profound understanding of the fulfillment of self-realization. In this regard, the idea of religiousness under discussion gives rise to a robust form of humanism with the purpose of developing toward a "transcendental existence or realm of an infinite completeness of truth, goodness, and beauty"; in the language of Confucianism, what this implies is the moral ideal of trying one's best to "attain sagehood" (*chengsheng* 成聖) by "giving full realization to one's heart-mind and knowing one's own *Xing*-nature" (*jinxin zhixing* 盡心知性) or "illuminating the heart-mind and finding the *Xing*-nature" (*mingxin jianxing* 明心見性).[6] Thus seen, the humanist spirit of realizing oneself to the utmost extent has played an essential role in formulating the moral relationship between man and Heaven in Confucianism. In brief, in terms of the ethics of self-realization, the moral ideal that Confucianism proposes involves an inner process of "ultimate self-transformation" that leads toward the actualization of the "authentic self."[7]

While the three key features of moral religion may represent a general moral picture of Confucianism, here I am chiefly concerned with Mou's elucidation on these topics, which, in many ways, interestingly resonates with Tang Junyi's insights.[8] This chapter serves several purposes. First and foremost, as indicated, despite Mou's reputation for "philosophizing" Confucianism through the Kantian frame, it remains the case that some crucial aspects of Mou's academic enterprise are greatly indebted to Hegel and that its "ultimate objective, which somewhat echoes that of Western post-Kantian philosophy, is to demonstrate the limits of Kant and what the contribution of Chinese thought may be to surpass him."[9] More exactly, in response to the "crisis of meaning" triggered by the "modernization" challenge to Chinese culture, Mou is devoted to reestablishing the moral character of Confucianism by reading Kant's idea of autonomy into the philosophy of Confucius, Mencius, and the Lu-Wang School of Song-Ming Neo-Confucianism. But, in my view, it is largely through Hegel's dialectical philosophy that Mou comes to merge the moral ideal of Confucianism with liberal democracy into an innovative form of liberalism in the Chinese context, namely, the Confucian liberalism grounded in an ethics of self-realization.

Here, instead of fleshing out Mou's political thinking, it suffices to restate that apart from the Hegelian idea of the "self-negation" (*ziwo kanxian* 自我坎陷) of *liangzhi* 良知 ("original knowing," or the "knowing-reality of enlightened awareness"), a central concept in Mou's democratic theory, Mou is also receptive to Hegel's understanding of history as the realization of human freedom, to the Hegelian principle of embodiment, or the particular principle of individuality or subjectivity that renders human action meaningful in history, and to Hegel's attempt to transcend Kant's definition of human reason with regard to the bifurcated world. Regarding moral religion in particular, Hegel's immanent theology actually provides Mou with a "prominent Western voice lending critical support for the inner sagehood (*neisheng* 內聖) of human beings";[10] in fact, I take it that thanks to the influence of Hegel, Mou's reading of Christianity reaffirms "Kant's many seemingly passing and unimportant remarks on religion in the first *Critique*."[11] In short, the presence of the Hegelian way of thinking did not prevent Mou from taking Kant's scheme as his pathway to reach out through a unique system of moral metaphysics across cultures; on the contrary, it makes a great addition to our understanding of Mou's momentous contributions to the creative transformation of Confucianism in modern times.

Moreover, in this sense, it is instructive to compare Mou with T. H. Green in relation to moral religion. Just as Green tries to bring together Kant's subjectivity and Hegel's immanent God in establishing his own idea of "eternal consciousness," it is widely agreed that the notion of moral subjectivity in Confucianism is a blend of transcendence and immanence.[12] By exploring the philosophical similarities between Mou and Green, I shall be able to make the key claim that although recent scholarship has largely directed attention to the connection between the Confucian self and the Kantian self, Mou's reconstruction of the Confucian self, in point of fact, bears a striking resemblance to a Hegel-inspired ethics of self-realization. Indeed, through a Hegelian reinterpretation of Mou's moral thinking, it is hoped that this book may go some way toward reshaping Mou's liberal political thinking in a new light.

That said, provided that there are salient affinities between Green and Mou in terms of moral religion, the ethics of self-realization, the idea of real subjectivity, the notion of embodied individualism, and so on, it is my conviction that a far-reaching dialogue between New Confucianism and British idealism can help bring to light the general picture of Confucian liberalism. This could be achieved through encouraging a reappreciation of the values of liberalism in terms of ethical democracy, civilized citizens, a nondominant concept of the common good, a perfectionist reading of freedom, and the social recognition of rights on the one hand, and broadening the cultural horizons of the Confucian legacy on the other.

Hegel: The Reconciliation of God and Humanity

Let me begin with a brief examination of Hegel's philosophical reflection on Christianity. Overall, what is essential to Hegel's philosophical enterprise is a self-awareness of the growing sense of alienation and estrangement in human feeling, caused, among other factors, by the snapping of the bonds between man and God. As Hegel states, "our religion wishes to educate men to be the citizens of heaven who always look on high, and this makes them strangers to human feeling."[13]

RETHINKING CHRISTIANITY

In fact, in his search for a "purely moral religion,"[14] Hegel's early writings displayed his aversion to the orthodox doctrines of Christianity. For example, in "The Positivity of the Christian Religion," Hegel comes to challenge Christian authorities on two main counts: his Romantic love for Greek "folk religion," whose ultimate truth was beauty, and his early devotion to Kantian ethical thinking in favor of autonomy and rationality. Although a "deep sympathy for the doctrine of the Gospel" as a resolution for his "inner struggle" is present in "The Spirit of Christianity and Its Fate,"[15] Hegel describes the tragedy of Christianity by remarking:

> In all the forms of the Christian religion which have been developed in the advancing fate of the ages, there lies this fundamental characteristic opposition in the divine which is supposed to be present in consciousness only, never in life.... Between these extremes of the multiple or diminished consciousness of friendship, hate, or indifference toward the world, between these extremes which occur within the opposition between God and the world, between divine and life, the Christian church has oscillated to and fro, but it is contrary to its essential character to find peace in a non-personal living beauty. And it is its fate that church and state, worship and life, piety and virtue, spiritually and worldly action, can never dissolve into one.[16]

What Hegel complains about here are the "extremes which occur within the opposition between God and the world, between divine and life."

As might be expected, this not only reiterates St. Paul's identification of the Christian as a "pilgrim in a foreign land," but also anticipates Hegel's later famous expression of "unhappy consciousness" in his *Phenomenology of Spirit*. In Hegel's statement, passing through ancient Stoicism and Skepticism, the self-consciousness emerging in the Christian spirit is so indifferent to human life that, although one is free in the "beyond," he is restricted in this world, as the "beyond" is "something that cannot be found."[17] As a result of this, the Christian is supposed to live in neither world and can never feel "at home." On this account, I think Judith Shklar is correct in remarking that "Hegel had a very deep sense of the enduring wounds that the 'unhappy consciousness' had inflicted on the European spirit" and that "there was one element in Kant's moral theory that Hegel hated even more than its passivity: its vestigial Christianity and craving for a 'beyond.'"[18]

It seems that Hegel never changed his mind about the failure of the orthodox doctrine of an external God, that is, to treat God as something out there to be reached. In *Phenomenology of Spirit*, there is a turn to philosophy. In other words, while Hegel continues to describe religion on rational grounds,[19] *Phenomenology of Spirit* finally offers a *philosophical* transformation of Christianity that could bring about a reconciliation of God and humanity.[20] The crucial point here is that Hegel does not reject Christianity entirely, but that he only accepts a kind of Christianity that has been "systematically reinterpreted to be a vehicle of his own philosophy."[21] Seen in this light, what is at issue is the "consciousness of absolute reconciliation," a "new consciousness of humanity" or a "new religion," that accounts for the "consciousness of a reconciliation of humanity with God."[22] It is exactly in this sense that Raymond Plant argues:

> For Hegel, therefore, the philosophy of religion is not just a specific branch of philosophy dealing with a specific set of intellectual problems within religion. It is much more profound and pervasive than that. The Christian religion, properly understood, provides us with an integrated account of human existence both historically and in the modern world. It is for Hegel the basis for a new humanity when it is philosophically transcribed and comprehended.[23]

Indeed, what Plant says here stands for the paradigmatic example of moral religion that I am seeking in this chapter, namely, that morality and religion are inseparable. In the case of Hegel (as well as Green), however, it should be remembered that this does not necessarily imply that philosophy and religion are identical:

> [Religion] is the consciousness of absolute truth in the way that it occurs for all human beings. Thus it is found in the form of representation. Philosophy has the same content, the truth; it is the spirit of the world generally and not the particular spirit. Philosophy does nothing but transform our representations into concepts. The content remains always the same.[24]

THE SELF-POSITING GOD

To understand Hegel's religious thought, one must therefore consider his philosophy. However, space does not permit me to introduce Hegelian dialectic in detail. Instead, I only intend to remark that the aim of his dialectic is to demonstrate how different stages of consciousness proceed from a lower level to a higher level as the "contradiction" in the former is unveiled[25] and that dialectic always involves an "inner process" of the subject's self-development. Furthermore, for Hegel "the Absolute, what is ultimately real, or what is at the foundation of everything, is subject,"[26] and the process of the unfolding of the Absolute "is the process of its own becoming, the circle that presupposes its end as its goal, having its end as its beginning; and only by being worked out to be its end, is it actual."[27]

In this context, we should note that for Hegel, the inner process of the development of the mind is *ensured* "because there is something analogous to the action of God united with human life and history whose action is the basis for the rationality of the process."[28] More precisely, according to Hegel, the rational necessity of the inner process is made certain because "God, as a conscious being, has this inner necessity, as all conscious beings do, to externalize himself in nature and in human life—that is to say in otherness—and through this process of externalization to come to full consciousness."[29] As Hegel puts it elsewhere: "The divine Idea is just this: to disclose itself, to posit the Other outside itself and to take it back again into itself in order to be subjectivity and spirit."[30]

On this reading, I think that Charles Taylor's argument is sensible in its keeping with Hegel's use of the term "posit" (*setzen*) to identify his concept of God as the "self-positing God," who eternally makes the "conditions of his own existence," and who is the "subject of the rational necessity" that reveals itself in the world.[31] More precisely,

> Like the theist view, he [Hegel] wants to see the world as designed, as existing in order to fulfill a certain prospectus, the requirements of the embodiment for Geist. But like the naturalistic, he cannot allow a God who could design this world from outside, who could exist before and independently of the world. His idea is therefore that of a God who eternally makes the conditions of his own existence.[32]

Here, we are arriving at the core of Hegel's "new religion," in which it is posited that God not only is internalized within human mind, but also is manifested in nature and history. In this sense, nature and history are, therefore, not in conflict; rather, they are just the essence of God embodied in different forms. Regarding the creation of the world, Hegel makes it clear that:

> Nature is the Son of God, not as the Son however, but as abiding in otherness, in which the divine Idea is alienated from love and held fast for a moment. Nature is self-alienated spirit; spirit, a bacchantic good innocent of restraint and reflection has merely been let loose into it; in nature, the unity of the Notion conceals itself.[33]

On the other hand, he also describes the "incarnation" of God in the embodied Christ as a historical truth.

> In order for it [this divine-human unity] to become a certainty for humanity, God had to appear in the world in the flesh [cf. *New Testament*, John: 1:14]. The necessity that God [has] appeared in the world in the flesh is an essential characteristic—a necessity deduction from what has been said previously, demonstrated by it—for only in this way can it become a certainty for humanity; only in this way is it truth in the form of certainty.[34]

The Realization of Self-Knowledge

Two crucial points can be derived from the above discussion. First, since God or the Spirit, as a conscious being, must externalize itself in otherness, an awareness of the "other" in which God is embodied, namely, nature and history in its manifold forms, is itself a "study of God."[35] To quote Hegel, "God can be known or cognized, for it is God's nature to reveal himself, to be manifest."[36]

Second, the principle of embodiment indicates that consciousness does not exist in isolation, that it always involves encounter with otherness, and that it requires recognition by what one is not. Therefore, it follows that the dialectical process of the development of self-consciousness is one in which subject comes to realize the Absolute by *historically* engaging with otherness to bring together nature, history, and all human knowledge under the name of the ultimate truth, that is, God. Indeed, it is only at the last stage of the development of self-consciousness that the ultimate reconciliation of God and humanity will become apparent to the philosophical mind as the Absolute Knowing. Thus, at the very end of *Phenomenology of Spirit* Hegel writes:

> The goal, Absolute Knowing, or Spirit that knows itself as Spirit, has for its path the recollection of the Spirit as they are in themselves and as they accomplish the organization of their realm. Their preservation, regarded from the side of their free existence appearing in the form of contingent, is History; but regarded from the side of their [philosophically] comprehended organization, it is the Science of Knowing in the sphere of appearance: the two together, comprehended History, form alike the inwardizing and the Calvary of Absolute Spirit, the actuality, truth, and certainty of his throne, without which he would be lifeless and alone.[37]

All this indicates that, for Hegel, freedom and reason can only be actualized and grasped in history, that the human mind must be historically conditioned, and that human practices always entail historical consciousness. Compared with Kantian *Moralität*, as a result, Hegelian *Sittlichkeit* suggests that "morality cannot be achieved by individuals, but only by an entire community or mankind as a whole, living in a wholly uncoercive, loving 'ethical commonwealth' for which [the] Lawgiver alone legislates."[38] And so, according to Charles Taylor, Kantian self-determination, based on the "conception of a noumenal agent,"[39] is understood as a form of "disengaged subjectivity," whereas Hegelian self-realization makes available an alternative version of "embodied subjectivity."

Green: The Humanistic Calling for God

The religious thought of British idealism was greatly influenced by Hegel. For our purposes, it is sufficient only to examine the Hegelian aspects of Green's idea of moral religion by bringing the following three issues into consideration: Green's criticisms of Catholicism, Green's notion of the "eternal consciousness," and the Christian self appearing in his writings.[40]

CRITICISMS OF CATHOLICISM

Paralleling Hegel's disapproval of the "unhappy consciousness" within Christian religion, Green criticizes Catholicism for failing to acknowledge the proper relation between God and man as it asserts "the opposition between the inward and outward, between reason and authority, between the spirit and the flesh, between individual and the world of settled right."[41] In Green's mind, the major problem with Catholicism is that, over time, it has developed into a "Christianity of ordinances,"[42] a "dogmatic theology," falling short of the "immediate consciousness" of a genuine religion or the "intuition" of the divine.[43] It is therefore not surprising that like Hegel, Green holds that Lutheran Protestantism, understood as a form of "revealed religion," has shed "inward light" upon the new Protestant subject by appealing to "justification by faith" and the "right of private judgment"[44] and that the Reformation has effectively had a positive impact upon the European Spirit, enabling it to move toward the reunification of humanity and God. According to Green, having "opened a breach in the substantial unity of Christendom,"[45] the Reformation spread the fresh idea of autonomous consciousness over humanity, calling for a humanistic reunderstanding of the connection between God and man. This is a "calling" that requires serious philosophical scrutiny because when the new Protestant subject is "released from the dogma of the church," it is likely that "he will make a dogma of his own."[46] In this sense, it can be said that the "calling" is nothing but a rational expectation for the advent of a "true philosophy." As Andrew Vincent eloquently articulates,

> For Green, religion should neither try to place itself above secular authorities, nor fix God's presence into symbolic sacraments. The only hope, for Green, is a consciousness which moves beyond this dualism, one which is "laboriously

thoughtful" and apprehends (what we call) God in the rational educated consciousness of humanity.[47]

Moreover, along the lines of Hegel, Green firmly argues that "all that was essential in Christianity was capable of being restated in terms of a rationally organized scheme of thought."[48] In fact, for Green, "philosophy does but interpret, with full consciousness and in system, the powers already working in the spiritual life of mankind."[49] That said, like Hegel, Green argues that a new religion capable of generating a true integration of human ethical personality within a community can be developed. "Christian dogma, then, must be retained in its completeness, but it must be transformed into a philosophy."[50] As Green's former pupil Arnold Toynbee puts it, "Other thinkers have assailed the orthodox foundations of religion to overthrow it. Mr. Green assailed it to save it."[51]

Following Hegel, then, Green sees one of the major tasks of philosophy as rearticulating the religiousness in Christianity in a rational way. In reviewing J. Caird's "Introduction to Philosophy of Religion," Green remarks:

> That there is one spiritual self-conscious being, of which all that is real is the activity and the expression; that we are related to this spiritual being, not merely as parts of the world which is its expression, but as partakers in some inchoate measure of the self-consciousness through which it at once constitutes and distinguishes itself from the world; that this participation is *the source of morality and religion*; this we take to be the vital truth which Hegel had to teach.[52]

In short, influenced by Hegel, Green's ethics is also embodied in a form of moral religion, as religion was seen to be "giving expression to God in the moral life."[53]

THE ETERNAL CONSCIOUSNESS

For Green, the religiousness under discussion is nothing less than the "eternal consciousness," expressing a philosophical appreciation of God, the divine, or the infinite as an idea of reason and morality.[54] In "Fragment of an Address on the Text 'The World Is Nigh Thee,'" Green writes:

> It has been sometimes remarked that if all the New Testament had been lost to us except some half-dozen texts, the essence of Christianity would have been preserved in these, so that out of them everything in it that is of permanent moral value might have been developed; and if there can be an essence within the essence of Christianity, it is the thought embodied in the text I have read; the thought of God, not as "far off" but "nigh," not as a master but as a father, not as a terrible outward power, forcing us we know not whither, but as one of whom we may say that we are reason of his reason and spirit of his spirit; who lives in our moral life, and for whom we live in living for the brethren, even as in so living we live freely, because in obedience to a spirit which is our self; in communication with whom we triumph over death, and have assurance of eternal life.[55]

Seen in this light, when Green says that "God has died and been buried, and risen again, and realized himself in all the particulars of a moral life"[56] and that "if Christ dies for all, all died in him: all were buried in his grave to be all made alive in his resurrection,"[57] he is clearly saying that the basis of our moral life is predicated on a rational understanding of the "eternal consciousness" of God embedded in us. Thus, sticking to Hegel's conception of an immanent God and the principle of embodiment, Green also sees the idea of incarnation as potentially serving a moral purpose throughout. Indeed, for Green, "Christ is realized in moral action"; "the incarnation of Christ is a moral idea implanted in the consciousness of the radically free subject."[58] In brief, Green retains Hegel's insight that the way to discover the divine is within man himself; for Christ has become "the necessary determination of the eternal subject, the objectification by this subject of himself in the world of nature and humanity."[59]

Now, it has become plain that Christ, as an idea of rationality and morality internalized within the human mind, actually speaks for man's own "true self,"[60] that is, the moral ideal to be sought in a course of action. To quote Green,

> There is a conception to which every one who thinks about himself as a moral agent almost instinctively finds himself resorting, the conception variously expressed as that of the

"better," the "higher," the "true" self. This conception, I believe, points the way to that true interpretation of our moral nature, which is also the only source of a true theology.[61]

It follows that the central theme of Green's moral religion holds the view that "Christ is the eternal act of God, perpetually re-enacted in individual human lives"[62] as they struggle to realize their own true selves. In other words, for Green,

> Christ is what all humans are in potentiality. The Christ figure is thus part of the eternal objectification of God in the world. This, for Green, is the root Christian idea. Religion becomes active morality. This is the substance to the radically free subject, the Christian citizen.[63]

To sum up what we have discovered so far, although, unlike F. H. Bradley, Green does not directly employ a dialectical method to establish his ethics, he clearly sets out to adopt Hegel's theology concerning moral issues. No matter how far Green was influenced by Kant regarding the idea of free will, his moral theory undeniably presents a typical Hegelian form of moral religion. Put succinctly, whereas for Kant religion is an "appendix to the ethical personality," and the philosophy of religion eventually becomes an "adjunct to moral philosophy,"[64] Green follows in Hegel's footsteps in seeing the philosophy of religion as "more profound and pervasive than that." The Christian religion, for Green, as for Hegel, is "the basis for a new humanity when it is philosophically transcribed and comprehended." In short, Green sees God as "immanent in individuals and in history";[65] that is to say, "immanent in the total structure of human experience, including science, history, and social and political life."[66]

THE TRUE SELF

Having touched on Green's "eternal consciousness," we are now in a better position to examine his discussion on the moral ideal of self-realization. In what follows, with the aim of this book in mind, I shall clarify Green's idea of self-realization by comparing him with both Kant and Hegel.

My argument so far has implied that only through a Hegelian reading of the "eternal consciousness," objecting to all the distinctions of duality between God and man, nature and morality, fact and value, phenomena and noumena, and so on, can we make real sense of Green's rejection of Kant's bifurcation in the first book of *Prolegomena to Ethics*. For Green, "there is but a single order of reality, nature, man and God being essentially one."[67] However, this is not to say that Green is entirely indifferent to Kant's transcendental philosophy. In fact, in spite of differences, Green's idea of free subject and his theory of knowledge and experience owe a great deal to Kant.

Briefly, as we have seen, what underlines Kant's transcendental argument is the view that the task of a philosopher is to discover the *postulates* or *conditions* that make knowledge and morality possible in the first place. This suggests that one of the main tasks of Kant's *Critique of Pure Reason* is to pose a critique "of the faculty of reason in general, in respect of all knowledge after which it may strive independently of all experience."[68] Indeed, Kant's epistemology addresses the point that the knowing subject goes before the object and that the ability to experience is prior to what is experienced.

Parallel to Kant's transcendental argument, Green argues in *Prolegomena to Ethics* that, since the motive for human action is not merely "felt desire," but "conceived desire," there must therefore be a self-distinguishing subject who is able to conceive and think. Unlike Kant's exclusion of human desires and feelings from the rational domain of morality, however, Green contends that since "all desire is the act of a subject which thinks in desiring, all thought the act of a subject which desires in thinking,"[69] it follows that subject precedes desire. And thus, following Kant, Green also calls the ability of the subject to conceive and think the will, that is, "free-cause":[70] "The will is simply the man. Any act of will is the expression of the man as he at the time is."[71] He, nonetheless, argues at the same time that the will is not so much a *postulate* but the moral ability to actualize reason and desire in real life situations.

More to the point, analogous to Kant's transcendental unity of apperception, arguing that the world of experience is the result of an expanded and unified application of *a priori* forms and categories on what is given, Green, too, adopts a unifying eternal subject. For Green, the self comes to comprehend the world through relations with others, which in turn implies an "eternal consciousness" that transcends individuals as particulars. "Human action is only explicable by the action of an eternal consciousness, which uses them as its organs and reproduces itself through them."[72] Unlike Kant, however, it seems that Green's "eternal consciousness," the Absolute, embraces both transcendence and immanence, resulting in criticism from David Brink, who asserts that, for the sake of clarification, "Green must choose whether the Absolute is transcendent or immanent."[73]

From the standpoint I am taking, however, it is exactly the two fundamental meanings of "eternal consciousness" which coexist in Green's thought that interest me the most in this chapter. As has been indicated, the most distinctive characteristic of Confucian moral subjectivity is also a combination of transcendence and immanence, which can be more compatibly reconstructed in terms of Hegelian moral religion than *solely* in terms of a Kantian transcendental argument. Before turning to examine the idea of moral religion in Confucianism, I shall now try to show how it is possible to accommodate both transcendence and immanence in Green's idea of self-realization from a Hegelian viewpoint of moral religion.

To start with, in contrast to Kant's attitude toward metaphysics, we should remember that Green's inherent concern about moral religion obviously signifies that "he is essentially a religious philosopher"[74] with a resolute hope in metaphysics. Following the line of reasoning that God is the "ideal self" for the individual to re-enact within his mind, it seems to me appropriate to argue that the transcendental feature of "eternal consciousness" in Green's thinking subject not only denotes "what is already within me" before the world makes sense to me, but, more importantly, it also implies the *spiritual breaking-through* of the self to reach out to the "ideal self" above me.

Second, it also follows that, in Green's thought, the "eternal consciousness" does not simply stand for the *postulate* of the existence of God. Far from espousing the Kantian use of the term, Green's "eternal consciousness" argues for the real embodiment of God within me to various degrees. In Kant's examination, since God, the soul, and the will are neither spatial nor temporal—no one can conceive of anything that is outside of time and space—they are thus merely things-in-themselves, which are inaccessible to my subjectivity. Therefore, it is completely useless to employ a subjective category regarding understanding transcendental experience: that is, to employ causality to prove the existence of God. This is why Kant tries to show that traditional metaphysics leads to insoluble "antinomies," in which no progress is made compared to physical science.

Counter to Kant's bifurcated world, Green never treated the existence of God, the immortality of soul, and the free will as things-in-themselves. In a personal letter to Scott Holland, Green explained that his philosophical conclusions overall are "the inevitable result of thinking together [about] God, the world and the history of man."[75] The crucial point here is that as with Hegel, Green is an advocate of Absolute idealism, caring about the real existence and true actualization of the eternal subject, rather than of Subjective idealism, simply being interested in the transcendental conditions of genuine knowledge.

In the sphere of morality, the subject matter of *Prolegomena to Ethics*, the key thread running through Green's work is as follows: given the necessary existence of the knowing subject and its will to conceive of desire that initiates action, it follows that the satisfaction of an action, namely good, must be *the actual realization of the capacities and potentialities of the self within community*, rather than the exercise of the free will as a postulate. That is to say, for Green, the moral import of human action lies in the idea of good unfolding through the gradual process of self-realization, and, consequently, the degree of good is dependent on how great the capacities and potentialities of the self are to be realized in that action. In short, self-realization is the "realization of the capacities of the human soul" or the "perfecting of man" in history.[76]

Here we can see the Hegel-inspired communitarian facet of Green's discussion of the moral self.[77] Put briefly, since the human world, as we have seen, is an unfolding of the eternal act of God, the world that we inhabit is a world of the rationalization of divinity. To realize one's own "ideal self," a person must at the same time internalize the "common norms" within an integrated community, starting from family and social relations, through civil society, to the state. In political terms, as we shall see where appropriate, this means that the aim of the state is to maintain a system of rights in a way that allows citizens to attain the actualization of real freedom, that is, the full accomplishment of self-realization.

This is not the place to explore the perfectionist liberalism in Green's political thought. Instead, we shall now observe two more philosophically important features of his idea of self-realization. On the one hand, just as with contemporary thinkers such as Charles Taylor and Alasdair MacIntyre, the communitarian dimension of Green's thought still emphasizes the value of the individual, or the idea of freedom or autonomy (in the broader sense). As Green puts it, "no one can convey a good character to another." "Everyone must make his character for himself."[78]

On the other hand, it is worth mentioning that, while Hegel seems to have thought that the Absolute or God has achieved full realization in his own time, Green, under the influence of F. C. Baur, holds that "the self-realization of God is never a finished process."[79] To quote Green himself:

> The revelation therefore is not made in a day, or a generation, or a century. The divine mind touches, modifies, becomes the mind of mind, through a process of which mere intellectual conception is only the beginning, but of which the gradual complement is an unexhausted series of spiritual discipline through all the agencies of social life.[80]

However, this does not affect the fact that Green essentially follows Hegel's endorsement that full self-realization can only take place within an integrated community. At root, the center of Green's moral thinking is Hegelian *Sittlichkeit* rather than Kantian *Moralität*. Moral action, as Green insists, is the "expression of man's character" because "it reacts upon and responds to given circumstances."[81]

Confucian Religiousness: A Hegelian Reconstruction

Thus far, we have unveiled the three main aspects of the idea of moral religion in the thought of Hegel and Green: (1) the disapproval of the orthodox Christian view that God is wholly external; (2) a reinterpretation of the attributes of God through internalization; and (3) the moral ideal of self-realization as the fulfillment of one's moral capacities through communicating with the way in which God works in history. In this section, I want to argue that Mou Zongsan's reconstruction of Confucian moral religion is heavily indebted to Hegel, and consequently, that his reexamination of ethical personality in Confucian thought bears a remarkable similarity to Green's idea of self-realization.

What Is Wrong with Christianity?

When Mou states that "whoever wants to provide a positive account and affirmation for moral religion will adopt the position of idealism in philosophy,"[82] he is self-consciously referring to the Hegelian revision of

Christianity. In rethinking the problem of the relation between God and man in the West, Mou also publicly acknowledges Hegel's contribution toward developing a humanistic version of Christianity.[83] As he remarks:

> The modern spirit of the West has forgotten about God and its transcendental medieval ideals. . . . This has had a humbling and alleviating effect on Christianity. While this could reflect an insufficiency or decline in the West's religious spirit, it also enables a greater unity between Heaven and man through giving "complete fulfillment to one's body"[84] and "full realization to one's *Xing*-nature" (*jianxing jinxing* 踐形盡性), so revitalizing the West's religious spirit and launching a new transformation. Hegel's *Philosophy of History* is an attempt to demonstrate this change by verifying the embodiment of God in a secular world from the perspective of historical development. . . . This is the only way that we can find a solution to the way things are in this world.[85]

It seems fair to indicate that Mou is interested in Christianity for two reasons: to examine the weakness of Western civilization, and to highlight the peculiarity of Chinese civilization. In Mou's terminology, the sharp distinction between orthodox Christianity and Confucianism can be singled out in terms of "distant religion" (*lijiao* 離教) and the "perfect teaching" (*yuanjiao* 圓教) that has been previously discussed. Put in other terms, Mou sees the conventional Christian religion as based on a separation between God and humanity but the spirit of Confucianism as entirely humanistic. He remarks:

> The life of Christ aimed to give up all things in reality, even to sacrifice his own life, in order to return to God. By returning to God, his religious spirit proved that only the true God is the pure absolute, above man. In this sense, the religion created by Christ is non-humanistic or trans-humanistic. Despite this, he reveals a criterion of truth, which has become the criterion of human activity and formed the cultural system of Western Christianity throughout its development. In his religion, he does not aim to pursue the union of God and man or install a moral subject that can relate man to God. This is the spirit

of a two-bladed knife [representing two separate worlds], so I refer to it as a distant religion.[86]

In contrast, what is central to Confucianism is a form of "perfect teaching" in relation to the "infinite heart-mind" (*wuxianxin* 無限心) and the "ontology of non-detachment" (*wuzhi de cunyoulun* 無執的存有論). Here, seen from the viewpoint of moral religion, the religiousness of Confucianism clearly sticks to the belief that as "humanity forms an inseparable unity with Heaven, earth, and the myriad things, its sensibility is in principle all-embracing"; accordingly, self-knowledge is neither "knowing that" nor "knowing how," but an "objectless awareness," a "realization of human possibility of 'intellectual intuition' (*zhi de zhijue* 智的直覺)."[87] That said, as in all other organized religions, "transcendence" is crucially important in Confucianism. However, more analogous to Hegel and Green than to orthodox Christianity, the "transcendence" at stake is not meant to signify the inaccessibility of God, but the "perfecting of man," the "true self," as God or Heaven has bestowed within the mind. In short, Confucian religiousness clearly implies the "ethical personality of sagehood."[88]

I shall return to the ideas of Heaven and self-realization in Confucian thought shortly. For now, we must note that this does not mean that man may easily arrive at sagehood; rather, it is only through a lifelong effort in the arduous practice of an ethical life that the full potentialities of one's moral ability can be actualized nearly in accordance with the teachings of sages. This explains why, instead of the Gospels and the Messiah, the core of Confucianism contains the rich teachings of actual practice (*gongfu* 功夫), meaning the continual practices of the perfecting of a great man.

Therefore, in answering the disputed question about whether Confucianism is a religion, Mou's insights, which have continued to influence future generations of New Confucians,[89] are as follows: in terms of "institutions," it is true that Confucianism has never developed into an organized setting of religious rituals; in terms of "principle," however, Confucianism is "highly religious" and represents an "extremely complete spirit of religion."[90] In other words, Mou thinks that, "although China has never come up with a religion such as Christianity, the most spectacular and complete moral consciousness, moral spirit or the state of moral affairs is already represented by Confucianism."[91] Based on the moral ideal of ren 仁 (humaneness), the central thinking about the human heart-mind and *Xing*-nature, and the "*Dao* of Heaven," Confucianism has achieved a complete "pathway to spirit life,"[92] gradually reaching toward the "conformity of Heaven and man in union." In short, Confucianism, properly understood, is a profound form of moral religion, containing the moral "basis of ordinary life" and the spiritual "motif of cultural creation."[93]

The Internalization of Heaven

By disclosing the religiousness of Confucianism from a Hegelian viewpoint, Mou is also making explicit its humanistic implications; indeed, the moral religion in his mind is one "upon which human dignity is based, and from which human value stems."[94] Therefore, it comes as no surprise that Mou's statements about the "conformity of Heaven and man in union," paralleling Hegel and Green, offer a further demonstration of the internalization of Heaven in Confucian thought.

To realize the interrelationship between Heaven and man, Mou actually traces the origins of the idea of Heaven back to an older tradition in Chinese culture. In that tradition, as Mou maintains, Heaven is understood in terms of "reverence" (*jing* 敬). "In reverence, our subjectivity does not face toward God; what we do is not self-negation, but self-affirmation."[95] That is to say, in sharp contrast to original sin and the fall, when the heart-mind is full of reverence, the more we come to know about Heaven, the more we will come to realize the holiness and completeness that we already have within our subjectivity.

Thus seen, Confucian moral religion certainly takes as its point of departure the idea that humanity or *Xing*-nature is deeply rooted in Heaven, rather than opposed to it. To quote the first sentence of the *Doctrine of the Mean* (*Zhongyong* 中庸): "*Xing*-nature is what Heaven imparts." Furthermore, as Mou accurately argues, we can only truly appreciate "inner morality" (*neizai daodexing* 內在道德性) as being nothing but the "universal reason regulated by humanity in harmony with divinity,"[96] if we view the framework of Confucianism from a perspective of moral religion. Therefore, Confucius's highest virtue of *ren*, or Mencius's four cardinal virtues—*ren* 仁 (humaneness), *yi* 義 (righteousness), *li* 禮 (ritual proprieties), and *zhi* 智 (wisdom)—are just different expressions of the universal reason within us: the universal moral ability to undertake self-affirmation endowed by Heaven. For this reason, Mou is likely to identify Confucianism as a form of "rational idealism" in Western philosophical terms.[97]

In accordance with "rational idealism," there is another sense in which Mou deliberately employs Hegel's philosophy of religion to reconstruct the idea of the "conformity of Heaven and man in union." In Hegel's terminology, as Mou reminds us, the very idea at issue actually stands perfectly for the "Real Unification" of subjectivity and objectivity, that is, the actualization of "Real Reality."[98] In other words, the Confucian way of grasping Heaven and man in union is reminiscent of Hegel's Absolute Spirit. Thus, it is no wonder that for Mou the idea of "inner sagehood" in Confucianism, which represents the capability of grasping the "heavenly, sagely or enlightened *Dao*," is equivalent to that of "knowing God" inwardly in the Hegelian revision of Christianity; as Mou articulates, Hegel's "learning is an understanding that attains an all-encompassing utter clarity of the development and realization of the heart-mind and *Xing*-nature," which in turn is advantageous for acknowledging Kant's "self-imposed barrier to metaphysical insight with his epistemology."[99]

More exactly, just as Hegel's Absolute Reason seeks a reunification of any possible divisions between God and man, morality and nature, mind and things, the term *ren* in Confucianism literally means "humanity" as a whole. Largely echoing Green's saying of the "realization of the capacities of the human soul," to "attain sagehood" is, for the most part, equivalent to developing the moral potentiality inherent in the subject as much as humanly possible. According to Chan Wing-Tsit's (陳榮捷 1901–1994) prevailing definition, *ren* leads to general virtue, "which is basic, universal and the source of all specific virtues," although Confucius "never defined it."[100] Furthermore, in Mou's interpretation, *ren* is not simply the highest virtue, the perfecting of man, or the ideal self, but it also implies the moral capacity and potentiality that are within us.

In the latter usage, *ren* has two general features, namely, "awareness" (*jue* 覺) and "constancy" (*jian* 健). While the former means the self-awareness of moral heart-mind—"only when one acquires awareness will he gain the heart-mind of four germs"—the latter demands that one should "abide by the constancy of the *Dao* of Heaven" so as to unify humanity and Heaven.[101] In this regard, the general picture of Confucius's moral thinking can be seen as his own personal struggle in seeking ethical personality, that is, "learning from what is around me" (*xiaxue* 下學) and "getting through to what is up above" (*shangda* 上達).[102]

In parallel with the internalization and externalization of the Absolute Knowing, Mou gives two similar meanings to *ren* through his Hegelian reading of Confucianism. He says that "the nature of *ren* is the all-embracing sensibility, while its function is to replenish the myriad things" (*ren yi gantong wei xing, yi runwu wei yong* 仁以感通為性, 以潤物為用).[103] Through the "practice" of putting *ren* into action, the moral sources within my heart-mind can therefore reverberate with the *Dao* of Heaven. Therefore, he argues that *ren*, just like Hegel's Absolute Spirit, can be well understood as the "real life," the "real substance," the "real subjectivity," or the "real self" in the deepest moral sense.[104]

In Hegelian theology, as we have seen, one of the most significant consequences stemming from the immanence of God is the corresponding inward tendency to reinterpret the incarnation of Christ. In contemporary New Confucianism, there is also an inclination to universalize the spirituality of an ethical life of Confucius. To quote Tang Junyi, "the life of Confucius is the stage of the incarnation of Chinese culture."[105] In a similar way, Mou argues that Confucius is not simply a great philosopher as commonly supposed in the West; far from it, his endeavor to conduct a meaningful ethical life manifests a concrete and real model of realizing the *Dao* of Heaven. Put clearly,

> The *ren*-reality (*renti* 仁體) in Confucius is the greatest fulfillment of *renti*. The *Spring and Autumn Annals* (*Chunqiu* 春秋, i.e., the historical work he revised) is full of strict *yi* and compassionate *ren*. This is impossible unless one has sympathy for the whole universe. And so, the expressions of Confucius reflect his cultural life and ideals, which in turn symbolize the perfection of "ethical life" or "human relations" (*renlun* 人倫), and the paradigm of *renlun*. In other words, his life as a whole represents (Chinese) cultural life, and his sayings as a whole represent (Chinese) cultural ideals, which (through historical practice) have transformed into the personality of "virtues and wisdoms" (*dehui* 德慧) as a whole.[106]

Or alternatively, the unity between Heaven and humanity has been thoroughly articulated in terms of Mencius's famous mottos about "giving full realization to heart-mind" (*jinxin* 盡心), "knowing *Xing*-nature" (*zhixing* 知性), and "knowing Heaven" (*zhitian* 知天). To quote from the *Mencius*:

> Mencius said, "For a man to give full realization to his heart-mind is for him to understand his own *Xing*-nature, and a man who knows his own *Xing*-nature will know Heaven. By

returning his heart-mind and nurturing his *Xing*-nature he is serving Heaven. Whether he is going to die young or to live to a ripe old age makes no difference to his steadfastness of purpose. It is through awaiting whatever is to befall him with a perfected character that he stands firm in his proper destiny."[107]

Seen in this light, as Mou continues, the "learning of the principles of *Xing*-nature" (*xingli zhi xue* 性理之學) underpinning Song-Ming Neo-Confucianism signifies nothing but the "learning of the heart-mind and *Xing*-nature" (*xinxing zhi xue* 心性之學), that is, an extraordinary extension of the "learning of inner sagehood" (*neisheng zhi xue* 內聖之學) initiated by Confucius and Mencius. More precisely, from the key point that the true connotation of "attaining virtue" (*chengde* 成德) is to "arrive at an infinite and perfect meaning within one's finite life," it follows that for Confucians "morality is religion, generating the accomplishment of a moral religion for humankind"; that is to say, "in Confucianism morality never stays within the boundary of finitude, unlike in the West where morality and religion are often treated as two opposite stages."[108]

All this indicates that the search for the "conformity of Heaven and man in union" in Mou's Hegel-inspired writings is, by and large, consonant with the Confucian moral metaphysics that he has finally set forth. That said, either Confucius's discussion of *ren* or Mencius's treatment of *Xing*-nature can generally be seen to have established the "real subjectivity," or the "authentic self," namely, the fullest realization of "moral subjectivity," in Confucianism.[109] "Since Confucius and Mencius represent the orthodoxy of Chinese Confucianism, the stress on subjectivity is central to the great tradition of Chinese thought. Therefore, Chinese intellectual thought can be generally described as the 'learning of the heart-mind and *Xing*-nature.'"[110]

THE AUTHENTIC SELF

In summary, then, Mou's notion of Confucian moral religion is strikingly reminiscent of the Hegelian turn toward an immanent theology. As a consequence, there are several things that can be said about the similarity of the moral ideal of self-realization—namely, the fulfillment of one's "inner morality" through a process of "immanent transcendence" toward the "real self"—in Confucianism and in Hegelianism, especially in Green's version.

First, the moral agency of Confucianism is similar to that of Green in the sense that the fundamental basis of morality is predicated on a Kantian subjectivity that is endowed with certain moral ability and potentiality. In the *Analects*,

> The master said, "Is *ren* really far away? No sooner do I desire it than it is here."[111]

> The master said, "It is Man who is capable of broadening the Way. It is not the Way that is capable of broadening Man."[112]

In a similar way, as I have previously cited, Mencius articulates:

> Humaneness, righteousness, the rites, and wisdom are not welded on to me from the outside; *they are in me originally*. And a different view is simply due to want of reflection. Hence it is said, "Seek and you will find them. Neglect and you will lose them."[113]

The upshot here is that Confucian subjectivity contains both immanence and transcendence; Confucius's *ren* and Mencius's idea of the "goodness of *Xing*-nature" are not only inherent in man, but they also serve as principles of transcendence leading toward the perfecting of man. "*Ren*," as Cheng Zhongying [Cheng Chung-Ying] (成中英) argues, "is rooted in one's very nature and being"; "it is a need to transcend oneself to a higher level of universality and spirituality and to a larger extension of the human interrelationship in well-being and unity at the same time."[114]

Second, as in Green, the pursuit of self-realization in Mencius's wing of Confucianism is to bring out the best of "what is in me originally," that is, to realize one's moral capacities and potentialities. Here, it is worth noticing that a lot of effort has been put into considering the connection between Mencius and Kant regarding the features of moral subjectivity. One of the most salient differences between Kant and Mencius is that, while for Kant, our inner moral ability in terms of free will is taken as a *postulate* that makes moral activity possible, for Mencius, as for Green, freedom is not just a thing-in-itself, but it is what is actually exercised in our action: the actualization of one's moral capacities and potentialities in concrete circumstances. Besides, as I shall mention in the next chapter, like Green, Mou's reading of Mencius also picks holes in Kant's specific way of treating moral feeling.

Third, Confucianism in general would agree with Green's argument that "everyone must make his character for himself." Indeed, it has been widely agreed that Confucianism is, above all, an ethics of self-cultivation or self-edification; for Confucians, one has to seek the inward light of morality by his own effort. One of Mou's most well-known pupils, Tu Weiming [Tu Wei-Ming] (杜維明), when trying to delineate the tradition of seeking self-realization in East Asian civilization, makes two essential points as follows: (1) "Each human being has sufficient internal resources for ultimate self-transformation; we can become a sage, a Buddha, or a true person through our self-effort because sageliness, Buddhahood, or the Way is inherent in our human nature." (2) "The path to the highest good, to nirvana, or to oneness with the Way is long and strenuous."[115]

Fourth, while Tu's first argument matches perfectly with the meaning of self-realization, his second point reflects to a great extent the difficulty of moral practice according to Green. In Green's mind, as indicated, man is not created complete with all his capacities and potentialities; rather he must strive for their full development through history in which God is immanent. Similarly, Confucius and Mencius are modest about the true realization of the ideal self. Furthermore, just as Green sees the self-realization of God in human history as an unfinished process, under no circumstance does Confucianism believe that the actualization of the *Dao* of Heaven can be easily exhausted. As Mou puts it, what Confucius and Mencius have done is "to realize that which Heaven has unveiled in *Xing*-nature, in *ren*, in morality, this is not to say that they can actualize the whole meaning or the infinite mystery in a complete sense."[116]

Finally, echoing Hegel's *Sittlichkeit*, the teachings of Confucianism encourage people to find self-realization in the activities, institutions, and relationships within their own society. As Mou articulates,

> According to Confucian doctrines, there is no isolated virtue, because *ren* and *yi* cannot exist in the individual independently. . . . Why is this so? This is because the virtues of *ren* and *yi* must be objectified in the world of humanity; their objectification even should spread over the whole of Heaven, earth and all things. This is why Wang Yangming [Wang Yang-Ming] (王陽明 1472–1529) says that "the great man

thinks of Heaven, earth, and the myriad things as oneness." In a similar way, Cheng Mingdao [Cheng Ming-Tao] (程明道 1032–1085) remarks that "the person of *ren* is related to Heaven, earth, and the myriad things in oneness." This is completely in accordance with the view that "the completion of the self necessitates that of things" (*chengji chengwu* 成己成物) in the *Doctrine of the Mean*, meaning that since "*chengji* is *ren*, *chengwu* is wisdom," what is implied by *chengji chengwu* is "the *Dao* of unifying inwardness and outwardness." This also reflects Mencius's teaching that: "All the ten thousand things are there in me. There is no greater joy for me than to find, on self-examination, that I am true to myself." In Confucian doctrines, the only way to accomplish virtues is by reaching this completeness and fullness.[117]

The Ethics of Self-Realization

To conclude, I argue that post-Kantian Western moral philosophy, including Kantianism, utilitarianism, and the Hegelian critics of Kant, take autonomy, freedom, independence, free will, self-interest, individuality, and so on, to be the cardinal condition of human conduct. Therefore, it may be appropriate to describe "human dignity" as the Western "overlapping consensus" on common humanity.[118] Even so, there are at least two relevant but non-identical idioms of "human dignity" that have hovered over the modern history of Western moral thinking, which, for the sake of argument, can be framed as the Kantian notion of self-determination or self-legislation, and the Hegelian notion of self-realization or self-fulfillment.

Here, I do not intend to deny that as far as the study of Mou is concerned, the Kantian approach is far more prevalent. From the previous discussion, nonetheless, it follows that the ethics of self-realization in pursuit of the full actualization of the ideal self is as significant in making sense of Mou's reconstruction of Confucianism from a comparative perspective. For one, the purpose of undertaking cross-cultural dialogue, as Mou sees it, is to seek mutual understanding between different civilizations by comparing similar ways of thinking about humanity as a whole, that is, the truth of the concrete whole in Hegel's usage. For another, it should be remembered that although Mou's "moral metaphysics" is based on his lifelong engagement with Kant's philosophy, it departs from

Kant's "metaphysics of morals" in some pivotally crucial ways. Again, both Hegel and the British idealists have never abandoned the chief heritages of Kant's philosophy, upon which Mou's reconstruction of the moral features of Confucianism is grounded, namely, "inner morality," the "vertical expression of the vertical system" (*zongguan zongjiang* 縱貫縱講), and the "perfect good" (*yuanshan* 圓善). In a basic sense, what has been said thus far amounts to giving a more detailed account of how the Hegelian insights, such as real subjectivity, the full meaning of reality, and concrete universal, have been at work in Mou's philosophical system.

In fact, the idea of the authentic self, real subjectivity, or what Taylor calls embodied subjectivity as expressed in this book, bears a significant resemblance to what William Theodore de Bary has referred to as "personalism in Confucianism" from a different angle. As de Bary states:

> When Western notions of liberalism and individualism reached East Asia in the nineteenth century, they had no precise equivalents in Chinese or Japanese parlance, and neologisms had to be invented for them. *Ko-jen chu-i* [*Geren zhuyi*] 個人主義 (Jap. *Kojin shugi*), the term devised for "individualism," emphasized the discrete or isolated individual. This contrasts with Confucian personalism referred to in my earlier lectures, which conceived of the person as a member of the larger human body, never abstracted from society but always living in a dynamic relation to others, to a biological and historical continuum, and to the organic process of the Way.[119]

To be sure, de Bary's aim here is to differentiate the way individuality matters in Confucianism from prevalent asocial individualism. On this reading, it is particularly interesting to note that even Zhang Hao [Chang Hao] (張灝 1937–2022), a distinguished disciple of Yin Haiguang [Yin Hai-Kuang] (殷海光 1919–1969), also draws attention to the *differentia* between Confucian personalism and atomistic individualism by remarking:

> On the one hand, this kind of "personalism" emphasizes a person's sociality and considers a person's sociality as indivisible from what makes a person human. Because of this, people must participate in society and politics. . . . On the other hand, the Confucians' idea of the "inner sagehood" possesses a transcendent consciousness. Confucians believe

that people's nature is endowed by Heaven, and, upon this basis, individuality can forever preserve its independence and autonomy and will not be swallowed by sociality. This type of "individualism" combines sociality and individuality and yet transcends both, eliminating the opposition between individualism and collectivism in modern Western culture. It can cure the defect of partiality found in both positions and provide a new perspective for modern social thought.[120]

All this, of course, does not mean that there are no noteworthy differences between Mou's New Confucianism and Hegel's Absolute idealism. For our purposes, there are several things that need to be mentioned, which, in turn, will help bring together British idealism and New Confucianism in dialogue. In the beginning, we need to bear in mind that for Mou, the overall dissimilarity between Western and Chinese thinkers is that while the former are devoted to pursuing knowledge, the latter are much more eager with wisdom. One could say that Western philosophers, including Kant, Hegel, and indeed, the British idealists, among others, often fall victim to taking seriously the positivity of human life and human reason; in contrast, the authentic Confucians, encouraged by Confucius and Mencius, are prone "to see 'all-under-Heaven' as the content of their personal responsibility, and to treat what they learn as the guiding principles of personal, political, and social practices."[121]

On the one hand, what this reaffirms is the key point underlining Confucian moral metaphysics, namely, that unlike Kant's rational belief in God, Hegel's self-positing God, or Green's immanent God, only Confucianism attributes "intellectual intuition" to the "infinite heart-mind" (*wuxianxin* 無限心) and regards it as a principle of moral creativity. That said, Mou is apt to swap God in the Western tradition for the "infinite heart-mind" as the ultimate source of humanity, morality, and the sensible world. Thus, as we have seen, he firmly insists that *Xing*-reality and *Dao*-reality are completely identical and that there is no point following Kant in differentiating the three postulates of the existence of God, free will, and the soul, as the "infinite heart-mind" is one and the same.

On the other hand, in view of this fact, Confucianism failed to develop a sufficient theory of scientific knowledge and an independent version of democratic politics out of the moral reasoning in association with "attaining sagehood." Rather than making a clear-cut distinction between morality and politics, however, Mou asserts that the anticipation of Confucian democracy, so to speak, lies in a dialectical reappreciation of the "indirect and specific" relationship between the two important domains of human affairs. To reiterate, it is against this context that the ethical liberalism of the British idealists may help expound the possibility and plausibility of reinterpreting Mou's political philosophy in a Hegelian vein.

More to the point, in addition to launching a criticism of Kant for his treatment of freedom as a postulate, Mou also expresses a deep reservation about Hegel's dialectic "being detached from [moral] praxis," because in his Logic Hegel basically treats the Absolute as a bare concept without moral import from the very beginning. At this point, it is extremely interesting to note that another leading founder of the ethics of self-realization in the school of British idealism, F. H. Bradley, has largely developed the crux of the Hegelian revisions of Kant in his writings and simultaneously resolved the very problem of the Absolute in Hegel's Logic. For this reason, the New Hegelian thinker was greatly appreciated by both Mou Zongsan and Tang Junyi. To round off my argument, it seems appropriate to engage in a potential dialogue between Mou and Bradley in respect of the endless pursuit of self-perfection, before leaving for Mou's political theory.

Chapter 3

The Endless Pursuit of Self-Perfection

Introduction

Unlike Tang Junyi's [Tang Chun-I] (唐君毅 1909–1978) high appraisal of the British idealists, Mou Zongsan only occasionally mentions these names. The fact that Mou did not go deeper into the traditions of idealism does not, it appears to me, necessarily prevent us from seeking a family resemblance between New Confucianism and British idealism. Historically speaking, as Mou confesses, it was through Tang's talking about F. H. Bradley's "reconciliatory dialectic" (*xiaorong bianzhengfa* 消融辯證法) that he came to realize the kernel of dialectical thinking and the importance of Hegel's philosophy;[1] besides, as we shall see, Mou clearly sympathized with Tang's notion that Bradley's "reconciliatory dialectic" can help elucidate Confucianism to some extent. In terms of moral thinking, not only do the British idealists aim to merge the Kantian moral subject with the Hegelian ideas of actualization and embodied individualism into an ethics of self-realization, but their famous formula of "my station and its duties" (to use Bradley's phrase) also echoes a good deal of Mou's discussion of the true self.

Above all, for the British idealists, self-realization means the perfection of human personality, namely, the full actualization of one's moral capacities and ends toward a higher self. By the same token, for Mou, the gist of Confucian moral practice can be sketched out by Mencius's "giving full realization to heart-mind" (*jinxin* 盡心), where the "heart-mind of humaneness" (*renxin* 仁心) is taken to mean a moral subjectivity bestowed with moral ability or moral spontaneity to develop and realize itself in concrete situations. In this regard, moral practice at once involves an endless process of "fulfilling virtue" (*chengde* 成德) toward the "perfect good" (*yuanshan* 圓善), namely, the final actualization of *ren* 仁 (humaneness); in moral activity one is driven to seek a "virtuous personality" by unceasingly exercising the skills of "attaining sagehood" (*chengsheng* 成聖).

The purpose of this chapter, accordingly, is to substantiate the parallelism between Bradley's endeavor to synthesize Kant and Hegel in respect of the ethics of self-realization and Mou's post-Kantian attempt to transcend the limits of Kant so as to specify the characteristics of Confucianism from different angles. Inasmuch as the intellectual enterprise of Mou involves an extensive engagement with Kant and Hegel, Bradley is of great significance for three major reasons. First, Bradley's revision of "reconciliatory dialectic" in relation to the "concrete universal" has considerably amended the pitfall of Hegel's dialectic that worries Mou, namely, that Hegel treats the Absolute as a bare concept without moral import from the very beginning. It is largely against this context that Mou thinks the "reconciliatory dialectic" may help bring to light the spirit of *ren*.

Second, as with Mou, Bradley criticizes Kant for treating freedom as a *postulate* from a Hegelian perspective. More precisely, upon examining the development of Western moral consciousness from utilitarianism, via deontology, to "my station and its duties," it becomes apparent that the ethics of self-realization upheld by Bradley, Green, and the like, is basically in agreement with New Confucianism on the account that both schools share an attempt to bring together human feeling and the moral law in providing a more comprehensive account of the highest good.

Third, at this point, it is equally important to note that another of Bradley's criticisms of Kant is about the relationship between the individual and community, or between the self and the whole. Bearing a striking resemblance to Mou's post-Kantian claim that "although man is finite, he can be infinite,"[2] Bradley's ethics of self-realization, in association with his "reconciliatory dialectic" and Hegel's "concrete universal" which both Mou and Tang appreciate, also effects a Hegelian reconciliation of the finite self and the infinite whole. Be that as it may, Mou's affirmation of "intellectual intuition" (*zhi de zhijue* 智的直覺) sets him apart from Bradley, in that Bradley clearly retains reservation on the ability of human reason to create the infinite whole, that is reality as such, or the thing-in-itself. At root, unlike the idealists we have surveyed thus far, including Kant, Hegel, Green, and indeed, Bradley, Mou's key point is that only Confucianism, with the notion of the "infinite heart-mind" (*wuxianxin* 無限心), supplies the basis for "intellectual intuition" as a principle of moral creativity. At the end of the day, this is the reason why Confucianism may arrive at a profounder wisdom of the "perfect teaching" (*yuanjiao* 圓教).

To make my point, the following discussion will be divided into four parts. I shall first make clear the meanings of "reconciliatory dialectic" and of the "concrete universal," followed by a brief account of Bradley's post-Kantian criticism of Kant's deontology. Then, I turn to see Bradley's reconciliation of Kant and Hegel in respect of the ethics of self-realization, otherwise known as "my station and its duties." In the course of examining Bradley's ideas, as might be expected, I shall incorporate Mou's insights into the dialogue. Finally, I am going to touch on the major difference between Mou and Bradley with regard to the issue of the "perfect teaching."

Absolute Idealism

Given that Mou's attention to Hegel and British idealism was greatly directed by Tang, it seems appropriate to begin this study with an assessment of the reception of Bradley's "reconciliatory dialectic" and Hegel's "concrete universal" in the works of both Tang and Mou.

Reconciliatory Dialectic

According to Tang, Bradley is "the philosopher of philosophers in the eyes of British Idealists"; in fact, as Tang confesses, it is thanks to Bradley's *Appearance and Reality* that he "was led to study the works of great idealists like Kant and Hegel."[3] For my purposes, I only intend to focus on the two principles within Bradley's "reconciliatory dialectic," which Tang sees as offering a remarkable starting point for the discussion of reality, namely, coherence and comprehensiveness.[4]

The principle of coherence, as Tang suggests, means that "all that we commonly take to be real," including primary and secondary qualities of things, space and time, motion and change, causation, activity, things, the meaning of the self, and even moral and religious experience, "are all phenomena which merely unveil certain degrees of reality, incapable of uncovering the Absolute reality."[5] Referring to *Appearance and Reality*, this is to say that for Bradley, whatever is self-contradicting, in the sense of its contents and existence being irreconcilable with each other, is phenomenal, that is, appearance; by way of contrast, "ultimate reality is such that it does not contradict itself; here is an absolute criterion."[6] Although Bradley has made every effort to vindicate his assertion that not only feeling but also all important forms of thought are anything but the Absolute reality, the crucial point is that "denying that something is real is equivalent not to saying that it is unreal but to saying that it is appearance."[7] In short, reality has never been absent in appearances.[8]

On this view, as Tang continues, the principle of comprehensiveness thereby implies that "the Absolute reality is absolute experience, [which Bradley otherwise calls] sentient experience," which "embraces all appearances in an inclusive harmony."[9] Accordingly, to say that an object is phenomenal is not equal to saying that it does not exist, but that it exists as parts, aspects, that is, appearances of the Absolute: "everything phenomenal is somehow real"; "reality without appearance would be nothing."[10] Thus, what Bradley's account of the Absolute really intends to show us is that the phenomena do exist, but not all exist to the same extent, that is, there are degrees of reality.[11] In short, as Bradley's famous quote says, "the world is the best of all possible worlds, and *everything* in it is a necessary evil."[12]

For the most part, Mou shares with Tang a similar reading of Bradley's "reconciliatory dialectic." To quote Mou:

> Bradley prescribes that the meaning of appearance is by itself contradictory and incomprehensible. How, then, do we fix this contradiction? . . . Bradley, a neo-Hegelian, follows Hegel's line of thinking and proclaims that all these contradictions should reconcile into the "immediate this," which is the "reality" that has all those contradictory phenomena as its rich contents. The "immediate this" is the Absolute. Bradley's argument is still different from Hegel's. Hegel begins with Absolute being, and Absolute being is empty. In a way called expansive dialectic, Absolute being fills its emptiness step by step through a dialectical development. Bradley's way, in contrast, can be called reconciliatory dialectic—all contradictory and conflicting phenomena are reconciled into the "immediate this." When this "immediate this" turns into

reality, all contradictions not only dissolve, but actually become the bountiful contents that enrich the "immediate this." This kind of reconciliatory dialectic is very meaningful.[13]

Put in other terms, as Mou articulates elsewhere, for Bradley "the so-called reality is the infinite whole which embraces and transcends all phenomena"; "while the infinite whole is able to reconcile all finite, contradictory phenomena, the contradictory phenomena in the infinite whole, because of the reconciliation of contradictions, will remain partially true."[14] This commentary, once again, reflects Bradley's viewpoint that "there will be no truth which is entirely true, just as there will be no error which is totally false."[15] Or alternatively, as Bradley's distinctive follower Michael Oakeshott puts it, "even if truth is difficult to come at, nothing can be dismissed as mere error," and "where error is impossible, truth is inconceivable."[16]

The Unity

Based on the above discussion, it seems to me that Tang is absolutely correct in remarking that Bradley's "reconciliatory dialectic" is distinctive, in that the mind "enters into reality through phenomena"[17] as "the reality itself is nothing at all apart from appearance."[18] Be that as it may, Bradley still agrees with Hegel that "reality is spiritual,"[19] that "the true is the whole,"[20] and that the Absolute reality is a "concrete universal," not a collection of discrete facts.

That said, another crucial thread underlining Bradley's writings is the Hegelian viewpoint of the "concrete universal," meaning that all ideas constitute a unity in the sense of being related to one another, that every distinct idea cannot be truly grasped without referring to the unity, and thus, that the purpose of philosophy is to reach a more complete understanding of the unity by reconciling all possible contradictions.

In *Ethical Studies*, Bradley's major work in moral philosophy, the task of reconciliation, takes on a typical Hegelian fashion of transcending the two opposite one-sidednesses of thinking as well. By implication, as we shall see, this means that a philosophical study of morality can be established by demonstrating the ways in which the contradictions and partialities of two prevailing moral creeds, namely, "pleasure for pleasure's sake" (utilitarianism) and "duty for duty's sake" (deontology), are to be reunited in "my station and its duties."[21] "Our true being," according to

Bradley, "is not the extreme of unity, nor of diversity, but the perfect identity of both."[22]

Furthermore, Bradley takes it that the starting point for a philosophical study of morality is the *fact* of ordinary experience, namely, "the world, both on its external side of the family, society, the State, and the work of the individual in them, and again, on its internal side of moral feeling and belief."[23] Also, following Hegel, Bradley insists that the business of the philosopher is to explain *the world as it is*.[24] It follows that for Bradley moral practice has its relative autonomy:[25] To be moral is to *act morally* within *Sittlichkeit*, whose existence does not depend on philosophical doctrines. As Green puts it, tradition exemplifies idioms of action and will "actuate men independently of the operation of the discursive intellect."[26]

Understanding *Ren* in the Hegelian Vein

I shall return to the task of philosophy in relation to the issue of reality later on. For now, it is more critical to point out that Mou leans toward believing Tang's story that "reconciliatory dialectic" gives "support to Chinese cosmology"[27] in general, including Buddhism and Daoism.[28] As regards Confucianism, Mou states in his earlier writings:

> In the sayings of Hegel, . . . you can find out the rich meanings of dialectic and its impact on the life or culture of the Germans, which ceaselessly confirms itself and negates itself toward a higher level, ceaselessly transcends and ceaselessly destroys. It yearns for absolute completeness (*juedui de yuanman* 絕對的圓滿), and yet the absolute completeness can never be reached, falling short of final realization. . . . My friend Tang Junyi once said to me that if we put the Absolute in the front, we can never arrive at it. This does not make sense, so far as *Dao*-reality [i.e., the reality of morality] (*daoti* 道體) is concerned. He agreed with Bradley's reconciliatory dialectic. According to this point of view, all of our developments have a grounding, which is the absolute completeness; all developments are to illuminate this absoluteness, and this is what is called "self-awareness in every single step" (*bubu zijue* 步步自覺). All developments are to be reconciled in this absoluteness at the same time, and this is what is called

"returning to the roots and reverting to what is originally in me" (*guigen fuben* 歸根復本). This, of course, shows a hint of Chinese Confucianism. However, this kind of reconciliatory dialectic can be used only after having "illuminated the heart-mind and found the *Xing*-nature" (*mingxin jianxing* 明心見性) and having "established the reality of morality and erected the ultimate ideal" (*jianti liji* 建體立極).[29]

From the standpoint I have been taking, this quotation is of great importance. On the one hand, it affirms that for Mou the key notion of *ren* in Confucianism is in some crucial respects equal to the fullest meaning of reality known as the Absolute in Hegel's philosophy.[30] As Mou puts it elsewhere, the life of *ren* "must be embodied" in society, and so, compared to "extensional truth" such as the "abstract universality" of mathematics, *ren* recognized as "intensional truth" is affiliated to what Hegel calls "concrete universality."[31] Moreover, although Mou blames Hegel for treating the Absolute as a logical necessity rather than a moral concept right from the outset, he clearly appreciates Bradley's "reconciliatory dialectic" as a profound analogy apt to clarify Confucian moral practice in terms of *bubu zijue* and *guigen fuben*.

On the other hand, the quotation at stake reestablishes that the most comprehensive ideal of Confucianism is to erect moral subjectivity. For this reason, the employment of "reconciliatory dialectic" in Confucianism is permissible only if moral subjectivity, characterized by the figurative expressions *mingxin jianxing* and *jianti liji* deriving from the language of Song-Ming Neo-Confucianism, has been firmly established. Returning to Mencius, this means that the moral practice of "giving full realization to heart-mind," namely, *bubu zijue* and *guigen fuben*, is deeply rooted in the matters of moral metaphysics concerning "knowing *Xing*-nature" (*zhixing* 知性) and "knowing Heaven" (*zhitian* 知天), namely, *mingxin jianxing* and *jianti liji*.[32]

In Mou's denotation, as we have seen, *mingxin jianxing* and *jianti liji* spell out a specific feature of the Confucian subjectivity, namely, "immanent transcendence" (*neizai chaoyue* 內在超越), which has remarkable affinity to Kantian moral autonomy. This affinity, however, does not affect the fact that Mou at the same time searches for the potentiality of effecting a Hegelian revision of Kant; indeed, my view is that, as with Bradley, Mou also conceives of an ethics of self-realization that is aimed at reconciling Kantian free will and Hegelian *Sittlichkeit*.

The Development of Moral Consciousness

While the formula of self-realization is grounded in the common source of British idealism, in Bradley's analysis of Western moral consciousness, there is a dialectical movement from "pleasure for pleasure's sake" (utilitarianism), via "duty for duty's sake" (deontology), toward "my station and its duties." Putting to one side the issue of utilitarianism,[33] here I shall merely concentrate on the similar ways in which Mou and Bradley offer a Hegelian revision of Kant's moral theory, leading to a post-Kantian ethics of self-realization.

Two Criticisms of Kant

At the outset, it may be appropriate to reiterate that although Kant's philosophy has close kinship to Confucian ethics, Mou's reconstruction of Confucian "moral metaphysics" is after all different from Kant's "metaphysics of morals." For the present context, it suffices to bring up two of Mou's criticisms of Kant. In the first place, as indicated, Mou believes that Kant is mistaken in treating the free will merely as a postulate. As a result of this, Kant's practical philosophy falls short of offering a far-reaching discussion of the full actualization of humanity in concrete situations and the importance of human feeling in shaping the basis of morality. In this regard, it can be said that the ethics of self-realization is advantageous to spelling out the philosophical similarities between Mou and the British idealists, mainly because it is committed to fusing the sensible world with the moral law, particularly with regard to an ethical reading of the organic relationship between the individual and community, otherwise identified as embodied individualism in this book.

It is true that for Kant, morality requires the moral subject to "act from duty, on maxim and out of the respect for the law," and hence, the grounding of morality subsists in human reason alone. This, however, does not mean that Kant entirely neglects the significance of human feeling in supporting the implementation of the moral law. According to Kant, our resolution of choice does proceed "*from* the presentation of a possible action *to* the deed through the feeling of pleasure or displeasure, taking an interest in the action or its effect," but the state of feeling in question falls into two categories which are poles apart, namely, "sensibly dependent" and "moral": the former is that feeling which is caused by external objects in the natural world and thus "precedes the presentation of the law," whereas the latter "can only follow upon it" and thus shows a *respect* for morality.³⁴ That is to say, Kant's idea of moral feeling is understood as a "*susceptibility* on the part of free choice to be moved by pure practical reason (and its law)," and "every man (as a moral being) has it in him originally"; for this reason, unlike the idea of "moral sense" in the Humean theory of moral sentiments, which implies a "theoretical capacity for perception directed toward an object," the idea of moral feeling in Kant's metaphysics of morals is "merely subjective, which yields no knowledge."³⁵ As a consequence, to say that Kant insists on "a strict contrast between reason and feeling" is not equivalent to saying that Kant excludes human feeling from the discussion of morality; rather, it says only that for Kant, "the moral law is the *Bewegungsgrund* of moral feeling" and that "it is the form of moral law, rather than sensible feeling that constitutes the *Bestimmungsgrund* of morality."³⁶

In the discussion that follows, I am equipped to examine more fully the topic of moral feeling, together with a restatement of embodied individualism from different angles. Before going any further, however, it is first necessary to point out that all things considered, the key difference between Mou and Kant in respect of moral feeling results from the second challenge that Mou poses to Kant: through the lens of Heidegger, Mou also thinks that in terms of philosophical anthropology the Kantian self is, in fact, a finite creature, lacking a comprehensive understanding of "intellectual intuition" that is unrestricted and infinite in potentiality.

By and large, it is in this manner that Mou highlights the moral spirit of Confucianism by saying that "although man is finite, he can be infinite," a saying that resonates with the voice of the British idealists in many significant ways. Be all this as it may, unlike the British idealists, who in offering a synthesis of utilitarianism and Kantianism within the Western tradition, are prone to incorporate human desire and self-satisfaction into the moral law, the moral feeling that concerns Mou is, on balance, what can be called "enlightened feeling" (*jueqing* 覺情), in keeping with the existence of "intellectual intuition" that lays the foundation for the Confucian moral metaphysics that Mou has finally established. In what follows, let me elaborate on these two criticisms in association with Bradley's viewpoints in turn.

THE POSTULATE OF FREEDOM

As regards the postulate of freedom, to begin with, the charge that Mou presses on Kant is not about the rational ability of the free agent to discover moral principle; but rather, his contention is that the "practical use of freedom" must at the same time contain a "meaning of presenting (*chengxian* 呈現) in moral practice,"³⁷ or more exactly, the presentation of heart-mind and feeling in concrete situations. That said, despite the merits, Kant's practical philosophy fails to consider morality and freedom from the standpoint of "enlightened feeling" mentioned above, largely due to the bifurcated world he left, namely, the dichotomy between the transcendental world of free will and the empirical world of sensations and desires. As far as Confucianism is concerned,

> such a transcendental kind of heart-mind and feeling can be traced to *ren* which was embodied in Confucius. . . . These are transformed into the nature of heart-mind in Mencius's sense: [the four germs] are at the same time feelings and principles (*li* 理). Principles are certainly transcendental, universal, and *a priori*. Nonetheless, these principles are not only universal in an abstract manner, but are also shown in the concrete heart-mind and feeling. Therefore, they are concretely universal. Insofar as heart-mind and feeling are concrete and genuine expressions of principles, they are also promoted to be transcendental, universal, and at the same time subjective and objective. They are no longer purely subjective on the factual level.³⁸

Put differently, in view of the fact that Kant is eager to separate morality from nature, which, in turn, leads him to deal with moral feeling on the factual level, within the Kantian binary framework we are unable to answer the vital questions of how freedom is *possible* in the real world and why men would be *interested in* following moral principle. In Mencius's context, by contrast, morality *simultaneously* involves the "heart-mind and *Xing*-nature" (*xinxing* 心性) and "enlightened feeling." As Mou puts it, "Enlightened feeling is at the same time reason: it neither precedes reason nor goes after reason; it is identical with reason."³⁹ Accordingly, although Mencius's view about the "goodness of *Xing*-nature" (*xingshan* 性善) echoes Kant's discussion of free will and moral principle to a great extent, in sharp contrast to Kant, the saying that "reason and righteousness please my heart-mind in the same way as meat pleases my palate"⁴⁰ at once implies that in the system of the *Mencius* there exists a tendency of "enlightened feeling" to develop toward goodness at the same time.

In short, in the ideal situation, moral principle created by the "authentic heart-mind" (*benxin* 本心) is coexistent with the pleasure of following it.

An excellent illustration of this moral scenario, once again, lies in Mencius's famous statement: Not only do the *moral potentialities* of humaneness, righteousness, the observance of rites, and wisdom "exist in me originally," but also, and equally important, there exist "four germs"—in accordance with these moral potentialities, namely, the *enlightened feelings* of compassion, shame, courtesy and modesty, as well as right and wrong—that may help guide the agent to actualize its "inner morality" (*neizai daodexing* 內在道德性) in the actual world.[41] All in all, that is the reason why Mencius articulates that "seek and you will find it; let go and you will lose it."[42]

> If this is the case, then seeking is of use to getting and what is sought is within yourself. But if there is a proper way to seek it and whether you get it or not depends on destiny, then seeking is of no use to getting and what is sought lies outside yourself.[43]

Thus seen, the moral theory of Mencius is superior to that of Kant in the sense that the actual presentation of freedom, that is, the "full realization of heart-mind," in concrete situations, has turned out to be *possible*. What is more, provided that Mencius's heart-mind embraces both moral reasoning and moral feeling, its self-realization through "seeking" all together explains why people would feel *interested in* respecting moral principle.

If the above discussion is correct, then it follows that undertaking a certain Hegelian revision of Kant will do good to the development of Confucian subjectivity for modern times. For one thing, Hegel does not discard the principal values that Kant conveys to underline modernity, namely, individuality, freedom, and human dignity. Furthermore, as Mou concedes, despite the fact that Hegel fails to bring to light the significance of "intellectual intuition," together with "enlightened feeling," in making sense of the ontological principle of moral creation, one of Hegel's most substantial modifications of Kant is to "take seriously and make stand out" the "principle of realization" or the "principle of actualization, embodiment" in relation to the constant practice (*gongfu* 功夫) of seeking, thanks to the fact that "Hegel places a stress on reality."[44]

The Post-Kantian Turn

That being said, I am now in a better position to contend that the British idealists such as Bradley and Green have likewise launched a critique of Kant's postulation of free will, focusing on Hegel's notion of realization, embodiment, or objectification. To cite Tang's comment again,

> Those who follow Kant, such as Fichte, Hegel, and Green, make a more systematic claim that all categories of knowledge are established by the mind, and explain more sufficiently the ability of man's free will to be autonomous, by bringing into account the objective will or objective spirit that not only prescribes the social ideal and the orientation of historical culture, but also accesses the will of the universe, the spirit of the universe.[45]

Bradley chiefly makes three points. Primarily, he maintains that to act "from duty," that is, to act by understanding the action as our own duty, is a contradiction. Because to act is to realize *yourself*, and to realize yourself is to materialize and particularize your *wills*; in this regard, the existence of a formal will without *contents* is impossible.

Again, as regards the presupposition of acting "on the moral principles," Bradley takes issue with their abstractness:

> Everyone knows that setting out, whether in religion, morals, or politics, with the intent to realize an abstraction, is a futile endeavor; and that what it comes to is that either you do nothing at all, or that the particular content which is necessary for action is added to the abstraction by the chance of circumstances or caprice. Everybody suspects, if they do not feel sure, that acting consciously on and from abstract principles means self-deceit or hypocrisy or both.[46]

Finally, as far as acting "out of the respect for the law" is concerned, Bradley writes:

> It is clear that in a given case I may have several duties, and that I may be able to do only one. I must then break some "categorical" law, and the question the ordinary man puts

to himself is, which duty am I to do? . . . All these points we admire are in one way a matter of law; but if you think to decide in particular cases by applying some "categorical imperative," you must be a pedant, if not a fool.⁴⁷

In other words, as another leading British Hegelian, R. G. Collingwood articulates, "acting according to rules always involves a certain misfit between yourself and your situation."⁴⁸

At this point, it is worth mentioning that despite lacking the notion of "enlightened feeling," the British idealists also think that Kant's moral theory simply neglects the importance of human feeling and desire. Along the lines of his revisions of Kant, Bradley writes that the world in which we live and which we wish to make better is one with "the morality already existing, ready to hand, in laws, institutions, social usages, moral opinions and feelings."⁴⁹ Similarly, in his "Lecture on Kant" T. H. Green makes it clear that "Kant's mistake is to assume there is no alternative between determination by natural desire for pleasure, and determination by abstract contemplation of moral law; for we often in all consciousness desire things other than pleasure."⁵⁰

In no way does this suggest that morality should be purely determined by want and impulse. On the contrary, for the British idealists, the real *motive* of human agency is predicated on the moral ability to seek "self-satisfaction" in transcending the present and actual situation so as to create for ourselves the *ends* which our action intends to actualize in the future state. Here, I do not intend to deny that unlike Kant's idea of moral feeling, which is, by default, non-cognitive, Green's discussion of "self-satisfaction" implies a cognitive power directed toward an object, that is, an end, and that unlike Mou's effort to explain "enlightened feeling" in a transcendent sense, none of the British idealists affirms the existence of "intellectual intuition." Be that as it may, the following description of Green's moral theory, it seems to me, may greatly help us to get hold of the post-Kantian discourse of moral ideal largely shared by British idealism and New Confucianism.

> [For Green], the motive determining an agent's will is always an idealized future state of his own self, a conception of himself as satisfied—whatever it may be that he seeks. For this reason, argues Green, moral action is the "process of self-realization," i.e., of making a possible self real. In historical terms, Green's

arrival at the formula of self-realization represents an important shift in ethical thinking. Instead of asking with the utilitarian, intuitionist, and even the Kantian philosophers of the day, "What ought I to do?" Green and many Idealists who followed him re-constructed ethical inquiry in the mould of an older question, "What kind of person ought I to be?"[51]

In short, in seeking the answer to the definitive question of "what kind of person I ought to be," both schools of thought not only regard the moral subject or the moral self as the crux of morality but also relate it to the ultimate meaning of human life in respect of the pursuit of self-perfection, that is, the higher self. To round off this key point, we must turn to "my station and its duties," which clearly entails a Hegelian aspiration to offer a synthesis of nature and morality, or more precisely, the particularity of pleasure in utilitarianism and the generality of Kant's categorical imperative, so as to *make real* the value of freedom in concrete situations.

My Station and Its Duties

As I expound on "my station and its duties," we shall have an opportunity to see more clearly how the ethics of self-realization encouraged by Bradley, among others, can provide us with a distinctive Hegelian standpoint for recounting Mou's delineation of the features of moral practice in Confucianism.

THE SOCIAL SELF

For the most part, the British idealists accept Hegel's notion of embodied subjectivity or embodied individualism that we have already touched on. That said, as far as the relationship between the individual and society is concerned, the British idealists basically look to Hegel's idea of concrete universality for their inspiration. As such, it comes as no surprise that apart from "utilitarian individualism," they also oppose Hebert Spencer's "organic individualism," which takes a "mechanical or biological" rather than "practical" reading of humanity.[52] In the words of Henry Jones, the idealists and the naturalists such as Spencer actually use the term "organism" in an emphatically different sense: while Spencer's "ethical teachings consist on the one hand of an inherited Hedonism, and on the other of elaborate analogies drawn between the physical structures and habits of animals and the mental structure and ethical habits of men," the real meaning of social organism, or moral organism undertaken by the idealists, denotes that "an individual has no life except that which is social, and that he cannot realize his own purposes except in realizing the larger purposes of society."[53]

More exactly, given that "man is self-conscious," that "morality from beginning to end is *self*-realization," and that moral action entails a reciprocal concern for others in society, it follows:

> The social organism is thus a concrete, living, self-interpreting, self-differentiating whole, apart from which neither the universal—the abstract society—nor the particular—the abstract individual—can be. Isolated from each other they are but names; sunder their relations and they cease to exist. They exist in and through each other, and are constituted by their relation.[54]

By the same token, Bradley's discussion of "my station and its duties" can be largely taken to be a "restatement of Hegel's *Sittlichkeit*" on the account that "the individual is nothing without society, and morality is through and through social."[55] To be sure, Bradley would agree with Hegel that the individual is inseparable from an "ethical substance" consisting of "laws and powers" and that "these substantial determinations are *duties* which are binding on the will of the individual."[56] Accordingly, for Bradley, as for Hegel, the so-called atomistic self must be deemed a "mere fancy," namely, an "abstraction," for "what we call an individual man is what he is because of and by virtue of community."[57] In short, to use D. G. Ritchie's terminology, the individual is obliged to seek a good life within a "community of self-interpretation."[58]

Against this backdrop, the first point I try to make is that Hegel's *Sittlichkeit* also plays a crucial role in Mou's reconstruction of Confucian moral practice. As previously said, Mou visibly appreciates Hegel's principle of realization. In Mou's phrase, "Confucius's *ren* and *yi* 義 (righteousness) are related not only to morals, but also to their objective realization."[59] It is basically in this Hegelian sense that Mou further remarks: "Although the Chinese people are prone to talk about the whole," for example, the Confucian aphorism has it that "Heaven and earth coexist with me" and that "the myriad things are identified with me," this does not imply a disapproval of individuality. Quite the contrary, as I have explicated vis-à-vis the term "personalism" employed by William Theodore de Bary and Zhang Hao [Chang Hao] (張灝 1937–2022) in the last chapter, Mou completely agrees that Confucianism is in essence featured by a "full-blown individualism," having a "complete respect for individuality,"[60] widely known as the practice of *self*-cultivation in community.

The Real Life

Furthermore, the idea of embodied subjectivity at the same time involves an appreciation of the concrete universal, recognizing the ultimate end of the self's continuous embodiment as the real self or the Absolute. In Bradley's words, a person's will is an act, and an act is a particular event; accordingly, "the self as a whole is, in the end, the content of our wills,"[61] and to fully realize ourselves is to make real all the content of our wills by means of action: In theory and practice, then, "my end is to realize myself as a whole."[62] Put in other terms, self-realization denotes the potentiality of a "universal life,"[63] insofar as "there is nothing which, to speak properly, is individual or perfect, except only the Absolute."[64]

As a matter of fact, the attempt to treat the moral self as fully rational, as both Kant and Hegel expect, is quite common to many British idealists. However, more greatly influenced by Hegel at this point, the British idealists' understanding of the true or ideal self, namely, the actualization of humanity as a whole in the fullest sense, is not merely a postulate; but rather, the ideal self is identified with a "universal life," that is, "concrete whole." For example, John Stuart Mackenzie argues that "the true self is what is perhaps best described as the *rational* self. It is the universe that we occupy in our moments of deepest wisdom and insight."[65] According to Bernard Bosanquet, "all the great contents of the developed human self—truth, beauty, religion and social morality—are all of them but modes of expression of the Ideal self."[66]

In the case of Mou, as we have seen, *ren* portrays the "concrete universal" of humanity as well as the "moral ability" of *benxin* that enables the agent to discover the rationality of moral principles defining the ultimate purpose of human life. Accordingly, Confucian moral practice in respect of the realization of *ren* can be captured as a dedication to "giving full realization to heart-mind" in a way that the highest state of human rationality, namely, "Real life," "Real substance," the "Real subject," or the "Real self"[67] can take shape in the real world. In short, moral practice regards an endless process of seeking the fulfillment of virtue toward an accomplishment of sagehood.

THE INFINITE WHOLE

Seen from the perspective of "my station and its duties," the actual realization of *ren* can therefore be heightened from two angles. In one sense, it involves the proper relation of the self to other selves in the ethical world; in another, it concerns the *reality* of a universal life, that is, the ultimate purpose of human life. Put in other terms, what truly underpins the meaning of self-realization is an understanding of the relationship between the finite self and the infinite whole.

In terms of moral practice, it must be stressed once again that for Bradley, as for Mou, the Hegelian viewpoint of *Sittlichkeit* does not necessarily imply a belittlement of the individual. Three main points can be added to this. First, Bradley makes it clear that the crux of moral activity is to "make the self-evolution of ourselves and of humanity the end."[68] That said, despite adopting Hegel's *Sittlichkeit*, Bradley retains Kant's essential principle on treating humanity as an end. Considering the purpose of this chapter, this view is of great consequence because it reminds us of the reason why Mou prefers Bradley's "reconciliatory dialectic" to Hegel's "expansive dialectic."

Second, community or ethical substance is anything but a *sufficient* condition for creating duties. On the contrary, as Bradley continues, the truth is that

> personal morality and political and social institutions cannot exist apart. And (in general) the better the one, the better the other. The community is moral, because it realizes personal morality; personal morality is moral, because and in so far as it realizes the moral whole.[69]

Similarly, Confucianism does not exert a divorce between the self and virtues, between the individual and social settings, or between personal morality and the moral whole. In Mou's denotation, as previously said, "there is no isolated virtue, because *ren* and *yi* cannot exist in the individual independently,"[70] but by no means does this mean that Confucianism is against the individual. The whole point is that Confucianism sees man as a dialogist, rather than a monologist, and thus, that the self to be realized in concrete situations is not a private self, but a social self.

Third, to say that moral progress in a society is indispensable for moral development in the individual is not equivalent to remarking that the individual should be deprived of freedom: "Choice is necessary for morality."⁷¹ In accordance with the "reconciliatory dialectic" that we have discussed, this means that in the course of self-realization, the agent "exhibits a greater degree of reality only insofar as it contains within itself more of the 'total Universal,' that is, insofar as it becomes transmuted, comprehensive and self-consistent"; or, to put it another way, "a self becomes more of a self to the extent to which it becomes less distinct from other selves."⁷²

In a like manner, not only does Mou maintain that Confucius's *ren*, Mencius's *Xing*-nature, or Wang Yangming's [Wang Yang-Ming] (王陽明1472–1529) *liangzhi* 良知 ("original knowing," or the "knowing-reality of enlightened awareness") parallels Kant's free will, but he also urges that Confucianism takes a practice-first viewpoint in examining the meaning of what it is to be a human being, implying that freedom is unavoidable for morality. However, as with Bradley, Mou does not deny that the fullest realization of the moral capability of *benxin* has to do with a dialectical movement toward a "total Universe." For example, following the view that self-cultivation and the moral whole cannot be set apart, Mou remarks that "in Confucian doctrines, the only way to accomplish virtues is by reaching this completeness and fullness."⁷³ Indeed, this is why Wang Yangming says that "the great man thinks of Heaven, earth, and the myriad things as oneness." Against this background, Mou thus concludes his view about Confucian philosophical anthropology by articulating that "although man is finite, he can be infinite."

Considerably echoing Mou's motto, Bradley writes that to take self-realization as the moral end is to argue that "what one desires is self as a whole," that "the self is to be realized as an infinite whole," and that "the only way a man can do that, given his finitude, is to know and will himself as a member in an infinite whole."⁷⁴ To quote Bradley,

> "Realizing yourself as an infinite whole" means, "Realize yourself as the self-conscious member of an infinite whole, by realizing that whole in yourself." When that whole is truly infinite, and when your personal will is wholly made one with it, then you also have reached the extreme of

homogeneity and specification in one, and have attained a perfect self-realization.[75]

The Limitation of Philosophy

Up to this point, we have unveiled a cluster of affinities between Mou and Bradley largely in respect of moral practice. However, in the field of moral ontology, they clearly have different views about whether a man is able to reach the infinite whole, the real self, or the Absolute in the end.

Ideal Morality and Religion

In Bradley's analysis, although "my station and its duties" ensures that the existence of duty is concrete, objective, and universal, the misfit between myself and my situation, between the moral self and the empirical self, has not yet been completely removed: First, as moral experience shows, in our social life it is difficult to entirely eradicate radical evils and moral conflicts; second, there are duties such as the social ideal of cosmopolitanism transcending one's community affiliation; third, some duties are even not related to my station but are produced by the nonsocial culture of science and art. Accordingly, the ideal self or ideal morality to be fully realized consists of the "objective world of my station and its duties," the "ideal of social perfection," and the "ideal of nonsocial perfection."[76]

On this account, "morality does involve a contradiction."[77] For, the essence of our moral life is to overcome the evil by pursuing the good; goodness and evil coexist in morality: "You cannot define moral goodness without bringing in evil"; "the evil is as much a fact as the good, and without our bad self we should hardly know ourselves."[78] The problem, however, is that it is always beyond our humanity to destroy evils in a complete sense; or alternatively, the paradox has it that were evils utterly annihilated, there would be no morality at all. Furthermore, neither the "ideal of social perfection" nor the "ideal of nonsocial perfection" can be completely realized in human life. As a result, it seems to be the case that "we are a self-contradiction: we never are what we feel we really are; we really are what we know we are not; and if we become what we are, we should scarcely be ourselves."[79]

It follows that morality, albeit entailing an endless process of self-perfection, "is imperfect, and imperfect in such a way as implies a higher, which is religion."[80] Like morality, "the object of religion is that same ideal self," that is, the complete reality;[81] in religious life our ultimate ideal is to effect a reconciliation of the divine and the human, that is, to arrive at oneness. Unlike morality, however, religion is based not on thought, but on faith; the main difference is that "what in morality only is to be, in religion somehow and somewhere really is, and what we are to do is done."[82] In this regard, there appears an intricate tension between the reflection on morality in *this* world and the faith in the coming of the world *beyond*. As with the Christian consciousness, then, "our morality is consummated in oneness with God, and everywhere we find that 'immortal Love,' which builds itself for ever on contradiction, but in which the contradiction is eternally resolved."[83]

Thus seen, there is immediately a limitation inherent in philosophy: To philosophize is to understand the "concrete universal," and if philosophy ceases to think, it "commits suicide"; however, it is beyond the ability of our mind to understand "this concrete universal in detail," although this offers "no good ground for our declining to entertain it."[84] In other words, philosophy (as well as religion) cannot verify the ultimate existence of morality; instead, we are living in an autonomous world of meanings, in which it is up to ourselves to undertake an endless process of self-perfecting.

Profound Wisdom

With regard to the principles of coherence and comprehensiveness mentioned above, it seems to be the case that for Bradley, the Absolute will never show up, and morality is after all "appearance," not "reality," as it commits self-contradiction, even religion cannot set it straight. All in all, Bradley upholds that there is an inherent restriction to human reasoning, in view of the fact that human beings do not have the *very kind* of "intellectual intuition" that Mou finds in Confucianism, namely, the ability to create *reality* as such, that is, the infinite whole.

In Mou's system, as it will be remembered, benxin is on balance the "infinite heart-mind" (*wuxianxin* 無限心), or the "heart-mind of infinite freedom" (*ziyou wuxianxin* 自由無限心). Apart from representing the notions of both subjectivity (that is, the moral ability which makes possible moral activity) and objectivity (that is, the highest good which features the purpose of moral activity), *benxin* also possesses "intellectual intuition" as a principle of moral creativity capable of realizing the "absoluteness that initiates reality."⁸⁵ Based on what has been established in the last two chapters, it seems appropriate to restate that Mou is enthusiastic about this faculty for two major reasons. On the one hand, with "intellectual intuition" it would then be logical to uphold the "conformity of Heaven and man in union" (*tianren heyi* 天人合一) that uniquely characterizes Confucianism. As Mou puts it,

> We may comprehend Heaven, earth, and myriad things in a comprehensive way that affirms a substance of transcendence (God or the *Dao* of Heaven) which creates them or makes them happen, and this is utterly determined by a human's moral heart-mind or the truthfulness of a human's moral creativity. That is to say, the reason why Heaven takes in the meaning of creating all things is to be completely confirmed by the point of the truthfulness of our moral creativity. . . . Thus, [as Mencius remarks,] to fulfill my heart-mind is to know my *Xing*-nature; to fulfill my heart-mind and to know my *Xing*-nature are to know why Heaven is Heaven.⁸⁶

On the other hand, the affirmation of "intellectual intuition" is closely related to the Confucian notion of the "perfect teaching." To quote Mou,

> So, the fullest accomplishment of the highest good [in Confucianism] is this: "The great man is he who is in harmony, in his attributes, with Heaven and earth; in his brightness, with the sun and moon; in his orderly procedure, with the four seasons; and in his relation to what is fortunate and what is calamitous, in harmony with the spirit-like operations (of Providence). He may precede Heaven, and Heaven will not act in opposition to him; he may follow Heaven, but will act (only) as Heaven at the time would do."⁸⁷ . . . This is the absolute perfect teaching. . . . There is no such thing in the West, and for this reason, morality and religion cannot be united in oneness on the one side, and morality and metaphysics cannot be united in oneness on the other. This is why so many Western philosophers have talked about reality, for example, Bradley has a book called *Appearance and Reality*.⁸⁸

In a nutshell, the "perfect teaching" in Confucianism is "perfect" because the archetype of moral perfection in question, namely, the true actualization of the full potentiality of *benxin*, is perfectly identified with the *Dao* of Heaven. In addition, it is "teaching" because, unlike Bradley's usage of "reality," which has its roots in the Western tradition, in the Confucian tradition whatever the sage says evokes a version of *profound wisdom* about the genuine meaning of a moral subject, that is, learning to become a human.

The Turn to Politics

To close this chapter, I want to make three points. First, it should have become clear by now that despite the differences largely in terms of "enlightened feeling" and "intellectual intuition," there exists moral resonance between Mou and Bradley in respect of the ethics of self-realization and that this resonance is grounded in the fact that both thinkers attempt to synthesize Kant and Hegel. From the standpoint I have been taking, this implies that the ethical thinking of British idealism bears a striking but often overlooked resemblance to that of New Confucianism.

Second, the ethics of self-realization embedded in the writings of Mou and Tang actually has had a significant impact on the later development of contemporary Confucianism. For example, to quote Cheng Zhongying [Cheng Chung-Ying] (成中英),

> *Ren* is the beginning and the end of a full process of humanizing a human person or, for that matter, a process of human perfecting. *Ren* is also such a process of continuing achievement and effort toward the end of humanization and perfection.[89]

Finally, although in comparison to either Kant's metaphysics of morals or Hegel's Absolute idealism, Confucian moral metaphysics and Confucian moral practice are full of profound wisdom, it remains true that Confucianism in general failed to develop democracy and political values related to it in the past. From the above discussion, it follows that what is required for the justification of Confucian liberalism, so to speak, would be a new Confucian political philosophy committed to resting democracy on the ethics of self-realization, which has thus far been demonstrated as a plausible reformulation of Confucian ethics in the post-Kantian context, characterized by the features of embodied individualism, the actualization of freedom in concrete situations, the moral worth of self-cultivation within a community, the potential assumption of a common good, and the like. To see more fully what I mean by Confucian liberalism, we must turn to examine the aspect of political innovation in Mou's democratic theory.

Part II
Civil Liberalism

Chapter 4

Democracy and the Politics of Innovation

Introduction

In spite of the great achievement of Mou Zongsan in theorizing on the prospect of democracy in the modern transformation of Confucianism, his Hegelian presentation of the "blossoming of democracy" (*minzhu kaichu* 民主開出) has been severely criticized by both anti-Confucian liberalism and antiliberal Confucianism.[1] Again, since the attack on Hegel's political philosophy, made by cold war liberals such as Karl Popper and Isaiah Berlin,[2] has had a great impact on the recognition of liberalism in the Chinese context, even Mou's disciples have turned to recast Confucian democracy in a Kantian fashion.[3] What is more, the landscape of contemporary Confucian political philosophy has been dramatically altered for the past two decades or so, owing to a variety of renovated perspectives, including Confucian pragmatism,[4] progressive Confucianism,[5] Confucian perfectionism,[6] civic Confucianism,[7] public reason Confucianism,[8] and so on, but the names of Mou and other leading New Confucians are only mentioned in passing.

In contrast to these perspectives, I take it that Mou's political thinking, if properly reconstructed in a Hegelian vein, will give us renovated ground to relocate a group of liberal elements, including democracy, individuality, citizenship, open society, freedom, and rights, into the Confucian forms of life. In other words, given that Mou's early political writings were largely inspired by Hegel and full of Hegelian terms, there is no point in excluding Hegel's insights when rebuilding Mou's political thought as presenting a form of civil liberalism rooted in the spirit of

116 | Confucian Liberalism

ren 仁 (humaneness). Indeed, unlike Mou's disciples, I totally agree with John Rawls's remark that Hegel "stands in the liberal tradition" and that Hegel is a "moderately progressive reform-minded liberal" as well as a "defender of the modern constitutional state."[9]

To make my case, I argue in this chapter that as for democracy, Mou actually raises three main questions: (1) Why did Confucianism not develop democracy in the past? (2) How can Confucianism develop democracy? And (3) what is the subtlest model of Confucian democracy? Taken together, they also constitute the three crucial aspects to be considered for a philosophical explanation of the "politics of innovation," namely, political crisis, political transformation, and political ideal. The crucial point here is that in the course of this explanation, Hegel's critical assessment of modernity, his discussion of objective spirit, and his ambiguous legacy for liberalism are all required to make better sense of Mou's political philosophy. Overall, the three questions of Confucian democracy concerned correspond to Hegel's thoughtful analysis of historical conditions of morality and politics in modern times to a great extent. Before going any further, it thus seems proper to account for the Hegelian scheme in a way that may help bring to light Mou's unique voice of Confucian democracy.

The Hegelian Scheme

Speaking of Hegel, Charles Taylor is absolutely accurate in remarking that "we have very good reason to use Hegel, but we have to use him with great care."[10] Instead of explaining which parts of Hegel's philosophy are dead,[11] however, my purposes allow me to focus on some of the main reasons why we should pay attention to "what is living" of Hegel when trying to get a better reunderstanding of Mou's political thinking.

The Politics of Civilization

To begin with, my turn to the Hegelian scheme in this book is largely predicated on the fact that some significant aspects of Mou's examination of Confucianism are akin to the core insights of Hegel's concrete philosophy, such as embodied subjectivity, the principle of actualization, the full meaning of reality, and the concrete universal. More exactly, Mou shares with Hegel the insight that parts are meaningful only if they are related to the whole, and thus, that the particular meanings of human practices and social organizations appearing in specific historical contexts and stages can be comprehensively apprehended only if they are related to the concrete universal of humanity and civilization in development. In short, methodologically speaking, it is mainly through the lens of Hegel that Mou comes to understand the issues of democracy with regard to objective spirit.

In this regard, it seems fair to remark that an essential part of Hegel's intellectual legacy that concerns Mou is the attempt to incorporate history, civilization, tradition, the forms of life, and so on, into the study of the nature of political life. In other words, thanks to Hegel's long-standing impact, Mou's political thinking, by and large, belongs to the category of what may be referred to as the "politics of civilization," or more broadly, the "politics of civility." Compared to some of the prevailing patterns of political theorization at the present time, such as the "politics of justice" and the "politics of rights," the "politics of civility" is essentially linked with a sense of historicity.

That said, granted that there are limitations in Hegel's philosophy, we still owe to him the "historical turning," the viewpoint that the mission of theory is "to come to grips with its own time," the viewpoint that "theory forms a unity with the history in which it emerges and which it strives to comprehend."[12] Accordingly, in practical terms, the main reason to maintain an interest in Hegel, despite the collapse of the final terminus of human history, is mainly because the course of his philosophical examination of the conditions of modernity is still "highly relevant to our time" and "very much to the point."[13]

At this junction, it is relevant to note that although Mou largely borrows from Hegel's philosophy of history in the course of explicating the "blossoming of democracy," this does not imply that he is on the same page with Hegel in terms of the idea of God's plan for an endpoint of human history. In what follows, the Hegelian scheme under consideration refers not so much to the Christian background of Hegel's philosophy but to the philosophical way of treating politics that Mou learns from Hegel.

Before turning to shed some more light on the manners in which the key elements of Hegel's political philosophy—namely, civilization, objective spirit, and liberal commitment—have penetrated Mou's writings, I now intend to follow in Charles Taylor's footsteps in providing a Hegelian diagnosis of the practical predicaments of our time—namely, the crisis of modernity, the challenge of radical freedom, and the moral weakness of liberal democracy. By this means, we shall be in a better position to reevaluate the importance of the Hegelian scheme in reestablishing Mou's Confucian liberalism.

Modernity, Radical Freedom, and Liberal Democracy

Let me begin by saying that even in the present, Hegel's work deeply captures the malaises of modernity in terms of the alienation of the self, the dissolution of public meanings, and the ascendency of instrumental reason,[14] to name only a few. To appreciate more fully the significance of Hegel in this respect, it can be restated that beginning with *Early Theological Writings*, Hegel's thinking consists of an attempt to work out the growing sense of alienation in the modern epoch. Even if, with the turn to philosophy in *Phenomenology of Spirit*, the focus of attention has been extended from the opposition between finite and infinite spirit, to the separation of man as knowing subject from nature, to the division between reason and desires within men, and to the distinction between the individual and community,[15] Hegel's writings unvaryingly spell out the crisis of modernity rooted in a deep perception of estrangement.

On this reading, the aim of Hegel's philosophy is to overcome the insufficient conditions of humanity such that reason and freedom can be actualized in a fuller sense. In other words, the expression of "self-positing *Geist*" not only means that *Geist* or subjectivity consists of reason, freedom, and self-consciousness, and has been embodied in the universe and human practices, but also implies that the self-realization of *Geist* involves an understanding of the world as a series of progressive phrases toward a more complete actualization of reason and freedom.

Returning to Mou, it seems that the problem of estrangement also plays a crucial part in his thought; however, Mou's deeper purpose for proposing Confucian democracy is to deal with the political crisis of modern China and the moral quandary of Western modernity at the same time. To do justice to Mou, he has never uncritically proposed a Western-centric conception of democracy for a new China. Rather, in addition to the profound reflection on the divorce between man and God (or moral sources), the obscure meaning of human life, and so forth, Mou's search for Confucian democracy can be seen as an adjunct to his far-reaching criticisms of the catastrophes of modernity with regard to atomistic individuality, radical freedom, the disrespect for civility and ethical life in politics, the hazards of technocracy and scientism, and so on. Overall, in keeping with Hegel's emphasis on ethical life, namely, the attempt to revive the "Greek harmony between individuals and public institutions within the new context presented by the free subjectivity of modernity,"[16] a key thread running throughout Mou's moral and political philosophy is to create a Confucian harmony between subjective freedom and Confucian *ethos* embodied in communal practices. Unlike Hegel, however, Mou tries hard to make a distinction between Confucian public virtue—more exactly, a specific set of *Confucian governing and civic virtues*—penetrating his political philosophy and Confucian morality as a whole presented in his moral metaphysics.

I shall touch on this important topic many times in this book where appropriate. For now, it can be added that another of the vital influences of Hegel on contemporary political theory is that he is extremely dissatisfied with subjective freedom (or with some qualifications, negative freedom in Isaiah Berlin's usage), which falls prey to a separation between subjectivity and objectivity. To be sure, Hegel firmly believes that freedom in its real meaning denotes "the freedom that man has in following his own essence, reason."[17] Accordingly, there is no doubt that the Hegelian conception of philosophical anthropology is poles apart from the one from which contemporary discussion of negative freedom stems, be it Hobbesian, Lockean, or utilitarian. In Taylor's words, the Hegelian embodied subjectivity, in line with both Aristotle and the Herderian "expressivist" viewpoint, "is characterized teleologically, as tending toward a certain perfection, that of reason and freedom."[18] In short, although Hegel failed to foresee that subjective freedom or radical freedom grounded in disengaged subjectivity is still vigorously at work in our time, his creative notion of embodied subjectivity and the idea of concrete freedom or situated freedom related to it entail a potentiality of seeing the continuous objectification of human freedom with regard to *Sittlichkeit* as the fulcrum of democratic practices.[19]

By the same token, for Mou and his followers, Confucianism anchors the world with a sense of purpose, that is, *ren*, which not only makes sense but is cardinal to all other virtues related to the ultimate meaning of human life. For this reason, it is adequate to regard *ren* as humanity as a whole which has as its features humaneness, dignity, reason, freedom, and subjectivity, and to see Confucianism for the most part as an ethics of realizing *ren* as fully as possible in concrete situations. Indeed, from my point of view, the Hegelian appreciation of embodied subjectivity, together with the Herderian "expressivist" notion of man, is similar to "personalism in Confucianism." And so, as with Hegel, Mou is clearly aware that the "abstract freedom of the individual" actually entails the strength of "absolute negativity," giving rise to the crisis of modernity featuring alienation and estrangement,[20] which, as indicated, can be transcended by returning to true freedom, that is, *ren*.

The crucial point here, however, is that compared to the fruits of Western modernity in terms of democracy and science, the stress on "inner sagehood" (*neisheng* 內聖) had never generated a true actualization of "outer kingliness" (*waiwang* 外王). In this manner, there is a serious deficiency embedded in Confucianism, namely, that it actually contributes nothing imperative to inaugurate what may be called the "way of politics" (*zhengdao* 政道), on which the legitimacy of political authority can be rightly based. To this, it can be immediately added that for Mou, democracy is just another expression of the "way of politics" on the account that the *political* meaning of democracy, by definition, is a "formal condition," or alternatively, an "aloof form" (*chaoran de xingshi* 超然的形式),[21] through which the *moral* cores of "humane government" (*renzheng* 仁政) can be actualized at the end of the day. All in all, what I have been trying to suggest is that in Mou's analysis, to resolve the political crisis of China, Confucianism has to generate a renovated form of politics.

Before analyzing Mou's definition of democracy in a complete sense, however, it is more crucial to point out that Hegel's dialectic can without a doubt be treated as a disclosure of the historical conditions of democracy. In brief, the goal of dialectic is to demonstrate how different stages of consciousness or spirit proceed from a lower level to a higher level as the contradiction or partiality in the former is unveiled. Taking an example from the *Philosophy of History*, the development of the idea of freedom via human agents roughly proceeds as follows: The "customary harmony of the Greeks" first showed itself to be partial when the worth of independent thought was discovered by Socrates; gradually, independent thought developed itself into individual conscience and free will, owing to the advent of Christianity and subsequent great events such as the Reformation. The "abstract freedom of the individual" as such, however, continued to reveal itself to be partial once it is taken as the basis of society, having brought out the chaos of the French Revolution. The one-sided positions of these two movements, nevertheless, were to be reunited in the emergence of the "German society of Hegel's time," in that a reconciliation of the individual and community is provided.[22]

Putting aside Hegel's disputable description of German society, what is important in the present context is that there are, accordingly, three main viewpoints grounded in Hegel's method of political theorization, which are needed for making sense of Mou's establishment of Confucian democracy. Put briefly, they are: (1) the dialectical relationship between politics and morality; (2) the importance of civility, tradition, and the forms of life in the understanding of politics; and (3) the revitalization of a common good and public meanings.

First, it is true, as we shall see, that for Mou the "blossoming of democracy" involves a divorce between the political subject and the moral subject. In accordance with the argument that Confucianism endorses embodied subjectivity, nonetheless, Mou also adopts the vital Hegelian point that the separation between the form of politics (democracy) and the content of morality (the spirit of *ren*) is only *transient*, that its reunion must be regarded as the next stage of the development of Confucian democracy. That said, given that in the dialectical process form and content are to be reunited in the end, Mou makes it clear that the political form of democracy cannot be permanently detached from its own ethical substance rooted in the spirit of *ren*. At root, Confucian democracy does not simply mean democratization, but it literally suggests that we should make efforts to rest democracy on Confucianism; indeed, what I mean by Confucian democracy, or in a broader sense, Confucian liberalism, is one that aims to reconcile the modern cry for liberal values with the Confucian quest for common meanings.

Second, in comparison to Hegel, however, it is my central argument that when merging democracy with the spirit of *ren*, Mou tries to modify a specific set of *Confucian governing and civic virtues* under the blueprint of the "way of governance" (*zhidao* 治道). The point I am trying to make here is that while the majority of scholarship on Mou's political theory focuses on the *modernity* of the "way of politics" alone, the Hegelian scheme will enable me to draw on the *tradition* of the "way of governance" at the same time. Accordingly, as I hope to make clear in chapter 5, the "way of governance" expressed by Mou actually can be regarded as a renovated reconstruction of Confucian civility, or the Confucian forms of life, in accordance with the ethical import of democracy, giving rise to a certain conception of "Confucian democratic civility." As such, as I shall continue to argue in chapter 6, given that the "way of governance," by and large, critically represents the Confucian political ideal widely known as "humane government," it becomes certain that for Mou the development of political democracy is unavoidable, because only through the *venue* of democracy can the spirit of *ren* be finally actualized in a modern open society.

Third, seen in this light, a study of Confucian liberalism is incomplete without paying attention to the topic of the common good. On this topic, my general premise is that no matter whether Hegel can be said to be a liberal or not, it remains true that Mou and the British idealists are greatly indebted to Hegel's insights for relocating a bundle of liberal expressions, such as subjectivity, individuality, citizen, the state, open society, freedom, and rights, into the forms of life characterized by a common good. That is to say, different from mainstream liberalism, the form of civil liberalism anticipated by Mou also shares with the British idealists a perfectionist reading of politics in association with the ethics of self-realization. In view of the fact that Hegel's theory of the state has been widely regarded by many scholars as antiliberal in the Chinese context, I plan to bring in the perfectionist liberalism of British idealism in chapters 7 and 8 to help clarify some of the long-term debates over Hegel's political philosophy, such as the dominance of social control and the problems of positive freedom and state interference. In a nutshell, provided that there are prominent similarities between New Confucianism and British idealism in respect of an ethics of self-realization, the political thinking of British idealism identified as a form of perfectionist liberalism is interestingly comparable to Mou's anticipation of Confucian liberalism.

Civilization, Objective Spirit, and Ethical Democracy

That being said, I now want to recast the significance of the Hegelian scheme by reference to the three questions concerning Confucian democracy at stake. Overall, from the above discussion, it follows that Mou's earlier political writings largely fall back on Hegel's *Philosophy of History* as the aim of his political philosophy is analogous to a historical survey of the crisis and transformation of Chinese culture and its place in the chains of human civilization in progress. In other words, sticking to the Hegelian scheme, Mou maintains that the political conundrums that we confront, for example, the political crisis of legitimacy in China, cannot be fully dealt with unless we consider the larger problem of the historical conditions of humanity (or spirit) involved. For this reason, Mou employs a cluster of Hegel's terms, such as objective spirit, subjective freedom, self-negation, dialectic, the forms of life, in explaining the absence of democracy in the past and the possibility and plausibility of Confucian democracy in the future.

In the Chinese context, it has been widely held since the May Fourth Movement (*Wu Si Yundong* 五四運動) that Confucianism is culturally at odds with democracy. As Mou's writings suggest, however, the reason that Confucianism failed to develop democracy was not because its intrinsic character rooted in *ren* contradicted the moral basis of democracy, but because its all-encompassing pursuit of "unceasing pureness of virtue" (*dexing zhi chun yi buyi* 德行之純亦不已) often overlooked matters of objectification and institutionalization, namely, the Hegelian viewpoint that "every institution is nothing but the objectification of Reason, the expression of objective spirit."[23] In other words, "Chinese culture has subjective spirit and absolute spirit, but it lacks objective spirit"[24] in the sense of developing rights, free subjectivity, the rule of law, civil society, constitution, sovereignty, and the state. More precisely, unlike Hegel's identification of objective spirit as such, the objective spirit manifested in the world of Confucianism is "decrees and regulations" (*dianxian* 典憲), normally understood as *li* 禮 (rituals, ritual propriety) with regard to "rule by virtue" (*dezhi* 德治). I shall return to this issue with regard to Mou's interpretation of Xunzi (荀子) in the next chapter. For now, I just want to remark that as Mou confesses, Confucianism, albeit morally perfect, is politically defective owing to its tendency to assimilate politics *entirely* into morality.

Accordingly, it also can be said that Confucianism is badly short of the "constructive presentation of reason" (*lixing zhi jiagou biaoxian* 理性之架構表現) in favor of the "way of politics," even if it is exceedingly good at demonstrating the "functional presentation of reason" (*lixing zhi yunyong biaoxian* 理性之運用表現) in favor of the "way of governance," which, through practice, has expressed the spirit of *ren* in the lived forms of life. Or alternatively, as Mou continues, the reason why Chinese culture did not care that much about democracy can also be attributed to the point that its mainstream presentations such as Confucianism lack the idea of the political subject in pursuit of subjective freedom.[25] And thus, focusing on Confucianism, the political transformation of modern China in terms of the "blossoming of democracy," as Mou famously articulates, depends on a process of "self-negation" (*ziwo kanxian* 自我坎陷) of the moral subject. Considering the purposes of this study, it is important to mention that Mou's own translation of *ziwo kanxian* as "self-negation" clearly implies that the "blossoming of democracy" actually involves a *dialectical* movement, by means of which the political subject associated with subjective freedom will be *temporarily* separated from the moral subject full of *ren*, namely, one's "original knowing in morality" (*daode liangzhi* 道德良知) or the "goodness of *Xing*-nature" (*renxing ben shan* 人性本善),[26] before moving on to be reconnected with the spirit of *ren* in an indirect and limited way.

Although my turn to the Hegelian scheme is therefore different from the Kantian approach offered by Mou's disciples, by no means does it abandon the idea of Confucian moral subjectivity echoing Kantian free will that Mou has arduously established; rather, my real point of following Hegel is to mark out the political implications of the actualization of the spirit of *ren* in a democratic society. More to the point, I actually admit that the idea of subjective freedom is emphatically linked to Kant's "morality," that what lies at the center of the modern world is the hope that everyone can be equally free, and that it is freedom as such that provides the basic condition making possible modern democracy. However, as it will be recollected, there are three stages of objective spirit presented in Hegel's *Philosophy of Right*, namely, "abstract right" (personal right), "morality" (subjective freedom), and "ethical life" (the family, civil society, and the state). Far from rejecting Kantian subjective freedom in total, a significant aspect of Hegel's political philosophy is to demonstrate "how personal right and subjective freedom can receive real contents through the institutions of the modern state."[27]

Here, I do not intend to deny that unlike Hegel, Mou says very little about the systems of civil society and the constitutional law of the state. However, it is more than clear that remarkably inspired by *Philosophy of History*, and perhaps, *Phenomenology of Spirit*, Mou keeps to the Hegelian scheme when elaborating on the aforementioned three questions of Confucian democracy, with the ultimate purpose of merging the political form of democracy with its ethical substance. What is more, as mentioned above, there are three main insights inherent in Hegel's method of political theorization, which seem to have influenced Mou's political thought to a great extent. In order to bring New Confucianism and British idealism together in dialogue on the topic of liberalism, it may be appropriate to restate these insights by reference to British idealism in a brief outline.

In the first place, although Mou's reunion of the "way of politics" and the "way of governance" rejects a clear-cut distinction between politics and morality, connoting some affinities between the two, Mou does not derive "outer kingliness" directly from "inner sagehood." Instead, as I shall explain in detail, what Mou demonstrates to us is a Hegelian version of relating these two spheres of human action in an indirect, or so to speak, dialectical, way. In this regard, it is worth mentioning that both New Confucianism and British idealism are prone to exert a *twofold* definition of modern political expressions, such as democracy, citizens, the state, and freedom; for Mou, as for T. H. Green, for example, liberal language can be understood *politically* and *morally, constitutionally* and *ethically, institutionally* and *civilly*, and the like.

Furthermore, in Mou's structure, the relationship between politics and morality is not merely "indirect" but also "specific," in that his rebuilding of the "way of governance," rather than imparting to the moral subject a "vertical theory" of the "perfect teaching" (*yuanjiao* 圓教) in "attaining sagehood" (*chengsheng* 成聖), delivers a set of public virtues grounded in the Confucian forms of life for the political subject. In other words, one of the theoretical outcomes resulting from "self-negation" points to a disparity between moral metaphysics and political philosophy. Insofar as democracy is required so as to restore the political order in crisis, what is at the heart of the moral basis of Confucian democracy, as we shall see in subsequent chapters, is not so much about a *complete* presentation of the "conformity of Heaven and man in union" (*tianren heyi* 天人合一) but about a *particular* actualization of the spirit of *ren* in the political sphere. All in all, I contend that echoing British idealism, Mou also rests democracy on an ethics of self-realization penetrating Confucianism, which in political terms demands that government should help the people to "attain accomplishment according to the individual's nature" (*jiu geti er shuncheng* 就個體而順成).

This way of thinking will at once bring us back to the challenging subject of the common good. At this point, it is interesting to note that Green's liberal conception of the common good, which alludes to a perfectionist reading of the state, citizen, and open society without sliding into authoritarianism, may help us a good deal to grasp Mou's discussion of Confucian *res publica* in chapter 7. Again, to round off my argument, I am going to make clear in chapter 8 that Mou's discussion of the double meaning of freedom actually bears a striking resemblance to Green, who has been considered the originator of the distinction between negative and positive freedom in the English context. Assuming that anti-Confucian liberalism and antiliberal Confucianism share a narrow understanding of liberalism closely related to the Lockean natural rights tradition, Millian utilitarianism, or Kantian deontology, my Hegelian reidentification of Mou's anticipation of Confucian liberalism in accordance with the forms of civil liberalism and perfectionist liberalism has the effect of enlarging our reception of the mapping of liberalism in the Chinese context.

To conclude, by engaging in a series of far-reaching dialogues between Mou Zongsan and the perfectionist liberalism of the British idealists, I shall be able to rethink a constellation of liberal ideas, including an ethical identification of citizenship, an elucidation of the misunderstanding of positive freedom, a critical reflection on the justification of state interference, an explanation of the common good that fits into a democratic society, an affirmation of human constants, an introduction to the rights-recognition thesis, and so on, in the third part of the book. In this way, I shall also be better equipped to explain away the misconceptions of Mou's Confucian liberalism launched by both anti-Confucian liberalism and antiliberal Confucianism.

Political Crisis: Why Did Confucianism Not Develop Democracy?

Having reshaped the Hegel scheme as such, for the rest of this chapter I am prepared to substantiate Mou's inquiries into the three questions concerning Confucian democracy in order. As stated, central to Mou's examination of Confucian democracy is a distinction between the "way of politics" and the "way of governance." Before clarifying this key pair of technical terms by reference to the binary meaning of democracy in chapter 6, I now intend to explain more fully the two different presentations of reason that set the "way of politics" apart from the "way of governance" in the first place.

Two Presentations of Reason

Unlike the anti-Confucian liberals, Mou keeps saying that the failure of Confucianism in developing democracy is not because its moral ideal is in conflict with the foundation of democracy, but because this ideal has never, through realizing the "authentic heart-mind" (*benxin* 本心), objectified itself toward establishing the legitimacy of political authority. For this reason, Mou's democratic theory is closely associated with a comparison between Chinese and Western philosophy, aiming to shed light on both the *moral* superiority of Confucianism and its *political* disadvantage owing to the lack of a proper way to actualize the true meaning of "outer kingliness." To this end, Mou thus sets forth a famous distinction between the "functional presentation of reason" and the "constructive presentation of reason" (hereafter, "functional reason" and "constructive reason"). In a nutshell, whereas the former denotes the endless pursuit of self-perfection in Confucianism, the latter stands for the "externalization of reason" featuring the Western understanding of empirical knowledge and democratic politics.[28]

Put clearly, the gist of "functional reason" is to reach the concrete whole, by avoiding any potential divisions or oppositions (*mian qu duili* 免去對立), and so there is an inherent constant tendency to build a relationship of "Sub-Ordination" (*lishu guanxi* 隸屬關係). In contrast, the crux of "constructive reason" is analytic, taking care of categories and differences, and thus entails a counterforce to move away from the moral meaning of practical reasoning for a virtuous life and to search instead for a nonmoral meaning of analytical or theoretical reasoning under the name of Understanding (*zhixing* 知性), resulting in a disparate relationship of "Co-Ordination" (*duilie guanxi* 對列關係). The point here is that although "functional reason," at which Confucianism is extremely excellent, is higher than "constructive reason,"[29] democracy and science, which have so rapidly developed in the West, stem from "constructive reason," rather than from "functional reason."

Put in other terms, while the Confucian tradition has arrived at a fabulous representation of "functional reason" by giving a full account of the moral subject in relation to Confucian moral metaphysics, the notions of the knowing subject and the political subject that make possible science and democracy were completely obscure in Chinese culture. Alternatively, it can be inferred that the quintessential character of Chinese philosophy is "virtue first," as opposed to the "knowledge-first" character of Western philosophy, and thus, that the achievement of Confucianism in offering a comprehensive explanation of moral subjectivity in respect of a "virtue-first" philosophy is, by nature, dissimilar to the triumph of the West in promoting science and democracy in respect of a "knowledge-first" philosophy.

The Paradox of Democracy

Seen in this light, there at once appears *a paradox of democracy in Confucianism*: China's failure to create democracy, from a philosophical viewpoint, is due to its remarkable success in the field of moral thinking; as previously said, Confucianism is so devoted to the moral ideal of a virtuous personality that it says almost nothing about the actualization of this moral ideal from the perspective of political subjectivity. In other words, even though Confucianism is superior to Kant in terms of the affirmation of "intellectual intuition" (*zhi de zhijue* 智的直覺), there is, paradoxically, a serious flaw in this superiority, namely, that the direction of Chinese culture has always looked *inward* to find the moral subject and never looked *outward* to develop the independent political subject, which we now call "citizenship" as a rule.

Or, to put it another way, although Confucianism entails a profound theory of the moral subject purporting to "make one's heart-mind upright" and "keep one's thoughts honest and sincere" (*zhengxin chengyi* 正心誠意), and an illuminating discussion of moral practice with regard to an "investigation of things" and an "extension of knowledge" (*gewu zhizhi* 格物致知),[30] it falls short of building the knowing subject and the political subject, upon which science and democracy are grounded. Accordingly, Confucianism has never truly realized the political ideal of the "outer kingliness," namely, "governing a state well" and "bringing peace to all-under-Heaven" (*zhiguo ping tianxia* 治國平天下).[31]

The Lack of Subjective Freedom

Based on what has been said, I am now going to review to what extent Hegel's statements would support Mou's discussion of the nonexistence of democracy in Confucianism. To begin with, Hegel denotes in *Phenomenology of Spirit* that in spite of the "enduring wounds that the 'unhappy consciousness' had inflicted on the European spirit,"[32] the appearance of Christianity has brought out the "freedom of self-consciousness," which has *eventually* helped Western modern politics take shape in favor of individual freedom. Put clearly, the "unhappy consciousness" rooted in Christianity, purporting to divorce the subject from the object, has historically resulted in the values of freedom and equality defining the modern self: "Only with the coming of Christianity, Hegel maintains, did people come to recognize that all human beings are in principle free because all are equal in the eyes of God."[33]

However, it should be noted that in the structure of *Encyclopedia of the Philosophical Sciences in Outline*, the appearance of the "abstract freedom of the individual," that is, practical reason identified as free will, basically falls "in the sphere of subjective spirit in general"[34] for the practical spirit as such is simply oriented to satisfy one's particular desires by a cluster of indeterminate and contingent choices. Furthermore, and more importantly, although *Geist* as the "unity of subjectivity and objectivity"[35] would carry on moving from subjective spirit to objective spirit (law, morality, and ethics) and from objective spirit to absolute spirit (art, revealed religion, and philosophy),[36] it is the modern mutation of the "abstract freedom of the individual" into abstract right and subjective freedom that inspires the spirit of modern democracy characterized by the trilogy of the French Revolution: freedom, equality, and popular sovereignty.

That is to say, as Hegel further argues in the *Philosophy of Right*, the novel identification of oneself as a *person* (endowed with personal right) and a *subject* (free to make possible moral principles) is what significantly characterizes European modernity. To quote Hegel,

> The right of the subject's *particularity* to find satisfaction, or—to put it differently—the right of subjective freedom, is the pivotal and focal point in the difference between *antiquity* and the *modern* age. The right, in its infinity, is expressed in Christianity, and it has become the universal and actual principle of a new form of the world.[37]

In contrast, in Oriental society there only existed what can be otherwise called "substantial freedom":

> Substantial freedom is the implicit rationality of the will which is subsequently developed in the state. But in this determination of reason, individual insight and volition are not yet present; in other words, subjective freedom, which can only determine itself in the individual and which constitutes the reflection of the individual in his own conscience, has not yet come into being. Where there is merely substantial freedom,

commandments and laws are regarded as firmly established in and for themselves, and the individual subject adopts an attitude of complete subservience towards them. Besides, these laws need not accord with the will of the individual, and the subjects are therefore like children, who obey their parents without will or insight of their own.[38]

In my view, then, it is basically against this Hegelian context that Mou thinks that the Chinese failure to develop democracy is owing to the point that "China only has the principle of universality, but lacks that of individuality"[39] in relation to subjective freedom, that is, the "free subjectivity of modernity." The crucial point here is that the appearance of subjective freedom in the West is historically rooted in the Christian "unhappy consciousness," resulting from the separation between subjectivity and objectivity, but such a kind of dualism has never occurred in Chinese culture as the moral spirit of Confucianism is inclined to assert "intellectual intuition," always taking the form of self-affirmation. To develop democracy in the Chinese cultural setting, as a result, Confucianism must endure a process of "self-negation," by means of which the subject and the object are to be set apart in the first place.

More exactly, given that the "universal subjectivity" in China has never undergone the process of "self-negation," Hegel seems to have been correct in observing that no clear consciousness of individual freedom was present in ancient China, that only one person, the emperor himself, was free in political terms. Thus, although Mou would strongly rebuff Hegel's Eurocentric opinion that "Cicero gives us *De Officiis*, a book of moral teaching more comprehensive and better than all the books of Confucius," that "for their reputation it would have been better had they never been translated,"[40] he does not completely deny a notorious comment that Hegel makes about China in his *Lectures on the Philosophy of World History*: "The Orientals do not yet know that the spirit of man as such is free in himself."[41]

All this, however, does not mean that China did not make any significant contribution to human reason. In truth, Chinese rationality has embodied itself in ways saliently different from the West: "Intellectual intuition," for one thing, involves an ethical personality of sagehood, a self-affirmation of the holistic embodiment of Heaven. Furthermore, Chinese society is in essence a "universe of personality"[42] continuously pursuing moral values. Thus seen, Hegel simply neglects the fact that

Chinese culture has developed an extraordinary representation of reason in morality, which can be identified as the "synthetic spirit of the fulfillment of reason" (*zonghe de jinli zhi jingshen* 綜合的盡理之精神). To be sure, that which goes with this intensity of moral reason is an "individuality that is dissimilar to the knowing subject"[43] and the political subject, otherwise known as the "analytic spirit of the fulfillment of reason" (*fenjie de jinli zhi jingshen* 分解的盡理之精神) accomplished by modern Western philosophy.

Political Transformation: How Can Confucianism Develop Democracy?

That being said, the following is a discussion of how Confucianism can develop democracy. My crucial task here, as might be expected, is to further explore the "self-negation" of the moral subject.

From Morality to Politics

Hopefully, it is clear now that at the heart of Mou's idea of "self-negation" is a separation between politics and morality, by means of which the political subject in respect of "constructive reason" and subjective freedom can be developed out of the moral subject full of the spirit of *ren* in Confucianism. In this regard, to say that classical Confucianism is short of the ideas of democracy, political subjectivity, and political freedom is to grant that "the Chinese people are living in life, not in a conceptual framework, in law, and in contract."[44] Accordingly, for Mou, the "blossoming of democracy" would be a deadlock, should we abide by the traditional manner of connecting moral ideals and political governing in a *direct* way (*zhitong* 直通); in contrast, the potential of Confucian democracy lies in a new scheme, reconnecting the two spheres in an *indirect* way (*qutong* 曲通).[45]

That is to say, in the face of the challenges posed by the achievements of Western democracy (as well as science), the political ideal of "outer kingliness" in association with "humane government" should alter its key meaning, moving from the old-fashioned belief that sages should govern "all-under-Heaven" (*tianxia* 天下) by virtue, to the innovative idea of relating morality and politics in an *indirect* way. This, however, denotes two *contradictory claims* at the same time. On the one hand, it implies that politics must be separated from morality such that the political subject can arrive on the scene; on the other, this separation cannot persist for good, otherwise the form of democracy that blossoms from it would be anything but *Confucian*. On this reading, Hegel is of significance once again, simply because the movement from the "separation of politics and morality" to the "reunification of politics and morality" echoes the moments of "self-negation" and the "negation of negation" in the dialectical sense. To make my case, I have strongly suggested that Mou's key word in realizing the "blossoming of democracy," namely, *ziwo kanxian*, should be translated as "self-negation" in accordance with his own gloss.

SELF-RESTRICTION OR SELF-NEGATION?

However, it is worthwhile to mention that the term *ziwo kanxian* has been eloquently taken by some distinguished scholars to mean "self-restriction" (*ziwoxianzhi* 自我限制) in English, even though Mou's own gloss is "self-negation." David Elstein, for example, offers two provocative reasons for the translation as "self-restriction."[46] First, since "functional reason" is superior to "constructive reason," the former needs to "restrict itself to a lower level"[47] such that democracy and science can be attained. Second, in place of relying on "sagely rulers and worthy ministers" (*shengjun xianxiang* 聖君賢相),[48] democracy is treated by Mou as a new instrument to bring moral concerns to politics. However, what is needed in developing democracy from Confucianism is "not a complete or permanent negation of moral reasoning"[49] because democracy itself is value neutral, whereas "the basis for democracy is Mencius's doctrine that human nature is good."[50] Thus, the "blossoming of democracy" involves a dialectical process in which the transitory separation of morality and politics will eventually be reunited again.

On this interpretation, I have three points to make. Overall, I agree with Elstein that since "Mou's goal is to justify democracy in Confucian terms and of course that entails using Confucian concepts," his understanding of liberalism, democracy, law, participation, and freedom is saliently different from that of John Rawls in *Political Liberalism*.[51] Unlike Elstein, however, here as elsewhere my central argument is that Mou's endorsement of liberal values can be better reinterpreted as encouraging a Hegelian form of ethical liberalism.

Moreover, while Elstein is correct in remarking that "functional reason" is superior to "constructive reason," he mistakenly conflates the idea of "self-restriction" with that of "self-negation." On the one hand, as we shall see, in different texts crossing over his early and later intellectual life, Mou holds on to a Hegelian understanding of the "self-negation" of "functional reason" when talking about how to develop democracy out of Confucianism. On the other, Mou's usage of the "self-restriction" of the sagely ruler in exerting political power is restricted to the context wherein he comes to reconstruct the ancient Confucian political ideal known as "humane government," by reference to the doctrine of "inaction" (*wuwei* 無為), namely, letting things take their own course. I shall give a detailed account of Mou's retreatment of the "way of governance" with regard to the principle of "self-restriction" in chapter 6. For now, I only want to single out that should we understand Mou's political thinking more thoroughly, "self-negation" and "self-restriction" actually play different roles in making manifest the possibility and plausibility of Confucian democracy.

Third, both Elstein and I have the same opinion that the current form of democracy is not the whole story for Mou robustly insists that Confucian democracy should be grounded in Confucian ethics, and thus, dialectical thinking is required for making sense of the ethical import of Confucian democracy. It is true that Mou once said that the moral foundation of democracy recognized as *ren*, the "goodness of *Xing*-nature" or *liangzhi* 良知 ("original knowing," or the "knowing-reality of enlightened awareness"), is equivalent to Kantian good will.[52] At the same time, nonetheless, he remarked that the spirituality of liberalism lies in "what Hegel means by freedom,"[53] which can only be realized in a rational system of public institutions—ethical life. In short, as for the reunion between politics and morality, Mou seems to have left his readers with two potential ways of reading—the Kantian universal principle of right and the Hegelian idea of ethical life.

Since the purpose of this book is targeted at offering a Hegelian reinterpretation of Mou's intellectual legacy for Chinese liberalism in the broader sense, I am determined to show in the next section that we are able to better comprehend the *political implications* of the actualization of *ren* in a democratic age, once Mou's reconstruction of the "way of governance" as he suggests, is understood as the Confucian forms of life through practices. For now, let me continue to unveil the

134 | Confucian Liberalism

manners in which Mou explains the meaning of "self-negation" in a Hegelian vein.

THE PROCESS OF SELF-NEGATION

At first, it must be noted that although Mou's explanation is utterly philosophical, this does not mean that he neglects the fact that in the course of history democracy has arisen from countless struggles and austere conflicts. In the words of Mou, the moment of "self-negation" comes into sight largely due to "restrictions from outside" (*ziwai xianzhi* 自外限制),⁵⁴ meaning that it is only through struggles to overcome the external obstacles that the disposition to equal freedom may gradually present itself to history. The upshot is that as a philosopher, Mou says very little about the emergence of democracy with regard to the relentless conflicts of personal interests, subjective freedoms, and different classes. Instead, he simply treats the call for democracy, together with the renovated political and legal culture, as *a newly emergent historical condition* that Confucianism must deal with so as to become involved in the modern world.

That being said, I may now delve into Mou's discussion of "self-negation" in detail. In a philosophical sense, *ziwo kanxian* implies that the historical revelation of political subjectivity, "constructive reason," and subjective freedom is possible only if the moral subjectivity intrinsic to Confucianism has endured a process of subject-object dualism. Seen in light of Hegelian dialectic, nonetheless, that which comes after "self-negation" is an "indirect" reconnection between morality and politics; that said, the essential aim of the "blossoming of democracy" is to rebuild a proper relationship between "inner sagehood" and "outer kingliness" for the modern transformation of Confucianism. To make my case, let me begin by requoting, this time in full, an important passage from Mou's *Lishi zhexue* 歷史哲學 (Philosophy of History).

> This means that what Chinese Confucianism had said about outer kingliness before is not enough. In the past, the Confucians used to remark that outer kingliness was derived directly from inner sagehood, in view of the fact that to "make one's heart-mind upright" and "keep one's thoughts honest and sincere" is enough to imply outer kingliness directly. . . . All this is the direct manner of outer kingliness. This direct man-

ner, however, is insufficient. Now we understand that outer kingliness in the positive sense, to realize outer kingliness fully and objectively, must undergo a "winding" (*quzhe* 曲折), that is, as previously said, to make a "detour" (*zhuan yige wan* 轉一個彎), so as to build a [legitimate] way of politics, a [democratic] institution, indirectly: This is the indirect manner of outer kingliness.⁵⁵

Later on, Mou fills out his view in *Zhengdao yu zhidao* 政道與治道 (The Way of Politics and the Way of Governance) by saying:

It is true that outer kingliness is extended from inner sagehood. But there are two ways of extension, direct and indirect. To extend in the direct way was what had been said before; to extend in the indirect way is what we are now going to make clear in relation to science and democracy.⁵⁶

Put differently, my key point here is that only if *ziwo kanxian* is to be understood as "self-negation" can we truly grasp the dialectical relationship between morality and politics in Mou's political writings. Although moral reason by nature must cry out for science and democracy, virtue, in its direct moral meaning and in its functional presentation, does not lead to the development of science and democracy, which as Mou keeps arguing, are related to the constructive presentation of reason. From the perspectives of science and democracy, therefore, the nature of the constructive presentation of reason that makes them possible must be "in opposition to" (*weifan* 違反) the moral meaning and functional presentation of virtue; this is what can be called the "opposition" between theoretical or analytical reason and practical reason. In other words, there must appear a sense of the "opposite" (*ni* 逆), seeking something that is opposed to its own nature. This, apparently, is a "contradiction" (*maodun* 矛盾).⁵⁷

Accordingly, to build democracy in China, the functional presentation of "inner sagehood" must go through a "sudden reversal" (*zhuanzhe de tubian* 轉折的突變), and the moral subject must "give way to" (*rangkai yibu* 讓開一步)⁵⁸ the knowing subject and the political subject. Another piece of first-hand evidence indicating Mou's intentional employment of Hegelian dialectic into the emergence of *subjectivity* in question can be found in Mou's later work, *Xianxiang yu wuzishen* 現象與物自身

(Phenomena and Noumena). When referring to the revelation of the understanding upon which science and democracy rest, Mou writes:

> This revelation is dialectical (in the Hegelian sense, not in the Kantian sense). It can be explained in this way: (1) Speaking from the outside, provided that man has both humanity and sagehood, scientific knowledge is in principle necessary and possible, otherwise the meaning of what a human being is would be insufficient. (2) Speaking from the inside, to accomplish this necessity, . . . [the activity of *Xing*-reality (*xingti* 性體)] must self-consciously endure the process of self-negation, turning itself into the understanding; only when this understanding is in opposition to things can these things become objects whose appearances will be investigated by the understanding in every way possible.[59]

Now, it seems clear that the subtexts of "opposition" and the like are just different expressions of the same thing, signifying that in order to establish Confucian democracy with regard to an "indirect" reconnection between "inner sagehood" and "outer kingliness," the moral spirit of *ren* must engage a Hegelian sense of "self-negation" in the first place, which literally connotes "self-denial" (*ziwo fouding* 自我否定),[60] the "denial of the marvelous application of original knowing and innate awareness" (*liangzhi benjiao de shenzhi miaoyong zhi fouding* 良知本覺的神智妙用之否定).[61]

Political Ideal:
What Is the Subtlest Model of Confucian Democracy?

I have indicated that in spite of the significance of "self-negation" in Mou's writings, neither abstract individuality nor subjective freedom elucidates the political ideal of Confucianism in a modern democratic society. To see more creatively Mou's account of the subtlest model of Confucian democracy, a disclosure of the movement from subjective freedom to ethical life is needed.

From Subjective Freedom to Ethical Life

Although Mou expresses approval of the "separation of politics from morality,"[62] resulting in the accomplishment that "politics has its independent meaning, making itself stand out as an independent domain," he soon adds that this is just "a temporary departure from morality."[63] Because, "seen in light of the wholeness of human activity or cultural ideal in the ultimate sense,"[64] it turns out that the relationship between politics and morality cannot be permanently separated. On balance, constructive and functional reasons are nothing but two *specific* presentations of the substance of spirituality (*jingshen shiti* 精神實體), that is, *ren*. And so, as the essence of humanity in the complete sense requires, political reason should be related to the concrete whole of *ren* in some way.

At this point, it is relevant to reiterate that Hegel's treatment of objective spirit in the *Philosophy of Right* consists of three main topics: the self-identification of a *person* in terms of abstract right; the self-determination of a *subject* in terms of morality (*Moralität*), including Kantian subjective freedom; and the self-realization of personhood and subjectivity in harmony with a *rational* system of social and political institutions developing through family, civil society (embracing the system of needs, the administration of justice, and the police and the corporation) and the state, known as ethical life (*Sittlichkeit*).[65]

Indeed, as I have said earlier, it is Hegel's suggestion that personal right and subjective freedom should receive "real contents" through the rational institutions of the modern state. In other words, Hegel thinks that "right and morality are only ideal moments," that "their existence is only in ethical life," and that "the actual morality is only the morality of the whole in ethical life,"[66] namely, the modern state. Seen in this light, for Hegel, the institutions of the modern state are "rational" insofar as they are based on the certainty of "truth concerning right, ethics, and the state."[67] In short, the rationality of the state is to make happen the "actuality of freedom"[68] in the modern world.

Be that as it may, since for Hegel *Geist* only absolutely actualizes itself in human thought and self-consciousness, the rationality of the modern state in the sense of being totally identical with freedom cannot be fully attained until its citizens all together come to understand "how and why they are free in it"; for this reason, the purpose of political philosophy, as Hegel sees it, is to offer a *reconciliation*, by means of which citizens are educated to comprehend in the end their "social world as a form of life in political and social institutions" that truly realizes the highest good of modernity, that is, the "basis of our dignity as persons who are free."[69] In short, Hegel's usage of ethical life as "customary morality" is meant "to refer simultaneously to a system of social institutions and to the moral attitude of the individual who identifies with and lives them."[70]

Here, I must confess once again that compared with Hegel, Mou falls short of providing a detailed analysis of civil society, a proper discussion of constitution, and a coherent theory of the state, largely because, like democracy, these institutions did not exist in ancient China. And thus, it is not surprising that Mou sometimes identifies them as parts of the "way of politics" in favor of "constructive reason" that waits to grow out of Confucianism in the face of modernity. However, strongly influenced by Hegel, Mou refuses to see law *solely* as a means of protecting rights and does not see the state *merely* as a neutral instrument to maintain a legal order; instead, Mou otherwise articulates law and the state as the "presentation of the objectification of reason" and an "organic official state"[71] respectively. To quote Mou,

> If Universal Spirit has never embarked on the self-awareness of individuality to become subjective freedom, the "opposition" between subjective spirit and absolute spirit cannot be manifested. If this is the case, then the "unification" represented by the "big reality" cannot be organically in harmony. If this is the case, then the objective spirit represented by the state and law cannot be truly actualized either.[72]

> The moral substance of spirituality recognized as *ren* and *zhi* (*ren qie zhi de daode jingshen shiti* 仁且智的道德精神實體) . . . in addition to the individual, has to reveal itself to society and Heaven, earth, and myriad things, so as to complete itself, to make itself stand out. That is, it has to objectify itself and make itself absolute. To objectify itself is to reveal itself to the state, politics, and law; in this regard, the state, politics, and law are the objectification of spirit, that is, objective spirit.[73]

Following Hegel, then, Mou seems to grant that the essence of the state and law cannot be detached from the "moral substance of spirituality recognized as *ren* and *zhi*" in his own expression, that the reunion of politics and morality under discussion can be seen as involving a further process of the "negation of negation," by means of which subjective freedom will be reunited with the ethical life of the state and law. As regards the "negation of negation," *Aufheben*, Mou remarks:

> By going through this extraction (of subjectivity and objectivity) and re-melting, the subjectivity is no longer *that* subjectiv-

ity in opposition, the objectivity is no longer *that* objectivity in opposition, and the Absolute is by no means *that* Absolute in its original harmony. By going through negation and the negation of negation, some has been phased out, and some has been preserved, this is what is called *Aufheben*.⁷⁴

THE SPIRIT OF SELF-RESTRICTION

However, it is important to bear in mind that among other things, Mou does not accept Hegel's belief in the necessity of divine guidance or God's will for the Absolute to arrive at its complete manifestation at the end-point of human history, nor does he think that the fullest actualization of the "moral substance of spirituality recognized as *ren* and *zhi*" can be reached in the realm of democratic politics. On the whole, Mou maintains that what the "moral substance of spirituality recognized as *ren* and *zhi*," or the concrete universal of *ren*, keeps actualizing in the political domain is the public virtue concerning "governing the people" (*zhiren* 治人), which, in the Confucian tradition, can be distinguished from the personal practice of "cultivating oneself" (*xiuji* 修己) toward "attaining sagehood."

I shall say something more about "governing the people" in relation to the "way of governance" in chapter 6. For now, I just want to stress that even though it is through the Hegelian scheme that Mou becomes able to propose an ethical version of Confucian democracy, leading him to resolve the political crisis of China (as well as the moral predicament of modernity) by actualizing the political ideal of "humane government" in a democratic society, largely due to the division between "governing the people" and "cultivating oneself," he is more susceptible than Hegel to the liberal principle, indicating that the functions of morality and politics are, after all, distinguishable. Put succinctly, regardless of the fact that the political form of democracy should be grounded in the ethical content of the Confucian ways of life, the business of the government, far from imposing a substantial good on the governed from the comprehensive standpoint of "cultivating oneself," is *restricted* to a specific set of public virtues in accordance with the gist of "governing the people," attempting to assist the people in "attaining accomplishment *according to the individual's nature*."

All this reaffirms that the spirit of "self-restriction" has actually been disclosed by Mou in his crucial but often neglected restoration of the "way of governance." Therefore, the meaning of "self-restriction" is not only dissimilar to that of "self-negation," from which the political subject associated with the "way of politics" emerges, but also, and equally important, it is interestingly consistent with the essence of liberalism. A full examination of the liberal aspects of the "way of governance" will require more space than is possible here. Instead, it suffices to say that while scholars every so often have reservations about Hegel's political philosophy, mainly because of the fear that his theory of the state, if mistakenly interpreted, "helps breed totalitarianism,"[75] my Hegelian reinterpretation of Mou's political thought avoids this outcome.

To make my case, I am thus going to give a more detailed account of what I have called "Confucian democratic civility" and to revisit the Confucian political ideal largely in terms of the liberal-oriented principle of "self-restriction" in the following two chapters. Taken together, it will be made clearer that Mou's reconstruction of the "way of governance" entails a Confucian conception of the common good related to a cluster of Confucian public virtues, or more exactly, a set of *Confucian governing and civic virtues*, which, although rooted in an ethics of self-realization, is compatible with liberal spirit. After all, for Mou, the subtlest model of democracy lies in a Hegelian reconciliation of political democracy and "humane government" that is recognized, not as the completest fulfillment of "inner sagehood," but as the embodiment of the spirit of *ren* in the lived forms of life along with the *Zeitgeist* of democracy.

The Confucian Forms of Life

To close this chapter, let me summarize what has hitherto been said by remarking that the essential problem of the "blossoming of democracy" in Mou's context involves a process of the "objectification of subjectivity"[76] in relation to Hegel's discussion of objective spirit. In view of the fact that the subtle model of Confucian democracy is, after all, an unity of subjective freedom and Confucian ethics, I contend that the key elements that Mou attributes to "humane government," such as the tenet of "stepping aside, spreading out, and leaving things as they are" (*rangkai sankai, wu gefu wu* 讓開散開, 物各付物), and the dictum of "being strict with oneself and lenient toward others" (*yanyiluji kuanyidairen* 嚴以律己 寬以待人), are equivalent to *Sittlichkeit*, rather than to *Moralität*. First and foremost, they stand for the "customary morality" about the historical actualization of the spirit of *ren* that has been practiced through time. Again, they clearly express the common meanings embedded in lived ways of life characterizing the Confucian political ideal. Furthermore, departing from the old-fashioned view that sages should turn "all-under-Heaven" into virtues, Mou's reconstruction of "humane government" has the purpose of demonstrating that its elements are compatible with political democracy, that is, the "way of politics." Finally, just as the "way of politics" stands for the "blossoming of democracy," what defines the ends of democracy in an open society hinges on the "way of governance" in association with "humane government."

In contrast to rights-based liberalism or "procedural republic,"[77] it is my conclusion that Mou's political ideal recognized as Confucian liberalism in support of an ethical version of Confucian democracy is akin to a Hegelian form of ethical liberalism,[78] be it civil liberalism or perfectionist liberalism. To fill out the whole picture of Confucian liberalism, I shall discuss the meaning of civility to shed light on the proper relation between modernity and tradition in the next chapter, followed by a disclosure of the cores of the "way of governance" in respect of the liberal spirit of "self-restriction." In so doing, the partialities of both anti-Confucian liberalism and antiliberal Confucianism will also be unveiled.

Chapter 5

Civility and the Renovation of Tradition

Introduction

It is true that the leading New Confucians have been widely labeled as conservatives in a negative sense. Having shown Mou Zongsan's project of establishing Confucian democracy in a Hegelian vein, I now turn to argue that an important aspect of his political philosophy is to concoct a fusion of cultural conservatism and political progressivism, with the purpose of reuniting the habitual practices of "Confucian democratic civility" captured by the "way of governance" (*zhidao* 治道) with the progressive values of liberal democracy, otherwise identified as the "way of politics" (*zhengdao* 政道). In short, my view is that a comprehensive study of the concept of "civility" may not only help explain away some of the misconceptions about the limited reception of modernity and liberal values in the writings of anti-Confucian liberalism, but it may also open the door to rebuilding what I call Confucian liberalism from a "civil" perspective.

More precisely, in light of the ideological debate regarding the encounter between Chinese culture and Western modernity, Confucian liberalism is proposed in objection to both anti-Confucian liberalism (that is, Westernized liberalism) and antiliberal Confucianism (that is, "traditionalistic"[1] Confucianism). And here, as opposed to the "standard viewpoint," which sees liberalism as a *modern* creation accommodating the values of individuality, democracy, freedom, and rights, and Confucianism as a *traditional* manner of thinking that appreciates community, meritocracy, "inner sagehood" (*neisheng* 內聖), and duty, I contend that

Mou's political philosophy can be seen as an endeavor to provide a philosophical reconciliation between the antitheses in question.

Overall, then, the purpose of this chapter is to direct attention to the significance of Confucian liberalism recognized as a form of civil liberalism by focusing on the link between modernity and tradition. To this end, the following discussion will be divided into five sections. In the beginning, I shall embark on a brief examination of the discourse of political modernity in the Chinese context with regard to the deep crisis of Chinese civilization caused by the conviction that "rule by *de*" (*dezhi* 德治) is contradictory to the "rule of law" (*fazhi* 法治). Putting aside antiliberal Confucianism for now, my central argument here is that largely mirroring the spirit of *total Westernization* sparked by the May Fourth Movement (*Wu Si Yundong* 五四運動), the prevailing form of Westernized liberalism is based on an uncritical, Western-centric stance and the misconception that liberal democracy draws a definite distinction between politics and morality, or alternatively, between democracy and civility.

Despite the difficulties involved in defining civility, I assert in the next section that civility, by and large, denotes both "good manners" and "public norms." In the former sense, it is similar to *li* 禮 (rites, ritual propriety) in Confucianism and by default related to tradition and civilization, whereas in the latter sense, it is for some thinkers analogous to public spirit, public virtue, public good, or a common good. In this regard, while Westernized liberalism is prone to detach democracy from civility in both senses, Confucian liberalism aims to relocate liberal democracy and its related values into a Confucian community where public good is embodied in the manners of behavior and the forms of life.

To introduce Confucian liberalism in a fuller sense, in the following two sections, I plan to challenge the Western-centric stance and the nonmoral concept of politics underlying Westernized liberalism, respectively. On the one hand, it seems to me that a Hegelian grasp of civility as civilization can greatly help us to reassess the proper relationships between civilization and barbarism, between modernity and tradition, and between individuality and community. On the other hand, I contend that civility recognized as public norms may further highlight the importance of civic virtue in substantiating a well-ordered civil society in respect of a common good, which in turn fosters liberal democracy.

Inasmuch as there are various forms of liberalism, I am going to make the case in the last section that the political thought of Mou fits perfectly into the scheme of civil liberalism, in an attempt to reunite the form of political democracy and the content of "Confucian democratic civility." All things considered, by employing the term "Confucian democratic civility," I am not suggesting an "inclusive notion" of *li* as the "ultimate point in pursuit of the Way and virtue,"[2] or the adoption of a "comprehensive doctrine" rooted in Confucian moral metaphysics. Rather, following Mou, I take it to imply a specific set of *Confucian governing and civic virtues*, which are consistent with the principles of democracy.

As a final point, considering the subject matter of the book, in this chapter I shall try to take into account the philosophical works of R. G. Collingwood and Michael Oakeshott, the other two great Hegelian thinkers with a British face, together with the remarkable opinions about civility offered by Edward Shils. Despite the differences, the Hegelian scheme that they share helps us to spell out more clearly the similarities between New Confucianism and Hegelian liberalism.

The Discourse of Political Modernity

Let me now sketch out a conventional grasp of "rule by *de*" in traditional Confucianism.

Rule by Virtue

For Confucius, as Benjamin Schwartz rightly puts it, *ren* 仁 (humaneness) is the highest good of humanity, and its associated *de* 德 (virtues) cannot be obtained "without the structuring and educative effects of *li*," meaning "all those 'objective' prescriptions of behavior, whether involving rite, ceremony, manners, or general deportment."[3] It is possible that virtues go astray and rites are mistaken; the righteousness and appropriateness of human practices, in the end, rely on the reflection and judgment that a person makes in his social life according to the spirit of *ren*. In general, then, *li* in Confucianism signifies the approved patterns of behavior, the established norms of human relations, and the general meanings of social practices; as such, it not only contains a sense of good feeling and emotional comfort,[4] but it is also able to show an individual the way to reach *ren* through self-effort. "Unless a man has the spirit of *li*," says Confucius, "in being respectful he will wear himself out, in being careful he will become timid, in having courage he will become unruly, and in being forthright he will become intolerant."⁵

As for the nature of government, Confucius is apt to encourage what may be called the "politics of virtue and talent" (*xianneng zhengzhi* 賢能政治), or simply "rule by *de*." According to the *Book of Rites* (*Liji* 禮記), the five main tasks for a virtuous king are "regulating what is due to his kindred," the "reward of merit," the "promotion of worth," the "employment of ability," and the "maintenance of a loving vigilance."⁶ Rather than endorsing the idea of the "rule of law," "rule by *de*" maintains that there are two ways of enhancing the effectiveness of *de*.⁷ Primarily, society must be guided by virtues, that is, the sources of human excellence and flourishing, rather than ruled by regulations;⁸ in addition, since virtue will not naturally permeate society, a leader must act as a virtuous role model for the people and influence people's behavior. Put in other terms, a political leader has two responsibilities, to imbue the people with virtue and to preserve and continue rituals and proprieties; both ends are accomplished through the deeds and conduct of a virtuous leader.⁹ It is quite clear from Confucius's views on governance being "rectification" or "correction"¹⁰ in terms of *de* that for him the purpose of governing is of special concern to the moral business in educating people to pursue a good life.

It is relevant to note here that the two most distinctive followers of Confucius in the Warring States Period (*Zhangguo* 戰國 403–221 BC), namely, Mencius and Xunzi, both subscribe to the "politics of virtue and talent" in general, but they have different views about the significance of *li* in becoming a sage and a true king. For the sake of structure, I shall return to the contrast between Mencius and Xunzi when drawing on "Confucian democratic civility" from Mou's perspective. For now, I just want to mention in passing that despite seeing Xunzi's proposal for "rule by *li*" (*lizhi* 禮治) as a vital presentation of objective spirit in the development of Confucianism, Mou's own rebuilding of the Confucian political ideal is largely in favor of Mencius's pursuit of "humane government" (*renzheng* 仁政). Even so, Mou concedes that there is a huge cleavage between the Western concept of democracy associated with the "rule of law" and the traditional pattern of "rule by *de*" as a whole. In brief, whereas democratic *modernity* spells out the division between the public and private spheres, the importance of freedom, and the protection of individual rights, in the Confucian *tradition*, the public (political) and private (moral) are never divided, and it lacks the ideas of civil society, citizenship, personal freedom, and political rights.

THE CRISIS OF CONFUCIAN CIVILIZATION

Facing the challenges of Western modernity, Mou and his companions fairly acknowledge that there are serious pitfalls of "rule by *de*" that need to be critically adjusted. To make a long story short, the encounter between Chinese culture and Western modernity arrived on the scene around the late nineteenth century, and from the very beginning, the episode took its roots in a wider interrogation of whether Confucianism was in conflict with Western modernity featuring democracy (and science).[11] To be sure, in this process the dramatic "linguistic paradigm shift" in modern China took place when "the traditional Chinese culture simply could not withstand the onslaught of a superior Western civilization and was forced to change its ways."[12] Another way of making the same point is to say that a good number of political expressions currently used in the Chinese context, including individuality, freedom, autonomy, the state, democracy, the rule of law, constitutionalism, rights, liberalism, socialism, and Marxism, which originate largely from a generalized European context,[13] came ashore in the Sinophone world while Chinese intellectuals were eagerly "in search of wealth and power."[14]

More precisely, the motivation behind the "linguistic paradigm shift" points to an unwavering "moral anxiety" driven by the deepest civilization crisis caused by Western imperialism. A famous contemporary philosopher has even borrowed Alasdair MacIntyre's conception of "epistemological crisis" to illustrate the predicament of Chinese culture,[15] meaning that in the actual world which Chinese people inhabit, the language of morality and politics, the system of beliefs, and even the way of life are in "the same state of grave disorder."[16] Therefore, some sort of "radicalism" that has strived to bring to the fore a gigantic change in the rudiments of Chinese culture has long been taken as the main source offering the meanings of "liberalism" and its related values for Chinese speakers, and many of its crucial features still hover in the minds of Chinese liberals. Also, many scholars have been devoted to interpreting the characteristics of Chinese liberalism within a larger framework of the "Chinese Enlightenment," aiming to launch a persistent pursuit of innovative versions of morality and politics for a new China.

The common belief in the antagonism between Confucianism and modernity then took shape in the Chinese cultural setting, and before long reached its high point during the May Fourth Movement. Instead of delving deeper into the historical formulation of the anti-Confucian trend,[17] there seem to have existed some long-standing misconceptions about Chinese liberalism with regard to its three famous slogans: *total Westernization*, *individualism*, and *democracy*. More precisely, since May Fourth was sparked by a profound sense of national humiliation and fervent patriotic sentiments,[18] it has been widely held in the Chinese context that what the new intellectuals in the New Culture period advocated was nothing but a *radical* form of liberalism, in an attempt not only to give away the Confucian tradition entirely for Western modernity, but also to bring about renewed morality of individualism and an advanced politics of democracy for an enlightened China.

The phrase of total Westernization, to begin with, usually has been related to what Lin Yusheng [Lin Yu-Sheng] (林毓生) notably refers to as "totalistic iconoclasm," that is, the tendency to place "the necessary priority of intellectual and cultural change over political, social, and economic changes."[19] In the words of Leigh K. Jenco,

> Convinced that the individual rights and political progress urged by early liberals could not advance on the basis of China's "traditional" political culture, May Fourth activists urged young people to "destroy the Confucian shop" that in their view shored up social hierarchies, inhibited individual growth and personal expression, discouraged rational scientific inquiry, and crippled necessary social transformation in the name of adhering to ancient sagely models.[20]

From this, it follows that the new intellectuals were clearly split by a sharp dichotomy, to borrow Joseph Levenson's term, between "value" and "history," confronting a radical choice of "either" the modernity of Western values "or" the tradition of Chinese culture.[21]

More to the point, "radical liberalism," so to speak, adopts simultaneously a fanatical notion of individualism: "rationalistic individualism." The new intellectuals of May Fourth, as Zhou Cezong [Chow Tse-Tsung] (周策縱 1916–2007) puts it,

> appealed to reason not custom, to nature not man-made law, and to humanitarianism and aesthetics not ethical rules and

religion. They doubted everything which appeared to them not proved. Their role in history was to loosen old habits and conventions, to reform thought and feeling, to destroy tradition, and to open the mind to change. In short, they prepared the way for a great revolution.²²

Finally, in political terms, a significant aspect of May Fourth's *radicalism* therefore gives enthusiastic approval to the idea that liberalism was the same thing as democracy, meaning the greatest political achievement of Western civilization, whereas *conservatism* stood for anything but an endorsement of democracy. In other words, along the lines of the alleged tension between the Enlightenment and the "established order," or to quote Alexis de Tocqueville, between the "revolution" and the "old regime," in the eyes of new intellectuals, the conservative elements, such as civility, virtue, order, and tradition, amount to the austere obstacles to realizing democracy in modern China.

Westernized Liberalism

The legacies of May Fourth discussed above explain to some extent why both the extremes of anti-Confucian liberalism largely based in Taiwan and antiliberal Confucianism recently reemerging from China share the "standard viewpoint" that there is an incompatible tension between Confucianism and liberal democracy.²³ Leaving aside antiliberal Confucianism, in this chapter I only want to draw on the version of anti-Confucian liberalism advocated by Taiwan's liberal thinkers such as Hu Shi [Hu Shih] (胡適 1891–1962), Yin Haiguang [Yin Hai-Kuang] (殷海光 1919–1969), and Zhang Foquan [Chang Fo-Chuan] (張佛泉 1907–1994) in the 1950s and 1960s as it was largely against this context that the alternative theorization on Confucian liberalism was envisaged by Mou and his fellow New Confucians. Accordingly, as I have said, there are two major matters that concern me here, namely, the *credulous* attachment to "Westernization" and *partial* reception of "liberalism" in the writings of Westernized liberalism.

To begin with, focusing on the issue of civility, the so-called Western-centric stance basically rests on three key assumptions: First, Western civilization is superior because it has entirely developed out of barbarism, which in turn assumes *an absolute divergence between civilization and barbarism*. Second, Western civilization is superior because it has succeeded in developing democracy and science, which in turn insinuates *a sharp contrast between modernity and tradition.* Third, Western civilization is superior because it gives priority to freedom and rights over communal ties, which in turn implies *an inner tension between individuality and community.*

When coming to liberal democracy, as a result, Westernized liberalism keeps *a clear-cut distinction between politics and morality.* It is apparently on this account that Yin Haiguang fiercely rebuffs the plausibility of justifying democracy in moral terms, especially in Confucian terms, by writing eloquently:

> If we take morality as the basis of democracy, then it will coincide with Hegelian pan-logicism, which in turn is one of the groundings of pan-politicism, laying a foundation for totalitarianism. Under the great influence or determination of modern technology, process becomes more important than goal. . . . Morality itself does not have the use of preventing immoral behavior from emergence. So, morality cannot serve as the basis of democracy at all. Even without these catastrophes, the truth is that morality belongs to the sphere of ethics, falling outside of institution. For this reason, morality and politics are two poles apart.[24]

Indeed, as we have seen, the marked distinction between outer political action regulated by laws and inner moral conduct governed by autonomy is completely blurred in traditional Confucianism. So, Zhang Foquan echoes Yin by remarking that in terms of morality, the "dignity of man consists of virtue," whereas in terms of politics, the "dignity of man consists of basic rights."[25] As a result, Zhang and many other Westernized liberals also further the point, basically in agreement with Isaiah Berlin, that real liberals should promote negative freedom (rights) and reject positive freedom (whether it be moral autonomy or self-realization) as the latter is apt to give rise to political totalitarianism.

At this point, it is interesting to note that even in today's China, as one scholar correctly puts it, political modernization simply denotes an entire acceptance of "universally applicable truths" offered by Westernized liberalism. That is to say, as regards liberal language, there exists a propensity to understand "democracy as defined by universal suffrage, free elections, and party politics," to treat freedom as a "gift" to make one's own choice, absolutely regardless of moral considerations and the traditional ways of life. In short, "Chinese discourse reflects not only a simplistic liberalism but also, and primarily, what Oakeshott called 'Rationalism.'"[26]

A significant part of this chapter, accordingly, makes the point that the assumptions of the Western-centric stance are doubtful and that the notion that the "dignity of man consists of virtue" is essential to what may be called the virtue of the citizen, or so to speak, the civic virtue appropriate to a liberal democratic society. Or to restate alternatively, civil liberalism holds that the civic virtue that is embedded in the manners of behavior and the forms of life can not only "serve as the basis of democracy" but also lay a foundation for the ethical order of civil society.

The Concept of Civility

In proposing a political theory of civil liberalism, I am aware that "even in scholarly discussion, *civility* rests on a much looser, less formalized (in any sense) set of meanings than, say, *justice*, *democracy*, or *equality*, which are the subjects of concerted efforts at definition and analysis."[27] To round off my argument, I am obligated to clarify the concept of civility by reference to its twofold meaning, namely, good manners and public norms.

GOOD MANNERS

In terms of etymology, just as courtesy originates from court and politeness has roots in *polis*, the Latin word for civility is *civilitas* and related to it, *civilis*, meaning refined and urbane.[28] Although there were numerous "courtesy books" in the Middle Ages, the popularity of the usage of civility in early modern times was largely thanks to Erasmus of Rotterdam's *De Civilitate Morum Puerilium*. In an original sense, civility denoted the styles and tastes of the upper classes, and with the rapid growth of the city and town life in the Middle Ages, a civilized person was gradually identified as an "urban gentleman" with a group of polished manners. To this, it can be immediately added that civility could be learned and taught and that the reverse of civility was incivility or rudeness underpinning a set of "invective behaviors."[29] As a rule, civility thus understood is akin to the notion of *li* in Confucianism.

Furthermore, as far as civil liberalism is concerned, there are two crucial terms that have bearing on our general understanding of civility, namely, tradition and civilization. On the one hand, the key character of civility recognized as a group of manners of behavior grounded in local cultures resembles that of a "tradition" or a *"practice"* in Oakeshott's connotation.

> A practice may be identified as a set of considerations, manners, uses, observances, customs, standards, canon's maxims, principles, rules, and offices specifying useful procedures or denoting obligations or duties which relate to human actions and utterances. It is a prudential or a moral adverbial qualification of choices and performances, more or less complicated, in which conduct is understood in terms of a procedure. Words such as punctually, considerately, civilly, scientifically, legally, candidly, judicially, poetically, morally, etc., do not specify performances; they postulate performances and specify procedural conditions to be taken into account when choosing and acting.[30]

On the other hand, civility also shares with the words "civilizing" and "civilization" a common etymology. For my purposes here, there are three things about civilization that must be pointed out at the outset: First, seen in light of the history of historiography, the idea of the "civilizing process" was actually put into practice much earlier than the beginning of modernity. For instance, as long ago as the twelfth century, the very idea had been envisioned by William of Malmesbury, the author of the *Deeds of the Kings of the English* (*Gesta Regum Anglorum*).[31] Be that as it may, it was, once again, "Erasmus who popularized the notion that some people were civilized and others uncivilized—and that the difference might have moral consequences."[32] That said, although the verb "civilize," from which "civilization" stems, did not *officially* appear in English until the seventeenth century,[33] during the sixteenth century "civility" had already started to absorb some of the connotations of "civilization" at the same time as the "opposition between the 'civil' and the 'barbaric' implicit in classical writings" was allegedly being developed in response to the "challenge presented by the discovery of the 'savage' inhabitants of the New World," and then applied in a "contrast between English civility and Irish barbarity."[34]

Second, it was not until the eighteenth century, the age of the Enlightenment, that the word "civilization" had at last come into view in the bulk writings of philosophers and historians.[35] To be sure, as Arnaldo Momigliano remarks, the main theme of history in the eighteenth century was the "idea of civilization."[36] And here, my purposes permit me to single out that according to J. G. A. Pocock's reconstruction of the linguistic context in which Edward Gibbon wrote *The History of the Decline and Fall of Roman Empire*, many important authors at that time, including Giannone, Voltaire, Hume, Robertson, Ferguson, and Adam Smith, were eager to write the history of the "Christian millennium" regarding the deterioration from classical antiquity into the darkness of "barbarism and religion," and to recount the advent from the later set of conditions of a "Europe" in which "civil society could defend itself against disruption by either."[37] For instance, the subject matter of Hume's *History of England*, completed in 1761, was about nothing but the process of civilizing England. To quote Hume, his work was written to fulfill the "curiosity entertained by all civilized nations" in the process of "inquiring into the exploits and adventures of their ancestors," and he closed volume 1 of *History of England* by remarking, "Thus we have pursued the history of England through a series of many barbarous ages, till we have at last reached the dawn of civility and science."[38]

Third, the above discussion of the civilizing process does imply that civility is associated with the formulation of the modern state.[39] The association that is taken up in what follows may be said to go hand in hand with, or be a part of, the civilizing process. What is important in the present context is that in Pocock's analysis, the historiography of the Enlightenment actually had two themes: "the emergence of a system of sovereign states—multiple monarchies, confederacies and republics—in which the ruling authority had the competence to maintain civil government and conduct an independent *Aussenpolitik*; and the emergence of a shared civilization of manners and commerce, through which, in addition to treaties and statecraft, the independent states could be thought to constitute a confederation or republic."[40]

At the heart of Pocock's historical inquiry of historiography, then, lies a vital thread running throughout this chapter, that is, in contrast to the universalistic, antitraditional viewpoint of Westernized liberalism, a crucial approach to understanding the emergence of sovereign states and its institutions has been in relation to a civilization of manners, virtue, and commerce.[41] This is to say that for many great thinkers of the Enlightenment, the philosophical attempt to conceive an "enlightened Europe" of which they themselves were a part, far from being *culturally blind* and *historically insensitive*, served to clarify which traditional manners and beliefs could be transformed into a new set of civic virtues appropriate to the advent of civil society in support of civil government. In short, this *method* of theorizing on politics matches with what I have said about civil liberalism to a great extent. To say something more about the character of this method, I now turn to the second facet of civility.

PUBLIC NORMS

We shall have an opportunity to resume the issues of civilization and tradition shortly. For the moment, it is more vital to point out that in terms of etymology, *civilitas* is lexically kin to the political expressions of *cive* (citizen) and *civitas* (civil association) as well.[42] And thus, we are not surprised that another aspect of civility "focuses on politics, citizenship, and community, and is related to good character and virtue."[43] Seen in this light, it appears that one of the key features of modern political thought is to elevate the "subject" to the "citizen," that is, to seek the public norm of civility appropriate to the new emergence of a civil society, which is made of multiple individuals. On this account, as K. H. Jamieson writes, "it makes practical sense to embrace civility as a norm" for "the rhetorical exchanges that occur between those in an ongoing relationship" and "those who have come together as a community to address problems."[44]

It goes without saying that what is essential to liberalism in general and to civil society in particular points to the notion of the individual. However, it is equally true that different liberal writers may have employed different methods in justifying the norm of civility regulating the interactions between multiple individuals in civil society. To fill in the main theme of this chapter, in what follows I intend to follow in Oakeshott's footsteps in dividing the liberal theorization on individuality into hypothesis-based and practice-based approaches, and then, I shall try to reach a common understanding on the norm of civility between these two approaches.[45]

First, in Oakeshott's denotation, those who take the hypothesis-based approach toward an understanding of the individual basically fall into three different versions: the Lockean theological or natural law vision, where "individuality is the gift of an omnipotent and infinitely wise Maker";[46] the Kantian metaphysical vision, where a "metaphysical and ethical context" is given to justify the experience of the individual;[47] the utilitarian vision, where each man is considered as having a natural character "to make his own choices for himself about his own happiness."[48] Despite the fact that Oakeshott finds the methods of political theorization of all three to be inadequate,[49] they provide the main sources for the identification of liberalism as a prevailing political tenet.[50]

In this understanding, it seems clear that what we today refer to as "rights-based liberalism" in the works of John Rawls and Ronald Dworkin, among others, is a modification of the hypothesis-based approach, apt to describe the public norm of a liberal society as what "defines the kinds of behavior that persons can rightfully expect from others." In the main, for liberals as such, the norm of civility consistent with liberal citizens and liberal culture, as Richard C. Sinopoli puts it, points to the manners in which we "treat others with the concern and respect they are owed as persons able to act upon plans advancing a conception of the good life."[51]

Moreover, as a consequence of the progress of deliberative democracy,[52] there also has been a tendency to relate the norm of civility to the "constructive engagement with others through argument, deliberation, and discourse."[53] Accordingly, the idea of deliberation, together with concern and respect, has turned out to be the core of civil norms in contemporary liberalism. Rawls, for example, argues that in a well-ordered civil society, the citizen is under a "duty of civility" to sustain the political values of public reason, implying "a willingness to listen to others and a fairmindedness in deciding when accommodations to their views should reasonably be made."[54]

By way of contrast, the practice-based approach is prone to take Herder's notion of linguistic context and Hegel's notion of *Sittlichkeit* into account when discussing the meaning of individuality, resulting in an alternative form of "embodied individualism" as opposed to the "abstract individualism" of the hypothesis-based approach. I shall say something more about Herder's philosophy of language shortly. What is more important in the present context is that in spite of the disparate methods of theorization on individuality and liberal values, these two approaches share a group of the elements of civil norms, such as humanity, dignity, respect, and concern.

In the case of Oakeshott, for instance, the practice-based approach is applied to explain the norm of civility in terms of a set of noninstrumental rules constituting what he famously calls *societas*. In brief, according to Oakeshott, *societas* stands for a *moral* mode of civil association in which human beings are "associated solely in being related to one another in terms of their common acknowledgement of the authority of rules of conduct (law)";[55] by contrast, what he calls *universitas* is one that is recognized as a *prudential* mode of enterprise association in which human beings are "associated in terms of their joint pursuit or promotion of a chosen substantive purpose or interest."[56]

Throughout his career, the contrast at stake has undergone a number of reformulations that include disparities between the "politics of individualism" and the "politics of collectivism,"[57] between the "politics of skepticism" and the "politics of faith,"[58] and between "*nomocracy*" and "*telocracy*."[59] Despite the different expressions and the slight shifting of focuses, what remains unchanged is Oakeshott's key point that "the language of civil intercourse is a language of rules; *civitas* is rule-articulated association."[60] That said, for Oakeshott, what lies in the norm of civility in question is a genuine meaning of the rule of law, to protect the dignity and freedom of every individual in making his or her own choices.

Civil Politics

From the standpoint I have been taking, however, there is another application of the practice-based approach in justifying the norm of civility in respect of humanity, dignity, concern, and respect that bears the most striking similarities to New Confucianism, that is, to see civility as what Montesquieu calls the public spirit embedded in the manners of behavior and the forms of life in a community. For Montesquieu, public spirit is "love of the republic," and "love of the republic in a democracy is love of democracy."[61] In this sense, civility known as public spirit is analogous to civic virtue, and to pursue civic virtue entails an endeavor to transfigure the good manners between persons into the concern for the common good in public affairs.[62]

On this account, Shils's landmark work on civility, *The Virtue of Civility*, warrants much more discussion. For the most part, Shils grants that civility is a "belief which affirms the possibility of the common good" within a "morally valid unity of society," that civility denotes an "attitude of concern for the good of the entire society," and that civility represents the "image of the common good inherent in the nature of collective self-consciousness."[63] In short,

> Civil politics are based on civility, which is the virtue of the citizen, of the man who shares responsibly in his own

self-government, either as a governor or as one of the governed. Civility is compatible with other attachments to class, to religion, to profession, but it regulates them out of respect for the common good.[64]

All this, however, does not imply that Shils's version of civil politics abandons the liberal commitment, nor does it endorse a form of *universitas* in Oakeshott's usage.[65] The upshot is that as with Rawls and Dworkin, Shils also firmly believes that "civility is basically respect for the dignity and the desire for dignity of other persons."[66] What is more, civility recognized as an "attitude of respect, even love, for our fellow citizens," as Stephen Carter powerfully adds, is based on the moral belief "that humans matter, that we owe each other respect, and that treating each other well is a moral duty"; or to put it another way, since "shared moral norms generate the mutuality of respect (especially for those who follow the norms) that in turn allows civilization and, thus, civility," civility will impose on the citizens of a liberal society a "duty to treat all human beings with equal respect."[67]

Now, based on what has been said, it becomes clearer that Westernized liberalism neglects the historical significance of incorporating a civilization of good manners and civic virtue into the making of civil society in the modern sense and that it adopts the hypothesis-based approach when introducing liberal values into the Chinese context. Owing to the dominance of Westernized liberalism, as a consequence, even in a liberal democratic society like Taiwan, the "standard viewpoint" is still at work. Contrary to this, what I mean by Confucian liberalism not only remains faithful to the practice-based approach but also endorses the merit of civil liberalism in combining the double meaning of civility—good manners and public norms—into a cultural convention of "Confucian democratic civility," upon which the political innovation of liberal democracy rests.

Civility as Civilization

In the following two sections, I am about to provide a more detailed analysis of the twofold aspect of civility. In so doing, my major goal is to defy the Western-centric stance and the nonmoral concept of politics attached to Westernized liberalism so as to arrive at a reaffirmation of the plurality of liberalisms from different angles. In this section, I plan to tackle the first topic by explaining away the three misconceptions concerned: the absolute disparity between civilization and barbarism, the sharp contrast between modernity and tradition, and the uncompromising tension between individuality and community.

CIVILIZATION AND BARBARISM

Putting aside the issue of "liberal imperialism,"[68] I just want to begin this section by remarking that it is misleading to claim that Western civilization is superior to other civilizations simply because it has absolutely developed out of barbarism into an *ideal* stage of civilization. This claim, together with the ultimate triumph of liberal democracy, is dubious because, as Collingwood claims, there are elements of barbarity, and thus, *incivility*, left over in Western civilization, which in turn gives rise to the predicament of liberalism. To make my point, let me cast light on the Hegelian insights of Collingwood's political theory.

For Collingwood, civilization is, by and large, equivalent to civility. More exactly, whereas civility is used for "the ideal condition into which whoever is trying to civilize a community is trying to bring it," civilization is the name for the *process* itself, that is, "the condition to which in a given case it leads."[69] In the Collingwoodian setting, that is to say, civilization stands for a process of the development of the human mind toward a superior lifestyle, a polished way of acting or a refined form of life that is worth pursuing. And thus, the civilizing process denotes a change for the better, that is, to arrive at a higher level of rationality, marking out the elements of civilization.

Furthermore, as Collingwood continues, the idea of a civilized society, or what he otherwise dubs a social community, can be seen as a "collection of individuals capable of free choice," attempting to pursue a common purpose with others "whom they deem equally as free and rational."[70] In Collingwood's eyes, the more rational its individual members have become, the more civilized a society will be. Thus seen, civilization denotes not only a *rationalizing* process in terms of which emotionally driven connections (e.g., members of the family) will gradually be replaced by connections based on rationality (i.e., members of a civil society), but also a *socializing* process in terms of which the "nonsocial community" will be transfigured into the "social community." That said, for Collingwood, the words "rational" and "social" are synonyms, and there is no straightforward distinction between the nonsocial and the social communities.

However, in Collingwood's scheme, the social community is not equivalent to the body politic. On the whole, the body politic is a mixed community embracing elements of both social and nonsocial community, and it is, by and large, governed by three basic laws: (1) a body politic is divided into a ruling class and a ruled class; (2) the barrier between the two classes is permeable in an upward sense; and (3) there is a correspondence between the ruler and the ruled.[71] Taken together, this implies that "the life of the body politic is that of the continuous process of conversion from the nonsocial to the social, that is, the dialectical process of growing up in a body politic to share the business of rule."[72]

From this, it follows that the purpose of a body politic is entirely consistent with the ideal of civility on the account that it is aimed at supporting the social community to make the most of the elements of civilization, such as education, wealth, law and order, and peace and plenty. Or alternatively, the major task of politics is to reduce the perils of barbarity that will bring about "hostility toward civilization"[73] by making every effort to maintain a civil order. Due to the following two factors, however, the elements of barbarity can never be completely wiped out.

For one thing, just as the lives on the earth are renewed again and again, the attendance of new members in the social community is incessant; therefore, the civilizing process is always an endless process in the face of numerous contingent matters. In other words, for Collingwood, there are always barbarity, rudeness, incivility, and cruelty remaining in the social community because every civilization in the process of civilizing must at the same time preserve the "primitive survivals" of the condition out of which it develops, that is, barbarity.

Again, in the real world, politics always involves the use of power. Accordingly, it seems undeniable that in every civilization the features of barbarity and civility often coexist and that the elements of barbarity can never be totally eradicated by the pursuit of civility because the transformation of the nonsocial into the social community involves an endless process, and the "transeunt rule exercised by the rulers over the nonsocial community in the body politic entails an element of force which is incompatible with the ideal of civility."[74]

On this reading, the big crisis confronting Western civilization is that the pursuit of a continuous progression toward the perfect state of knowledge and society commonly undertaken by the dominant schools of thought in our time, including scientism, realism, positivism, and indeed, the hypothesis-based approach in political theory, is basically *culturally blind* and *historically insensitive*; as such, they all fail to notice that the survival of barbarism will precipitate the total collapse of liberal democracies. For this reason, Collingwood furthers his diagnosis by saying that a serious defeat rooted in the classical liberalism of Hobbes, Locke, and Rousseau is that none of them has succeeded in providing a thorough discussion of the nonsocial community in respect of barbarism.

In comparison to Hobbes's *Leviathan*, then, the important message that Collingwood's *New Leviathan* delivers to us is that there are always situations and moments in which a civilized society will *return to the state of barbarity*. In this regard, liberal democracy per se is certainly not the *panacea* for the future of Chinese civilization, for the truth is rather that even today the exercise of liberal democracy is entwined with the uncivil behaviors associated with populism and the uncivil discourse appearing on the internet and in social media, for instance. In short, democracy is, as it always has been, at risk of self-dissolution, largely thanks to the radical evils of *incivility* in human nature.

This is not to say that we should give up pursuing liberal democracy. But rather, it means that just because "man seeks to be inherently both a law-maker and a law-breaker,"[75] when considering the stability of liberal democracy, we should bear in mind both the danger of incivility and the norm of civility. With this understanding, my search for civil liberalism in this study is predicated not only upon the fact that it echoes the gist of Confucian liberalism in relating the basis of liberal democracy to the public spirit of civility embedded in the Confucian forms of life, but also upon the deep worry about the pitfalls of mainstream liberalism. Before going any further, it thus seems well to resume my criticisms of the hypothesis-based approach with regard to the other two misconceptions.

Modernity and Tradition

As regards the sharp distinction between modernity and tradition, I have three general points to make. First, instead of assuming a unitary Enlightenment project,[76] I am driven to follow in Pocock's footsteps in maintaining that there is a "family of enlightenments."[77] Accordingly, in objection to the stance of Westernized liberalism asserting that the *future* of Chinese civilization lies in an actualization of the *past* achievement of Western modernity, what underscores Confucian liberalism is the view that the *future* of Chinese civilization lies in a synthesis of the *habitual* practices of the Confucian ways of thinking, idioms of doing and forms of life, with the achievement in democracy (and science) resulting from Western modernity accompanied by the appearance of the modern state. That is to say, as with the writers such as Hume, who seem to have encouraged a "conservative enlightenment,"[78] it is to Mou's credit that he tries to merge the *newly emergent* historical condition featuring democracy (which for Hume is commerce) with the *enduring establishments* of Confucian dictums and mottos (which for Hume are the customs and habits of English Constitutionalism).

Also, in keeping with Pocock's thesis, it seems that for many distinguished writers of the eighteenth century, modernity is, after all, a continuous process of tradition. That is to say, they bear out the way of thinking that we had better give new ideas to the new world without entirely "breaking up with the past." To quote Hume once again, "almost all improvements of the human mind had reached nearly to their state of perfection about the age of Augustus." Thus, he was driven to find a middle course between modernity and antiquity by remarking at the same time that "it may be justly affirmed, without any danger of exaggeration, that we, in this island, have ever since [1688] enjoyed, if not the best system of government, at least the most entire system of liberty, that was ever known amongst mankind" and that it was largely through numerous contingent habitual practices that "a civilized nation like the English [had] established the most perfect and most accurate system of political liberty that was ever found compatible with government."[79]

As a final point, it seems to me that the contrast between modernity and tradition rests on a profound confusion between tradition and traditionalism. As Shils correctly puts it, while tradition embraces the sources of the meanings of life that make possible the exercise of freedom in a real sense, "traditionalism is almost always ideological and extremist."[80] In this sense, "traditionalism is not only hostile to liberty, it is also radically hostile to tradition"; in short, traditionalism is "the greatest enemy of the tradition of civility which is essential to its life."[81] Or alternatively, in the words of Jaroslav Pelikan, tradition accommodates the "living faith of the dead," but traditionalism holds on to the "dead faith of the living."[82]

INDIVIDUALITY AND COMMUNITY

The third misconception that I wish to deal with is about the uncompromising tension between the individual and the community in which he or she lives. On this matter, it can be restated in the beginning that Shils's understanding of tradition as the "vicissitudes of the human mind"[83] is analogous to Oakeshott's definition of a "practice" mentioned above. In a word, a practice, just like a language, "is not the creation of grammarians"; but rather, it is made by speakers."[84] Accordingly, as regards the relationship between freedom and practice or between individuality and community, Oakeshott writes that

> the "freedom" which can be pursued is not an independently premeditated "ideal" or a dream; like scientific hypothesis, it is something which is already intimated in a concrete manner of behaving. Freedom, like a recipe for game pie, is not a bright idea; it is not a "human right" to be deduced from some speculative concept of human nature. The freedom which we enjoy is nothing more than arrangements, procedures of a certain kind.[85]

Thus read, I think Timothy Fuller is right in remarking that "Oakeshott was an individualist, but not an abstract individualist. Individuality is a self-understanding composed in responding to others in a certain tradition of behaviour. We understand ourselves to be individuals because we are self-conscious within a context of innumerable self-conscious agents."[86] In a nutshell, the real point concerning Oakeshott's connection to liberalism is not about whether Oakeshott is "a lover of liberty"[87] or not, but about whether his love of freedom has the same quality as that of mainstream liberals who adopt the hypothesis-based approach.

Overall, if the term "individualism" is taken to mean views about the relationship between the individual and communities (such as societies, cultures, languages, and traditions), then there are likewise two distinguishable forms of individualism related to the two approaches of liberal political theory under discussion, namely, "embodied individualism" (or "concrete individualism") and "atomistic individualism" (or "abstract individualism"). Considering the aim of this chapter, it seems advisable to reiterate what I mean by "embodied individualism" by drawing attention to the two crucial points related to Herder's philosophy of language[88] that I have elucidated elsewhere.[89]

First, I contend that Charles Taylor's deconstruction of the "disengaged reason,"[90] Michael Sandel's critique of the "disencumbered self,"[91] and Alasdair MacIntyre's repudiation of the "emotivist self"[92] can all be understood as attempts to revitalize the Herderian "expressionist self" or the Hegelian "embodied subjectivity." Seen in this light, Oakeshott's discussion of a free agent in terms of self-disclosure and self-enactment is likewise a regeneration of the Hederian-Hegelian pursuit of the value of the individual.

Second, it is to Herder's credit that he makes every effort to reconcile the sharp contrast between reason and tradition as defined by the Westernized liberals; for Herder, human reason, properly understood, is precisely the ability to express oneself as one wishes by means of language. In some sense, Herder's idea of context dependence accords perfectly with Hegel's *Sittlichkeit*, implying that ethical principles are specific to a certain community, and thus, that human reason and freedom, as the principle of embodiment shows, can only be completely achieved within a concrete context. From my point of view, it seems evident that the historicist emphasis on context-dependence or *Sittlichkeit*, which has had great impact on British idealism and philosophical communitarianism, also plays an important role in making sense of Oakeshott's idea of a "practice."[93]

To conclude, it is my understanding that the practice-based approach not only resonates with the ethical turn toward liberalism underlining the rationale of the book, but it also leads to a different way of appreciating liberal values by taking seriously the value of tradition and the diversity of civilizations.[94] In short, the practice-based approach is anything but the pursuit of total Westernization.

Civility as Public Good

Having touched on the idea of civilization and its related issues, let me now turn to object to the view that the proper understanding of liberal democracy implies a clear-cut distinction between politics and morality. My alternative opinion is that civility understood as public good comprises the moral grounding of civil society, which not only plays a crucial part in nourishing an ethical version of democratic citizenship, but also helps prevent political discourse from sliding into rudeness and incivility.

Civil Society

As we have seen, civility covers both polite and political spheres: polite civility is the "acquisition of social etiquette and manners," whereas political civility concerns the components of a common good such as the "display of respect."[95] Focusing on the liberal tradition, a further distinction can thereby be made between the "civility of etiquette" for personal lives and the "liberal civility" for public affairs.[96] All this, of course, does not imply that political civility is in separation from polite civility. Rather, it hints only that political civility is a subset of polite civility.[97] More precisely, although civility shifts over time, there appears an overall consistency that is aimed at promoting the central values of "respect, tolerance, and considerateness" underlining both polite and political civility. In short, "civility interweaves politeness and political respect; it undergirds modern notions of republicanism, civil society, and the public good."[98]

For classical liberal thinkers such as John Locke, the modern world is characterized, among other things, by the appearance of civil society, wherein counter to barbarism, the state of nature, and ancient civilized society, the rights to life, freedom, and property are legally protected by a legitimate civil government. Following the republican tradition, by contrast, Adam Ferguson claims that civil society is grounded in something older than property, namely, public virtue and communal bonds, and thus, that "it is in conducting the affairs of civil society, that mankind find the exercise of their best talents, as well as the object of their best affections."[99] Again, in Hegel's redefinition, civil society is a part of ethical life, which consists of the system of needs (market), the administration of justice (law), and the police and the corporation (regulation).[100]

Although this book aims to reconstruct Mou's Confucian liberalism via the Hegelian scheme, here I do not intend to discuss Hegel's notion of civil society in detail. This is mainly because, rather than following in Hegel's footsteps in building a full-fledged theory of civil society, Mou's Hegel-inspired political theory asserts that the quality of political life largely depends on a normative concept of society that conducts its interactions with regard to the lived forms of life. Put in other terms, for Mou, political civility is of great significance in buttressing the exercise of democracy as his understanding of democracy is akin to the tradition of Montesquieu and Tocqueville, among others, which sees democracy as both a "type of government" and a "system of manners," a "form of social life."[101] For this reason, what I mean by civil society does not exclude the import of "civilized society" or "good society."[102] In short, my usage of "civil society" basically implies a "society of civility in the conduct of the members of the society toward each other."[103]

Civic Virtue

As a consequence, the political aspect of civility that concerns me here points to an "ethical version of democratic citizenship" in association with civic virtues, namely, "the civil capacities of contemporary liberal democratic societies."[104] In short, civic virtue is the virtue of the citizen in that it delivers an "appreciation of attachment to the institutions"[105] that constitute civil society.

Furthermore, in the words of Shils, the identification of civility as civic virtue evokes a call for the common good:

> The common good is a pattern which permits or enables the living of a good life, by individuals, collectivities and the entire society—or at least a better life than they otherwise might live. The civil society is the common good. Civility is the concern for the maintenance of the civil society as a civil society. Civility is therefore a concern to reconcile—not abolish—divergent interests.[106]

The idea of the common good proposed by Shils is a *liberal* one, seeing as it treasures the liberal values of humanity, dignity, respect, tolerance, and open-mindedness. At the heart of "liberal civility," or what I have otherwise called "democratic civility," lies one's "willingness to consider respectfully the views of others, with an understanding that we are all connected and rely on each other."[107] This at once brings us back to Rawls's definition of the "duty of civility" mentioned above. Once more, my key point here is that whether civility is understood as a "civil duty" or a "civic virtue,"[108] it accommodates the values of "respect, tolerance, and considerateness,"[109] and thus, that what sets civil liberalism apart from rights-based liberalism is not so much about their attitudes toward the basic liberal ideals but about the ways of justification.

As a final point, I do not intend to deny that on some occasions "democracy may require withdrawal from *civility* itself."[110] For instance, one writer remarks:

> The civility movement is deeply at odds with what an invigorated liberalism requires: intellectual clarity; an insistence upon grappling with the substance of controversies; and a willingness to fight loudly, openly, militantly, even rudely for

policies and values that will increase freedom, equality, and happiness in America and around the world.[111]

However, I still firmly believe that a liberal conception of the common good is of great significance in making possible the stability of liberal democracy. For one thing, we are living in an age of "ideological politics" characterized by *radical* "progressivism."[112] And so, "being civilized, having good manners, controlling one's behavior, and showing restraint in expression are necessary (even if not sufficient) for the civility needed in a strong democratic polity."[113] Again, civility may protect liberal democratic society from the "danger of extremes of partisanship" by diminishing "the real losses which are bound to be inflicted on a society in which conflicts are both inherent—they are inherent in all societies—and provided for by its liberal democratic constitution."[114]

CITIZENSHIP

It follows that civility is a key constituent of citizenship, that is, "full membership in the community," or put differently, "citizenship without civility is empty."[115] More precisely, citizenship can be defined as enjoying "mutual membership" with regard to *political equality* in a civil society. In the general description of "rights-based" citizenship, as T. H. Marshall famously states, the equality of citizenship lies in a set of equal rights, developing from the stage of civil rights, through that of political rights, to that of social rights.[116] By way of contrast, I agree with David Miller on the point that a more robust understanding of citizenship, apart from enjoying a "set of equal rights," also includes a "set of obligations," "being willing to take active steps to defend the rights of other members of the political community, and more generally to promote its common interests," and to "play an active role in both the formal and informal arenas of politics."[117]

In the subsequent chapters, we shall have opportunities to see how the *republican* version of understanding civil society, civic virtue, and citizenship sketched above is largely consistent with my reconstruction of Mou's Confucian liberalism. That said, Confucian liberalism as a form of ethical liberalism, be it civil liberalism or perfectionist liberalism, does not necessarily exclude the civic tradition associated with republicanism. Indeed, by coining the term "Confucian liberalism," I have been using "liberalism" in a broader sense.

From the above discussion, we may arrive at the conclusion that the ordinary understanding of liberal expressions in the Chinese-speaking world is one-sided since what Westernized liberalism represents to us is just a peculiar side of liberalism. More precisely, if the ideas of individuality and freedom have most vitally underlined liberalism, then there are different ways of defending the free agent in the modern history of political thought. The intellectual legacy of Oakeshott, as indicated, offers an excellent example. In fact, in the recent development of political theory, there has been a tendency to revitalize the importance of Hegel in marking the ethical, historicist, or civilized turn toward liberalism, leaving us space to reflect on the possibility, plausibility, and creativity of Confucian liberalism from a Hegelian point of view.

Put in other terms, instead of regarding liberalism as a single, undivided whole, there exist several alternative groupings of liberalism in recent scholarship. As I have given some examples in the introduction, we have, with John Gray, rationalistic liberalism versus agonistic liberalism,[118] with Richard Rorty, Kantian liberalism versus Hegelian liberalism,[119] and with Charles Taylor, procedural liberalism versus communitarian (or republican) liberalism.[120] For my purposes here, it seems sufficient to indicate that all these writers share the understanding that the meanings of liberalism have been redefined at least in part by a growing sense of its *historicity*, a sense that increases our awareness of the plurality of ways of thinking and forms of life in the modern world. As a result, it may not be inappropriate to reformulate the two faces of liberalism as "hypothesis-based liberalism" versus "practice-based liberalism." Based on this schema, it at once appears that the Westernized liberalism advocated by Yin and Zhang and the Confucian liberalism promoted by Mou, as a matter of fact, belong to the streams of "hypothesis-based liberalism" and "practice-based liberalism" respectively.[121]

Confucian Democratic Civility

That being said, I now try to bring to light what I mean by "Confucian democratic civility."

Wenming and Gongde

Hopefully, it is clear now that the notion of *li*, by and large, embraces the twofold facet of civility that we have discussed. More precisely, given that *li* is literally translated as ritual propriety, "ritually shaped activity" not merely implies good manners and politeness, but also refers to "patterning" (*wen* 文) in Confucianism, meaning that which may enable the flourishing of "culture, community, and civilization."[122] In this regard, it may be said that *li* taken as a whole is equivalent to the idea of civilization (*wenming* 文明), and thus, that the crisis of Confucian civilization in the modern era can be regarded as an extensive collapse of ritual order, bringing about a cry for the transformation of values.

As I have said, it is basically against this context that Mou's political philosophy consists of an attempt to incorporate the "blossoming of democracy" (*minzhu kaichu* 民主開出) into the Confucian political ideal, resulting in a "politics of innovation." Unlike Westernized liberals, however, Mou strongly urges that a context-sensitive theorization on democracy cannot be attained without simultaneously bringing into account this vital question: How can democracy work at all in a cultural setting traditionally fostered by Confucianism? In other words, seen from the perspective of civil liberalism, Mou's theory of democracy at the same time engages a reassessment of the possibility and plausibility of Confucian civility as the public spirit or public virtue (*gongde* 公德) in a democratic society, namely, "Confucian democratic civility."

Accordingly, if to develop democracy out of Confucianism requires a "significantly different political philosophy,"[123] then the essential task of a Confucian political philosopher in favor of liberal values is to further a *Confucian* explanation of civil society, civic virtue, and citizenship, *accompanied by* the "blossoming of democracy." Or, to put it another way, inasmuch as Mou's Confucian liberalism is a combination of the "way of politics" and the "way of governance," he is obligated to demonstrate how and in what sense democracy can be grounded in the public good that is embodied in the Confucian forms of life. In short, at issue is how to develop a Confucian conception of the common good with regard to the socially established norms rooted in Confucian culture.

In view of the fact that there is a deep conflict between the "politics of virtue and talent" and the "politics of democracy," Mou's proposal for the "new outer kingliness" (*xin waiwang* 新外王), as I see it, thus makes every effort to embark on a renovation of the tradition of "rule by *de*." There are at least three vital arguments that Mou has made in an attempt to make sense of the subtlest model of democracy in Confucian terms: first, to prefer Mencius's "*ren*-centered" reading of *li* to Xunzi's "inclu-

Civility and the Renovation of Tradition | 169

sive" understanding of *li*; second, to make a further separation between "cultivating oneself" (*xiuji* 修己) in pursuit of sagehood and "governing the people" (*zhiren* 治人) in terms of "self-restriction" (*ziwoxianzhi* 自我限制), resulting in a *specific* restatement of Confucian public virtue; third, to give a renewed account of Confucian ethical citizenship by explicating how the principle of "self-restriction" originally underpinning the "governing virtue" of the leader can be further transmuted into the "civic virtue" of the citizen that fosters civil society.

To illuminate: due to the absence of democracy, the idea of equal citizenship did not exist in ancient Confucianism. As such, the public virtue that used to elucidate the asset of "governing the people" in terms of "self-restriction" was nothing but the "governing virtue" of the leader. With the "blossoming of democracy," however, a significant part of Mou's theory of democracy is organized to reformulate the moral character of the political subject, namely, the citizen, by transforming "governing virtue" into "civic virtue" in respect of the "way of *zhongshu*" (*zhongshu zhi dao* 忠恕之道). The "way of *zhongshu*," together with the principle of "self-restriction," as we shall see, is advantageous to spelling out the significance of democratic civic virtue in a Confucian vein as it "combines three character traits: tolerance, patience, and self-restraint."[124] All in all, "Confucian democratic civility" stands for a group of *Confucian governing and civic virtues* suitable for a democratic society.

For the rest of this chapter, I am only about to initiate these lines of reasoning in a way that may direct the attention to some of the extremely insightful but still less discussed parts of Mou's political thought. In the course of the succeeding chapters, I shall move on to substantiate these key arguments such that the picture of Mou's Confucian liberalism can be more fully completed.

A *REN*-CENTERED READING OF *LI*

Let me now begin the first issue by remarking that *li* in Confucianism stands for a form of *de*. The following passage from the *Book of Rites*, for example, lucidly explicates the moral aspect of *li*.

> In the visible sphere there are ceremonies and music; in the invisible, the spiritual agencies. These things being so, in all within the four seas, there must be mutual respect and love.

> The occasions and forms of ceremonies are different, but it is the same feeling of respect (which they express).[125]

In a philosophical sense, this means that *li* may take countless forms according to various circumstances, but at the heart of *li* lies the "deep-rooted character trait," which is equipped with "durable emotions, aptitudes, and dispositions"[126] toward "mutual respect and love." As Zhu Xi [Chu Hsi] (朱熹 1130–1200) puts the point from another angle, "If one is dutiful today, but not tomorrow, then one has not attained dutifulness in oneself, and this cannot be called virtue (*de* 德)."[127] In short, *li* recognized as communally established norms reasserts the social aspect of morality that we have previously discussed.

Even so, Mencius and Xunzi, as indicated, have different attitudes toward the significance of *li* and its place in the mapping of *de* as a whole. For my purposes here, there are three main points that can be made as follows. First, in Mou's diagnosis, Xunzi basically falls outside the pattern of orthodox Confucianism presented in chapter 1. More exactly, Mencius's idea of the "goodness of *Xing*-nature" (*xingshan* 性善), as we have seen, implies the notion of "inner morality" (*neizai daodexing* 內在道德性) rooted in the moral subject. In contrast, Xunzi tries to replace the "goodness of *Xing*-nature" with the "depravity of man's sociality," implying that ordinary people are compelled to go after "outer guidance," that is, *li*, which has already been established by the ancient sages and the former kings.[128] In brief, while both Confucius and Mencius apprehend the character of society "from inside," treating politics as an extension from morality, Xunzi considers the order of society "from outside," seeing rituals and rules as the crux of politics.[129]

Put in other terms, Xunzi does not adopt a "vertical expression of the vertical system" (*zongguan zongjiang* 縱貫縱講); rather, he takes *li* to signify the "deliberate effort" (*wei* 偽) by means of which humanity may be led to "beautify itself."[130] As such, in contrast to Mencius's thesis on the "unity of the heart-mind and *Xing*-nature" (*xin ji xing* 心即性), Xunzi is devoted to "modifying humanity through the heart-mind" (*yi xin zhi xing* 以心治性) with the purpose of enabling one to distinguish right from wrong in the *empirical* world.[131] That said, for Xunzi, the key point of conducting a moral life is not so much to fully realize the moral potentiality toward sagehood but to abide by the actuality of human experience because "the sage is the product of people's accumulated efforts" and "becoming a sage is something that people achieve through accumulation."[132] Accordingly, while for Xunzi the prerequisite for a positive and active leader in establishing the order rests on the "heart-mind of knowing" (renshi de xin 認識的心), or the "heart-mind of intelligence" (lizhi de xin 理智的心),[133] at the heart of Confucius's and Mencius's prescription of a "virtuous" leader lies the principle of "self-restriction" in accordance with the "heart-mind of morality" (daode de xin 道德的心).

Second, Mencius, of course, does not deny that a society should convey an order of ethics supported by a series of human relations,[134] that whether in politics or in social life there exists an ethical order between the superior and inferior, between the more and less noble, between the young and the old, and between relatives and strangers. But the upshot is that for Mencius, while the four leading virtues are listed as ren 仁 (humaneness), yi 義 (righteousness), li 禮 (ritual propriety), and zhi 智 (wisdom),[135] the appropriateness of li is dependent on a further evaluation of the "heart-mind of ren" (renxin 仁心). As Xu Fuguan [Hsu Fu-Kuan] (徐復觀 1904–1982) explains, li in the Analects (Lunyu 論語) is mainly used in three different contexts: reviving rituals that have already existed, extending religious rites to everyday life, and developing new meanings of li out of the "sources of li" (li zhi ben 禮之本). It is clearly against the last meaning that Mencius goes further to refer to the "heart-mind of modesty" (cirang zhi xin 辭讓之心) as the "germ of li," bringing about a significant consequence of "internalizing li as a kind of de within the heart-mind."[136] To quote Mencius, "A gentleman differs from other men in that he retains his heart-mind"; "That which a gentleman follows as his Xing-nature, that is to say, humaneness, righteousness, the rites, and wisdom, is rooted in his heart-mind."[137] And thus, Mencius's idea of "humane government" concentrates on the ruler's "heart-mind of ren": "The benevolent (humane) man has no match."[138]

Conversely, Xunzi's usage of li has nothing to do with the idea of "inner autonomous morality"[139] that we have previously unveiled; the cultivation of li in Xunzi's system of thought only entails an instrumental value. With the "depravity of man's sociality," Xunzi essentially admits that men's social position cannot be equal, that "total equality is not order," and that only "ritual and yi are the beginning of order."[140] As a consequence, a true king is one who is able to maintain social order by use of "outer establishments": "Ritual is that which the ruler of men uses as the yardstick and test for his various subjects, and then the classes of people are marked out completely."[141]

Third, in view of the fact that ren is the highest virtue of all virtues, namely, the fullest realization of one's moral ability, Mencius is obviously prone to undertake a "ren-centered" appreciation of li, in the sense that the "heart-mind of *ren*," after all, "goes beyond and can critique any given set of rituals."¹⁴² This way of reading *li*, for example, can be found in quite a few statements in the *Book of Rites*: "The rules of ceremony (*li*) are the embodied expression of what is right (*yi*)"; "humanity (*ren*) is the root of right, and the embodying of deferential consideration."¹⁴³ In other words, "the rules of ceremony (*li*)" represent the "elegant forms," whereas the "true heart and good faith" (*zhong xin* 忠信) are their "radical elements."¹⁴⁴ "In ceremonial usages we should go back to the root of them (in the heart-mind), not forgetting what they were at first" (*fanben xiugu* 反本修古).¹⁴⁵

On the other hand, Xunzi adopts an "inclusive" reading of *li*, on the account that *li* "should govern virtually every aspect of a person's life."¹⁴⁶ And so, Mou articulates that for Xunzi, "the entire body is ritual propriety and righteousness" (*tongti shi li yi* 通體是禮義). To quote Xunzi again, "Scales are a standard for goods, and ritual is a standard for proper regulation. One uses scales in order to establish the quantity of things, and one uses ritual in order to set the proper grades of people."¹⁴⁷ Thus, as Xunzi continues, "learning comes to ritual and then stops, for this is called the ultimate point in pursuit of the Way and virtue."¹⁴⁸ In this fashion, just as being a sage "is due to exercising vigilance over these things through ritual,"¹⁴⁹ being a true king is to "make divisions and distributions according to ritual."¹⁵⁰ Interestingly, other passages from the *Book of Rites* also endorse the "inclusive" notion of *li*. To take an obvious example: "The rites to be observed by all-under-Heaven were intended to promote the return (of the heart-mind) to the beginning (Creator of all); to promote (the honoring of) spiritual Beings; to promote the harmonious use (of all resources and appliances) of government; to promote righteousness; and to promote humanity."¹⁵¹

Li as Objective Spirit

Counter to Xunzi's version, then, what I mean by a "*ren*-centered" reading of *li* echoes to a great extent Xu Fuguan's insightful observation, indicating that "the cultural spirit [the essence of *li*] established by Confucius and Mencius according to the nature of *ren* can be everlasting, but the agenda concerning human relations [the forms of *li*] exercised by them must change with time."¹⁵²

However, none of this is to say that the New Confucians depreciate Xunzi completely. In Mou's opinion, Mencius and Xunzi carry forward

Confucius's legacy in two different directions: Mencius makes a groundbreaking contribution to the learning of "inner sagehood," whereas Xunzi reaches a high point of the theorization on "outer kingliness" (*waiwang* 外王).[153] Without a doubt, Xunzi's appreciation of Confucius's ideal of "outer kingliness," together with his stress on the "heart-mind of intelligence" and the institutionalization of rituals, makes manifest what Hegel refers to as objective spirit in an *initial* sense.[154] In addition, given that scientific knowledge is based on the notion of the "knowing subject" in relation to the natural world, "it is a big misfortune for Chinese history that the study of Xunzi has often been neglected by people, that his spirit has often been undiscovered to people."[155] Thus seen, another pressing task for the modernization of Confucianism consists of an attempt to "fuse Xunzi" with the Confucian tradition,[156] that is, to "pay serious attention to the positive worth [of Xunzi's thought] in connection with Confucius and Mencius."[157]

It is beyond the scope of this book to fulfill this task. As an alternative, I feel compelled to explain to some extent why Mou does not follow in Xunzi's footsteps in illuminating the "blossoming of democracy." To begin with, it will be remembered that for Mou, the gist of Confucian democracy is to actualize the spirit of *ren* in a modern civilized society formed by independent "political subjects" *as a whole*. In asserting modifying humanity through the "heart-mind of intelligence," nonetheless, the notion of the "knowing subject" in Xunzi's connotation is applied to the sagely king alone. For this reason, rather than endorsing the idea of "subjective freedom" in the Hegelian sense, Xunzi's viewpoint intensively endorses what Hegel has otherwise called the "freedom of one person" in ancient Oriental societies, meaning that all but the king himself was substantially free.[158]

By way of contrast, Mencius holds that *every* person is bestowed with the "subjective freedom of morality" (*daode de zhuti ziyou* 道德的主體自由),[159] which, in turn, implies a firm belief about the moral equality of *all* humankind in keeping with the moral grounding of democracy. The real problem confronting Mencius's version of "outer kingliness," as stated, is simply due to the fact that he falls short of developing the "political subject" out of the "moral subject." To amend this flaw, Mou calls for a Hegelian process of self-negation of the "goodness of *Xing*-nature."

Moreover, even if the presentation of objective spirit is drastically manifest in the work of Xunzi, this is clearly *not* the kind of "objective spirit that appears along the trajectory of a constitution."[160] In other words, Xunzi's attempt to actualize *li* with regard to "rule by *li*" cannot be confused with the "rule of law" in the sense of maintaining the social and political order by means of "objective and effective law"[161] under the jurisdiction of a legitimate constitution. That is why Mou thinks that as regards Xunzi's political thinking, no restraints are set in place to prevent the king's arbitrary use of power and absolute control over decisions, and thus, that "the ordinary man is unable to become a citizen, an individuality of self-awareness."[162] That said, Xunzi's primitive disclosure of object spirit is not compatible with the moral outlook of democracy, in that it leaves the moral worth of the individual out of consideration.

On the other hand, Mou considerably agrees with Xu on the point that the main course of "governing the people" in Confucianism, far from considering *li* to be an expedient tool in establishing social order, is always steered to "rectify the hearts of men" (*zheng ren xin* 正人心)[163] in ways that may enable them to respect *li* in accordance with their own "goodness of *Xing*-nature." In short, both Mou and Xu robustly adhere to Mencius's model of a "*ren*-centered" reading of *li* when trying to recount the modern implications of the Confucian tradition of "governing the people," otherwise known as the "way of governance."

The Duality of Subjectivity

What is more, the contrast between Mencius and Xunzi also touches on a longstanding debate concerning the "origin of power" (*quan yuan* 權原),[164] or what we today refer to as the legitimacy of political authority, in Chinese political discourse. In the words of Xu, apart from the Legal School (*Fajia* 法家),

> Chinese political thought can be largely said to have advocated the "principle of the people as fundamental" (*minben zhuyi* 民本主義), that is, to consider the people to be the subjectivity of politics. But the real politics in China for several thousand years was despotism in the sense that the origin of political power actually came from the emperor, not from the people; as a result of this, the emperor became the real subjectivity of politics. . . . This duality of subjectivity constitutes an unresolvable antagonism.[165]

On this matter, it seems evident that Mencius claims that the political subjectivity of the people is superior to that of the emperor, but Xunzi's position is the other way around. Therefore, despite the fact that the characteristics of Xunzi's thought taken as a whole are related to Confucianism rather than to the Legal School, his political thinking does "contain ingredients which may resort to dictatorship."[166] Leaving Xunzi aside, a greater tradition of Confucian political thought is, in fact, directed to make the case that the real task of a virtuous emperor is not so much to increase his own talents and capabilities but to develop a different sort of "virtue-competence" (*de liang* 德量)[167] regarding "governing the people" in relation to the principle of "self-restriction."

On the whole, because traditional Confucianism is apt to build a direct connection between "inner sagehood" and "outer kingliness," a rigorous bond between morality and politics, the starting-point for "rule by *de*" lies in an motivation to show a deep "respect for humankind," a sincere "trust in humanity."[168] This, however, does not mean that Confucianism neglects the differentiation between the pursuit of "perfect teaching" (*yuanjiao* 圓教) associated with "cultivating oneself" and the growth of "governing virtue" related to "governing the people." As a matter of fact, it is Xu's central argument, strongly supported by Mou, that for both Confucianism and Daoism, "only if the emperor is 'inactive' (*wu wei* 無為) can the ministers be 'active' (*you wei* 有為), and can all-under-Heaven be 'active'; this is the true meaning of the way of governance."[169]

From this, it also follows that unlike the relationship between father and son, which is absolute and unchangeable, the relationship between the emperor and ministers is conditional upon the principle of *yi* 義 (righteousness). In political terms, what this specifies is the point that the emperor is obligated to enrich his own virtue-competence in "governing the people," that there is a sense of "mutuality" underpinning his treatment of ministers, and that "the ministers are not the private tools owned by the emperor."[170] In a like manner, whereas *xin* 信 (trustworthiness) as a personal virtue can be found in Confucius's sayings such as "Make it your principle to do your best for others and be trustworthy in what you say,"[171] *xin* as a governing virtue is closely related to the "principle of the people as fundamental." For example, when Confucius says that "when there is no trust, the common people will have nothing to stand on,"[172] he is clearly seeing *xin* as a governing virtue, rather than a personal virtue.

To round off his point, Xu cites two insightful passages from the *Book of Rites*:

> The Master said, "Under Heaven there is only a man (here and there) who loves what is proper of humanity [*ren*] without some personal object in the matter, or who hates what is contrary to humanity without being apprehensive (of some evil). Therefore the superior man reasons about the path to be trodden from the standpoint of himself, and lays down his laws from (capabilities of the) people."[173]

> The Master said, "Long has the attainment of perfect humanity [*ren*] been difficult among men; it is only the superior man who is able to reach it. Therefore, the superior man does not distress men by requiring from them that which (only) he himself can do. Hence the sage, in laying down rules for conduct, does not make himself the rule, but gives them his instructions so that they shall be able to stimulate themselves to endeavor, and have the feeling of shame if they do not put them in practice."[174]

All this indicates that while the paramount principle for "cultivating oneself" is to actualize *ren* in the fullest sense, the most celebrated ruler in respect of "governing the people" is one who is willing to "lay down his laws from (capabilities of the) people," that is, to "lay down rules for conduct" in everyday life.[175] Therefore, the reasonable standard for "governing the people," or what we today call the business of the government, is "to love what the people love, and to hate what the people hate" (*minzhisuohao haozhi, minzhisuowu wuzhi* 民之所好好之, 民之所惡惡之).[176] Accordingly, as regards the use of power, authentic Confucianism believes that the exercise of "cultivation" must abide by the principle of "self-restriction," or alternatively, the "way of *zhongshu*," which can be learned in the dictums of daily language such as "being strict with oneself and lenient toward others" (*yanyiluji kuanyidairen* 嚴以律己寬以待人).

As we shall see in the next chapter, Mou effectively agrees to Xu's distinction between "cultivating oneself" and "governing the people" mentioned above. In Mou's words, the pursuit of personal achievement in "attaining sagehood" (*chengsheng* 成聖) from the perspective of moral metaphysics, in spite of everything, must be distinguished from establishing Confucian democracy from the standpoint of political philosophy. For Mou, as for Xu, the virtuous ruler, who grows a "heart-mind of *ren*," should try his best to "step aside, spread out, and leave things as they are" (*rangkai sankai, wu gefu wu* 讓開散開，物各付物) as stated by the principle of "self-restriction," such that the ruled are capable of "attaining accomplishment" *according to their own nature*.

Democracy and the Emergence of the Political Subject

Before delving deeper into the cores of the "way of governance" embedded in Mou's writings, however, I want to stress once more that in Xu's analysis, democracy is of great importance for the further development of Confucianism as it is only by stabilizing the supremacy of the political subjectivity of the people with a constitution that the political predicament captured by the "duality of subjectivity" can be resolved once and for all. Under no circumstances, however, does Xu or Mu identify "cultivating oneself" with "governing the people," nor do they fail to differentiate the "principle of the people as fundamental" from the "political form of liberal democracy." On the contrary, their key point is rather that the moral grounding of liberal democracy in respect of legitimacy is not at odds with a common belief entrenched in Chinese culture, that is, to actualize the spirit of *ren* in the affairs of "governing the people" on the authority of "humane government."

Thus seen, as Xu famously puts it, the followers of Confucianism needn't object to liberalism. For one thing, *ren* understood as the "source of human dignity," which keeps evoking my "self-awareness" and "self-reflection" regarding what it is really meant to be a human being, is perfectly coherent with the moral ideal of liberalism.[177] Again, even if the notion of rights originates from Western culture, this gives us no sufficient reason to deny that Confucius's thinking, if properly understood, entails the version of a "free society" as well.[178] The truth is:

> While in the West the spirit of freedom first set a brisk pace in understanding, in China it did so in virtue. But the spirit of freedom, [by nature], has to extend itself to the domain of politics, to attain concrete achievements in politics, such

that it can in the end act as a lucid system which provides an unchangeable pledge for the freedom of both understanding and virtue.[179]

This is to say that there is a philosophical affinity between *ren* and freedom,[180] that the spirit of *ren* or freedom at least consists of two ways of presentation. In one sense, the *moral* presentation of *ren* involves the "learning of the heart-mind and *Xing*-nature"; in another, the *political* presentation of *ren* is simply to "treat a human being as a human" (*ba ren dang ren* 把人當人).[181] Given that the two presentations are, after all, no more than two different aspects of humanity as a whole, Xu thus arrives at the same conclusion as Mou has suggested, that a promising prospectus of Confucianism in keeping with the development of human reason is to conflate the "way of politics" related to the rise of subjective freedom with the "way of governance" grounded in the Confucian cultural tradition.[182]

To be sure, inasmuch as liberal democracy must at the same time contain the ideas of open-mindedness, mutual respect, and pluralism, there is no point in eliminating the cultural essence of Confucianism from an open society. More to the point, for the robust supporters of humanism such as the New Confucians, who appreciate to the highest degree the importance of history and culture in making sense of the meaning of human life, it is hoped that any way of life or mode of thinking that is compatible with the basic values of liberal democracy should "enjoy a right and bear a duty to be merged with" the public culture of a democratic society.[183] That said, Confucian liberalism as a form of civil liberalism, on top of appealing to a list of equal rights for the people, is committed to suggesting in a further step that the citizen, as the rights-bearer, should try to return to the "cultivation of civility" (*li de taoye* 禮的陶冶),[184] that is, to cultivate "Confucian democratic civility" in a way that may help sustain the harmonious order of a liberal society.

Unlike the civic tradition in the West, however, there did not exist such a thing as "citizen" in traditional Confucianism. And so, the Confucian public virtue represented in the "way of governance" *was* far more related to the quality of political leadership than to that of democratic citizenship. In other words, thanks to the lack of the political subject, the idea of civic virtue—the virtue of the citizen—was literally absent in ancient China.[185] For this reason, Thomas Metzger writes that "civility as the public virtue of the merely decent person is not even a word that can be translated into Chinese."[186]

In response to Metzger, it is my central argument that with the "blossoming of democracy," Mou actually suggests that the cores of the "way of government," or the elements of "humane governance," can be transformed into a set of civic virtues associated with democratic citizenship. That is to say, Mou actually comes to clarify the liberal implications of the cores of the "way of government" from two related but distinguishable viewpoints. On the one hand, seen in light of political leadership, as we shall see in chapter 6, Mou's retreatment of the Confucian political ideal in relation to the elements of "humane governance" clearly denotes a set of *Confucian governing virtues*, which, in my view, are strongly supportive of an ethical version of democracy opposed to the recent revitalization of Confucian meritocracy. On the other hand, seen in light of democratic citizenship, the dictum about "being strict with oneself and lenient toward others," or alternatively, the "way of *zhongshu*," as I shall demonstrate in chapter 7, is mainly taken to imply a set of *Confucian civic virtues*, including human dignity, equal respect, reciprocal concern, and so on.

Taken together, what I mean by "Confucian democratic civility," a Confucian conception of the common good, or simply, Confucian *res publica*, conveys the virtues of both the ruler and the citizen, which in turn are embedded in the lived forms of life characterizing Chinese civilization. As far as the formation of Confucian liberalism is concerned, my major contribution is to make the point that the cores of the "way of governance" coined by Mou are full of insights for a political theory of virtuous leadership (chapter 6), together with good citizenship (chapter 7), in a democratic society. My discussion of Confucian ethical citizenship, as might be expected, will rely on the sources of British idealism once again, whereas the self-restrained character of a virtuous leader, as I see it, is a pivotally important issue that Western democratic theorists may learn from Confucianism.

THE CONSERVATIVE ENLIGHTENMENT

I conclude this chapter by making several points. First, insofar as the subtlest model of Confucian democracy is a synthesis of the "way of politics" and the "way of governance," Mou's rebuilding of the "way of governance" can be suitably seen as an endeavor to engage in a *democratic restatement of Confucian virtues*. That said, in addition to developing a fresh version of the "way of politics" in respect of the "blossoming of democracy," an equally important but often ignored aspect of Mou's political philosophy is to reconstruct the "way of governance" in a way that involves a reevaluation of Confucian civility (both as civilization and public good) from a "*ren*-centered" standpoint, leading to what has been referred to as "Confucian democratic civility." After all, this is the reason why, instead of adopting Xunzi's *entire* identification of *li* with *gongde*, Mou's treatment of the "way of governance" is largely based on Mencius's search for "humane government," which, in his eyes, is one that truly gets hold of Confucius's "*ren*-centered" model of "rule by *de*."

Second, while at the center of the purpose of government in Mou's connotation lies the assertion on "attaining accomplishment according to the individual's nature" (*jiu geti er shuncheng* 就個體而順成) associated with an ethics of realization, as I shall clarify subsequently, by no means does Mou's Confucian liberalism stipulate that the people must be led to pursue *the* good life predetermined by government. One of the main reasons is that which underpins Mou's understanding of the "virtuous" leader points to the "capacities of the subject" (*zhuti zhi neng* 主體之能) in accordance with the principle of "self-restriction." In addition, Mou and his New Confucian companions keep arguing that "the practice of humaneness depends on oneself alone" (*weiren youji* 為仁由己).[187] Moreover, in line with the principle of "self-restriction," Mou's well-known expression of "stepping aside, spreading out" and the tenet of "being strict with oneself and lenient toward others" can be perfectly understood as ingredients of "liberal civility" or "democratic civility," such as "tolerance, patience, and self-restraint."

Third, to reject the connection between the moral spirit of Confucianism and democracy simply on the account that morality and politics are two different things is thereby misleading. On the one hand, even the so-called rights-based liberalism of Rawls and Dworkin grants that the moral basis of liberal democracy depends on the norm of civility anchored in "respect and concern." On the other hand, seen from the perspective of civil liberalism, the moral grounding of liberal democracy hinges on the civic virtue embedded in the manners of behavior and the forms of life in a given community. Accordingly, in pursuit of Confucian liberalism, my real point is not that the "politics of virtue and talent" is compatible with the "politics of democracy"; rather, my central argument is that Mou's version of Confucian liberalism is remarkably akin to civil liberalism as it is aimed at incorporating liberal democracy and its related values into a certain conception of "Confucian democratic civility" that deeply reflects the Confucian forms of life.

Finally, in spite of the differences, Collingwood's philosophical account of civility, Oakeshott's practice-based approach to individuality, and Shils's social theorization on the virtue of civility all tend to validate the Hegelian viewpoint that a genuine understanding of politics cannot be insulated from the larger parts of the concrete whole, be they objective spirit, ethical life, civilization, tradition, or the forms of life. All in all, in contrast to Westernized liberalism, central to Confucian liberalism is an analogous endeavor to relocate the moral basis of liberal democracy into the public virtue that manifests itself in the Confucian manners of behavior and forms of life. In short, far from embracing "traditionalism" in the usage of Shils, Confucian liberalism is one that aims to synthesize political progressivism of modern democracy and the cultural conservatism of Confucian civility with the hope of bringing about a "conservative enlightenment" for Chinese civilization.

Chapter 6

The Confucian Political Ideal Revisited

Introduction

In the last chapter, I demonstrated that Confucian liberalism recognized as a Hegelian form of civil liberalism is aimed at reuniting the innovated form of political democracy with the ethical content of Confucian civility, that the gist of Confucian civility in question, or more exactly, "Confucian democratic civility," is related to a set of Confucian governing and civic virtues, and that the Confucian governing and civic virtues stemming from the ideal of "humane government" (*renzheng* 仁政) can be further examined from the perspectives of leadership and citizenship. What remains unexplored, nonetheless, is the essential scope of Confucian governing and civic virtues that, in Mou's explanation, are by all accounts consistent with the essence of liberalism. Leaving *Confucian civic virtue* for the next chapter, my major task here is to flesh out the liberal features of "Confucian democratic civility" in respect of *Confucian governing virtue*.

To be sure, due to the lack of the political subject—the notion of citizenship—the Confucian political ideal in pursuit of "humane government" used to place huge emphasis on the character of the virtuous leaders; as such, it is no wonder that one of the main traits in the recent revitalization of antiliberal Confucianism lies in a bid to replace Western democracy with "Confucian meritocracy" or "political meritocracy." Counter to this, the purpose of this chapter is to give substance to Mou's synthetic approach to incorporating "humane government" into an ethical modification of liberal democracy, or so to speak, "ethical democracy," from the standpoint of Confucian governing virtue. In Mou's words, ethical democracy arises from a synthesis of the "way of politics" (*zhengdao* 政道) related to liberal democracy and the "way of governance" (*zhidao* 治道) underlining "humane government." Rather than restricting his focus to a process of selecting virtuous leaders, Mou's project has the deeper purpose of resting the basis of liberal democracy on a set of governing virtues rooted in his liberal rebuilding of "humane government." For this reason, the cores that Mou attributes to the "way of governance" are, by and large, consistent with the ethical import of democratic life from a Confucian perspective.

Seen in this light, Mou's version of ethical democracy is immediately exempt from the severe criticisms of liberal democracy and its Western-centric bias launched by the defenders of political meritocracy. In brief, while Mou also wishes to regenerate the Confucian political ideal as a means to overcome the moral weakness of liberal democracy, unlike them, Mou's ultimate aim is not so much to replace liberal democracy with political meritocracy but to assign ethical import to liberal democracy. Hence, apart from critically appreciating the merits of "humane government" as a form of meritocracy, Mou is equally concerned with its long-term political pitfalls, such as falling short of laying the solid foundation for the legitimacy of authority, lacking a sufficient account of political modernity in respect of the characteristics of a modern state, and failing to provide mechanisms (e.g., the rule of law) for avoiding the abuse of power.

In what follows, I shall first illuminate the main features of the discourse of political meritocracy. Then, I am prepared to delve into Mou's idea of ethical democracy, followed by a detailed analysis of Confucian governing virtues in terms of the legitimacy of authority, the purpose of government, and limits on the abuse of power.

Political Meritocracy

Overall, the current revitalization of political meritocracy can be seen as a part of the movement of antiliberal Confucianism appearing in China. This is not to say that all of those who attempt to revive Confucian meritocratic thinking reject liberal values in a complete sense. On the contrary, most of them are driven to hybridize democracy with meritocracy so as to offer their own versions of Confucianism-based political proposal, and surely, not each of them stands up for an authoritarian state unreservedly. However, contrasted with Mou's Confucian liberalism, antiliberal Confucians declare at large that the *full* acceptance of democracy and liberal values is unrealistic on the failure of liberal democracy and the political problems confronting China, unauthentic toward the political tradition of Confucianism, and uncritical of Western-centrism. For the sake of concentration, let me here take the works of Daniel A. Bell and Jiang Qing (蔣慶) as examples.[1]

THE CHINA MODEL

Early in his career, Bell delivered a strong devotion to communitarianism,[2] arguing that even if the basic political and legal institutions have been fairly established in a society, this does not necessarily mean that the true freedom of individuals can then be fully actualized. According to Hegel, the upshot is that

> *the many* as single individuals—and this is a favorite interpretation of [the term] "the people"—do indeed live *together*, but only as a *crowd*, i.e., a formless mass whose movement and activity can consequently only be elemental, irrational, barbarous, and terrifying. . . . [For] its basis is then merely the abstract individuality of arbitrary will and opinion, and is thus grounded only on contingency rather than a foundation which is *stable* and *legitimate* in and for itself.[3]

On this reading, as Bell continues, Hegel's saying that "individuals come to take an interest in common enterprise and to develop a certain degree of political competence only by joining and participating in voluntary associations and community groups"[4] actually anticipates Tocqueville's emphasis on the significance of civil society in fostering civic virtue. Following Hegel, it thus seems plain that the pursuit of a collective good life, at the end of the day, rests on our joint concern for a common good. All in all, Bell greatly agrees with his teacher, Charles Taylor, on the key point that "Hegel may not have been a democrat in the sense of favoring universal suffrage, but he was still a kind of liberal, concerned with articulating the social framework within which freedom can be realized."[5]

Reflecting the main theme of this book, Bell obviously shares with Mou a profound anxiety about the moral weakness of liberal democracy. Their responses to the pitfalls of liberal democracy, however, are poles apart. As we shall see shortly, based on the twofold meaning of democracy, that is, the political and the moral, Mou makes it clear that the political meaning of democracy, that is, the "objective form" of democracy, is definitely *universal*, whereas the vital role that Confucianism can play in an open society is to reinforce the "moral foundation" of democracy from a Confucian standpoint. That said, insofar as democracy is taken as a legitimate way of running the government and arranging political power in terms of constitutionalism, the rule of law, and the like, it is absurd to insist on "democracy with cultural particularity."[6] Quite the reverse, what really concerns Bell is the cry for institutional design in quest of "democracy with Chinese characteristics."[7]

Therefore, facing an irresolvable crisis of governance in Western democracies, Bell in his recent work *The China Model* sets forth a mixed regime called "democratic meritocracy" in respect of three key features: "democracy at the bottom, experimentation in the middle, and meritocracy at the top."[8] For Bell, this model is not only an "ideal unique to China," but also an alternative to liberal democracy, in that "Chinese-style political meritocracy can be viewed as a grand political experiment with the potential to remedy key defeats of electoral democracy" with the "one person, one vote" principle.[9]

Overall, it is Bell's core argument that the endorsement of meritocracy in Confucianism can provide a decisive solution to the issues associated with competitive election, which, "instead of allowing for the flourishing of human goodness that underpins social harmony, almost counters human nature" and exacerbates social conflict. In Bell's analysis, political meritocracy in favor of a "government of the best and brightest"[10] is an answer, mainly because it by definition means that "political power should be distributed in accordance with *ability* and *virtue*" and that the business of the government is by all means "for the people."[11] Moreover, by excluding irrational voters, short-term policies, and greedy politicians from democratic elections, the political leaders in China seem to have led the country to success in economic growth.[12] What is more, a combination of limited democracy and virtuous leaders resonates with the political ideal of harmony in Confucianism as well.[13]

POLITICAL CONFUCIANISM

Speaking of the Confucian political ideal, the name Jiang Qing is now an institution. In the words of Bell, Jiang "has written the most systematic and detailed defense of political Confucianism since the establishment of the People's Republic of China."[14] More precisely, along with the distinction between "spiritual Confucianism" or "heart-mind Confucianism" (*xinxing Ruxue* 心性儒學) and "political Confucianism" (*zhengzhi Ruxue* 政治儒學), Jiang in his earlier writings pressed charges against Mou's political insensibility and his adoption of a "Western standard as the orientation for the development of Chinese culture."[15] By way of contrast, central to Jiang's writings as a whole is a bid to restore and boost "Chineseness" (*Zhongguoxing* 中國性). As such, far from following the comprehensive theory of "moral religion" established by Mou through the lens of Kant and Hegel, Jiang is keen to rebuild a state-supported "Confucian religion."

In Jiang's view, the key text that sets the tone for political Confucianism is the *Gongyang* commentary of the *Spring and Autumn Annals* (*Chunqiu Gongyang Zhuan* 春秋公羊傳),[16] aiming to actualize the "spirit of ritual and music" (*liyue jingshen* 禮樂精神), the "ideal of the kingly way" (*wangdao lixiang* 王道理想),[17] the "wisdom of great unification" (*da yitong zhihui* 大一統智慧), a "historical development in three phases" (*san shi xueshuo* 三世學說), and the "son of Heaven at the top rung" (*tianzi yi jue* 天子一爵).[18] Against this context, Jiang has more recently set out to design an ideal Confucian constitution in favor of a tricameral legislature,[19] posing strong objections to democracy as well.

More to the point, in line with Bell and others, Jiang also criticizes the atomistic individualism underscoring mainstream liberalism and maintains that the individual and community are not separable. Furthermore, he attacks democracy as a "secular form of politics," which disregards the "sacred values of political life," such as "the wellbeing of the environment, the welfare of future generations, and humanity as a whole,"[20] resulting from the liberal divorce of morality and politics. In short, liberal democracy is concerned with a "matter of head counting, having no regard for morality."[21]

Thus seen, despite the fact that Jiang and Mou are both aware of the shortcomings of liberal democracy in respect of atomistic individualism, they have emphatically different arguments on the Confucian political ideal, especially on the moral character of the ruler. In a nutshell, while Mou and his companions pay serious attention to the principle of "self-restriction" (*ziwoxianzhi* 自我限制) underpinning "humane government," Jiang, together with Bell, is more likely to advance the tenet of "elitism" through advocating an efficient and competent government. Or alternatively, for the New Confucians, democracy is indispensable for the future development of Confucianism because "if inner morality cannot be objectified to the outer world," to quote Xu Fuguan [Hsu Fu-Kuan] (徐復觀 1904–1982), then "there is no genuine practice" of humanity in the full sense.[22] As regards political Confucianism, the Confucian political ideal can be reached independently of its moral commitment grounded in the "heart-mind of ren" (renxin 仁心), in that the utmost goal of government is to sustain a harmonious order.

Cultural Relativism

It has been indicated that Mou's "spiritual Confucianism" is based on a "rooted global philosophy" of ren 仁 (humaneness), which, in turn, involves a philosophical task of participating in the enterprise of cross-cultural dialogue. Yet, it is evident from the above discussion that both Jiang's retrieval of political Confucianism and Bell's advocacy of the China model hinge on a belief in an anti-Western-centric position and cultural particularity, even though Bell is more enthusiastic than Jiang about the feasibility of merging liberal values with Confucian meritocracy. At this junction, it is interesting to note that a similar contrast also exists between Chen Ming (陳明) and Kang Xiaoguang (康曉光), the other two leading thinkers associated with political Confucianism.

Unlike Jiang's state-supported "Confucian religion,"[23] to begin with, Chen's Rousseau-inspired version of "civil religion" remains liberal to a certain degree.[24] In brief, Chen takes as point of departure the view that in the modern state the public spirit and the religious spirit, as Rousseau urges, are inseparable. Therefore, apart from treating Confucianism as something like "everyday ethics" in the private sphere,[25] what is truly important in the public sphere, in Chen's view, is to rebuild Confucianism as a form of "civil religion" so as (1) to rearrange the legitimacy of political authority in a way that may take seriously national interest and the duty of humankind; (2) to stimulate social organisms in a way that may settle the quandaries of atomistic individualism; and (3) to nurture the sense of cultural belonging in a way that may fix the fracture of historical narratives and refurbish cultural characteristics.[26] In short, rather than denying liberal values wholeheartedly, Chen's "civil religion" looks for a Confucianism-inspired common good supportive of what he calls "constitutional republicanism."[27]

On the other hand, Kang takes an extremely radical type of cultural relativism by claiming that "China should reject democratization, because this is a choice that will 'wreck the country and bring calamity to the people' (*huoguo yangmin* 禍國殃民)";²⁸ as an alternative, the political plan that Kang comes up with is the prospect of a "cooperative state."²⁹ In a recent work edited by two younger antiliberal Confucians, it is further held that China should try to set up its own agenda for universal values as opposed to Western hegemony.³⁰ One of the editors even depicts Western culture as a "turtledove taking over the nest of a magpie" (*jiu zhan que chao* 鳩佔鵲巢), meaning that the pursuit of democracy and freedom has for so long occupied the central place belonging to Chinese culture that it is time now for the Confucians to "eliminate the heresy."³¹

Ethical Democracy

In contrast to political meritocracy, I now turn to examine Mou's establishment of Confucian democracy as a form of ethical democracy.

CONSTRUCTIVE REASON AND FUNCTIONAL REASON

Without repeating Mou's Hegelian presentation of Confucian democracy with regard to the questions of "why Confucianism did not develop democracy" and "how to develop democracy out of Confucianism," we only need to bear in mind that for Mou, the "subtlest model of Confucian democracy" can only be actualized when Confucian "functional reason" (moral reasoning) and democratic "constructive reason" (political reasoning) are reconnected in a rather indirect and limited way.

Put in other terms, while Confucianism is short of an appreciation of the "constructive presentation of reason" (*lixing zhi jiagou biaoxian* 理性之架構表現) in favor of the "way of politics" upon which democracy rests, it is excellent at exerting the "functional presentation of reason" (*lixing zhi yunyong biaoxian* 理性之運用表現) in favor of the "way of governance," the political ideal of "humane government," which, through practices, has kept embodying the spirit of *ren* in the Confucian forms of life.³² In view of the fact that there is nothing morally wrong with "humane government" per se and that democracy is critical only because it is through this venue that the Confucian political ideal can be truly realized in the end, by no means does Mou intend to replace "humane government" *entirely* with liberal democracy.

Quite the opposite, it should be remembered that central to Mou's theorization of Confucian democracy is a bid to make real "humane government" in a democratic age by harmonizing the two presentations of reason. Contrary to the sharp divorce between politics and morality that antiliberal Confucianism (as well as anti-Confucian liberalism) takes liberal democracy to be, the consequence of Mou's democratic theory is a Hegelian appreciation of the dialectical relationship between politics and morality, aiming to iron out the longstanding view about the incompatibility between democratic politics and "humane government."

The Way of Politics and the Way of Governance

To understand this key argument in a fuller sense, we may draw further attention to the discrepancy between the "way of politics" and the "way of governance." In a nutshell, the "way of politics" stands for the source and transmission of the "legal limits" (as opposed to moral or prudential limits) on the transfer and acquisition of "political power" (*zhengquan* 政權);[33] that said, the "way of politics" is largely concerned with the *objectification* of the legitimacy of political authority in respect of the ideas of sovereignty, constitutionalism, democracy, and so forth. In contrast, the "way of governance" basically has to do with the employment of "governing power" (*zhiquan* 治權) in running the government; thus seen, what lies at the center of the "way of governance" is the recurrent question of how to go about governing in a kingly way.

What is important in the present context is that a vital facet of liberal democracy is to tell the "way of politics" apart from the "way of governance." That is to say, one of the significant consequences of democratic practice in the West is to establish a formal concept (*xingshi gainian* 形式概念) of the "way of politics," which is still obscure and shadowy in the traditions such as Confucianism saliently featuring the "way of governance." In Mou's view, this explains once again why Confucian political thinking has for a long time been captured by the meritocratic search for "sagely rulers and worthy ministers" (*shengjun xianxiang* 聖君賢相),[34] which, in the real world, has been unfortunately enveloped in the mist and clouds of "personal rulership" (*jia tianxia* 家天下).[35] As a result, we are not surprised that the transfer of political power in imperial China was accomplished by conquest or hereditary succession, in preference to democratic election. In short, the failure of Confucianism in developing democracy is predicated on the fact that it falls short of developing a formal concept of the "way of politics," in terms of which the legitimacy of political authority can be properly institutionalized.

All this, however, does not mean that the "way of politics" is superior to the "way of governance," nor does it imply that liberal democracy is morally impeccable. On the contrary, Mou signifies that both the "way of governance" and the "way of politics" are equally *insufficient* in the sense that each of them only presents a *partial* understanding of democracy, and thus, that to overcome the *political failure* of the "way of governance" and the *moral weakness* of the "way of politics," these two concepts must be reunited in the end. Indeed, Mou's search for the subtlest model of Confucian democracy consists of a Hegelian endeavor to fuse the horizon of Confucian ethics with that of liberal democracy.

POLITICAL DEMOCRACY AND GOVERNING DEMOCRACY

The "way of politics" and the "way of governance" actually represent two different meanings of democracy: the political and the ethical. On the one hand, what is related to the "way of politics" supported by "extensional reason" can be called the "extensional meaning of democracy" (*minzhu zhi waiyan de yiyi* 民主之外延的意義), characterized by sovereignty, constitutionalism, the rule of law, freedom, equality, rights, and so on. On the other hand, what is central to the "way of governance" fostered by "intensional reason" can be referred to as the "intensional meaning of democracy" (*minzhu zhi neirong de yiyi* 民主之內容的意義). From time to time, Mou also defines the former as "political democracy" (*zhengquan de minzhu* 政權的民主) and the latter as "governing democracy" (*zhiquan de minzhu* 治權的民主).[36]

In this respect, as Mou explains, even if Confucianism falls short of providing a proper appreciation of "political democracy," its contributions to "governing democracy" cannot be overlooked. The upshot here is that echoing Hegel's revision of Kant that sees freedom not as a postulate, but as what is actually realized in a rational system of institutions, not only are the mottos and dictums that Mou reattributes to "humane government" consistent with the ends of democracy (which, as we shall see, can be recognized as being advantageous to "attaining accomplishment"), but also, and equally importantly, they are embedded in the Confucian forms of life. Moreover, Mou's discussion of "humane government," as indicated, largely reflects the distinction between "cultivating oneself" (*xiuji* 修己) and "governing the people" (*zhiren* 治人) that Xu Fuguan has famously made, literally meaning that even in classical Confucianism, "public" virtue is not completely identical with "moral" virtue as a whole.

For the most part, Mou's renewal of "humane government" at least embraces three basic principles, which, taken together, lay the moral basis for liberal democracy. In order to spell out the idea of Confucian public virtue in a fuller sense, let me here lay out these three categories as follows: First, as regards *the legitimacy of authority*, Confucianism adopts the principle of "obtaining all-under-Heaven by virtue" (*yi de qutianxia* 以德取天下), or in a stricter sense, "public rulership" (*gong tianxia* 公天下), which, for instance, emblematizes an appeal of what Mencius has referred to as "government for the people" or "the people as fundamental" (*minben* 民本).

Second, as regards *the purpose of government*, Confucianism asserts the principle of "ruling all-under-Heaven by virtue" (*yi de zhitianxia* 以德治天下), that is, "rule by virtue" (*dezhi* 德治).[37] In Mou's renovated rebuilding, however, the stress is largely placed on the "direction of the people's hearts" (*minxin suoxiang* 民心所向), the tenet of "stepping aside, spreading out, and leaving things as they are" (*rangkai sankai, wu gefu wu* 讓開散開, 物各付物), the endeavor to "attain accomplishment according to the individual's nature" (*jiu geti er shuncheng* 就個體而順成), and the like.

Third, as regards *the use of power*, authentic Confucianism firmly believes that the exercise of "cultivation" (*jiaohua* 教化) must abide by the principle of "self-restriction," or alternatively, the "way of *zhongshu*" (*zhongshu zhi dao* 忠恕之道), which can be learned in the dictums of daily language such as "being strict with oneself and lenient toward others" (*yanyiluji kuanyidairen* 嚴以律己寬以待人). In a nutshell, while "being strict with oneself" implies "looking into yourself" (*fanqiu zhuji* 反求諸己), "being lenient towards others" contains, among other things, the aim of "making the people wealthy before cultivation" (*xianfu houjiao* 先富後教).

In what follows, I plan to demonstrate an *archetype* of Confucian public virtue by examining these three categories in order. In so doing, we shall be in a better position to make clearer how and in what sense Mou's version of ethical democracy is not only free from the accusations against liberal democracy raised by Bell and Jiang, but also likely to reveal the insufficiency of political meritocracy.

The Legitimacy of Authority: The People as Fundamental

In theoretical terms, what sets the tone for the transmission of political power in the authentic tradition of Confucianism initiated by Confucius and Mencius is the ideal of "obtaining all-under-Heaven by virtue." Here, "all-under-Heaven" literally means rulership, the empire, the kingdom, or the community of all the people.

Public Rulership

Historically speaking, this ideal was made known by the legendary story about Yao (堯) giving the throne to Shun (舜) and Shun giving it to Yu (禹). As Mou quotes the *Mencius* (*Mengzi* 孟子) in explaining,[38] the abdication (*shanrang* 禪讓) of Yao and Shun can be understood as proposing a pattern of "Heaven conferring, people conferring" (*tianyu renyu* 天與人與).[39] It is true that when the disposal of the throne came to Yu, he did not pass it on to Yi (益), but to his son Qi (啟). According to Mencius, nonetheless, it was still justifiable to say that this was the choice of the people given that Yu had "the people enjoy the bounty for a long time" and that "Qi was good and capable, and able to follow in the footsteps of Yu."[40] Thus,

> Mencius said, "A common man who comes to possess the Empire must have not only virtue of a Shun or a Yu but also the recommendation of an Emperor. That is why Confucius never possessed the Empire. On the other hand, he who inherits the Empire is only put aside by Heaven if he is like Jie (桀) or Zhou (紂). That is why Yi, Yi Yin (伊尹) and the Duke of Zhou (*Zhou Gong* 周公) never came to possess the Empire."[41]

Against this context, as Mou argues, the righteous way to transfer political power is to "present" (*tuijian* 推薦) the candidate to the people and let them make their "choice" and "selection" (*puxuan* 普選) by coming into contact with "his personal conduct and conduct of affairs." In short, the pattern of "Heaven conferring, people conferring" is patently expressed in this motto: "Heaven sees with the eyes of its people. Heaven hears with the ears of its people" (*tianshi ziwominshi, tianting ziwominting* 天視自我民視, 天聽自我民聽). In its original meaning, the principle of "obtaining all-under-Heaven by virtue" therefore connotes that the virtuous leader should rule the empire in accordance with the splendid ideal of "public rulership," alleging that all-under-Heaven is equally shared by all.[42]

The Grand Union and the Small Tranquility

By no means, however, does Mou intend to suggest that this motto is identical with democracy; again and again, his point is that without advancing a formal concept of the "way of politics," this way of thinking has never become a real thing in Chinese history. Undeniably, after the Three Dynasties of Xia (夏) (founded by Qi), Yin (殷) [or Shang (商)], and Zhou (周), the ideal of "public rulership" was entirely replaced by the routine of "personal rulership." Consider the following statements made by Huang Zongxi [Huang Tsung-Hsi] (黃宗羲 1610–1695):

> In ancient times all-under-Heaven were considered the master, and the prince was the tenet. The prince spent his whole life working for all-under-Heaven. Now the prince is master, and all-under-Heaven are tenets.[43]

> The "Law of the Three Dynasties" safeguarded the world for the sake of all-under-Heaven. . . . The laws of later times have "safeguarded the world as if it were something in the [prince's] treasure-chest."[44]

In an important sense, then, the cardinal notion of the "kingly way" (*wangdao* 王道) in Confucianism refers to the Three Dynasties.[45] For example,

> The Master said, "Whom have I ever praised or condemned? If there is anyone I praised, you may be sure that he had been put to the test. These common people are the touchstone by which the Three Dynasties were kept to the straight path."[46]

Inasmuch as there are different levels of political ideal, however, there appears to be a major difference between the abdication exercised by Yao and Shun and the hereditary system established in the Three Dynasties. For, according to the *Book of Rites* (*Liji* 禮記), Confucius otherwise makes a clear distinction between the Grand Union (*Datong* 大同) and the Small Tranquility (*Xiaokang* 小康) accessible to the Three Dynasties, in which what the "eminent men" had achieved was the "kingly way of Small Tranquility" (*Xiaokang zhi wangdao* 小康之王道).[47]

In any case, it is hardly surprising that the original Confucian ideal of "public rulership" entails a crucial aspect of "governing democracy." The thing, however, is that starting from Confucius and Mencius, through the Song-Ming Neo-Confucians, to the eminent scholars in the late Ming dynasty, including Huang Zongxi, Gu Yanwu [Ku Yen-Wu] (顧炎武

1613–1682), and Wang Fuzhi [Wang Fu-Chih] (王夫之 1619–1692), the "extensional meaning of democracy" stays opaque by different degrees, largely due to the absence of "constructive reason." At the end of the day, the spirit of seeking "political achievement" (*shigong jingshen* 事功精神) in relation to the "way of politics" has never been on a par with that of attaining "moral achievement" in relation to the "way of governance."

THE KINGLY WAY AND THE HEGEMONIC WAY

Before moving on to the next section, nevertheless, there is one more thing about the acquisition of political power that requires discussing. As is well known, Confucius lived during the Spring and Autumn Period (*Chunqiu* 春秋 770–476 BC), in which "rites and music (*li yue* 禮樂) were in ruins,"[48] meaning that society was in disarray. Mencius was born in the Warring States Period (*Zhanguo* 戰國 475–221 BC), a time of chaos caused by various states battling against one another. In other words, the historical context in which Confucius and Mencius worked was one in which the "kingly way of Small Tranquility" had collapsed and the "eminent men of the Three Dynasties" had gone. And so, the main task of both great thinkers was to "rebuild the order."

To this end, a criterion was established to make a further distinction between the kingly way and the hegemonic way.[49] Referring to what has been said earlier, there are accordingly three levels of political order in Confucianism. The highest one is the Grand Union envisaged by the legendary emperors (*di* 帝) such as Yao and Shun; the middle layer is the "kingly way of Small Tranquility" pursued by the virtuous kings (*wang* 王) full of talents and merits, including Yu, Tang (湯), King Wen (*Wenwang* 文王), King Wu (*Wuwang* 武王), and so on; and the lowest case is the hegemonic way under the control of the depraved tyrants (*ba* 霸)[50] such as Jie and Zhou.[51]

While it is against this context that Mencius offers his assessment of rebellion by saying, "I have indeed heard of the punishment of the 'outcast Zhou,' but I have not heard of any regicide,"[52] Mou makes it quite clear that this is not meant to imply the notion of popular sovereignty. Insofar as "political democracy" is closely related to the "way of politics," the significance of this dictum falls into the domain of the "way of governance" or "governing democracy," emblematizing an appeal of what Mencius has famously referred to as "government for the people" or "the people as fundamental."[53] It is true that for Mou, that which is needed to effectively cope with the problem of the legitimacy of authority is "political democracy," not "government for the people." From the standpoint I have been taking, nonetheless, a reconsideration of the purpose of government in relation to "rule by virtue" will help us to a great extent to appreciate the meaning of democracy from an *ethical* viewpoint.

The Purpose of Government: Rule by Virtue Reconsidered

Echoing the tenet of "the people as fundamental," Mou maintains that "rule by virtue" in Confucianism actually entails the deepest respect for "individual life in existence" (*cunzai de shengming geti* 存在的生命個體);[54] in other words, the value of individuality, rather than the interest of the ruler, is the benchmark on which the "kingly way of virtuous rule" (*dezhi zhi wangdao* 德治之王道) is based.[55] To this end, "rule by virtue" is anchored in the principle of "stepping aside exhaustively" (*quanfu rangkai* 全幅讓開) with an attempt to let the individual be able to fulfill the meaning of life according to his own nature.[56] Seen in this light, as stated, what is essential to "rule by virtue" is not so much a process of selecting talented leaders but the duties that a *virtuous* leader should impose upon himself when exercising the art of governing and cultivation. In other words, Mou grants that there exists a significant distinction between "cultivating oneself" as a moral person and "governing the people" in a way that enables every individual to "attain accomplishment" according to his own nature. In the discussion that follows, let me try to elaborate on the insights of "governing democracy" rooted in this vital instruction in terms of three codes: (1) the "direction of the people's hearts"; (2) the tenet of "stepping aside, spreading out, and leaving things as they are"; and (3) the endeavor to "attain accomplishment according to the individual's nature," namely, to attain "*self*-accomplishment" or to fulfill "*self*-realization."

The Direction of the People's Hearts

"Rule by virtue" is, first and foremost, an art of governing that is concerned with the "direction of the people's hearts." Concretely speaking, this is to suggest that the will of the subjective party (the king) should obey that of the objective party (the people) (*zhuguan fucong keguan* 主

觀服從客觀).⁵⁷ To make his case, Mou first draws attention to Mencius's saying that the virtuous ruler should be full of "sympathy of joy and sorrow" for the people;⁵⁸ in other words, as Mencius remarks, the virtuous ruler need not abstain from the pleasures of wealth and beauty, as long as he can "share this fondness with the people."⁵⁹

The stress on the "direction of the people's hearts" also can be found in the *Great Learning* (*Daxue* 大學), which states that a celebrated ruler of virtue is one who "loves what the people love, and hates what the people hate" (*minzhisuohao haozhi, minzhisuowu wuzhi* 民之所好好之, 民之所惡惡之). Moreover, the *Doctrine of the Mean* (*Zhongyong* 中庸) asserts that "the superior man governs men, according to their nature, with what is proper to them" (*yiren zhiren* 以人治人). In short, "rule by virtue" is an ideal for running the government as it enables every individual to "fit his own nature" (*ge shi qi xing* 各適其性) and to "fulfill his own life" (*ge sui qi sheng* 各遂其生).⁶⁰

STEP ASIDE, SPREAD OUT, AND LEAVE THINGS AS THEY ARE

To make this goal happen, the ruler must have the "heart-mind of *ren*." In principle, this means that the honorable ruler should "step aside, spread out, and leave things as they are," such that various individuals are capable of "attaining accomplishment" according to their own nature. And here, it is obvious that the worthiest rulers, who follow the spirit of *ren* to make real this core in running the government, are Yao and Shun. To quote the *Analects* (*Lunyu* 論語),

> The Master said, "Great indeed was Yao as a ruler! How lofty! It is Heaven that is great and it was Yao who modelled himself upon it. He was so boundless that the common people were not able to put a name to his virtues. Lofty was he in his successes and brilliant was he in his accomplishment!"⁶¹

> The Master said, "If there was a ruler who achieved order without taking any action, it was, perhaps, Shun. There was nothing for him to do but to hold himself in a respectful posture and to face due south."⁶²

At bottom, the real benefit driven from the core of "stepping aside, spreading out" is to restore a harmonious social order, capturing the concreteness of the "human relations" (*renlun guanxi* 人倫關係) that already exist in a community: "to bring peace to the old, to have trust in my friends, and to cherish the young."[63] In other words, the gist of the tenet at stake is to prevent the ruler from twisting the order of things and distorting human nature at his disposal in accordance with the spirit of "self-restriction" or "self-constraining." To borrow the term from the famous Song Confucian Cheng Yichuan [Cheng I-Chuan] (程伊川 1033–1107), Mou thus infers that the tenet of "stepping aside, spreading out" is just another expression of "leaving things as they are."[64]

Here, it should be noted that while "leaving things as they are" denotes a sense of "inaction" (*wuwei* 無為), this is not meant to say that the ruler should care nothing about the public affairs of the people. Rather, it suggests that instead of "using what he loves and hates as the criterion in governing the people," the virtuous leader should try his best to "help and inspire the people to manage their own matters,"[65] that is, to lead a good life in their own way.

Attain Accomplishment According to the Individual's Nature

From this, it follows that enabling the people to "attain accomplishment according to the individual's nature" is *the deepest moral appeal* of "rule by virtue." There are, accordingly, three crucial points that can be made as follows. First of all, for Mou, as for other leading new Confucians, since the moral spirituality of Confucianism consists in an ethics of self-realization leading to an "endless pursuit of self-perfection," i.e., "attaining sagehood" (*chengsheng* 成聖), the ultimate purpose of "rule by virtue" is to make happen *the moral appeal of self-realization and self-accomplishment*. To quote Xu Fuguan once again,

> In Confucianism, every individual is considered to be an existence of personality (*renge de cunzai* 人格的存在); as such, Confucianism shows considerable respect to the achievement of every individual's personality. As regards the purpose of politics, this is to say that [the ruler] has to assist [the people] in attaining the achievement of personalities, making every individual capable of performing like a gentleman, with the purpose of initiating a world of humanism.[66]

Furthermore, here as elsewhere in this study, I use the term "*self*-realization" or "*self*-accomplishment" because Confucianism, in actuality, puts the accent on the value of the individual. It is true that the manner of looking up to individuality (human dignity, freedom, equality, and so on) in Confucianism is saliently different from the way in which the mainstream theory of "political democracy" deals with it. However, for this reason, in contrast to the so-called abstract individualism or atomistic individualism under attack by antiliberal Confucians, Mou deliberatively claims that Confucianism has arrived at a "pinnacle of individualism,"[67] akin to what has previously been referred to as embodied individualism or personalism. In short, as Mou lucidly puts it, the real meaning of individualism "is to lay emphasis on the individual, not to place the individual before everything"[68] because the authentic meaning of human life that the individual is after can never be separated from "the concrete existence of the life relation and the social relation."[69]

What is more, according to the moral appeal of self-accomplishment, we are not far away from another of Mencius's famous mottos: "The people are of supreme importance; the altars to the gods of earth and grain come next; last comes the ruler."[70] Considering Mou's distinction between the two different meanings of democracy, Mencius's viewpoint of "the people as fundamental" is surely not equivalent to "political democracy." What is vital in the present context, however, is that in Mou's mind the expression of "the people as fundamental" deeply rooted in the ethics of self-realization is not incompatible with "political democracy" either. At the end of the day, it is to Mou's credit that he aims to rest the moral basis of democratic politics on the common Confucian beliefs such as "the people as fundamental," purporting to deem "attaining self-accomplishment" or "fulfilling self-realization" a common good.

One serious problem arises. How, then, is it possible to relate ethical democracy further to a theory of the common good without resulting in social domination and exploitation by the state? Before delving deeper into this crucial issue from the perspective of *civic virtue* in the next chapter, here I just want to say something more about the features of *governing virtue* in Mou's "liberal" treatment of the task of "cultivating the people" for a virtuous leader. In contrast to political meritocracy, central to Mou's project is an attempt to rebuild a set of governing virtues apt to obligate the virtuous ruler to abstain from abusing power. The caution about the proper use of power, as might be expected, is after all associated with the principle of "self-restriction," in keeping with the principle of "stepping aside exhaustively" under discussion.

The Limits on the Abuse of Power: Cultivation and Its Limitation

Put succinctly, the purpose of cultivation[71] is to improve a man by leading him to be a "being of humanity" (*rendao de cunzai* 人道的存在),[72] capable of conducting a morally worthy life within human relations. To do justice to Confucianism, however, Mou contends that Confucian thinkers always bear in mind the spirit of "self-restriction" when dealing with cultivation. That said, Mou draws his attention not merely to cultivation, but also, and more importantly, to its limits.

Being Strict with Oneself

For the most part, the principle of "self-restriction" can be found in the dictums of daily language such as "being strict with oneself and lenient toward others." Let me first account for the first part of this dictum.

Along with the "heart-mind of *ren*," it seems to be the case that Confucianism regards the "capability of the subject" (*zhuti zhi neng* 主體之能)[73] as the most important agency in "attaining sagehood" as well as in going about governing. This, of course, does not mean that the virtuous leader should "force" or "compel" the people to become moral persons; rather, it simply says that the truly virtuous manner of "governing the people" consistent with the spirit of *ren* is to "be strict with oneself" in such a way that the people are inspired and enlightened by nothing more than his honorable conduct. There are a number of texts in the *Analects* that exhort leaders to adopt this way of thinking:

> The Master said, "The rule of virtue can be compared to the Pole Star which commands the homage of the multitude of stars without leaving its place."[74]

> Ji Kang Zi [Chi Kang Tzu] (季康子) asked Confucius about government. Confucius answered, "to govern is to correct.

If you set an example by being correct, who would dare to remain incorrect?"[75]

The Master said, "If a man is correct in his own person, then there will be obedience without orders being given; but if he is not correct in his own person, there will not be obedience even though orders are given."[76]

Ji Kang Zi asked Confucius about government, . . . Confucius answered, "In administering your government, what need is there for you to kill? Just desire the good yourself and the common people will be good. The virtue of the gentleman is like wind; the virtue of the small man is like grass. Let the wind blow over the grass and it is sure to bend."[77]

Why does Confucius think about cultivation this way? The reason is that he firmly believes that one's moral accomplishment can only be attained through personal efforts. To be sure, at the center of the ethics of self-realization, namely, the moral appeal of "attaining accomplishment according to the individual's nature," is a kind of "moral autonomy" that Mencius refers to as "looking into yourself":

Mencius said, "If others do not respond to your love with love, look into your own benevolence; if others fail to respond to your attempts to govern them with order, look into your own wisdom; if others do not return your courtesy, look into your own respect. In other words, look into yourself whenever you fail to achieve your purpose. When you are correct in your person, the Empire will return to you. The Book of Odes (Shi Jing 詩經) says,

> Long may he be worthy of Heaven's Mandate,
> And seek for himself much good fortune."[78]

In short, one cannot put somebody on the right path by force as morality, after all, is a matter concerning innate moral awareness.[79]

Furthermore, as Mencius elaborates, the spirit of ren is everlasting, whereas might and self-interest are temporary. Seen in this light, the difference between the kingly way and the hegemonic way is that while in the latter case the people may be "happy" for a time, in the former situation they are "expansive and content."[80]

The problem, however, is that because of this fashion of thinking, Confucianism is apt to neglect the importance of institutions and regulations in protecting the "political rights" of the people. In a sense, this is the backdrop against which the *Analects* points out:

> The Master said, "Guide them by edicts, keep them in line with punishments, and the common people will stay out of trouble but will have no sense of shame. Guide them by virtue, keep them in line with the rites, and they will, besides having a sense of shame, reform themselves."[81]

As a result of this, the huge responsibility for running the government falls on nobody save the virtuous ruler. As Mencius remarks:

> A gentleman transforms where he passes, and works wonders where he abides. He is in the same stream as Heaven above and Earth below. Can he be said to bring but small benefit?[82]

Elsewhere Mencius writes: "Goodness alone is not sufficient for government; the law unaided cannot make itself effective."[83] According to Mou, what Mencius means by "the law" here is not the positive law but the principle of "rule by virtue." And consequently, what is needed to make the government effective at spreading goodness throughout "all-under-Heaven" is cultivation of the people by the personal conduct of the virtuous ruler. Or alternatively, as the *Doctrine of the Mean* says, "with the right men growth of government is rapid, just as vegetation is rapid in the earth" (*rendao minzheng, didao minshu* 人道敏政, 地道敏樹).[84]

Being Lenient toward Others

Overall, the second part of the dictum known as "being lenient toward others" designates the relationship between the self and others in terms of reciprocity, mutual help, a sense of sharing, and the like, which, as we shall see, plays an essential part in shaping the characteristics of Confucian civic virtue. Here, focusing on Confucian governing virtue, it seems to imply, for instance, an instruction to run the government with the aim of "making the people wealthy before cultivation." In keeping with Mou's expression of "individual life in existence," Xu Fuguan takes it that for Confucius and Mencius, "the political value of governing the people is, first and foremost, ascribed to the needs of people's natural life,"[85] that is, the wealth and interest of every individual's ordinary life.

Put in other terms, there are three things that have been described in both the *Book of History* (*Shang Shu* 尚書) and the *Spring and Autumn Annals* (*Chunqiu* 春秋) as the kernels of "rule by virtue," namely, the "rectification of the people's virtue" (*zhengde* 正德), the "conveniences of life" (*liyong* 利用), and the "securing abundant means of sustenance" (*housheng* 厚生). And here, it seems plain that while the first item restates the gist of cultivation, the other two suggest that deprived of material well-being, the people would be in a difficult position to carry out their own moral mission.

MORALITY AND POLITICS RECONSIDERED

Based on what has been said thus far, it would then be misleading to remark that Confucianism completely blurs the distinction between morality and politics. The truth is rather that Confucianism, as Mou maintains, sorts out this crucial problem in ways that are dissimilar to the "standard viewpoint." Considering the goal of this chapter, it seems appropriate to round off the argument concerning the *specific* relationship between morality and politics in Mou's reconstruction of the Confucian political ideal by making three further points.

First, in consort with the principle of "self-restriction," the cores of "stepping aside, spreading out, leaving things as they are," and "being strict with oneself and lenient toward others" are taken by Mou as permanent political principles, keeping a tight rein on the abuse of power. As Mou puts it, "this 'cannot' is a matter of principle, that is, a limitation intrinsic to politics."[86]

Second, the public concern (*res publica*) of Confucianism in respect of the "way of governance" is to fulfill a common good, that is, to "attain accomplishment according to the individual's nature." In this sense, the rationale of cultivation is, without a doubt, to realize the spirit of *ren* thoroughly by enlightening the people. According to the spirit of "self-restriction," however, Mou makes it clear that even in traditional Confucianism this objective is limited in the sense that unlike *morality as a whole*, it only involves a "minimal and universal humanity" (*qima er pupian de rendao* 起碼而普遍的人道).[87]

Finally, in Mou's view, in comparison to personal moral achievement, a "sagely king" (*shengwang* 聖王), or what is today called a "great statesman," is one who is aware of the necessity of setting limits on cultivation. To make his case, Mou quotes a famous statement from Wang Fuzhi: "Let us investigate principle as we come into contact with things but never set up principle to restrict things" (*youjishi yiqiongli, wulili yixianshi* 有即事以窮理, 無立理以限事).[88] In brief, this denotes that in contrast to panmoralism (*fan daodezhuyi* 泛道德主義), the real meaning of the "way of governance" is not to "set principle to restrict" the diversity of human affairs in advance, but to "investigate principle as one comes into contact with" public interests in concrete situations.

The New Outer Kingliness: A Reevaluation

Up to this point, I have given a detailed analysis of "humane government" with regard to the "intensional meaning of democracy"; in so doing, I have brought to the surface an ethical version of democracy in relation to several Confucian governing virtues. Since my exploration rests on the assumption that Mou conveys a Hegelian reading of the two meanings of democracy, I now intend to take up again Mou's plan to overcome the political pitfalls of Confucian meritocracy and the moral weaknesses of liberal democracy and discuss how it leads to the "subtlest model of Confucian democracy," otherwise known as the "new outer kingliness" (*xin waiwang* 新外王).[89]

The Moral Weaknesses of Liberal Democracy

It should have become clear by now that for Mou, the Confucian political ideal "is not [morally] incorrect," but rather, "it is [politically] insufficient."[90] As such, the modern transformation of Confucianism must be carried out through the venue of democracy. "Political democracy" on its own, however, is not theoretically unbeatable, nor is it morally impeccable.[91] On the contrary, as with the advocates of political meritocracy, Mou also takes issues with liberal democracy. To make the contrast easier to grasp, Mou juxtaposes the moral weaknesses of "political democracy" with the moral merits of "humane government."

First and foremost, the "extensional presentation of reason" laying the foundation for "political democracy" is abstract and empty, in comparison to the concreteness and comprehensiveness of the "intensional presentation of reason" underpinning "humane government" in association with an ethics of self-realization. In my view, this contrast between extensional and intensional reason can be recaptured in that between abstract individualism and embodied individualism. More precisely, given that to assist the individual with "attaining accomplishment" according to his or her own nature is the deepest moral appeal of "rule by virtue," in no way does Mou's version of Confucian democracy pass over the "flourishing of human goodness."

Again, for this reason, "political democracy" fails to answer the crucial questions of how to relate (1) the individual to the state, (2) freedom to the ultimate meaning of human life, and (3) rights to the Confucian forms of life, in a perfectionist sense. To the best of my knowledge, this is exactly the reason why an extended examination of the idea of ethical citizenship, the connection between negative and positive freedom, and the relation of rights to *a nondominant theory of the common good* is required to illuminate more fully Mou's anticipation of Confucian liberalism. Instead of going into the details of these fundamental issues, I merely want to mention in passing that on this reading, Mou's political thinking bears a striking resemblance to the "perfectionist liberalism" of the British idealists such as T. H. Green.[92]

Furthermore, in opposition to the spirit of *ren*, "political democracy" neglects to provide a profound treatment of "universal humanity as a whole." In terms of morality, to properly understand "universal humanity," it would be advisable to engage in a cross-cultural dialogue in respect of the issues of human constants and moral practices. In terms of politics, this at once implies that Mou's ethical democracy also sees to "the wellbeing of the environment, the welfare of future generations, and humanity as a whole," to quote Jiang Qing again.

The Political Pitfalls of Confucian Meritocracy

What categorically sets Mou apart from Jiang and Bell is his different conception of the Confucian political ideal. In general, Mou takes a "liberal" stance in objection to authoritarianism, and thus, he makes every effort to get rid of the three major pitfalls of the meritocratic aspects of "humane government" as well. First, as regards the acquisition and transmission of "political power," the original ideal of "public rulership" is not up to scratch, in that due to the absence of the "extensional meaning of democracy," *the legitimacy of authority* has never been successfully resolved by means of establishing nonpersonal institutions such as democracy, constitutionalism, the rule of law, and so forth.

Second, in order to put "rule by virtue" into practice, the ruler is committed to educating the people. "Therefore, the administration of government," as contemporary meritocratic writers argue, "lies in getting proper men":

> Such men are to be got by means of the ruler's own character. That character is to be cultivated by his treading in the ways of duty. And the treading in those ways of duty is to be cultivated by the cherishing of benevolence [humaneness] (*gu weizheng zai ren, quren yishen, xiushen yidao, xiudao yiren* 故為政在人, 取人以身, 修身以道, 修道以仁).[93]

The crucial point here, however, is that the virtuous ruler is good to have but is not guaranteed and that the moral enlightenment of the people does not always happen. Moreover, there will appear an asymmetry in terms of political responsibility because, while the ruler is supposed to take the entire burden in running the government, the people play no fair part in enhancing the quality of public life. Overall, for Confucianism to adjust its political ideal to the modern world, it has to acknowledge the historical condition and convey *political modernity* in respect of the characteristics of a modern state.

This vital point, together with the principle of "self-restriction" disclosed above, alludes to the contention that rather than assigning the business of thriving human goodness to the virtuous leaders, the purpose of a modern democratic state is to create the conditions and environments that may help every individual to conduct a good life. To be sure, a significant thread running throughout Mou's political theory is to reconcile the moral development of the political subject (ethical citizenship) with a perfectionist version of the state, grounded in *a nondominant theory of the common good* that I plan to flesh out in the following chapter.

Third, for the same reason, as far as the exercise of "governing power" is concerned, there appears to be a tension between the ideal of "rule by virtue" and that of the "rule of law." That said, simply because Confucianism believes that "with the right men growth of government is rapid, just as vegetation is rapid in the earth," the worst case is captured by "let there be the men and the government will flourish; but without the men, their government decays and ceases" (*qiren cun, ze qizheng ju; qiren wang, ze qizheng xi* 其人存, 則其政舉; 其人亡, 則其政息).[94] Accordingly, the principle of "self-restriction" in Confucianism is, as it were, short of developing some sort of "objective" mechanism in avoiding *the abuse of power*, tending to give rise to social dominance and oppression.

A SYNTHESIS OF THE TWO MEANINGS OF DEMOCRACY

On the whole, then, the political thinking of Mou with the purpose of recovering the "intensional meaning of democracy" is not simply to "transplant" liberal democracy in Chinese soil; rather, his intention is at the same time to overcome the crisis of current democracy by reevaluating the essence of politics from an ethical point of view rooted in the spirit of *ren*.[95] All this reaffirms that both "political democracy" and "governing democracy" are insufficient and that the subtlest model of Confucian democracy points to a Hegelian synthesis of these two partial meanings of democracy. Put differently, to arrive at a fuller understanding of democracy grounded in the spirit of *ren*, we must give weight to Confucian moral reasoning as well as Western political reasoning. In short, Mou's "new outer kingliness" is a philosophical hybrid identified as "Confucian ethical democracy," paving the way for a political theory of Confucian liberalism.

To conclude, Mou's version of Confucian democracy is committed to transcending the moral weakness of liberal democracy by taking seriously the flourishing of human goodness and the pursuit of the common good in a community since its ultimate aim is to relocate democracy and liberal values into the public good that is embodied in the Confucian lived forms of life, or so to speak, the dictums and mottos of "humane government." On the other hand, by adopting democracy as an instrument to sort out the problems of "who governs" and "why and how to govern," Confucian ethical democracy is exempt from the political pitfalls of meritocracy, such as falling short of giving institutional ground to legitimacy, lacking a sufficient account of political modernity in respect of the characteristics of a modern state, and failing to provide mechanisms (e.g., constitutionalism and the rule of law) for avoiding the abuse of power. In short, Mou's version of Confucian liberalism is neither Western-centric nor Sino-centric; rather, it is a philosophical mixture that may go some way toward transcending the predicament of liberal democracy in a Confucian way.

Part III
Perfectionist Liberalism

Chapter 7

Confucian *Res Publica*

Citizens and the State

Introduction

I have hitherto argued that facing a crisis of political legitimacy, Mou Zongsan, the most extraordinary thinker in the New Confucianism of Taiwan and Hong Kong, declares that not only does Confucianism need to tackle the "way of politics" (*zhengdao* 政道) related to constitutional democracy, but also, and equally important, it must relink the "way of politics" with the "way of governance" (*zhidao* 治道) expressing the elements of "humane government" (*renzheng* 仁政). That said, by claiming that democracy can be developed out of Confucianism, Mou does not mean that the ethical content of "humane government" is identical with the political form of democracy; rather, his real point is to assert that the actualization of Confucian democracy at the end of the day depends on a reconciliation between the "way of politics" capturing political modernity and the "way of governance" bearing the customary cores of "humane government."

Seen in this light, a significant aspect of Mou's political philosophy is to embark on a critical reexamination of *the proper relationship between morality and politics*. The key point here is that in contrast to anti-Confucian liberalism, Mou clearly endorses a *perfectionist* viewpoint of politics when he says that the ultimate end of governing is to help every person to "attain accomplishment according to the individual's nature" (*jiu geti er shuncheng* 就個體而順成), but unlike antiliberal

Confucianism, his identification of a common good is largely consistent with the spirit of liberalism. In other words, whereas both camps in question adopt a joint recognition of mainstream liberalism, purporting to maintain a clear-cut distinction between morality and politics, as well as between civility and politics, Mou's version of Confucian liberalism can be reconstructed not only as a civil form of liberalism but also as a perfectionist style of liberalism.

This at once brings us back to the fact that there exist various forms of liberalism. For example, there has been a debate between "liberal perfectionism" and "liberal neutralism" in contemporary political theory.[1] Moreover, considering the themes of this book, it is extremely worthwhile to mention that the notion of "perfectionist liberalism"[2] in the work of the British idealists such as T. H. Green bears a striking resemblance to Mou's theorization on Confucian liberalism. Seeing that these two post-Kantian thinkers share an ethics of self-realization, a stance on political perfectionism, and a viewpoint of using Hegel's ethical life to shape the relationship between citizens as well as their lived forms of life in a community, I am devoted to opening a far-reaching dialogue between Mou and Green in the following two chapters. In so doing, we shall be able to reevaluate to some extent Mou's remarkable achievement in relocating another vital group of liberal expressions—largely including citizens, open society, the state, freedom, and rights—into the Confucian forms of life.

The reason why I put these terms together is mainly because they constitute the public concern of a liberal democratic society. Put differently, Mou's Hegel-inspired political thought, as I see it, contains a liberal version of Confucian *res publica*, stemming from the elements of "humane government." I have pointed out in the last chapter that Mou's liberal treatment of the cores of the "way of governance" consists of a set of Confucian governing and civic virtues, which can be seen from the perspectives of leadership and citizenship respectively. Having revisited the Confucian political ideal from the angle of a virtuous leader, a significant goal of the third part of the book is directed to widen the insights of the "kingly way" (*wangdao* 王道) from the viewpoint of a democratic citizen.

Leaving freedom and rights for the next chapter, I plan to begin this chapter by arguing that Mou's appreciation of liberalism, for the most part, consists of three facets: (1) the "object form" of constitutional democracy; (2) the "social vision" of an open society; (3) the "moral ideals" of individuality, human dignity, tolerance, equal respect, and so forth.³ In a nutshell, Mou's prospect of Confucian liberalism is predicated on the historical condition that with the advent of "modern spirit,"⁴ China needs to develop the "object form" of constitutional democracy. To lay a rational ground for constitutional democracy in the Chinese cultural setting, nonetheless, it is equally important to assert that the Confucian political ideal is by all accounts consistent with the "social vision" of an open society and that the "way of *zhongshu*" (*zhongshu zhi dao* 忠恕之道) underpinning the spirit of *ren* 仁 (humaneness) is not necessarily in conflict with the "moral ideals" of liberalism.⁵ Thus, the following examination of Mou's liberal thinking reiterates some of the key elements of "humane government" from different angles. By this means, it is hoped that Mou's philosophical proposal for combining Confucianism with liberalism can be displayed in a fuller sense. All in all, Mou's political philosophy can be represented as a form of Confucian liberalism in that it has the effect of recasting liberal language in a Confucian fashion.

This is to say that the subtlest model of Confucian democracy in Mou's connotation, although retaining *a Confucian perfectionist version of politics*, accords with liberal values at the same time. For this reason, Mou's discussion of a "perfectionist state" and "ethical citizenship," far from resulting in the abuse of state power and the depravity of social oppression, comes up with a reestablishment of Confucian *res publica* as *a nondominant theory of the common good*. On this reading, as I hope to show, not only is Mou's political theory free from the charges of anti-individualism, monism, and panmoralism (*fan daodezhuyi* 泛道德主義)⁶ made by anti-Confucian liberalism, but it also aims to transcend the moral weaknesses of mainstream liberalism in respect of atomism, apathy, selfishness, and exploitation acclaimed by antiliberal Confucianism. In short, Confucian liberalism is established with an aim of ironing out the perils caused by the extremes of both "panmoralism" and "pan-liberalism."

Against this context, I contend that Mou's persistent attempt to offer a synthesis of the "way of politics" and the "way of governance" is entirely comparable to Green's Hegelian approach to disclosing the twofold meaning—the institutional and the ethical—of the liberal expressions at stake. Both thinkers have common roots in what Mou calls "humanistic idealism," which not only shows great respect for individuality and humanity but also maintains that democracy, by dint of protecting basic human rights, is "supportive of the self-accomplishment of one's character."⁷ As a result of this, undertaking a comparative study of Mou's and Green's opinions about the double meaning of the state and the ethical version of citizenship characterized by the civic virtues of "ethical mutuality," "helping others do good," and "caring about the worst-off" will lead us to unveil in a fuller sense the striking affinities between New Confucianism and British idealism under the blueprint of perfectionist liberalism.

Constitutional Democracy

Let me now begin this chapter with Mou's examination of the first facet of liberalism.

A System of Rights and Duties

In Mou's eyes, unlike the constancy of "inner sagehood" (*neisheng* 內聖), the hunt for a new version of "outer kingliness" (*waiwang* 外王) must "conform to the trend of the times."⁸ This, however, does not mean that in politics "anything goes." Rather, as Mou quotes the *Mencius* (*Mengzi* 孟子) in saying, "the sun and moon being possessed of brilliancy, their light admitted even through an orifice illuminates,"⁹ meaning that the political innovation in support of democracy is unavoidable for the future development of Confucianism because the real motivation standing behind this change is nothing less than to carry out the permanent moral ideal of Confucianism.¹⁰ Put in other terms, as indicated, Mou firmly believes that only through the venue of democracy can the spirit of *ren* be finally realized in the field of modern politics. In fact, Mou thinks that modernization, after all, is a *political* business, which in turn implies democratization.¹¹

In line with the "way of politics," in his public lectures, Mou adds that liberal democracy, by definition, is a political regime or a set of political institutions, aiming to protect freedom (rights) by establishing a system of checks and balances and separated powers to prevent totalitarianism.¹² That said, democracy, together with a constitution exercising the mechanism of checking and balancing power, serves as an "objective form," making possible the individual's freedom of speech, freedom of thought, freedom of assembly, freedom of the press, and so on, in an open society.¹³ Given that what politically defines "modernity" as a value concept in the West is the pursuit of freedom as opposed to totalitarianism,[14] the primary task of a Confucian political theory in the face of modernity, accordingly, is to take into consideration the "way of politics" in respect of the state and a system of rights and duties associated with citizenship.

On the one hand, it is largely through the venue of a modern state that different peoples and clans can "all live together peacefully and well-orderedly within a highly rationalized political system" and that the transmission of power can be "arranged by a peaceful and rational legal institution."[15] On the other hand, as Mou continues, unless the people can participate in "state affairs," their "rights and duties" cannot be truly protected by the law of a state; to this end, the people must engage in the enterprise of "elevating" their own status from the "subject of an emperor" to the "subject of rights and duties," that is, the "citizen" in the modern sense.[16]

This legal aspect of the state and citizenship immediately implies the idea of constitutional democracy in association with the rule of law, and so Mou is prone to take "constitution" as the "constant thing" in modern politics.[17] To put it in a Hegelian vein, constitution is constant because it exhibits the "objective form" of "co-ordination" (*duilie geju* 對列格局), by means of which the "arbitrary will" of the "absolute supremacy" can be legally delimited;[18] that said, the first principle of modern politics in pursuit of freedom is that of "co-ordination."[19] In this manner, it also can be said that a "constitutional democratic state" historically resulted from a process of transfiguring the "sub-ordination" (*lishu guanxi* 隸屬關係) between the emperor (*jun* 君), the intellectuals (*shi* 士), and the people (*min* 民) into the "co-ordination" among all citizens, wherein the "limits to the power" (*quanxian* 權限) of the state are *objectively* systematized.[20] In short, the "political sphere" is a "sphere of treatment" (*duidai lingyu* 對待領域)[21] in which the role of the state is limited to maintaining a fair system of rights and duties that all citizens share via the rule of law.[22]

A PERFECTIONIST STATE AND ETHICAL CITIZENSHIP

Be all this as it may, Mou's deeper purpose for launching constitutional democracy is to actualize the "kingly way" in the modern world. Instead of recapping Mou's reconstruction of the elements of "humane government," here I only intend to stress again that Mou's understanding of political language contains both legal and ethical viewpoints. Therefore, on top of maintaining a system of rights and duties, the business of the state, in keeping with the legitimate principle of treating "the people as fundamental," is simultaneously "perfectionist" in the sense of making every effort to help the people "attain accomplishment according to the individual's nature." To take a salient example, as Mou further remarks, the Confucian political ideal of "bringing peace to the old, having trust in friends, and cherishing the young"[23] is likewise of great significance in a constitutional democratic state.

Moreover, Mou articulates in his later political lectures that a modern state is responsible for the task of "cultural cultivation."[24] In general, as we have seen, the gist of cultivation is to carry out the goals of the "rectification of the people's virtue" (*zhengde* 正德), the "conveniences of life" (*liyong* 利用), and the "securing abundant means of sustenance" (*housheng* 厚生) in accordance with the principle of "self-restriction" (*ziwoxianzhi* 自我限制). On the whole, Mou agrees with Xu Fuguan [Hsu Fu-Kuan] (徐復觀 1904–1982) on the argument that the modern image of a "perfectionist state" upholding the Confucian political ideal is one that aims at "making the people wealthy before cultivation" (*xianfu houjiao* 先富後教) and simultaneously maintaining constitutional order to objectively avoid the abuse of power.

By the same token, we may easily add an ethical side to Mou's appreciation of citizenship. In a nutshell, "ethical citizenship" means that there exists a moral relationship between citizens in respect of a common good that defines the fair system of rights and duties shared by them. In Mou's words, in a constitutional democratic state every person is committed to "*accomplishing himself according to his own will* through the arrangement of a system of rights and duties between men" (emphasis mine).[25] This clearly reasserts that Mou's conception of the common good, Confucian *res publica* at stake, can be generally identified as "attaining self-accomplishment," thoroughly echoing the ethics of self-realization that I have disclosed in the previous chapters. From the standpoint I have been taking, there are accordingly some decisive things that must be illuminated as follows.

To start with, it should be remembered that for Mou, the absence of democracy in ancient Confucianism is largely owing to the lack of the independent political subject, namely, a "political concept" of citizenship "prescribed by rights and duties."[26] Another way of making the same point is to remark that citizenship denotes a newly emergent form of social relationship coming together with the "way of politics." Given that the subtlest model of Confucian democracy lies in a mixture of the "way of politics" and the "way of governance," the core principles of the "way of governance" applied to morally restrict the virtuous rulers, such as the "way of *zhongshu*," can thereby be transformed into a set of Confucian civic virtues in an attempt to help shape the moral character of democratic citizens. All things considered, as I hope to make clear, the cores of the "way of governance" contain not only the idea of a "perfectionist state" consistent with the liberal values of an open society, but also that of "ethical citizenship" denoting the moral ideals of liberalism. Hence, Mou's reexamination of the Confucian political ideal can be seen as an endeavor to propose a liberal version of Confucian *res publica*.

Here as elsewhere in this study, at the heart of Mou's liberal disclosure of Confucian *res publica* lies the principle of "self-restriction" that sets both the tone for the purpose of government and limits on the abuse of power. In other words, Mou is surely aware that the fullest manifestation of Confucian perfectionism, apart from falling short of constructive reason, is likely to give rise to social oppression and domination by the state in an open society. As such, he intends to bring together Confucian *res publica* and the principle of "self-restriction" in balance. It is for this reason that I have tried to make a distinction between the principle of "self-restriction" at the center of Confucian *res publica* and the process of "self-negation" (*ziwo kanxian* 自我坎陷) concerning the "blossoming of democracy" (*mingzhu kaichu* 民主開出) in the preceding chapters.

Also, it follows that when Mou talks about the affinities between Confucianism and both the values of an open society and the moral ideals of liberalism, the Confucianism he has in mind is not so much about the "perfect teaching" (*yuanjiao* 圓教) of Confucianism but about the "political ideal" of Confucianism in keeping with the principle of "self-restriction." This is to say that for Mou, the essential task of a Confucian political philosophy is distinguished from that of Confucian moral metaphysics in that it only needs to seek the actualization of "humane government" in a democratic society, without referring to the ontological significance of "intellectual intuition" (*zhi de zhijue* 智的直覺).

That being said, I am now trying to make the case that the idea of Confucian *res publica* under discussion is thoroughly associated not only with the liberal values of autonomy, plurality and openness, which depict an open society independent of the state, but also with the civic virtues of "ethical mutuality," "helping others do good," and "caring about the worst-off," broadening the moral horizons of liberalism to a considerable extent.

Open Society

As regards the "social vision" of liberalism, I have three main points to make. First, despite the fact that Confucianism lacks the "way of politics," the Confucian political ideal is not at odds with an open society, to use Karl Popper's phrase.[27] Second, Mou's treatment of a "perfectionist state" accords with a *specific* distinction between morality and politics in a Confucian perspective, and thus, it is in every sense restrained to respecting the liberal values of *autonomy*, *plurality*, and *openness* characterizing an open society. Third, inasmuch as Mou's idea of a "perfectionist state" does not impose a "comprehensive conception of the good life" on citizens, it is immune from the symptoms of an authoritarian state, such as anti-individualism, absolutism, and panmoralism.

A Harmonious Order

Without explicating Popper's discussion of an open society in detail, it suffices to note that Confucian *res publica* identified as "fulfilling accomplishment according to the individual's nature" implies that what Confucianism is really after is a "harmonious order" in which every person is able to "fit his own nature" (*ge shi qi xing* 各適其性) and to "fulfill his own life" (*ge sui qi sheng* 各遂其生).[28] To be sure, a "perfectionist state" related to the "kingly way" is one that is committed to "governing men, according to their nature, with what is proper to them" (*yiren zhiren* 以人治人).

Against this context, in his later political writings, Mou states that the ideal of an open society in Confucianism can be reached by keeping to the principles of "obtaining what one deserves" (*ge de qi suo* 各得其所) and "fulfilling one's own life."[29] To make his point more clearly, Mou quotes the *Doctrine of the Mean* (*Zhongyong* 中庸) and the *I Ching* (*Yi Jing* 易經):[30]

> Let the states of equilibrium and harmony exist in perfection, and a happy order will prevail throughout Heaven and earth,

and all things will be nourished and flourish (*zhi zhong he, tian di wei yan, wanwu yu yan* 致中和, 天地位焉, 萬物育焉).³¹

The method of *Qian* is to change and transform, so that everything obtains its correct nature as appointed (by the heart-mind of Heaven), and (thereafter the conditions of) great harmony are preserved in union. The result is "what is advantageous, and correct and firm" (*qian dao bianhua, ge zheng xing ming, baohe dahe, nai li zhen* 乾道變化, 各正性命, 保合大和, 乃利貞).³²

In short, according to Mou, an open society is analogous to the "kingly way" that Huang Zongxi [Huang Tsung-Hsi] (黃宗羲 1610–1695) has famously recognized as "safeguarding the world for the sake of all-under-Heaven" (*cang tianxia yu tianxia* 藏天下於天下).³³

From this, it follows that Mou takes seriously the distinction between an open society and the coercion of a state. Although the state is devoted to promoting a common good identified as "attaining accomplishment," the following words "according to the individual's nature" all at once confine the role of the state, deferring to the liberal features of an open society in respect of *autonomy*, *plurality*, and *openness*. That said, Mou is dissimilar to mainstream liberalism, not because he misidentifies politics with *morality as a whole*, but because he is eager to make a specific distinction between morality and politics in ways that correspond to Confucian teachings.

Autonomy

First of all, as Mou puts it, at the heart of the human rights movement is a bid to separate the "political" from the "personal," resulting in an "emphasis on individuality"³⁴ in the public sphere, that is, the "free subjectivity of modernity." Tellingly, this is why in a constitutional democratic state the individual "has the right" to a system of rights, such as religious freedom and the right to private property.³⁵ In this manner, the moral appeal standing behind the rights discourse of political modernity, as it has been established previously, largely points to the idea of autonomy that underlies the philosophy of Rousseau, Kant, Hegel, and Green, among others.

Instead of repeating Mou's lifelong endeavor to rebuild a New Confucian moral metaphysics through the Kantian frame, we only need to mention in passing here that for Mou the Kantian idea of autonomy is completely resonant with the moral spirituality of Confucianism. Thus, Mou urges that a "perfectionist state" by all means cannot coerce the people to arrive at the "fulfillment of virtue" (*chengde* 成德). For one thing, "the practice of humaneness," as Confucius says, "depends on oneself alone" (*weiren youji* 為仁由己).[36] Or alternatively, in the words of Mencius, in moral practice you are always committed to "looking into yourself" (*fanqiu zhuji* 反求諸己).[37] Thus, the state cannot put somebody on the right path by force, simply because morality concerns the autonomy of the subject.

Or, to put it another way, since "the reason that makes a human being a *human*" rests on one's enjoyment of a "personal life belonging to himself, without being interfered with by others and being dominated and controlled by government,"[38] the Confucian version of a "perfectionist state" is anything but an authoritarian state as it is in every respect limited to maintaining a harmonious order largely with regard to a legal system of rights and duties. In short, in opposition to an "illusionary ideology," members of an open society "live in actual life" with freedom to choose,[39] hence state action is legitimate only if it makes every effort to assist citizens with "attaining accomplishment according to the individual's nature," without setting forth a dominant conception of the highest good in advance.

PLURALITY

Furthermore, modernization implies the "plurality of human reasons," purporting to assert that "science belongs to science, religion belongs to religion, politics belongs to politics," and indeed, "morality belongs to morality."[40] In a like manner, in the age of pluralism "family cannot be reduced to the state, and society cannot be reduced to government."[41] Seen in this light, the distinction between the "personal" and the "political" also entails a distinction between a comprehensive theory of moral metaphysics in pursuit of the fullest accomplishment of *ren* as the "unity of Heaven, earth, and all myriad things"[42] and a *specific* law of political affairs identified as the "kingly way." Put differently, although almost every religion or every philosophical system unavoidably presumes a certain notion of "absolute completeness" (*juedui de yuanman* 絕對的圓

滿),⁴³ or a "comprehensive conception of the good life" in contemporary political theory, central to an open society is a plurality of values and beliefs, rather than absolutism.

All this explains why Mou, despite admiring the importance of scientific knowledge, argues against the "dogmatism of scientism" in an open society.⁴⁴ What is more, the view that the actualization of the "kingly way" belongs to the specific domain of politics reminds us of the key point that for Mou, as for Xu Fuguan, there is a discrepancy between "cultivating oneself" (*xiuji* 修己) and "governing the people" (*zhiren* 治人) in Confucianism.

OPENNESS

As a final point, the value of openness suggests that the harmonious order is not subject to any "theory" or "dogma."⁴⁵ Mou quotes Lao Siguang [Lao Sze-Kwang] (勞思光 1927–2012) in articulating that although personal development begins with "common sense," only in an open society can one strive to "go beyond the limits of [the dogma] of common sense toward a virtuous subject able to actualize values"⁴⁶ in the real world. In other words, "a truly free man must have within himself a strong sense of human life," manifested as the lighting of the candle of functional reason to "illuminate and eradicate the darkness" of a society.⁴⁷

Thus seen, as Mou continues, even though the Chinese cultural tradition did not develop democracy largely thanks to the nonexistence of constructive reason and lacked the notion of rights caused by class struggle, the idea of functional reason, once conforming to the principle of "self-restriction," still plays a crucial role in preventing an open society from being overshadowed by the state. All in all, it is Mou's central argument that "since the spirit of 'stepping aside, spreading out, and leaving things as they are' (*rangkai sankai, wu gefu wu* 讓開散開, 物各付物) and the principle of 'attaining accomplishment according to the individual's nature' in essence denote a society of openness, they accord with the spirit of liberalism emphasizing the importance of individuality."⁴⁸

All this amounts to reaffirming that there is a distinction between "morality as a whole" and the specific contents of "political morality," so to speak. To refine his point, Mou quotes this famous statement from Wang Fuzhi [Wang Fu-Chih] (王夫之 1619–1692) once again: "Let us investigate principles as we come into contact with things but never set up principles to restrict things" (*you jishi yi qiongli, wu lili yi xianshi* 有

即事以窮理，無立理以限事).⁴⁹ According to Mou, what Wang means by "principles" (*li* 理) are moral principles regarding the ultimate concern of human life, whereas the term "things" (*shi* 事) refers to political affairs that involve experience, judgment, and practical wisdom.⁵⁰ On this reading, a "sagely king" or what is today called a "great statesman," is one who instead of "setting up principles to restrict" the diversity of human affairs in advance, "investigates principles as he comes into contact with" public interests in concrete situations so as to retain the value of openness.⁵¹ In my view, far from sliding into panmoralism, the discrepancy between "things" and "principles" at stake echoes to some extent what Kant has famously distinguished between a "moral politician" and a "political moralist."⁵²

In Mou's scheme, then, the state is simultaneously connected with and detached from society in a *specific* way: On the one hand, the state is *morally* related to an open society by promoting a common good rooted in an ethics of self-realization; on the other hand, it is *legally* constrained to respecting the liberal values of autonomy, pluralism, and openness, which are resonant with the spirit of Confucianism. Overall, Mou's stance on Confucian *res publica* is akin to what Joseph Chan (陳祖為) powerfully refers to as "moderate perfectionism," even though the extent to which Mou accommodates liberal values is broader than Chan's "Confucian political perfectionism."⁵³ It is not within the scope of my book, however, to give a detailed analysis of Chan's project. Instead, it suffices to remark that Mou's bid to reconnect the spirit of Confucianism with the values of an open society is anything but panmoralism.

Liberal Moral Ideals

Let me now move to the third facet of liberalism, that is, the moral ideals of individuality, human dignity, tolerance, equal respect, and so on. By this means, my purpose is to substantiate the key argument that the "way of *zhongshu*," if properly reconstructed, can be seen as presenting a liberal theory of the common good, displaying a set of Confucian civic virtues—such as "ethical mutuality," "helping others do good," and "caring about the worst-off"—which are resistant to social suppression. In response to antiliberal Confucianism, I then contend that Mou's Confucian liberalism is eager to transcend the moral weakness of mainstream liberalism, or what Mou dubs "pan-liberalism," surrounded by the drawbacks of atomism, apathy, selfishness, and exploitation.

The Way of Zhongshu

Let me begin by elucidating the significance of the "way of *zhongshu*." There is a famous conversation in the *Analects* (*Lunyu* 論語):

> The Master said, "Shen (參)! There is one single thread binding my way together."
>
> Zengzi [Tseng Tzu] (曾子) assented.
>
> After the Master had gone out, the disciples asked, "What did he mean?"
>
> Zengzi said, "The way of the Master consists in doing one's best (*zhong* 忠) and in using oneself as a measure to gauge others (*shu* 恕). That is all."[54]

Overall, the virtue of *zhong*, literally meaning "doing one's best," is completely parallel to the dictum about "being strict with oneself" (*yan yi luji* 嚴以律己); by way of contrast, the virtue of *shu*, literally meaning "using oneself as a measure to gauge others," is entirely analogous to the dictum about "being lenient toward others" (*kuan yi dairen* 寬以待人). Taken together, the "way of *zhongshu*" represents nothing but the appropriate pathway for one to put *ren* in practice. Truly, as Confucius puts it, "if one sets strict standards for oneself and makes allowances for others when making demands on them, one will stay clear of ill will."[55]

More precisely, *zhong* understood as "being strict with oneself" is a testament to the virtue of "faithfulness" or "authenticity" (*cheng* 誠), shedding light on the ethics of self-realization that we have previously discussed in terms of moral metaphysics, moral religion, and moral perfection. This is to say that *zhong*, together with the mottos of "overcoming the self,"[56] "watching over himself when he is alone" ("vigilance in solitude"),[57] and "illustrating illustrious virtue,"[58] points to the "inner morality" (*neizai daodexing* 內在道德性) of human dignity attached to the moral subject. For this reason, a discussion of *zhong*, as we shall see, may help bring to light the ideas of individuality and human dignity in Confucianism from different angles.

On the other hand, *shu* recognized as "being lenient toward *others*" is characteristically an other-regarding virtue. In general, *shu* is equivalent to the capacity of "empathy," entailing a "sympathetic understanding" about what others experience within their frame of reference. Therefore, in sharp contrast to apathy, *shu* is by and large taken to mean placing oneself in another person's position, and thus, it stands for an exertion to link the self with the other. In practice, *shu* is closely related to the phrase of "being magnanimous with others" (*kuanda wei huai* 寬大為懷), embracing the virtues of "magnanimity" (*kuanda* 寬大), "leniency" (*kuanhou* 寬厚), "generosity" (*kuanhong* 寬宏), "forbearance" (*kuanshu* 寬恕), and the like. Moreover, in the Confucian tradition the usage of *shu* has strong affinities with what Mencius calls the "heart-mind of compassion" (*ce yin zhi xin* 惻隱之心),[59] designating an insightful meaning of "lamenting the state of Heaven and pitying the conditions of mankind" (*beitian minren* 悲天憫人). In brief, as I shall elaborate shortly, the virtue of *shu* plays a vital role in shaping the liberal ideals of tolerance and equal respect from a Confucian standpoint, in that it denotes a deep sense of "caring about others."

Before turning to examine in detail how the "way of *zhongshu*" may help broaden the moral horizons of liberalism, however, it is important to bear in mind that inasmuch as what concerns Mou here is a *political* concept of citizenship, his examination of *zhong* and *shu* in this manner is certainly sticking to the "objective form" of constitutional democracy and the "social version" of an open society. Hence, once again, central to Confucian civic virtue is not a comprehensive doctrine of *zhong* and *shu*, but a restatement of the habits of *zhong* and *shu* as essential ingredients of "ethical citizenship" in accordance with the principle of "self-restriction." At last, it is on this account that Mou stands up for a perfectionist version of liberalism by rejecting what he calls "pan-liberalism" or "pseudo-liberalism,"[60] that is, the attempt to use liberty in a "negative and incautious" way, without scrutinizing in any way the specific connection between the business of the state and the significance of erecting one's own "moral personality and moral character" in a communal life.

Ethical Mutuality: Recasting Individuality and Human Dignity

Primarily, I take it that the "way of *zhongshu*" alludes to a civic virtue of "ethical mutuality," which is in turn beneficial to recasting the ideas of individuality and human dignity in the Confucian fashion. To make my case, it is worth mentioning at the start that the discussion of the "way of *zhongshu*" has long been associated with the famous dictum about "helping others to take their stand in so far he himself wishes to take his stand, and getting others there in so far as he himself wishes to get there" (*jili liren, jida daren* 己立立人, 己達達人). To quote the *Analects*:

> Zigong [Tzu Kung] (子貢) said, "If there were a man who gave extensively to the common people and brought help to the multitude, what would you think of him? Could he be called benevolent?"
>
> The Master said, "It is no longer a matter of benevolence [humaneness] with such a man. If you must describe him, 'sage' is, perhaps, the right word. Even Yao (堯) and Shun (舜) would have found it difficult to accomplish as much. Now, on the other hand, a benevolent man helps others to take their stand in so far as he himself wishes to take his stand, and gets others there in so far as he himself wishes to get there. The ability to take as analogy what is near at hand can be called the method of benevolence [humaneness]."[61]

An important question immediately arises: whether the dictum quoted above is most properly related to the virtue of *zhong* or to that of *shu*. According to Liu Baonan [Liu Pao-Nan] (劉寶楠 1791–1855), "taking one's stand and getting oneself there is *zhong*, whereas helping others to take their stand and getting others there is *shu*" (*jili jida zhong ye, liren daren shu ye* 己立己達, 忠也, 立人達人, 恕也).[62] Liu's connotation actually reflects Zhu Xi's [Chu Hsi] (朱熹 1130–1200) critical comment that "making the most out of oneself is called *zhong*, whereas doing unto others as you would have them do unto you is called *shu*" (*jinji zhiwei zhong, tuiji zhiwei shu* 盡己之謂忠, 推己之謂恕).[63]

Seen in this light, it becomes obvious that the "way of *zhongshu*" involves two fundamental categories of virtues, namely, the self-regarding virtue known as "making the most out of oneself" (*jinji* 盡己) and the other-regarding virtue recognized as "doing unto others as you would have them do unto you" (*tuiji* 推己) or "putting oneself in another person's place" (*tuiji jiren* 推己及人). Instead of delving deeper into the wholesale picture of Confucian virtues by reference to *zhong* and *shu*, it is more important to indicate here that in the Confucian setting the "way of *zhongshu*" in favor of an ethics of self-realization toward the accomplishment of *ren* implies that *zhong* is morally and practically inseparable from *shu*: one is incapable of "doing his best" unless he is committed to "putting himself in the place of others" who share common meanings with him. It is largely based on the bond between the self and the other in this manner that the "way of *zhongshu*" makes perfect sense of "ethical mutuality," tending to bind all individual members together in an ethical community.

To my knowledge, the significance of "ethical mutuality" in Confucianism can be properly elucidated with regard to Confucius's saying that "of neighborhoods humaneness is the most beautiful (*liren weimei* 里仁為美). How can the man be considered wise who, when he has the choice, does not settle in humaneness?"[64] Undeniably, as Confucius continues, "virtue can never stand alone. It is bound to have neighbors."[65] Thus, just as "a craftsman who wishes to practice his craft well must first sharpen his tools," those who wish to become a gentleman "should, therefore, seek the patronage of the most distinguished Counsellors and make friends with the most benevolent gentleman in the state where you happen to be staying."[66] On the other hand, as Zengzi remarks, the gentleman is a virtuous person who "makes friends through being cultivated, but looks to friends for support in humaneness."[67] In short, a key thread running throughout the Confucian tradition is to reach the common goal of "attaining sagehood" (*chengsheng* 成聖) by mutual learning.[68]

Returning to the moral ideals of liberalism, it should be noted that the idea of "ethical mutuality" so understood is by no means opposed to the value of individuality. Rather, Confucianism is as much concerned with individuality as it is with mainstream liberalism; Confucianism, as Mou argues, is even at the "pinnacle of individualism."[69] What really sets Confucian liberalism apart from mainstream liberalism is the fact that Mou's reference to individuality is remarkably akin to the Herderian-Hegelian vision of "embodied individualism," rather than to "atomistic individualism." That said, in line with "ethical mutuality," Mou's treatment of individuality is closely related to the moral ability to "fully develop the interest and talent that define one's own character"[70] with regard to human relations and social relations. This is because the notion of rationality in Confucianism is so "concrete"[71] that its true actualization, namely, the fulfillment of one's moral potentiality, is impossible without taking into account the forms of life that have existed in a community.

Or, to put it another way, while *zhong* understood as "making the most out of oneself" is thoroughly associated with the virtue of "faithfulness" or "authenticity," illuminating the core value of human dignity, the Confucian self is not an "atomistic self" utterly free from communal bearings, but an "embodied self" who is willing to consider others in their places, and do good with them by mutual learning. Translated into Hegelian terminology, this means that one's dignity and esteem recognized as freedom and reason (i.e., *zhong*) cannot be fully realized unless he simultaneously brings in consideration of the conditions and opportunities for others to realize freedom and reason (i.e., *shu*) in a similar way.

HELPING OTHERS DO GOOD: REAPPRECIATING TOLERANCE

All this reaffirms that *shu* identified as an other-regarding virtue encompasses an ethical import of "caring about others." For my purposes here, however, it is essential to clarify the two main usages of *shu* in the Confucian context, namely, the dictum about "helping others to take their stand in so far he himself wishes to take his stand, and getting others there in so far as he himself wishes to get there," and its matching part, "do not impose on others what you yourself do not desire" (*jisuo buyu, wushi yuren* 己所不欲, 勿施于人).⁷²

The virtue of *shu* used in the first sense, to begin with, is anything but egoism or selfishness. For this reason, Confucius highly praises Zilu [Tzu Lu] (子路) when the latter says, "I should like to share my carriage and horses, clothes and furs with my friends, and to have no regrets even if they become worn."⁷³ What is more, according to Confucius, *shu* refers to an enthusiastic attempt to "help others to realize what is good in them" (*chengren zhi mei* 成人之美), in place of "helping them to realize what is bad in them."⁷⁴ In the words of Mencius, to make this point is equivalent to remarking that "there is nothing more important to a gentleman than helping others do good" (*yuren weishan* 與人為善),⁷⁵ which is clearly reminiscent of Zengzi's saying quoted above, namely, that a virtuous man should "look to friends for support in humaneness" (*yi you fu ren* 以友輔仁).

It follows that along the lines of "ethical mutuality," the social merit of "helping others to realize what is good," or "helping others do good," adds a quintessential part to our examination of a liberal theory of the common good at issue. For, what may be properly called goodness in Confucianism, as it should have become clear by now, always refers to an other-regarding state of affairs under the heading of *shu*. Given that *zhong* and *shu* are inseparable and that "helping others do good" is indispensable for one's own actualization of goodness, the idea of the common good in Mou's Confucian liberalism thereby corresponds to a "good for each and all," a "mutual good" supporting the suggestion that each individual member of a community should be held accountable for the conditions and opportunities of others, especially the less advantaged, in pursuing a good life.

Before discussing the second aspect of *shu* in relation to the feebler, I think it is sufficient to make the case that *shu* as an other-regarding virtue denotes something more than the legal aspect of "tolerance" (*kuanrong* 寬容) in mainstream liberalism: to be tolerant of the words and deeds of a person or a group could simply mean that you show a *legal* respect to those who are in disagreement with you without showing any *affection* toward them, while *shu* linked with the emotion of "sympathetic understanding" is meant to denote a virtue of treating people with affection, which involves sharing, helping, caring, and compassion, in Confucianism. In a nutshell, unlike "tolerance," which can be exhibited without reciprocal concern, *shu* functions as a higher moral standard, involving an awareness of "caring about others."

In a basic sense, it seems to me that Mou is aware of this distinction between "tolerance" and *shu*. For instance, Mou observes that compared to the notion of "tolerance" in the human rights movement, which is concerned with "objective" social issues such as religion, class, and despotism, the consideration of *shu* in Confucianism is interrelated with *zhong* in respect of mottos such as "overcoming the self," "watching over himself when he is alone," and "illustrating illustrious virtue." However, adhering to the specific distinction between morality and politics, Mou soon adds that in the age of democracy the fullest realization of "illustrating illustrious virtue" in the personal sphere is indisputably different from the arduous struggle for human rights in the public dominion and that the persistent exercise of erecting one's moral subjectivity by "overcoming the self" needs to be distinguished from the "kingly way" of "bringing peace to the old, having trust in friends, and cherishing the young."[76] This, of course, does not mean that we should give up the virtue of *shu* for the sake of seeking the legal protection of human rights alone. Rather, it denotes that pursuing *shu* in accordance with the objective form of constitutional democracy and the social version of an open society is of great significance for avoiding the moral pitfalls of "pan-liberalism," in that it may go some way toward developing a more substantial version of civic literacy than the common belief of "tolerance" in treating others as one should.

Caring about the Worst-off: Reshaping Equal Respect

Another emblematic aspect of *shu*, as indicated, is linked with the aphorism "do not impose on others what you yourself do not desire." On this reading, the virtue of *shu* is obviously contradictory to the exploitation and manipulation of the less advantaged in a community. Tellingly, it has been widely held in the Confucian tradition that the practice of *shu* will give rise to a customary belief in caring not merely about others, but also, and more significantly, about the "worst-off" in a community. For Confucians, it is morally improper to achieve one's own wants while being completely indifferent to the suffering and pains that the weaker bear. In short, apart from "helping others do good," an alternative way of treating *shu* as a civic virtue is to identify it with a profound "care about the worst-off."

Shu so understood, as might be expected, has much to do with Mencius's description of the "heart-mind of compassion" as the germ of *ren*. There are, accordingly, a number of statements that can be cited to expound the moral character of *shu* like this. For example, Mencius articulates that the gentleman is liable to be "benevolent toward the people and looking after all things" (*renmin aiwu* 仁民愛物),[77] and thus, that he learns to "look upon himself as responsible for others who starve" (*renji jiji* 人飢己飢) and to "look upon himself as responsible for those who drown" (*renni jinni* 人溺己溺).[78] In a like manner, Zhang Zai [Chang Tsai] (張載 1020–1077) states that "all people are brothers; creation is part of me" (*min bao wu yu* 民胞物與).

This way of grasping *shu*, as I see it, is resonant with Confucius's instruction about the purposes of self-cultivation for a gentleman too: "He cultivates himself and thereby achieves reverence"; "he cultivates himself and thereby brings peace and security to his fellow men"; "he cultivates himself and thereby brings peace and security to the people."[79] All things considered, an uncompromising picture of Confucian civility associated with *shu* is to make real the hope that "elderly men with no spouses or children, widows, orphans, elderly people without children or grandchildren, the handicapped, and the ill–*are all provided for*" (*guan gua gu du feiji zhe jie you suo yang* 鰥寡孤獨廢疾者皆有所養).[80]

Considering the themes of this book, it is interesting to note that to talk about *shu* in light of the aphorism "do not impose on others what you yourself do not desire" is equivalent to evoking the Kantian formula of "the end in itself," namely, the duty of treating humanity always as an end, never merely as a means. Indeed, as we have seen in the previous chapters, Confucianism as a moral theory grants that one should convey equal respect to every person. And here, with the aphorism at stake, it can be added straight away that seeing as no one would desire being treated as a means, you should not impose exploitation of any sort on others.

Unlike Kant, however, Confucianism does not belittle the pursuit of well-being or common interest. For one thing, Confucian *res publica* recognized as "attaining accomplishment according to the individual's nature" does not prevent a "perfectionist state" from "making the people wealthy before cultivation" by seeking the "conveniences of life" and "securing abundant means of sustentation." Also, as Mou remarks, the "way of *zhongshu*" can be deemed the highest principle of politics, largely because it aims to create a "happy order" that "prevails throughout Heaven and earth" and "nourishes and causes to flourish all things."[81] In short, the phrase "bringing peace and security to the people" has long been deemed an ultimate Confucian political ideal.

From the standpoint I have been taking, this is to say that adopting the Kantian approach alone is insufficient to fully reveal the multifaceted structure of Mou's political philosophy. This is because Mou's political thinking aims to incorporate the elements of "humane government," or what I have otherwise referred to as *Confucian civic virtue*, into the "objective form" of constitutional democracy and the "social version" of an open society, resulting in a Confucian form of perfectionist liberalism. Accordingly, based on the Hegelian revisions of Kant's philosophy that I have unveiled, my key point here is that Mou's idea of Confucian *res publica* in terms of "attaining accomplishment according to the individual's nature" consists of a bid to bring together the Confucian goal of "all being provided for" (*jie you suo yan* 皆有所養) and the Kantian formula of "the end in itself." For this reason, as we shall see shortly, Mou's discussion of Confucian *res publica* is interestingly reminiscent of Green's theory of the common good in aid of the weaker.

To conclude, Mou's Confucian liberalism is immune from the major criticisms against liberal tenets launched by antiliberal Confucianism because it clearly departs from mainstream liberalism in trying to get rid of the shortcomings of atomism, apathy, selfishness, and exploitation. Given that liberal democracy, for Mou, is much more than a "matter of head counting, having no regard for morality,"[82] we may make a rejoinder to Jiang Qing (蔣慶) again by saying that Mou's search for Confucian *res publica* pays serious attention to "sacred values of political life" in a pluralist open society, such as "the welfare of future generations and humanity as a whole."[83] All in all, both antiliberal Confucianism and anti-Confucian liberalism largely neglect one of the most significant consequences of the fashion of "embodied individualism" in contemporary political theory, which is to shift the focus of discussion from contractarianism, natural rights theory, and utilitarianism to a general concern about the quality of public life and the character of the citizen in a liberal society.[84] That said, the Herderian-Hegelian tradition of stressing the historicity of human action and the importance of ethical life plays a crucial role in promoting the ethical turn to liberalism, encouraged by the British idealists and the philosophical communitarians or liberal republicans such as Charles Taylor, to name only a few. In short, perfectionist liberalism associated with an ethics of self-realization, far from falling victim to totalitarianism and absolutism, stands for a different approach to justifying liberal values in a new light.

The Perfectionist Turn to Liberalism

For the rest of this chapter, then, I am prepared to make better sense of Mou's notion of Confucian *res publica* by explicating Green's theory of a common good from two angles, namely, the state and citizenship.

THE DOUBLE MEANING OF THE STATE

The key concept of Green's political philosophy is political obligation,[85] focusing on the reasons why the citizen is under an obligation to obey the law issued by the authority of the state. A philosophical survey of legitimacy with regard to political obligation, accordingly, has everything to do with the twofold meaning of the state that we have found in Mou's writings.

In ethical terms, Green basically follows Hegel in seeing the state as the "society of societies," the society in which "all their claims upon each other are mutually adjusted."[86] Although Green's appreciation of the state therefore denotes a common good grounded in the ethics of self-realization, the moral temperament of the state is limited to the point that it should serve as an "instrument for the moralization of man,"[87] that is, to help the citizen to arrive at the fuller actualization of his or her moral potentiality. That said, even if the state is of moral significance, its task is not so much to define the ultimate meaning of human life but to maintain legal order beneficial to the self-realization of its members.

In legal terms, it thus seems that in contrast to the stereotype of the reception of Hegel's theory of the state, Green does not come to see the state *itself* as an end in the absolute sense. Instead, the phrase an "instrument for the moralization of man" implies that the state cannot impose a predetermined comprehensive version of the common good on the citizen. On the contrary, influenced by Kant, Green holds that the major task of the state is to maintain and adjust a system of rights by means of which the citizen may enjoy equal conditions to achieve his or her own accomplishment. To be sure, as a new liberal, Green's political theory is apt to present the state as a "body of persons" who are mutually recognized as "having rights, and possessing certain institutions for the maintenance of those rights"[88] all together.

Putting aside Green's theory of freedom and rights, it suffices to remark that just as Green's approval of positive freedom by no means excludes the importance of negative freedom, the moral trait of the state in association with an ethics of self-realization is in full harmony with the legal character of the state defined as sustaining a system of rights. Taken together, a quick portrait of Green's perfectionist version of politics gives us the impression that the main business of the state is to make happen a system of rights (and duties) with the purpose of enabling citizens to realize their own moral potentiality in a legally ordered community.

New Liberal Politics: Removing Obstacles to Self-Realization

To see this issue from another angle, it is essential to point out that although Green's ethics of self-realization appreciates the cultivation of human excellence, it emphasizes the values of autonomy, pluralism, and openness all the way through. In parallel with the Confucian stance that "the practice of humaneness depends on oneself alone," as indicated,

Green argues that "no one can convey a good character to another" and that "everyone must make his character for himself."[89] For this reason, Green contends that it is *not* possible for the state to force citizens to be *good*; quite the reverse, nobody save the individual can realize his or her own moral potentiality in every single concrete situation.[90] In other words, what the state can provide to citizens is only "conditions and encouragements"[91] beneficial to their endless pursuit of self-perfection, rather than mandating actions of any kind.

Put differently, the extent to which a state can exercise its power legitimately and tolerably is not to bring about the whole package of a rational life plan, but to sustain a system of rights allowing citizens to conduct a better life in their own ways. This explains why the proper office of the state in Green's mind is, by and large, restricted to removing any obstacles to self-realization, to eliminate the hindrances to the actualization of equal moral power for every citizen. To quote Green: since the lawful action of the state, that is, the "community acting through law" is to promote "habits of true citizenship," it seems necessary to confine the main task of the state to the removal of obstacles "to the realization of the capacity for beneficial exercise of rights without defeating its own object by vitiating the spontaneous character of that capacity."[92]

On this reading, it seems adequate to stress that Green's perspective "qualifies as modern liberal politics," or more exactly, a perfectionist version of new liberal politics, as his theorization of moral perfection is "critically dependent upon freedom of choice and personal responsibility"[93] in a pluralist society. That said, in no way does Green's moral conception of the state underestimate the value of the individual; quite the opposite: the state and social "institutions have worth only to the extent that they sustain and promote the possession and exercise of virtues by individual citizens."[94] To quote Green again,

> The value then of the institutions of civil life lies in their operation as giving reality to these capacities [of will and reason], as enabling them to be really exercised. . . . In their general effect, apart from particular aberrations, they render it possible for a man to be freely determined by the idea of a possible satisfaction of himself instead of being driven this way and that by external forces, [and thus they give] reality to the capacity called will. . . . *[T]hey enable him to organize his*

> reason, i.e., *his idea of self-perfection, by acting as a member of a social organization in which each contributes to the better-being of all the rest* [emphasis mine].⁹⁵

The statement that I italicized is of great significance as it clearly denotes the core meaning of Green's comprehension of a common good identified as self-perfection or self-realization. To be sure, in Green's work, the overarching structure of the state is characterized by a "publicly promulgated system of rights and obligations," which is in turn vindicated by a "publicly articulated conception of the common good"⁹⁶ recognized by all members. Green's conception of the common good, nevertheless, cannot be confused with the principle of the greatest happiness, the appeal to the general will, or the substantial satisfaction of welfare, safety, or prosperity in a collective sense;⁹⁷ in other words, it has nothing to do with what Michael Oakeshott refers to as *civitas cupiditatis*.⁹⁸

Individualist Perfectionism

Hopefully, it is clear now that the mode of perfectionism underpinning Green's political thought is to a great extent akin to what scholars call "individualistic perfectionism," purporting to maintain that "human flourishing—the term for perfection (and virtuous activity) in Aristotelian ethics—is something real, but it is at the same time highly individualized, agent-relative, inclusive, self-directed, and profoundly social."⁹⁹ And so, while it is the notion of the common good that provides the definitive answer to the interrogation of political obligation and political authority, the justification of the common good (which is "inclusive and profoundly social") is entirely based on the common recognition of the citizen (who is "individualized, agent-relative, and self-directed"). Undeniably, the common good identified as a "good for each and all" is one that calls for the self-reflection of the *individual* citizen in realizing what is good for himself and for *others*. As Green puts it, an "interest in common good" is

> the ground of political society, in the sense that without it no body of people would recognize an authority as having a claim on their common obedience. It is so far as a government represents to them a common good that the subjects are conscious that they ought to obey it, i.e., that obedience to it is a means to an end desirable in itself or absolutely.¹⁰⁰

In this context, the very end desirable in itself is nothing but to realize one's moral capability (i.e., moral good), which, according to the British idealists, is closely interconnected with the equal conditions of other people to fulfill their moral good. To truly grasp what Green means by the common good, we must now turn to the viewpoint of "ethical citizenship."

A Good for Each and All

In the milieu of British idealism, "ethical citizenship" means that in addition to a system of rights, citizens "have special duties to one another as equal members of a shared community based on some form of common good,"[101] and so, a crucial aspect of the new liberal politics initiated by the British idealists is the stress on the "correlation of rights and duties."[102] In what follows, I am going to illustrate Green's identification of the common good as a "good for each and all" by reference to the three main ingredients that have been attributed to Confucian civic virtue, namely, "ethical mutuality," "helping others do good," and "caring about the worst-off." In the course of this examination, we shall have an opportunity to see how Green's theory of a common good aims to merge utilitarianism with Kantianism.

Mutual Membership: The Problem of Equality in Utilitarianism

Above all, it must be remembered that on the topic of individuality, Green's idea of self-realization is likewise predicated upon an "embodied self," expressing and acting within human relations and social relations. Hence, it is not surprising that Green's ethical capture of citizenship holds that citizens have "mutual membership"[103] in a community in which they try to obtain mutual recognition of a common good. In this regard, I think Avital Simhony is absolutely correct in articulating that Green's different expressions of "mutual membership," "mutual interest," "mutual dependence," "mutual helpfulness," and "mutual recognition" all lead to the same point, that the common good is one that pins down the "terrain of social and moral connectedness" where one's good and others' good are "non-contingently interwoven."[104]

In this regard, the common good from start to finish is a "good common to the person conceiving it with *others*, and good for him and them";[105] in other words, for Green, as for Mou, the *commonality* of the good binding together the members of a community points to a specific form of "ethical mutuality." And here, to use Bradley's terms, the genuine import of "goodness" in question is not "pleasure for pleasure's sake" (utilitarianism) or "duty for duty's sake" (deontology), but the actualization of one's moral potentiality in concrete situations known as "my station and its duties" (the ethics of self-realization).[106]

As regards utilitarianism, to begin with, Green picks holes in Bentham's defense of the equal respect for humanity. In order to assess utilitarianism from the standpoint of moral practice, Green actually makes two main points: On the one hand, vis-à-vis the principle of equality, he grants that utilitarianism is inclined to give equal consideration to the happiness of everyone. In Green's own words, with the slogan that "every one should count for one and no one for more than one," the movement of utilitarianism has tried to make obvious the moral vision that every human person should be "deemed an end of absolute value, as much entitled as any one else to have his well-being taken account of in considering the justifiableness of an action by which that well-being could be affected"; that said, as with Kant on this point, the leading utilitarian thinkers such as Bentham also pay attention to "the duty of treating all men equally."[107]

On the other hand, however, when dealing with the principle of promoting "the greatest happiness for the greatest number," Bentham is at once different from Kant. This is largely because the *equality* that concerns Bentham is not the Kantian categorical imperative to "act so as to treat humanity, whether in your own person or in that of others, always as an end, never merely as a means,"[108] but the equal measurement of men's different kinds of pleasure. That is to say, *for practical purposes*, the Benthamite maintains that "[that which] is of value in itself" is not every person but every pleasure at the end of the day.[109] There is, however, every reason to contend that different men may have different perceptions of pleasure in most different degrees, and therefore, it is hard for the Benthamite to "afford any positive ground for that treatment of all men's happiness as entitled to equal consideration" in the name of "beneficence."[110]

Thus seen, Green's argument against utilitarianism is based on its lack of positive ground, not its lack of equal consideration. Indeed, for Green, what makes Kant's deontology so distinguished is that he has built a more solid ground than utilitarianism for guaranteeing the equal treatment of the self-esteem of every person. After all, as far as the duty to humanity is concerned, Kant affords a better solution than Bentham, simply because utilitarianism is in many ways a resilient form of hedonism, maintaining that the end in morality is *dependent on* one's calculation of pleasures and pains.

EQUAL ATTAINMENT: THE PROBLEM OF OPPRESSION
IN UTILITARIANISM

All this, however, is not meant to say that Green discards utilitarianism completely. The truth is rather that Green highly appreciates its endeavor to reject traditional natural rights theory by emphasizing the social meaning of rights, and more essentially, that Green considers the empirical cognition of the "better-being of all the rest" an essential aspect of the common good. Thus, to be exact, in Green's view, the major failure of utilitarianism is not that it cares about "all men's happiness," but that when pursuing "all men's happiness," it is unable to provide sufficient positive ground for treating "all men's dignity" equally, and consequently leaves room for potential "oppression of the weaker by the stronger" in public life.

In other words, thanks to the potential pitfall of treating others as a means, the formula of the "greatest happiness for the greatest number" is often subject to seeking the well-being of the lucky majority at the expense of the greater well-being of the unfortunate few. Put differently, while the principle of equality in Bentham's system is intended to alleviate the distress of the weaker by raising the "total amount of happiness," another shortcoming embedded in the principle of maximization is that it would justify a society that permits the "total amount of happiness" always in favor of the pleasure of the stronger, completely regardless of the pain of the weaker. Based on the premise that different men are prone to pleasure "in most different degrees," Green thus continues to express his concern about the problem of class oppression or social oppression by saying:

> Certainly no absolute rule could be founded on [utilitarianism], prohibiting all pursuit of happiness by one man which interferes with the happiness of another, or what we commonly call the oppression of the weaker by the stronger; for the stronger being presumably capable of pleasure in higher degree, there could

be nothing to show that the quantity of pleasure resulting from the gain to the stronger through the loss to the weaker was not greater than would have been the quantity resulting if the claims of each had been treated as equal.[112]

Another way of making the same point is to say that for Green, the idea of "mutuality" or "reciprocity" characterizing the common good denotes not only that we are related to each other in an ethical sense, but also that "others are not regarded as a mere means to one's own good but, rather, are fellow citizens who share identical goods (ways of acting/being treated) with one another."[113] In Green's thinking, "citizenship only makes the moral man" because citizenship only provides that self-respect, "which is the true basis of respect for others, and without which there is no lasting social order or real morality."[114]

To conclude, then, utilitarianism is unable to tackle the problem of inequality caused by the "oppression of the weaker by the stronger," not because utilitarianism lacks equal consideration, but because there is a tension between the principle of equality and the principle of maximization coexisting in utilitarianism. Or alternatively, we may say that in the development of morality, utilitarianism falls short of founding civil society on the idea of a common good in relation to the "less favored members of society," as the good sought by the Benthamite admits of "being competed for" and "cannot be equally attained by all."[115]

Shared Language: The Problem of Actualization in Kantianism

From this, it follows that unless the element of equal respect for human dignity deeply rooted in Kant's deontology is adjoined, one cannot prevent utilitarianism from enabling the "oppression of the weaker by the stronger." Nonetheless, it cannot be overlooked that Green takes issue with Kant's deontological defense of the formula of "duty for duty's sake" as well. For Kant, as we have seen, morality is a system of laws of freedom known as the categorical imperatives, specifying what ends the fully rational beings ought to choose for themselves and how they ought to act with regard to these ends. In Kant's system, then, the formula of "the end in itself," spelling out the moral demand of equal respect, is just a sign of the truth that human beings are bestowed with equal rationality to exercise their free will. However, this freedom is *transcendental* in the sense that it is beyond the realm of cognitive knowledge; it is a rational guide for action in light of which a person can have faith in the postulate *that he is free*.[116] Accordingly, a typical Hegelian critique of Kant's viewpoint of "two-worlds" has been often launched, on the account that it treats free will simply as a *postulate*, lacking a consideration of the objectification of freedom in ethical life.

Along with this criticism, in "Lecture on Kant" Green complains that Kant unnecessarily disconnects desire (the empirical self) with moral thinking (the moral self). According to Green, as stated, "Kant's mistake is to assume there is no alternative between determination by natural desire for pleasure, and determination by abstract contemplation of moral law; for we often in all consciousness desire things other than pleasure."[117] Here, it is worth mentioning that in Green's system the idea of a good is the "idea of something that will satisfy a desire" and that "only if some pleasure is the object of desire does the anticipation of the satisfaction of the desire yield the idea of pleasure as a good."[118] This is to say that for Green, to fulfill oneself in the moral sense is, in point of fact, a satisfaction of desire, an actualization of will.[119] Seen in this light, the formula of "duty for duty's sake" is thereby of "empty abstractness" as it does not deal with human desire and cognition; it is an "idea of nothing in particular to be done,"[120] resulting in the "paralysis of will"[121] in the end.

Furthermore, Kant ignores the fact that there are different moral rules, bringing about conflicts of duties in the actual world, or what R. G. Collingwood calls the "misfit between yourself and your situation."[122] To resolve this misfit, for Green, we must alter the focus of attention from the Kantian interrogation of "what I ought to do" to that of "what kind of person I ought to be,"[123] engaging in an endless pursuit of self-perfection, otherwise known as the true self. The true self, by definition, is not an "isolated self" in the Kantian sense, but rather, an "embodied self" seeking his own good, the "bettering of his life," with regard to the good of others, the "bettering of others' lives" in ethical life.

In this regard, it seems to me that largely in keeping with the "way of *zhongshu*," Green also attributes the virtues of "ethical mutuality" and "helping others do good" to his identification of the common good without abandoning the Kantian formula of "the end in itself." As Green powerfully articulates:

> Social life is to personality what language is to thought. Language presupposes thought as a capacity, but in us the capacity of thought is only actualized in language. So human

society presupposes persons in capacity—subjects capable each of conceiving himself and the bettering of his life as an end to himself—but it is only in the intercourse of men, each recognized by each as an end, not merely as a means, and thus as having reciprocal claims, that capacity is actualized and that we really live as persons.[124]

Surely, it is against this context that Green comes to define the conception of virtue in terms of three basic conditions: first, virtue is meant to imply "social merit as founded on a certain sort of character or habit of will"; second, virtue springs from the individual's effort to "satisfy himself with some good conceived as true or permanent"; third, "it is only as common to himself with a society that the individual can so conceive of a good."[125] In consequence, as Green concludes, unless the common good that we are after appears to be a "state of mind or character of which the attainment, or approach to attainment, by each is itself a contribution to its attainment by every one else," our social life can never arrive at a harmonious order as "new vistas of hostile interests, with new prospects of failure for the weaker," are continually opening.[126] Indeed, one of the most distinctive features underpinning the notion of the common good shared by Mou and Green is the civic virtue of "caring about the worst-off."

A Synthesis of Kantianism and Utilitarianism

Thus far, we have established that while Green maintains the gist of the Kantian critique of utilitarianism, sticking to the point that citizens should mutually recognize each other "always as an end, not merely as a means," he does not intend to utterly relinquish the utilitarian care about the "better-off of all the rest" too. According to Green, to truly discover one's own pleasures and pains, one needs to appreciate the pleasures and pains of others because the satisfaction of the self includes a moral concern about the satisfaction of others, "not simply as a means to our own pleasure, but as ends in themselves deserving their own satisfaction."[127] In other words, "man cannot contemplate himself as in a better state, or on the way to the best, without contemplating others, not merely as a means to that better state, but as sharing it with him."[128]

On this reading, the ethics of self-realization identified as an endless pursuit of self-perfection toward a higher self can be suitably seen as an attempt to bring together the Kantian belief in the "equal respect for human dignity" and the utilitarian concern about the "better-being of all the rest" at one go. The politics of the common good promoted by Green and his fellows brings into consideration not only the *form* of the formula of "the end in itself" but also the *content* of "the well-being of others." As a result of this, it has the merits of actualizing our freedom and moral ability in concrete situations and removing the "oppression of the weaker by the stronger" at the same time.

On the whole, it seems evident that Green's discussion of the common good grounded in an ethics of self-realization is parallel to Bradley's dialectical analysis of the development of moral consciousness through "pleasure for pleasure's sake," via "duty for duty's sake," toward "my station and its duties." Indeed, by giving weight to the question of "what kind of person I ought to be" in respect of the true self, the British idealists have succeeded in bringing to light an identification of the common good as a "good for each and all" in accordance with the exercise of liberal politics. Through the above discussion, we may thus arrive at the conclusion that New Confucianism and British idealism share not only an ethics of self-realization but also a perfectionist understanding of political ideas such as citizenship and the state.

A Nondominant Theory of the Common Good

Before putting the finishing touches on the picture of perfectionist liberalism in terms of freedom and rights, I shall close this chapter by shedding some light on the similarities between Mou's and Green's nondominant theory of the common good.

Noncentralization: Against the Coercion of State Power

On the one hand, seen from the perspective of the state, Green's notion of the common good identified as a "good for each and all" demands that the state should strive to remove obstacles to every citizen's self-realization, meaning that the business of the state is to create equal conditions for all citizens to attain self-realization by sustaining a system of rights and duties. At the heart of Green's perfectionist version of politics, therefore, lies a principle of *noncentralization*, purporting to prevent the state's power from abusing the common good as a weapon to threaten the values of autonomy, plurality, and openness that mark out an open society.

For this reason, when Green writes that the state is an "institution for the promotion of a common good,"[129] he does not intend to say that the individual citizen should sacrifice his self-interest for the common interest of the state, nor does he have it in mind that the state is permitted to promote some sort of common interest in favor of those who are stronger in utilitarian terms. Instead, the principle of noncentralization denotes that the proper office of the state is to maintain the equal "conditions and encouragements" for every citizen to realize his or her own moral potentiality in a way that "contributes to the better-being of all the rest."

It is true that in comparison to Green, Mou does not establish a thorough theory of freedom and rights, and he fails to define the legal aspect of the state in a sufficient way. However, given that these two thinkers share an ethics of self-realization and a Hegelian bid to reconcile the twofold meaning of a modern state, I contend that what Green has said about the character of the state can help us to fill in these lacunas in Mou's political writings.

More exactly, since a significant aspect of Mou's Confucian liberalism is to unite the "way of governance" with the "way of politics" in a manner that generates a perfectionist state together with a system of rights protected by the rule of law, I cannot see why Mou would not be in agreement with Green's major argument that the main business of the state is to maintain "conditions and encouragements" for citizens to erect their own "moral personality and moral character," even though Mou does not bring up the slogan of "removing obstacles to self-realization." In fact, from the above discussion, it seems clear that the Confucian governing virtue of "making the people wealthy before cultivation" is consistent with the crucial task of "removing obstacles to self-realization" in a significant way. On the whole, I consider it appropriate to remark that for Mou, "to govern is to correct" the state of affairs that are preventing the citizen from "attaining accomplishment according to the individual's nature."

Nonselfishness and Nonexploitation: Against the Oppression of Social Life

On the other hand, seen from the perspective of the citizen, there are prominent resemblances between Green's theory of the common good and

Mou's rebuilding of Confucian civic virtue. Corresponding to the notion of "ethical mutuality" attached to Confucianism, Green maintains that "the common good is mutual good: no one can achieve self-realization in separation from and independent of others; one's development is dependent on and is reciprocal with others."[130] In consequence, Green would highly appreciate the Confucian dictum about "helping others do good" too as he asserts in a similar way that a profound consideration about the "bettering of other's life" is essential to the realization of the "bettering of one's life." As a final point, Green's attempt to resolve the "oppression of the weaker by the stronger" by bringing into consideration Kant's equal treatment of human dignity is in parallel with the Confucian endeavor to "care about the worst-off" in light of the empathic connotation of *shu*.

To see this from another angle, it can be said that the social merits of "helping others do good" and "caring about the worst-off," largely resulting from the key concept of "ethical mutuality," are consistent with the principle of nonselfishness and that of nonexploitation, respectively. In brief, whereas the first one requires the citizen to not seek his "dominant interests to an object private to himself in which others cannot share," the second principle holds that "the humanity in the person of every one is to be treated always as an end, not merely as a means."[131] More exactly, if the second principle of nonexploitation reiterates the Kantian formula of "the end in itself," denoting equal respect among all rational beings, then the first principle of nonselfishness aims to retrieve the utilitarian concern about the "better-being of all the rest."

These two principles also work for Confucian liberalism. For, if a person is willing to "help others to take their stand and get others there," he will not have "dominant interests to an object private to himself in which others cannot share." Again, when a person is self-restricted from "imposing on others what he does not desire," he is apt to abide by the prescription of treating every person always as an end. On the whole, in an ideal society full of the "way of *zhongshu*," everybody would love to care for others, and nobody would desire being treated merely as a means. And if it is the case that the weaker are in danger of being treated as a means once permanently repressed by the stronger, then it is the main task of the state to put an end to social oppression by correcting what actually prevents the citizen from "attaining accomplishment according to the individual's nature" so as to adjust the propriety of the moral relationship between the self and others.

Chapter 8

Freedom and Rights

Introduction

This chapter aims to explore more fully the picture of Confucian liberalism as a Hegelian form of perfectionist liberalism by focusing on the interconnected ideas of freedom and rights. The following discussion will be organized into two major parts, dealing with the longstanding dispute about the twofold meaning of freedom and the plausible justification of rights in the Chinese cultural setting. By this means, it is hoped that the merits of Confucian liberalism in transcending the two extreme poles of anti-Confucian liberalism and antiliberal Confucianism can be further illuminated.

To begin with, largely thanks to Isaiah Berlin's "Two Concepts of Liberty" and Zhang Foquan's [Chang Fo-Chuan] (張佛泉 1907–1994) *Ziyou yu renquan* 自由與人權 (Liberty and Human Rights), an asymmetry emerged in conceptualizing negative and positive freedom in the Chinese context.[1] Overall, this development suggests, first, that whereas negative freedom represents a genuine appreciation of liberalism, positive freedom only leads to an extremely repressive society; second, that the relentless search for true freedom in Confucianism, as the "standard viewpoint" shows, is thus in deep conflict with liberalism. Indeed, for the anti-Confucian liberals, the pursuit of "humane government" (*renzheng* 仁政) in Confucianism needs to give way to a universalistic calling for human rights because the Confucian political ideal is predicated upon an obsolete perfectionist view about human reason, while what lays the foundation for the modern democratic state is the negative freedom of the individual. The asymmetry in question, however, has given rise to serious confusion that is rooted in Chinese political discourse about the meaning of liberalism. In order to make possible the promise of Confucian liberalism, I therefore argue that a more convincing reexamination of the idea of freedom can be advantageous for correcting these points of confusion. For instance, the appreciation of positive freedom displayed by the leading British idealist, T. H. Green, discloses a Hegelian form of perfectionist liberalism that greatly enriches our understanding of liberalism, as well as individualism and common humanity, from different perspectives.

That said, it is worthwhile to rework Green's theory of freedom for three reasons. First, as we shall see, both Berlin and Zhang refer to Green when making their distinctions between negative and positive freedom; indeed, "Green has frequently been portrayed as the originator of this distinction"[2] with regard to his perfectionist understanding of humanity. Second, be that as it may, Green's stress on the full actualization of human potentialities in concrete situations, or what I have called embodied individualism, still retains Kantian autonomy as one of the primary principles in politics even while revising it in a Hegelian vein. As a result, there is room to make the point that Green's holistic defense of positive freedom is free from political totalitarianism. Third, seen in this light, Green's philosophical scrutiny of freedom reflects a perfectionist expression of liberalism, which takes both an individual's moral ability and its embodiments (the family, civil society, and the state) into account, without giving up the hope of seeking a common good in politics. To be sure, "Green's message was concerned with an internal reform of the liberal tradition; it was not his aim to create a breach within liberalism."[3]

Based on what has been said, I then reveal the prominent similarities in theorizing the idea of freedom that Green shares with Mou Zongsan and his companions. The upshot here is that the leading New Confucians all attempt to keep hold of the double meaning of freedom in their political writings. That is to say, as with Green, a significant but rarely discussed aspect of Mou's political thinking is to relate the idea of true freedom in Confucianism to positive freedom grounded in an ethics of self-realization, without casting aside the political worth of negative freedom commonly known as rights.

Once focusing on the expression of rights, it seems to me that the three main objections to the anticipation of Confucian liberalism raised by the antiliberal Confucians can immediately be restated as follows: First, they argue that the stress on rights is utterly Western-centric and that there is no such thing as rights in classical Confucianism. Second, they make a case that the search for Confucian liberalism simply overlooks the major distinctions between Chinese and Western cultures; for example, in contrast to liberalism, Confucianism is apt to proclaim the priority of community and tradition over the individual and rights. Third, instead of accommodating liberal democracy in the Chinese cultural setting, they resort to finding faults with its moral weakness.

Against this context, I contend that the legacy that Mou has left us for reconstructing a political theory of Confucian liberalism actually contains two possible ways of interpretation, namely, Kantian and Hegelian, and that the latter is more beneficial than the former in responding to those objections in association with rights discourse made by antiliberal Confucianism. Here I do not intend to deny that given Mou's great contribution to making manifest the moral resonance between Confucianism and Kant, a number of his distinguished disciples are, unsurprisingly, driven to construe his political thought in a Kantian vein. Also, I concede that it is, by and large, Kantian autonomy that sets the tone for rights discourse and democratic imagination for the time being. But it seems to me that insofar as Confucian liberalism is, by default, a cultural hybrid, the *direct* application of the Kantian theory of rights into the Chinese context is problematic, simply because the Kantian approach is *culturally blind* and *historically insensitive*.

Two Concepts of Freedom Revisited

Let me now begin this chapter with a brief examination of Berlin's and Zhang's accounts of freedom, followed by a reflection upon the diverse meanings of liberalism, individualism, and common humanity.

Isaiah Berlin

In his renowned essay "Two Concepts of Liberty," Berlin makes a decisive distinction between negative freedom and positive freedom. In Berlin's understanding, negative freedom "consists in the absence of obstacles not only to my actual but, to my potential choices—to my acting in this or that way if I choose to do so," and "political liberty in this sense is simply the area within which a man can act unobstructed by others."[4] Historically, Berlin traces the origins of negative liberty, as such, through the works of Hobbes, Locke, Bentham, and J. S. Mill in England, and those of Constant and Tocqueville in France.

By contrast, Berlin defines positive freedom as that "which consists in being one's own master."[5] This sense of freedom evolves from Kant's "retreat to the inner citadel" in pursuit of self-determination or autonomy, to the ideal of self-realization, as in Hegel's full actuality of one's "true self," or as in Marx's rational emancipation from being enslaved.[6] While both Hegel and Marx treat freedom as the ability to grasp the rational necessity of history and nature, I am here concerned with the former thinker and his British disciples such as Green.[7] According to Berlin, Green's statement that "true freedom is the maximum of power for all the members of human society alike to make the best of themselves," "apart from the confusion of freedom with equality," entails a holistic tendency to depreciate personal enjoyment. The interesting thing for Berlin, however, is that "Green was a genuine liberal: but many a tyrant could use this formula to justify his worst acts of oppression."[8]

Berlin's dichotomy of freedom has been criticized for its conceptual misleadingness,[9] historical limitation,[10] philosophical prejudices,[11] and practical implausibility.[12] For my purposes, I only intend to single out two key matters. First, the motive standing behind Berlin's preference of negative freedom over positive freedom is to maintain the liberal division between politics and morality, such that the value of individuality in terms of freedom to choose can be ensured. Second, Berlin's dismissal of positive freedom actually comes from his concern about the political evils that might occur when false expectations for the "perfect state" of humanity are applied to the political sphere. In other words, for Berlin, there are certain connections between philosophical holism and political totalitarianism.

Zhang Foquan

Roughly four years before Berlin's inaugural lecture, Zhang Foquan published his landmark work on the history of Chinese liberalism, *Ziyou yu renquan*, in which he also undertook a redefinition of the meaning of freedom.[13] For Zhang, as for Berlin, there are two designations of freedom that must be distinguished: whereas negative freedom means the "political protection of freedom," positive freedom denotes a "certain state of the inner life of a man."[14] To make his case, Zhang quotes A. D. Lindsay, John C. Murray, and Edward Corwin to reveal that freedom, so far as its proper political and legal usage is concerned, simply means rights in the Western liberal tradition.[15] In stark contrast, he cites Confucius's famous expression in the *Analects* (*Lunyu* 論語) that "at seventy I followed my heart's desire without overstepping the line" to highlight the moral and spiritual aspects of positive freedom in Confucianism.[16]

Put briefly, Zhang asserts that there are three crucial differences between negative and positive freedom: first, the protection of the former requires coercion, while the exercise of the latter involves autonomy; second, the definition of the former is general, certain, and formalistic, while that of the latter is various according to people's different ways of life; and third, the former deals with the external relation between men, while the latter points to the inner life of a man.[17] In short, as with Berlin, what underpins Zhang's distinction is the liberal separation of politics from morality.

At this point, it is crucial to note that Zhang also acknowledges that Green, in his "On the Different Senses of 'Freedom' as Applied to Will and the Moral Progress of Man,"[18] has clarified the two implications of freedom. In Zhang's reading, Green is aware of the differentiation between the "primary meaning" of freedom, or "outward or juristic freedom," which deals with our "social and political relationships," and the reflective meaning of freedom, or "true" freedom, which accounts for our "inner life."[19] Later in the text, he adds that the distinction at stake echoes perfectly the distinction between the legal force of "obligation" and the moral autonomy of "duty" that Green has made elsewhere.[20] Overall, although Zhang severely criticizes philosophical holism by connecting it with political totalitarianism, his influential definition of "freedom as rights" in political and legal terms owes a great deal to British idealism.

However, in defending his own version of liberalism, Zhang surely does not endorse the whole package of British idealism. Despite admitting Green's distinction between legality and morality, he thinks that Green falls short of keeping this distinction in the end. This is because, according to the ethics of self-realization encouraged by Green, among other British idealists, it is eventually the "true" freedom associated with the notion of a common good that provides justification for the obedience of the "normal law of a state." Again, he blames Green for defending the confusing idea of eternal consciousness and a close relation between society and the state. Throughout *Ziyou yu renquan*, nevertheless, it is

Bernard Bosanquet's *The Philosophical Theory of the State* that receives most of Zhang's disapproval. Similar to Berlin, Zhang remarks that what is terribly wrong with the endorsement of positive freedom in the case of British idealism is that it often gives enthusiastic approval to the ultimate authority of the state over the individual.

According to Zhang, the justification of negative freedom therefore points to a solid confirmation of human dignity.[21] At root, his liberal thinking replicates the mainstream individualist conviction that the existence of society is for the sake of the individual, that "individuals are the only and final units in all kinds of human associations and the sources of every value," and that only men, not groups or the state, can have the legitimate subjectivity of rights.[22] Zhang's liberalism, without a doubt, entails the universalistic belief that there are common human values, namely, human rights, transcending various traditions and cultural barriers.

Freedom as Rights

It has been shown that primarily because both Berlin and Zhang use the liberal division between morality and politics to bolster the worth of individuality in terms of values such as human dignity, self-determination, and freedom to choose, their discussions on freedom seem to have something in common. In addition, their aversions to positive freedom and to the ethical features of the state strongly reflect the ethos of the Cold War. It is, therefore, no wonder that Berlin is so frequently considered an essential authority for Westernized liberals who aggressively critique New Confucianism[23] and that Zhang's legendary remark about "freedom as rights" is still taken as the "standard viewpoint" of Chinese liberalism.

Indeed, the clear-cut distinction between outer political action regulated by laws and the inner moral conduct governed by autonomy is completely blurred in Confucianism. By contrast, in mainstream liberal thinking, morality and politics are to be separated; as Zhang puts it, in terms of morality, "the dignity of man consists in virtues," whereas in terms of politics, "the dignity of man consists in basic rights."[24] Echoing Yin Haiguang [Yin Hai-Kuang] (殷海光 1919–1969), another leading liberal thinker, Zhang thus summarizes his objection to positive freedom by articulating that "it is a necessary conclusion that panmoralism (*fan daodezhuyi* 泛道德主義) turns out to be pan-politicism (*fan zhengzhizhuyi* 泛政治主義)"[25] and that this is the reason "why politics and ethics must be divorced, why political means cannot be mixed up with ethical ideals, and why 'inner sagehood and outer kingliness' (*neisheng waiwang* 內聖外王) cannot be taken as a democratic ideal."[26]

The crucial point here, however, is that if the separation of politics from morality is a vital means to reach the liberal ends of human dignity, self-determination, freedom to choose, and so on, it seems that there are divergent ways of appreciating the individual in the history of moral and political thought, which in turn allows us to understand the significance of common humanity in diverse ways.

More to the point, seen from the perspectives of the recent scholarship on the British idealists, especially on Green, it appears that philosophical holism relative to true freedom or positive freedom does not necessarily entail political totalitarianism. In fact, in the case of Green, philosophical holism is successfully employed to reevaluate liberal values in ways that are able to broaden our grasp of the horizons of liberalism, individualism, and common humanity currently in question. When searching for the possibility and plausibility of Confucian liberalism as a Hegelian form of perfectionist liberalism, then, attention must be directed not only to the confusion in identifying the *singularity* of liberalism as one that denies the moral consideration of positive freedom in terms of a common good, but also to the *diversity* of liberalisms that the Hegelian thinkers such as Green have tried to make manifest.

Four Concepts of Freedom Extended

What has been said so far reaffirms the three reasons for reworking Green's theory of freedom that I pointed out at the outset, which in turn correspond to the three main topics underpinning this book, namely, the diversity of liberalisms, individualisms, and notions of common humanity. In the discussion that follows, it seems reasonable to rework them by reference to Green's provocative theory of freedom. Here, let me begin with the last topic, that is, Green's perfectionist understanding of humanity.

A Perfectionist Understanding of Humanity

Apart from his well-known books, *Prolegomena to Ethics* and *Lectures on the Principles of Political Obligations*, Green has written two important essays on freedom: "Lectures on Liberal Legislation and Freedom of Contract,"[27] in which the implications of negative and positive freedom in the political context are discussed, and "Freedom," in which he clarifies the meanings of "juristic" freedom and "true" freedom in the personal context.[28] These two essays are interwoven in the sense that "a dual meaning of freedom is already established in the usage of the word in the personal realm, and it is this dual usage that underpins the conceptual pair of positive and negative freedoms in the political realm."[29] Put briefly, while positive and "true" freedoms are related to "moral action," negative and "juristic" freedoms are related to "ordinary action." On this reading, there are four concepts of freedom in Green's thought—negative freedom, positive freedom, juristic freedom, and "true" freedom—which can be illustrated in the table drawn up by Maria Dimova-Cookson below.[30]

Moreover, Green's examination of freedom is associated with the three important aspects of his moral theory that we have previously discussed—the perfectionist ethics of self-realization, freedom as the development of moral ability, and the Hegelian internal revision of Kant's self-determination or autonomy.[31] First, Green's assessment of "true" freedom is driven by his perfectionist ethics of self-realization. In a nutshell, the key thread running through Green's *Prolegomena* can be reiterated as follows: given the necessary existence of the knowing subject and its will to conceive desire that initiates action, it follows that the rational satisfaction of an action, that is, goodness, must be the actual realization of the capacities and potentialities of the self within the community, rather than the independent exercise of the free will as a postulate. That is to say, whereas will is the endeavor to seek self-satisfaction in terms of desires and wishes, reason is the capacity and potentiality to reach a better state of self-satisfaction, in which the "self" is treated as an end. This means that for Green, the moral import of human action lies not outside human action, but in the idea of goodness found in the process of one's own self-realization. Consequently, the degree of goodness in an action is based on the fulfillment of the rational

Table 8.1. The Meaning of Freedom in the Personal and Political Context

	Ordinary Action	Moral Action
Political Context	Negative Freedom	Positive Freedom
Personal Context	Juristic Freedom	"True" Freedom

capacities and potentialities of the self promised in the action. In short, self-realization is the "realization of the capacities of the human soul" or the "perfecting of man"[32] in history; in the moral ideal of self-realization, will and reason are eventually to be united in one.

Green's characterization of self-realization as the unity of will and reason follows in Hegel's footsteps by seeing willing as inseparable from thinking, and freedom as the rational ability to carry out one's own desires and wishes.[33] Indeed, when Charles Taylor says that "freedom is important to us because we are purposive beings,"[34] he is simply echoing the goal-oriented, self-realizing dimension of freedom in Hegel's heritage that likewise captures Green's mind: "willing constitutes freedom."[35] As Green puts it, "a man is subject to the law of his being, in virtue of which he at once seeks self-satisfaction, and is prevented from finding it in the objects which he actually desires, and in which he ordinarily seeks it."[36] In this regard, "true" freedom denotes what Hegel means by "rational will," that is "the will completely *within itself*, because it has reference to nothing but itself, so that every relationship of *dependence* on something *other* than itself is thereby eliminated."[37]

Second, unlike the view held by Berlin and others that "freedom is carefully and insistently distinguished from power and ability," and the idea that "there is a difference between *being free* and *being able to*,"[38] Green basically identifies freedom with ability and power. Along these lines, Green thus refuses to see juristic (and negative) freedom as the absence of obstacles and "true" (and positive) freedom as the ability to do something; instead, for Green, whereas juristic freedom signifies the "first form of self-enjoyment—of the joy of the self-conscious spirit in itself,"[39] "true" freedom stands for a rational reflection upon the previous self-enjoyment. This means that the two concepts of freedom actually represent two different stages of the actualization of one's rationality and moral ability in the course of completing the act of self-realization: a high level of freedom is always waiting to be achieved as long as the exercise of juristic freedom ceases to bring a proper feeling of self-satisfaction. Hence, as stated, the significance of "moral action" does not lie outside human action; what is moral is to seek the "realization of the capacities of the human soul," which allows a higher actualization of freedom.

Third, regarding Hegel's revision of Kant's autonomy, there are three important things to note: In the first place, Hegel critiques Kant's ethics on the grounds that the categorical imperative is empty and self-contradictory. In the language of *Elements of the Philosophy of Right*,

Hegel argues that the idea of morality (*Moralität*) represented by Kant's categorical imperative and the earlier moment of formal rights "are both abstractions whose truth is attained only in *ethical life* (*Sittlichkeit*). Thus, ethical life is the unity of the will in its concepts and the will of the individual, that is, of the subject."[40] In other words, "the unity of the subject with the objective good which has being in and for itself is *ethical life*."[41]

It is, by and large, Hegel's *Sittlichkeit* that generates British idealism's ethics of self-realization in reference to the dictum "my station and its duties." For instance, in line with *Prolegomena*, Green maintains that self-realization must be undertaken in a system of social relations "with laws, customs and institutions corresponding."[42] Put clearly, Green and his fellow British idealists basically accept Hegel's principle of embodiment and maintain that human consciousness is not isolated, always involves an encounter with otherness, and requires recognition of what one is not. Hence, in Green's mind, "for the self to become actual or real, the individual, to employ Hegelian terminology, has to externalize his or her capacities"[43] in the social reality.

In the second place, with respect to the individual-community relationship, Hegelian *Sittlichkeit* implies what has been called embodied individualism, maintaining that since human agency must be historically conditioned, human reason and freedom can only be fully actualized in a certain historical context. In this regard, as Green puts it, Kant's moral doctrine was found unsatisfactory by Hegel as he "seemed to make freedom an unrealized and unrealizable state." In contrast, for Hegel, "freedom, as the condition in which the will is determined by an object adequate to itself, or by an object, which itself as reason constitutes, is realized in the state."[44]

At first glance, it does seem that Green consents to the Hegelian allegiance that the modern state should be treated "as including all the agencies for common good of a law-abiding people."[45] A closer look, however, shows that Green actually creates an innovative conception of the common good, which allows him to make a holistic defense of positive freedom and offers a liberal version of state intervention without succumbing to political totalitarianism. I shall return to these two aspects of Green's perfectionist liberalism shortly. For now, it seems appropriate to put in a quick word about Hegel's effort to overcome any possible divisions of humanity made by Kant, including the divisions between the subject and the object, phenomena and noumena, and history and nature. As with Taylor, once again, Green also aims to rebuff both Hume's and Kant's opposed views of the self in a Hegelian fashion. According to Avital Simhony,

> They both defend a view of a divided self, which results from segregating reason and desire. With Hume, reason is impractical: it can neither set ends of action nor furnish any motives for action. This is expressed, for Green, in Hume's famous statement that reason is the slave of passions. Although Kant recognizes the constructive role of reason—which Hume neglects—he excludes the only material that reason needs to construct action: namely desires. Reason, however, cannot be practical if it is empty of desires.[46]

A Holistic Defense of Positive Freedom

Setting aside the disputable issue of whether Hegel himself is a liberal thinker,[47] what is more important in the present context is to examine Green's perfectionist presentation of Hegelian liberalism. In Green's view, as I have indicated, juristic freedom is set apart from "true" freedom, not by distinctive categories of "being free" and "being able to," but by the different degrees of our rational reflection. Similarly, the same logic applies to the primary distinction between negative freedom and positive freedom in the political context. However, it is to Green's credit that in collective life our rational reflection cannot but gain a specific purpose, that is, to look for a common good. Thus, while "freedom in all the forms of doing what one will with one's own, is valuable only as a means to an end," "freedom in the positive sense," by definition, is "the liberation of the powers of all men equally for contributions to a common good."[48]

In Green's writings, the common good in question, for the most part, stands for *the equal moral power or capacity for all citizens to pursue their own self-realization*: when we speak of freedom as something more than "merely freedom from restraint or compulsion," or "freedom to do as we like irrespectively of what it is that we like," we mean "a positive power or capacity of doing or enjoying something worth doing or enjoying," something that we do or enjoy "in common with others."[49] On this reading, Green's idea of the common good represents a state of mutual recognition in which the actualization of my own desires and wishes does not exclude the possibility that others could also have the same moral power as I do to pursue their own. In this regard, I think Avital Simhony is correct in pointing out that, in preferring to specify the substance of a common good, Green is more likely to give the agent two moral boundaries for his or her "dominant interests" in the process of self-realization: nonselfishness and nonexploitation. As stated in the last chapter, while the first constraint requires the agent not to seek his "dominant interests to an object private to himself in which others cannot share," the second reiterates the Kantian motto "that the humanity in the person of every one is to be treated always as an end, not merely as a means."[50]

One of the major themes underlying this book is that there exist different ways of appreciating the import of individuality, human dignity, and the like, which in turn can help us to grasp the plural forms of individualism as well as liberalism. Against this context, I have suggested that Hegelian embodied individualism be treated as a critical refinement of Kantian atomistic individualism rather than a total rejection of the significance of the individual. To be sure, Hegel's revision of Kant's ethics signifies "a culmination of the tradition of reflection on freedom and politics that begins with Rousseau and runs through Kant and Fichte" in terms of self-determination.[51] In short, Hegel's approach is to revise Kant's idea of autonomy, rather than abandon it completely. In the deepest sense, self-realization is the real and full actualization of self-determination, not only because it takes human desires and ethical life into consideration, but also because it aims to ensure that the realization of *my-self* does not contradict that of other *selves*.

By the same token, the Hegelian influence on Green's thought does not imply that he utterly discards Kant's idea of self-determination. Despite the important way in which Green links positive freedom with "true" freedom in terms of Hegelian self-realization, it remains the case that Kant's self-determination in terms of personal judgment, choice, and decision making, or to use the expression in *Prolegomena*, the necessary existence of the knowing subject and its will to conceive desire, plays an indispensable role in Green's theory of freedom. Indeed, when Green remarks, "No one can convey a good character to another," that "Every one must make his character for himself,"[52] he is referring to Kantian self-determination. In this way, Green's idea of a common good relative to positive freedom does not presume a single highest form of life; instead, it is more plausibly conceived as "a common conception of autonomy

Freedom and Rights | 257

which denotes the habitual tendency to act in accordance with one's highest (i.e., distinctively human) capacities."[53]

This, together with the view that the distinction between juristic and "true" freedom consists merely of the degree of rational reflection, suggests that the two concepts of freedom in question actually *coexist* in the political sphere; that is to say, for Green, positive freedom entails the enjoyment of negative freedom, and therefore, he is apt to promote negative freedom insofar as he favors positive freedom. In other words, the *political* aspect of negative freedom, in accordance with positive freedom, connotes the legal opportunities to contribute to a common good in public space. Negative freedom, in every sense of the political world, is equivalent to the notion of rights Green describes elsewhere in *Lectures*. To quote Green,

> Only through the possession of rights can the power of the individual freely to make a common good his own have reality given to it. Rights are what may be called the negative realization of this power. That is, they realize it in the sense of providing for its free exercise, of securing the treatment of one man by another as equally free with himself, but they do not realize it positively, because their possession does not imply that in any active way the individual makes a common good his own.[54]

To sum up, I have tried to make four points. First, for Green, there is no categorical distinction between negative and positive freedom; second, the advocacy of positive freedom can be justified if it meets the requirement of obtaining the "liberation of the powers of all men equally for contributions to a common good"; third, negative freedom is just as valuable as positive freedom since it serves as the prerequisite for making a contribution to a common good; finally, Green's innovative idea of a common good rooted in the ethics of self-realization is very close to a "common conception of autonomy."[55] Bringing these views together, it seems to be the case that Green's holistic justification of positive freedom in terms of a common good has nothing to do with totalitarianism; far from it, what Green has established is something like a "principle of justice," by means of which we may redistribute rights and powers among citizens. The real purpose of politics, as Green understands it, is to embark on our rational reflection upon social reality (i.e., practical reasoning in context) so as to realize a common good. The practical lesson that we may have learned from Green, as opposed to a "confusion of freedom with equality,"[56] is "the next great conquest which our democracy, on behalf of its true freedom, has to make."[57]

A Liberal Version of State Interference

Green's realistic concerns about tackling widespread social evils have irrefutably pushed him to turn away from the state neutrality found in an older form of liberalism and move toward a new liberal approval of state intervention. Based on the idea of a common good, it is not surprising that for Green the proper office of the state is to remove any obstacles or hindrances to the realization of equal moral power for every citizen.

Clearly, from Green's nondominant concept of the common good discussed in the last chapter, it follows that he does not commit to justifying state intervention in favor of the "total triumph of any one principle."[58] Quite the opposite, even though the state's business is to maintain a common good, we have said that everyone has the right to conduct his own good life, as long as he or she does not break the principles of nonselfishness and nonexploitation. On the other hand, in keeping with the tenet of self-determination or autonomy, Green makes it clear that "it is the business of the state, not indeed directly to promote moral goodness, for that, from the very nature of moral goodness, it cannot do, but to maintain the conditions without which a free exercise of the human faculties is impossible."[59]

Therefore, we can return to the time when Green aimed to challenge the old liberal idea of state nonintervention. While facing the problem of employers's liability in the 1880s, for instance, the old liberals argued that "it is not for the state to step in" because "the workman should be left to take care of himself by the terms of his agreement with employer."[60] By contrast, we find that Green's argument for state intervention was not that personal voluntary agreement is unimportant, but because it is so important that the state should ensure the social conditions capable of maintaining an environment where all citizens have the same opportunity to exercise their equal moral power. Likewise, in defending public health and necessary education, Green wrote, "Until such a condition of society is reached, it is the business of law or the state to take the best security it can for the young citizens growing up in such a health and with so much education as is necessary for their real freedom."[61] In short, for Green, it is morally right for the state to sustain the standard of well-being for its citizens, only because the pursuit of a common good as he defines it is the best way to realize the politics of self-determination initiated by Rousseau and Kant.

Beyond Negative Freedom

Having accounted for Green's theory of freedom, its detachment from political totalitarianism, and the alternative version of liberalism it endorses, my next task is to unveil some of the striking similarities between New Confucianism and British idealism with regard to the perfectionist reading of humanity, as well as the various meanings of individualism and liberalism.

REN AS TRUE FREEDOM

It is interesting to note that like Green, the New Confucians also realized the twofold meaning of freedom in respect of moral action and ordinary action under legal protection, despite the fact that they did not scrutinize these two concepts of freedom in both the personal context and the political context as Green did. Xu Fuguan [Hsu Fu-Kuan] (徐復觀 1904–1982), for instance, famously writes that the "spiritual condition of life" (*shenghuo de jingshen zhuangtai* 生活底精神狀態) underlying liberalism points to "self-awareness," "being one's own master" (*zi zuo zhuzai* 自作主宰),[62] whereas the legal sense of freedom stands for one's "lawful rights to existence," which cannot be interfered with by any arbitrary exercise of political power.[63] Similarly, Mou articulates in a Hegelian tone[64] that "freedom must be affiliated with moral reason and a person's self-awareness," whereas "various rights are merely the outcomes of its objectification, protected by the Constitution in a democratic regime."[65] In other words, as Mou continues,

> The acquisition and enjoyment of rights, in point of fact, are apparently not ready at hand. Hegel extracts and condenses the expression that "men were born free and equal" into an "idea of humanity," concerning what the nature of humanity should be [through the development of history]. Man, being a man as such, according to the necessity of his nature, is free.

> Here freedom is taken to mean a self-aware, active creativity essentially bestowed upon a man to actualize his necessity.[66]

The above distinction between "freedom" and "rights" echoes a good deal what Zhang Foquan and Isaiah Berlin have referred to as positive freedom (in Hegel's usage) and negative freedom (i.e., rights).[67] However, in keeping with Green's argument, Mou contends that a more plausible understanding of freedom should embrace both facets concerned because liberalism today has lost its "moral ideals," or "moral spirituality," in the sense that "the presentation of [its] freedom is negative and incautious,"[68] while the real sense of freedom is embedded in the "moral heart-mind."[69] And here, in his attempt to retrieve the "moral spirituality" of liberalism, Mou admits that by "spirituality," he means the spirit of *ren* 仁 (humaneness), or the "unity of subjectivity and objectivity in rationality," that is "freedom (in Hegel's definition),"[70] rather than the kind of freedom that current liberalism takes it to be.

Without a doubt, the view that *ren* is analogous to "true" freedom, the fullest actualization of one's moral potentiality, is widely held by the New Confucians. For example, the supremacy of "fulfilling virtue" (*chengde* 成德) and "fulfilling oneself" (*chengji* 成己) in Confucianism was prominently emphasized in the famous "Declaration on Behalf of Chinese Culture Respectively Announced to the People of the World" (*Wei Zhongguo wenhua jinggao shijie renshi xuanyan* 為中國文化敬告世界人士宣言 1958). In other words, Mou's endeavor to define "true" freedom as the actualization of "moral reason and a person's self-awareness" significantly reflects the "spirit of humanism" (*renwen jingshen* 人文精神) underpinning New Confucianism. In short, as Mou remarks, *ren* means man (*ren zhe ren ye* 仁者人也) and the attributes of humanness; "when these two are conjoined the result is *Dao*."[71]

According to Tang Junyi [Tang Chun-I] (唐君毅 1909–1978), to take another salient example, the final end of freedom is nothing but to make happen the "spirit of humanism," that is, the craving for the completest affirmation of "humanity, human relations, the human way, human personality, and the existence and value of human culture and history."[72] Seen in this light, the "highest form of freedom" or the "ultimate meaning of the self" has been exquisitely expressed in Confucius's golden rule that "the practice of humaneness depends on oneself alone" (*weiren youji* 為仁由己),[73] meaning that the "heart-mind of *ren*" (*renxin* 仁心) presents the fullest actualization of freedom and humanity.[74] In summary, either Tang or Mou would admit that *ren* is just another expression of what Berlin has referred to as positive freedom, that is, "being one's own master," in the words of Xu Fuguan.

On this reading, as Tang continues, Confucius is the sage who sets the tone for the understanding of real freedom and ethical personality in Chinese culture for what Confucius has achieved in the end is the "completest style of a sage."[75] Moreover, in spite of crucial differences, the Confucian way of understanding freedom is akin to the idealistic tradition of Kant, Hegel, Fichte, and so on[76] because these Western thinkers put stress on the significance of real freedom in a similar way. Along this line of reasoning, Tang therefore concludes by remarking that the idea of freedom in the mainstream liberalism of Britain (ranging from Locke to Mill) actually falls short of taking seriously the humanist depth of freedom and the ultimate meaning of human life. Instead, the theory of freedom that matches the spirit of Confucianism, as Tang confesses, is one that has been encouraged by the British idealists, including T. H. Green, F. H. Bradley, and Bernard Bosanquet.[77]

Seen in light of Green's theory of freedom, there are, accordingly, three crucial points that must be clarified. First, even if *ren* understood as "true" freedom grounded in the "spirit of humanism" is capable of boosting the "moral spirituality" of liberalism, by no means does this signify that the New Confucians misidentify *ren* with "juristic" freedom, that is, rights protected by law. On the contrary, as indicated, they basically adhere to Green's vital point that "true" freedom is conceptually differentiated from "juristic" freedom, in spite of the existence of a moral link connecting these two aspects of freedom. Second, from the standpoint I have been taking, it seems undeniable that Mou also agrees with Green on seeing rights (negative freedom) as the objectification or externalization of "true" freedom (positive freedom) in the political context. In Mou's scheme, this is to say that rights did not exist in traditional Confucianism, but they will come to the surface in relation to the political subject as a consequence of the "blossoming of democracy" (*minzhu kaichu* 民主開出). Third, inspired by Green's essential claim that negative freedom and positive freedom are morally interrelated in respect of a common good rooted in an ethics of self-realization, there is room to fill out Mou's picture of perfectionist liberalism by further establishing a Confucian theory of rights with regard to Confucian *res publica*. Instead of giving a full analysis of this important topic, which requires much more space than is possible here, I shall merely introduce Green's rights recognition thesis by reference to the debate between Kantian liberalism and Hegelian liberalism in the next section.

CRITICAL INDIVIDUALISM

As far as the rationale of this book is concerned, Tang's aforementioned comments are of great significance. For it immediately reminds us of the fact that the leading New Confucians are familiar with the works of British idealism. And thus, it is not surprising that in response to the anti-Confucian liberals's comments on Bosanquet, Mou powerfully articulates:

> Uncritical individualism only has the particularity of achieving selfishness, lacking universality in the sense of rationality and justice; it thus falls short of the real meaning of individuality. On this issue, Hegelians wish to unveil universality by criticizing [uncritical] individualism in such a way that while individuality can be rescued, developing into an individual of real meaning or an actual reality on the one hand, the universality, on the other hand, can also be saved, making rationality, ideals, justice, associations, and wholeness possible. That is to say, universality is full of real meaning and able to develop into a state of real wholeness or unification; it is certainly not rootless, empty, or bent by force. In any event, it is twisted to say that this theory takes away the freedom of individuality by enhancing totalitarianism.[78]

What Mou says here simply resumes the key point that he has made earlier, that Confucianism, far from depreciating the value of individuality, reaches the "pinnacle of individualism"[79] in the Hegelian sense. To be exact, for the category of individualism, Mou is apt to agree with the two arguments that we have thus far established. First, in contrast to abstract individualism or uncritical individualism, embodied individualism or critical individualism is a more coherent way of grasping the moral agency of individuality with regard to ethical life. Second, as in Green's work, to encourage a common good or positive freedom from the standpoint of philosophical holism does not automatically end in political totalitarianism. Indeed, as it has been previously established, Green's claim about "removing obstacles to self-realization" is saliently comparable to Mou's anticipation of Confucian liberalism. Put succinctly, seeing that there are family resemblances between Mou and Green in respect of an ethics of self-realization, a common good, ethical citizenship, a perfectionist state, positive freedom, embodied individualism, and so forth, it seems appropriate to comment that the liberalism that Mou has in mind is, for the most part, in concert with Green's perfectionist liberalism.

THE SOUL OF LIBERALISM

As a matter of fact, the leading New Confucians all share a perfectionist definition of liberalism. Thus, in the eyes of Tang Junyi, the highest principle of liberalism is based on the golden rule mentioned above, that "the exercise of humaneness [i.e., true freedom and free will] depends on oneself." In Xu Fuguan's observation, to resolve the current predicament of liberalism captured by a dominant form of "realistic individualism" in favor of "negative and utilitarian freedom," our grasp of liberalism should be extended toward an endorsement of "freedom in idealism," or "freedom in personalism,"[80] such that the moral ideal of liberalism in "being one's own master" can be reached. In the case of Zhang Junmai [Carsun Chang] (張君勱 1887–1969), it is equally argued that "the foremost value of a theory of freedom lies in its capacity of cultivating independent personality and good citizenship."[81]

In a similar way, Mou makes it quite clear that the general spirit of liberalism is individualism. By individualism, however, he does not mean the "individualism of selfishness." For the most part, as Mou continues, "the idea of individuality stressed by individualism *in political terms* [emphasis mine] is one that is prescribed by rights and duties"[82] in relation to constitutional democracy. The pursuit of individualism and liberalism as such, however, may turn out to be a dogmatic hunt for "uncritical individualism" and "pan-liberalism," if we completely wipe out the good manners, shared norms, governing and civic virtues, and the lived forms of life in a community.

By contrast, to borrow the terms from Hegel, Mou accentuates once again that although ancient China did not have the notion of "subjective freedom," from which mainstream individualism and liberalism stem, it should not be forgotten that "subjective freedom" is not the end of the journey; instead, a philosophical understanding of freedom would be insufficient unless we further account for the actualization of "objective freedom" represented by the state, law, and politics.⁸³ In line with Hegel, this is to say that what is central to a restoration of the profound meaning of individualism and the moral ideals of liberalism is the "self-awareness of the individual" (*geti de zijue* 個體的自覺),⁸⁴ that is, to associate the subjective freedom of the individual with the objective meanings of culture, tradition, and history.⁸⁵

In this regard, the "soul of liberalism" lies in a display of "individuality and values," which, in turn, provide us with the moral "sources of liberal democracy and academic culture."⁸⁶ From this, it also follows that the idea of individuality in question, more than enjoying a list of rights and duties, is taken by Mou to imply the gist of embodied individualism. To quote Mou,

> Individuality is the particular manifestation of humanity in the concrete and actual individual [through practice]. If you respect humanity, you must respect individuality. Only by respecting individuality can we create culture and make possible [the spirit of *ren*].⁸⁷

Indisputably, what Mou means by "culture" here amounts to "accomplishing humaneness by cultivation" (*renwen huacheng* 人文化成); thus, as Mou adds, its springs consist of "humanity, the human way, individuality, and values."⁸⁸ In summary, the combination of the political form of liberalism and the ethical import of Confucianism points to a Hegelian form of perfectionist liberalism because, all things considered, Confucian ethics is associated with an endless pursuit of self-realization.

Rights Justification: Kantian or Hegelian?

Up until now, I have shown that Green's political theory deserves much more attention in the Chinese context, if only because it helps us to a great extent to clarify the longstanding misperception that the commitment to "true" freedom in Confucianism conflicts with liberalism's pursuit of the "negative freedom of the individual," that is, rights. There is, however, another vital issue concerning Mou's studies that remains largely unexplored: the fashion of relating the legacy of Mou's political thought to Kantian liberalism, or alternatively, "autonomy-based liberalism,"⁸⁹ or "rights-based liberalism." For the rest of this chapter, I am prepared to argue that while Kantian liberalism, by and large, represents a form of Westernized liberalism, the Hegelian scheme that I have been establishing is exempt from the criticisms of Westernized liberalism launched by antiliberal Confucianism.

THE UNIVERSAL PRINCIPLE OF RIGHT

Before turning to study the attempt adopted by Mou's disciples to formulate Confucian liberalism from the Kantian perspective, I shall recharacterize Kantian liberalism in a brief outline. When coming to politics, Kant clearly realizes that it is differentiated from morality in a fundamental sense; that is to say, whereas moral actions are completely autonomous, the *legal* aspect of political life must entail coercion. More precisely,

> The moral decision of the inner man finds outward expression in legality, i.e., in an action conforming with law. But man's inner life must not be subject to coercion. Because we cannot know for certain anything about another person's inner life, it ought not to be the task of political action or legislation to change or in any way to condition another person's thought. As men we are free. Our freedom implies that we have a hypothetical right to acquire anything in the world of a nature which we are potentially capable of acquiring.[90]

Accordingly, as long as we want to connect politics with morality in some ways, the laws we issue for regulating political affairs cannot break the fundamental condition making possible morality in the first place, namely, the mandate that every individual must equally enjoy a hypothetical right. In other words, the only legitimate principle of duty that is capable of binding the free agents together would be a specific duty of right, which, far from using force, focuses on how to reconcile *my* freedom with the freedom of *the other* in accordance with a universal law. In Kant's words, the counterpart of the duty of right is therefore *a universal principle of right*. It reads: "Every action which by itself or by its maxim enables the freedom of each individual's will to co-exist with the freedom of everyone else in accordance with a universal law is *right*."[91]

A full examination of Kant's political thinking is beyond the scope of this book. For my purposes, it is sufficient to remark that the political stance that Kant derives from his moral theory is, without a doubt, universal respect for the "equal rights of others." That is to say, the formulas of the categorical imperative previously unveiled, in point of fact, are equivalent to arguing that "we cannot make exceptions in our own favor," that "we must acknowledge the universal right to autonomy," and that "we must endeavor to realize the ideal of equal freedom." In short, Kant's theory of rights is equivalent to obliging an agent to acknowledge the objective rights and equal entitlement of all agents "who are, like himself, blessed with a first-person perspective."[92]

It goes without saying that the Kantian universal principle of right is exactly the cornerstone of John Rawls's insistence on the "priority of the right over the good" and Ronald Dworkin's famous dictum stating that "rights are trumps." Or, to put it another way, "autonomy-based liberalism" is a vital form of what Charles Taylor has referred to as "primacy-of-right theories." To quote Taylor:

> Primacy-of-right theories in other words accept a principle ascribing rights to men as binding unconditionally, binding, that is, on men as such. But they do not accept as similarly unconditional a principle of belonging or obligation. [Rather], the obligation to belong is derived in certain conditions from the more fundamental principle which ascribes rights.[93]

Confucianism as a Kantian Liberalism

To summarize what has been said thus far, I think there are two major reasons that motivate Mou's disciples to interpret his political thinking in particular, and sometimes to recast the political ideal of Confucianism in general, *entirely* from a Kantian viewpoint.

First, it has been effectively argued by Mou himself that there are close similarities between the spirit of Confucianism and Kant's moral philosophy in respect of "inner morality" (*neizai daodexing* 內在道德性), a "vertical expression of the vertical system" (*zongguan zongjiang* 縱貫縱講), and the endless pursuit of the "perfect good" (*yuanshan* 圓善). Certainly, for Mou's pupils, we have good reasons to follow in Mou's footsteps in connecting Confucianism with Kantian liberalism, simply because Mencius's insistence on "inner morality," or alternatively, the "innerness of humaneness and righteousness" (*renyi neizai* 仁義內在) is parallel to Kant's autonomous ethics.[94]

Second, the Kantian universal principle of right is indisputably what lies at the heart of the rights discourse and democratic imagination in our time. That said, Kant's viewpoint "remains the paradigmatic and most influential attempt to vindicate universal moral principles without reference to preferences";[95] according to Kant's renowned claim in "What Is Enlightenment?" the motto of enlightenment is "Have courage to use your *own* understanding," and for this enlightenment, "All that is needed is *freedom*."[96] Hence, I think Taylor is correct in saying that "formalistic theories get their plausibility from the fact that they are grounded on certain moral intuitions that are almost unchallenged in modern society, based as they are in certain preconditions of moral discourse itself combined with a thesis about the radical homogeneity of humanity which is pretty hard to challenge" in a "de-parochialized" contemporary culture.[97]

Taken together, Kantian liberalism seems capable of actualizing the Confucian moral subject that Mou has tried intensely to erect in a way that accords with the liberal democratic culture in our time. According to Jiang Nianfeng [Chiang Nien-Feng] (蔣年豐 1955–1996):

> The formalistic character of moral subjectivity spelled out by Kant's metaphysics of morals can be turned into legal-political subjectivity in a way that coexists with moral subjectivity. It is for this reason that we may remark that the idea of moral subjectivity in Confucianism has reserved a place for [the development of] legal-political subjectivity.[98]

If this is the case, then, as Jiang continues, "the tie between Rawls's new liberalism and Kant's philosophy has provided us with a new perspective, by means of which the thesis on the 'blossoming of democracy' encouraged by New Confucianism can be reevaluated"[99] in a fresh light. In short, as Li Minghui [Lee Ming-Huei] (李明輝) concludes, even though Mou rests on "dialectic" to make his case for the "blossoming of democracy," "we still have good reason to assert that his argumentation is Kantian," because the "framework of doctrine" (*yili jiagou* 義理架構) that fosters his dialectic is Kantian.[100]

RIGHTS AND CULTURE

Be that as it may, it is my understanding that the Kantian approach on the table is problematic, partly because Kant's theory of rights confronts a set of challenges posed by the antiliberal Confucians, and partly because Mou's students fail to take more seriously Mou's reservations on Kant and his heavy reliance on the Hegelian scheme for grounding the endeavor to merge constitutional democracy with what I have called "Confucian democratic civility," or alternatively, Confucian public virtue.

To start with, it has been argued by the antiliberal Confucians that the expression of rights is utterly Western-centric as there is no such thing as "rights" in Confucianism; that primacy-of-right theories fall short of tackling the cultural particularity of Confucianism in proclaiming the importance of the common good; that rights discourse, shorn of the materials of civility, civilization, public spirit, and the forms of life embedded in a given community, is likely to cause serious flaws for liberal democracies, such as incivility and selfishness.

At this point, as indicated, Kantian liberalism has often been treated as one of the most influential forms of "rights-based liberalism" in relation to the "politics of rights," so to speak. For one thing, in Kant's explanation, morality derives neither from traditions and communities, nor from feelings and emotions, but from "pure reason" alone; thus, in the political domain "we have a hypothetical right to acquire anything in the world of a nature which we are potentially capable of acquiring." This clearly implies that Kant's justification of rights, rooted in the very idea of autonomy, is related to *a theory of natural rights*, absent in the practice of classical Confucianism. In other words, despite the fact that Confucianism and Kant share some salient features of moral subjectivity, it remains the case that *the political and legal culture* in the Chinese world is sharply different from Western practice.

Again, from the separation of the self from its community, it follows that Kant's "rights-based liberalism" also takes on board a form of *formalism*, which in turn claims the priority of the right over the good. Another way of making the same point is to remark that for Kant *rights exist prior to society*, without reference to the historically contingent condition of human agency. By no means, of course, does this mean that Kant neglects virtues or the good. The real point is that for Kant the identification of "political morality" can only be restricted to a duty of right; or put differently, the only legitimate political principle is the universal principle of right. As Li Minghui indicates, in Kant's system, political principle "has something in common with moral law as it is not only driven by the mandate of pure practical reason, but itself is also a formalist principle. But on the other hand, it is different from moral law as it only regulates the outward action without reference to one's thought."[101] The problem, however, is that sticking to the formalistic character of political principle, "the issue of rights is solely a political concern effectively indifferent to cultural influence"[102] for the liberal as such. And thus, with Kantian liberalism, we are not far away from the notions of "disembodied self," "disengaged self," and the like, underpinning the crux of modern democratic politics.

Facing the triumph of Kantian liberalism, it is therefore no wonder that the communitarian-pragmatic Confucian thinkers such as David Hall and Roger Ames urge that

> Chinese society cannot be interpreted as a complex of distinct and autonomous individuals who hold sovereignty over their own interiority, and whose togetherness is most significantly regulated by codes of law. Nor is such a society an organization wherein personal autonomy is to be protected by natural rights.[103]

To see this issue from another angle, if the Confucian moral subject resonant with Kantian autonomy were able to "find outward expression in legality, i.e., in an action conforming with law," then China would have long ago developed political subjectivity, democracy, and the rule of law. The tie that links Kant's moral autonomy with the universal principle of right is not simply based on a philosophical deduction, but also, and more importantly, it is embodied in the *historical practice* of natural law and natural rights tradition highlighting Western culture. Without experiencing that tradition, it is difficult to relate morality and politics in a Kantian way. Or alternatively, if we choose to defend the "rights of others" from a Kantian perspective, then, as the anti-Confucian liberals or cosmopolitans would argue, there is no point in taking seriously the cultural particularity of Confucianism in the first place. In short, taking a Kantian approach to seek the fusion of Confucianism and liberalism is doomed to fail as it is inevitably on the horns of a dilemma: it struggles to uphold either the political priority of the right or the cultural influence of the Confucian manner of thinking.

On the other hand, it seems to me that Mou's students have paid too little attention to the importance of Hegel. In the course of this book, by contrast, I have gone some way toward filling this huge lacuna in Mou's studies. In the first place, as we have seen, although Mou thinks extremely highly of Kant's revolutionary contributions to the enterprise of philosophy, his lifelong endeavor to rebuild a Confucian "moral metaphysics" is, after all, aimed at transcending the limitations of

Kant's "metaphysics of morals." Besides, Mou clearly appreciates Hegel's idea of concrete philosophy in respect of real subjectivity, the principle of embodiment, a full theory of reality, and the concrete universal.

More to the point, it should have become clear by now that not only are Mou's political writings and lectures full of Hegelian terms such as "self-negation," "self-awareness," "subjective freedom," and "objective freedom," but also he is apt to adopt a Hegelian revision of Kant's treatment of free will as a postulate, a Hegelian analysis of the crisis of modernity, and the moral weakness of liberal democracy. In particular, it has been largely overlooked in the Chinese context that Hegel, as Rawls concedes, stands firmly in the liberal tradition, emphasizing the worth of autonomy and freedom initiated by Rousseau and Kant.[104]

In terms of methodology, a key thread running throughout this book is to make the case that, inspired by Hegel, Mou's political philosophy contains a tenacious attempt to reunite the political form of constitutional democracy (and its related values such as rights) with the ethical import of Confucian civility consistent with the principle of "self-restriction." To be sure, here as elsewhere in this study, my central argument is that Mou's version of Confucian liberalism, echoing Green's perfectionist liberalism, is intended to incorporate a nondominant conception of the common good into liberal politics with the purpose of avoiding the dominance of social control and exploitation by the state.

As a result of all this, as far as rights discourse is concerned, my observation is that the Hegelian scheme is immune from the main criticisms raised by antiliberal Confucianism, only if the subtlest model of Confucian democracy so constructed, rather than taking liberal democracy for granted, rests on a critical transformation of the Confucian forms of life and ways of thinking. To avoid misunderstandings, however, it should be remembered that what I have argued against Kantian liberalism is not so much about the *value* of rights but about the *justification* of rights in the Chinese context. In what follows, instead of completing a Confucian theory of rights with regard to Confucian *res publica*, my purpose permits me only to sketch out the potential links between Mou's version of Confucian liberalism and Green's Hegel-inspired method of rights justification, normally labeled the "rights recognition thesis."

RIGHTS AND RECOGNITION

As opposed to a theory of natural rights, formalism, and atomistic individualism, my stance is that Mou's political thought may have room for a Hegelian recognition theory of rights advocated by Green, among others. For the most part, Green's rights recognition thesis asserts that no rights are prior to a society without being mutually recognized by its members with regard to a common good; thus, to deliberate the reasons why I should "have rights," one has to refer to the existing ways of life and manners of thinking in a given community. Unlike Kantian liberalism, there are, accordingly, three key features of the rights recognition thesis that can be juxtaposed: mutual recognition, a common good, and practical judgment in a situation.

Let me quickly begin with mutual recognition. Although Green severely criticizes traditional natural rights theories (including those of Hobbes, Locke, and Kant), he does not deny that some rights are so fundamental that they should be granted to all human beings. The crucial thing here, however, is that rights make no real sense unless the social and cultural settings are taken into account. Hence, even though it is the case that civil and political rights stem from natural rights, this alone gives us no sufficient reasons to ensure their actual existence. For the question remains why in our social relations with others "powers are recognized by people as those that ought to be exercised or secured for possible exercise."[105] Put differently, while the mainstream theories of rights, including utilitarianism and deontology, hold that "the possession of rights is entirely independent of facts about a subject's social milieu,"[106] mutual recognition is Green's key to open a communal window for rights discourse.

More exactly, given that morality, as we have seen, begins with one's "will" to conceive desire that initiates action, followed by his "power" to perform conduct properly in concrete situations, Green is prone to define rights as "those powers possessed by an individual that others recognize as necessary for the achievement of a shared good."[107] Put in other terms, along with the point that negative freedom (rights) and positive freedom (moral ability) are distinguishable but not separable, Green contends that

> the conception expressed by the "should be" is not identical with the conception of a right possessed by some man or men, but one from which the latter conception is derived. It is, or implies on the part of whoever is capable of it, the conception of an ideal, unattained condition of himself, as an absolute end. Without this conception the recognition of a power as a right would be impossible. A power on the part of anyone is so recognised by others, as one which should be exercised,

when these others regard it as in some way a means to that ideal good of themselves which they alike conceive: and the possessor of the power comes to regard it as right through consciousness of its being thus recognised as contributory to a good in which he too is interested.[108]

Instead of suggesting that civil and political rights should "function as trump cards held by individuals,"[109] then, it is recognition that "makes and acknowledges rights"[110] in Green's philosophy of rights. By no means, however, does this imply that rights are might. On the contrary, the "achievement of a shared good" mentioned above immediately reaffirms that for Green, rights are morally justified as long as they make contributions to a common good. In line with the ethics of self-realization shared by New Confucianism, Green makes it clear that a right, although necessarily involving the exercise of a power, is concurrently *moral* on the condition that the members of a community have mutually recognized each other as the equal possessors of it in a joint attempt to fulfill man's "vocation as a moral being."[111] To be sure, for Green, as for Mou, human rights are "natural" or "universal" because "they arise out of, and are necessary for the fulfillment of, a moral capacity without which a man would not be a man."[112]

Based on what has been said thus far, it seems clear that what Green refers to as a "shared good" is not a substantial good predetermined by the state; rather, it designates the nondominant idea of a common good, namely, *the equal moral power for all citizens to pursue their own self-realization*. What is more, consistent with the notion of embodied individualism, Green argues that the theorists of natural rights fail to take into account the fact that personal development begins with family and society and that the individual is inseparable from social norms. By way of contrast, with the emphasis on mutual recognition, Green's theory of rights at the same time urges us to exercise practical judgment *inside* our own community with regard to a common good. According to Green,

> In analysing the nature of any right, we may conveniently look at it on two sides, and consider it as on the one hand a claim of the individual, arising out of his rational nature, to the free exercise of some faculty; on the other, as a concession of that claim by society, a power given to the individual of putting the claim in force by society. But we must be on our

guard against supposing that these distinguishable sides have any really separate existence. It is only a man's consciousness of having an object in common with the others, a well-being which is consciously his in being theirs and theirs in being his—only the fact that they are recognised by him and he by them as having this object—that gives him the claim described.[113]

As space is limited, a comprehensive exploration of the rights recognition thesis[114] and its promising advantages in shifting the focus of rights discourse in non-Western societies may need to be left for another study. Here, let me briefly reiterate my rejoinder to antiliberal Confucianism in respect of the expression of rights. First, to exclude rights discourse from the Chinese context simply on the account that natural law and natural rights tradition is Western-oriented and that the political and legal culture of protecting individual rights did not exist in original Confucianism is not plausible to me. For the most part, the antiliberal trend in Confucianism, as I see it, is entwined with a negligence of the philosophical legacy of New Confucianism in relocating political modernity into the Confucian forms of life, a narrow understanding of the divisions of liberalism, and a partial appreciation of the multiple facets of modernity. And thus, it falls short of seeing more clearly the possibility and plausibility of bringing together the practical reasoning of rights recognition and Confucian *res publica* in a democratic society. In other words, even though the notion of "natural rights" was absent in classical Confucianism, seen in light of the rights recognition thesis, the "way of *zhongshu*" (*zhongshu zhi dao* 忠恕之道), for instance, at once gives us a solid ground for approving human rights as an essential prerequisite to fulfilling "man's vocation as a moral being" in the Chinese context, which, in turn, underpins human dignity as a potential *human constant* across cultures.

Moreover, in keeping with the Hegelian scheme, the rights recognition thesis is anything but culturally blind. For, inasmuch as human rights are nothing but basic moral powers mutually recognized as "necessary for the achievement of a shared good," they are "historically derived concerns resourced in the community that accords and protects."[115] The pursuit of human rights in association with Confucian liberalism, rather than taking Western criteria for granted, endeavors to go beyond the partialities of both Western-centrism and Sino-centrism, by taking seriously a cross-cultural dialogue between the Chinese and Western worlds.

As a final point, the articulation of mutual recognition presupposes a version of embodied individualism, which calls for an honest appraisal of what might be the right judgment in any situation. In brief, *ren* as the "achievement of becoming human in the best sense" not only stands for the first-person view of an autonomous moral agent in the sense of moral metaphysics, but also refers to the third-person view made by "those who participate effectively in the ritualized roles and relationships that characterize traditional norms of social living in Chinese society"[116] in political terms. Accordingly, if asked how and in what sense the Chinese people should accept Brian Barry's universalistic definition of human rights, which suggests "human rights are what all human beings need in order to live minimally decent lives,"[117] I think the proper answer is, after all, related to the enterprise of practical judgment. For it is the historical agents who live *here and now* that are supposed to ponder whether they should take civil and political rights more seriously, when deciding what "decent lives" are. Indeed, seen in this light, the future of Confucian liberalism has much to do with the reasons citizens take action in this historically given, practical world.

Conclusion

So far, I have made an effort to demonstrate that there is an intellectual case to be made for bringing together both New Confucianism (particularly the thought of Mou Zongsan) and Hegelian liberalism (mainly including the writings of the British idealists) with regard to the ideas of moral religion, self-realization, individuality, embodied subjectivity, democracy, civility, citizenship, open society, public good, the state, freedom, and rights. In the main, the undertaking of this far-reaching dialogue is dependent on the premise that Mou and the British idealists such as Green are post-Kantian philosophers who share a cluster of philosophical commitments; for instance, both of them take Kant's moral subjectivity as the starting point for their philosophical ventures, but they are eager to critically transcend the limits of Kant's idea of freedom by bringing into account the Hegelian principle of embodiment. Accordingly, a significant part of this book has been arranged to take seriously the crucial relationship between Mou and Hegel in an attempt to open new ground for cross-cultural philosophical development, as well as a wide range of the British idealists who help fill in many of the details in the cross-cultural encounter. By this means, it is genuinely hoped that the Hegelian reconstruction of Mou's Confucian liberalism presented in this book may go some way toward bringing about a culturally sensitive way of appreciating liberal language in the Chinese context, forging a reconciliation between the two extreme poles of anti-Confucian liberalism and antiliberal Confucianism and perhaps shifting the terrain of contemporary Confucian political philosophy in a certain way.

Overall, as we have seen, Confucianism liberalism takes a form of civil liberalism, in that it rests the objective form of liberal democracy on the moral content of "Confucian democratic civility." That said, apart from developing a fresh version of the "way of politics" (*zhengdao* 政道) in respect of the "blossoming of democracy" (*minzhu kaichu* 民主開出), an equally important but often ignored aspect of Mou's political philosophy is to reconstruct the "way of governance" (*zhidao* 治道) in a way that involves a democratic restatement of Confucian civility. Additionally, Confucian liberalism at the same time stands for a type of perfectionist liberalism that endorses a nondominant concept of the common good surrounded by a set of Confucian governing and civic virtues. In brief, if it is the Hegelian process of "self-negation" (*ziwo kanxian* 自我坎陷) that triggers the "blossoming of democracy," then central to the liberal conception of Confucian *res publica* embedded in Mou's political writings is the principle of "self-restriction" (*ziwoxianzhi* 自我限制) pinning down the Confucian political ideal, largely identified as "humane government" (*renzheng* 仁政).

This certainly does not mean that there are "exact parallels" between New Confucianism and British idealism. But based on the salient affinities between Mou's philosophical transformation of Confucianism and the Hegelian turn to moral and political thinking, it is my conviction that a Hegelian reidentification of perfectionist liberalism, and indeed, civil liberalism, in the works of Mou and his fellow New Confucians may contribute to expanding our understanding of liberal values in relation to the Confucian forms of life on the one hand, and to enlightening the search for the possibility and plausibility of merging Confucianism with liberalism, on the other. In this regard, the upshot of this book is predicated on the belief that, despite the prevalence of the "standard viewpoint" still hovering over Chinese political discourse, engaging a cross-cultural dialogue between New Confucianism and British idealism can help us a great deal to answer the fundamental question of how and in what sense Confucianism entails liberal values. Taken as a whole, the book makes some contributions to several fields of study.

First of all, as for Chinese ideological debate, the book is largely intended to challenge the "standard viewpoint" that has extensively captured the political imagination of Chinese people, namely, the opinion that we can only choose *either* liberal democracy *or* Confucian civilization, or alternatively, *either* the voyage of Westernization *or* the maintenance of tradition. In order to make possible the reunion of Confucianism and liberalism, nonetheless, I have tried hard to clarify the complicated meanings of liberalism in relation to the multiple facets of Western modernity. Seen in this light, one of the substantial consequences of the book, as I hope to bring up, is to abolish the austere dichotomy between liberalism and conservatism in Chinese political discourse. More exactly, in view of the fact that this research aspires to incorporate the ideas of tradition, civility, established norms, the lived forms of life, community, civic virtue, and so on into a "liberal" understanding of individuality, morality, and politics, Confucian liberalism can be seen as a philosophical alloy embracing the elements of both liberalism and conservatism, as well as those of communitarianism and republicanism.

Furthermore, as for seeking mutual understanding across cultures, this comparative work aims to reveal certain surprising resonances and overlaps of meanings, particularly over the comprehension of the purpose of human life and the idea of the self. Through the lens of an ethics of self-realization, this book unveils a salient "overlapping consensus" of appreciating the common values of mankind, such as human dignity, mutual respect, and care about others. More precisely, as opposed to atomism, or what I have otherwise called the hypothesis-based approach to political philosophy, a key thread running throughout my exploration is to bring to light an alternative mode of comprehending the meaning of individuality and its true actualization in concrete situations with regard to the Hegelian expression of embodied subjectivity or embodied individualism. This at once reminds us of the viewpoint that for Mou, inasmuch as the purpose of cross-cultural dialogue is to arrive at mutual understanding, only when we get hold of truths that are universal in different cultures can the exchange of ideas, say, between Chinese and Western philosophy, become significant.

Moreover, as for comparative political thought, I take it that the ethics of self-realization so *universally* reconstructed may at the same time help expound the depth and breadth of liberalism in general. On balance, to the extent that the moral insights of New Confucianism can be well reinterpreted in terms of an ethics of self-realization from a cross-cultural perspective, the wing of Hegelian liberalism is advantageous to "liberalizing" the political philosophy of New Confucianism in a new light. In this regard, once again, British idealism is highly relevant to my inquiry, not only because it is, by and large, identified as a fashion of new liberalism associated with the chief concerns of communitarianism and republicanism, but also, and more importantly, because this school of thought has received its main philosophical inspirations from both Kant and Hegel.

More to the point, as for the modern transformation of Confucianism, in no way have I dismissed the reason that makes Mou Zongsan, presumably the most important Chinese philosopher of the twentieth century, an ideal candidate for seeking a synthesis of Confucianism and liberalism, namely, that he is clearly well read and well versed in both Chinese and Western thought. Beyond doubt, Mou is most famous today for his Kant-inspired characterization of Confucian ethics in terms of "inner morality" (*neizai daodexing* 內在道德性), a "vertical expression of the vertical system" (*zongguan zongjiang* 縱貫縱講), and the pursuit of the "perfect good" (*yuanshan* 圓善), accompanied by his lifelong quest for a Confucian "moral metaphysics" in contrast to Kant's "metaphysics of morals." For the reasons that have been advanced in the course of this book, however, I contend that Mou's engagement with Kant has dominated our appreciation of his political philosophy in ways that are problematic and that the turn to Hegel and beyond will not result in relinquishing the moral traits of Confucianism that Mou has arduously rebuilt via the Kantian framework.[1] While retaining a real appreciation for the importance of Kant and Kantianism, I have endeavored to make the case that adopting the Hegelian scheme, in point of fact, allows a much more plausible theorization on the political ideas of democracy, civilized society, public good, freedom, rights, and so on, in Confucian terms. All things considered, what makes political thought of Mou so unique is the robust belief in making possible the philosophical hybridity identified as Confucian liberalism from a Hegelian perspective.

What is more, as for the study of Mou Zongsan, this is the first book-length examination of his moral and political philosophy in a Hegelian vein. By bringing into account the relevance of Hegelian liberalism, Mou has been reinterpreted as a thinker who has achieved so much in recasting liberal language from a Confucian standpoint. Under the blueprints of civil liberalism and perfectionist liberalism, I have shown that Mou's philosophy is of great significance in forging a Hegelian reconciliation between reason and its actualization, between the individual and community, between politics and morality, between citizenship and the state, between open society and a common good, between negative freedom and positive freedom, and the like. The spirit of reconciliation at stake also explains why, in my view, to fully understand the subtlest model of Confucian democracy in Mou's own context, the "way of politics" (political democracy) and the "way of governance" (governing democracy) are equally important. Above all, it is the retrieval of the "way of governance" that enables me to decipher Mou's political thought as a Hegelian version of ethical liberalism, be it civil liberalism or perfectionist liberalism. Indeed, as it will be remembered, my restatement of "Confucian democratic civility" and Confucian *res publica* is, as a rule, grounded in a liberal reading of the key ingredients of "humane government."

Finally, as for contemporary Confucian political theory, my ultimate purpose of rebuilding Confucian liberalism lies in a bid to reflect on a number of crucial disputes from fresh stances, including deliberating the debate between Confucian democracy and Confucian meritocracy, illustrating democracy's institutional and moral values, making better sense of Confucian *res publica* as a nondominant conception of the common good, ensuring the possibility of separating a group of governing and civic virtues from the totality of moral virtues in Confucianism, removing the asymmetry between negative and positive freedom, and reconciling the conflict between rights recognition and the common good. Up to now, I hope it has become evident that the intellectual legacy of the New Confucianism of Taiwan and Hong Kong deserves much more attention in the recent renewal of contemporary Confucian political theory. In particular, the general picture of Confucian liberalism that I have delineated is diametrically opposed to the discourse of "political meritocracy" appearing in China: the former aims to relocate democracy and its related liberal values *altogether* in the Confucian forms of life, whereas the latter's attempt to merge the meritocratic principle—that political power should be distributed in accordance with personal virtues and talents—with a *limited* adaptation of elections, as I see it, utterly overlooks the liberal insight toward avoiding the damages of humanity caused by political evils and is likely to give priority to an authoritarian, one-party rule over liberal commitments.

On the whole, then, my pursuit of a political theory of Confucian liberalism is devoted to "continuing" (*jiezhu* 接著) rather than "repeating" (*zhaozhu* 照著) what Mou and his New Confucian companions have talked about, namely, the panorama of the "new outer kingliness" (*xin waiwang* 新外王).[2] It is true that the consideration of the compatibility of Confucianism and liberalism has a long history entwined with the emergence of the discourse of Chinese modernity. While I appreciate the fruits of previous studies, in this book I am concerned specifically with the diversity of liberalisms, individualisms, and notions of common humanity from a Hegelian viewpoint. Now, after a laborious examination, if it is the case that we may legitimately identify civil liberalism or perfectionist liberalism as an alternative form of liberalism, I cannot see why Confucian liberalism is a contradiction in terms.

The celebrated historian Yu Yingshi [Yu Ying-Shih] (余英時 1930–2021) has once conveyed the metaphor of a "wandering soul" to identify the predicament of modern Confucianism, thanks to the historical fact that "the connection between Confucianism and the political and social systems was broken, and institutionalized Confucianism died."[3] Given that the spirit of Confucian humanism may justifiably lay a moral foundation for democracy, it seems appropriate to close this book by remarking that for New Confucian philosophers such as Mou Zongsan, Tang Junyi [Tang Chun-I] (唐君毅 1909–1978), and Xu Fuguan [Hsu Fu-Kuan] (徐復觀 1904–1982), developing democracy is morally essential to the future advancement of Confucianism in the Chinese context, not because political democracy is identical with Mencius's idea of "the people as fundamental" (*minben* 民本), but because the initiation of the "way of politics" amounts to "providing the people's life with an entrustment" (*wei shengmin li ming* 為生民立命)[4] at the end of the day.

Notes

Notes to the Introduction

1. "Rooted global philosophy means to work within a particular living philosophical tradition—thus its rootedness—but to do so in a way that is open to stimulus and insights from other philosophical traditions—thus its global nature." Stephen C. Angle, *Contemporary Confucian Political Philosophy* (Cambridge: Polity, 2012), 9; see also *Sagehood: The Contemporary Significance of Neo-Confucian Philosophy* (Oxford: Oxford University Press, 2009), 6.

2. In this regard, the work of Charles Taylor is inspirational, because his striving for potential "human constants" in respect of a "language of perspicuous contrast" between different linguistic matrixes is associated with a robust attempt to transcend the pitfalls of both cultural relativism (or what he calls the "incorrigibility thesis") and Western universalism (or what he refers to as the problem of "ethnocentrism"). Charles Taylor, *Philosophy and the Human Sciences: Philosophical Papers 2* (Cambridge: Cambridge University Press, 1985), 116–33; and *Philosophical Arguments* (Cambridge: Harvard University Press, 1995), 146–64. For a skeptical attitude toward seeking mutual understanding in comparative political theory, see Leigh K. Jenco, *Making the Political: Founding and Action in the Political Theory of Zhang Shizhao* (Cambridge: Cambridge University Press, 2010), 6–12.

3. For a comprehensive historical account of British idealism, see William J. Mander, *British Idealism: A History* (Oxford: Oxford University Press, 2011). For a general guide to the school's moral and political philosophy, see Peter P. Nicholson, *The Political Philosophy of the British Idealists: Selected Studies* (Cambridge: Cambridge University Press, 1990); David Boucher and Andrew Vincent, *British Idealism and Political Theory* (Edinburgh: Edinburgh University Press, 2000); David Boucher and Andrew Vincent, *British Idealism: A Guide for the Perplexed* (London: Continuum, 2012); and Colin Tyler, *Common Good Politics: British Idealism and Social Justice in the Contemporary World* (Basingstoke: Palgrave Macmillan, 2017).

4. I am aware of the comment that "comparative political theory is still in its infancy," all too often engaging in "parallelisms rather than comparisons." Michael Freeden and Andrew Vincent, "Introduction: The Study of Comparative Political Thought," in *Comparative Political Thought: Theorizing Practices*, ed. Michael Freeden and Andrew Vincent (London: Routledge, 2013), 12. On the other hand, some scholars maintain that a true appreciation of the distinctions of Oriental philosophy can help Western civilization to expand its own self-understanding and to rethink its ongoing predicaments from sharply different angles. See, for example, David Hall and Roger Ames, *Thinking Through Confucius* (Albany: State University of New York Press, 1987); *Anticipating China: Thinking through the Narratives of Chinese and Western Culture* (Albany: State University of New York Press, 1995); and *Thinking Through the Han: Self, Truth, and Transcendence in Chinese and Western Culture* (Albany: State University of New York Press, 1998).

5. Angle's work (see below) is exceptional as he is quite an admirer of Mou Zongsan.

6. See, for example, Isaiah Berlin, *Four Essays on Liberty* (Oxford: Oxford University Press, 1969); and Karl Popper, *The Open Society and Its Enemies*, vol. 2, *The High Tide of Prophecy: Hegel, Marx, and the Aftermath* (London: Routledge and Kegan Paul, 1962).

7. For a detailed account on the historical origins and philosophical features of New Confucianism (*Xinrujia* 新儒家), see Liu Shuxian [Liu Shu-Hsien] (劉述先), *Essentials of Contemporary Neo-Confucian Philosophy* (Westport: Praeger, 2003).

8. John Makeham, "The Retrospective Creation of New Confucianism," in *New Confucianism: A Critical Examination*, ed. John Makeham (Basingstoke: Palgrave Macmillan, 2003), 25, 43.

9. See, for example, Huang Yong (黃勇), "New Confucianism," in *A Concise Companion to Confucius*, ed. Paul R. Goldin (Oxford: Wiley Blackwell, 2017), 352–74; Liu Shuxian, *Ruxue de fuxing* 儒學的復興 (The Confucian Renaissance) (Hong Kong: Tiandi tushu, 2007), 110–20; and *Rujia zhexue de dianfan chonggou yu quanshi* 儒家哲學的典範重構與詮釋 (Reconstructing and Interpreting the Confucian Philosophical Paradigm) (Taipei: Wanjuanlou tushu, 2010), 3–18.

10. Quoted in Makeham, "The Retrospective Creation of New Confucianism," 39.

11. Mou elucidates the idea of "three unities" (*santong* 三統) in the so-called "three books of the new outer kingliness" (*xin waiwang sanshu* 新外王三書), namely, *Lishi zhexue* 歷史哲學 (Philosophy of History), *Zhengdao yu zhidao* 政道與治道 (The Way of Politics and the Way of Governance), and *Daode de lixiangzhuyi* 道德的理想主義 (Moral Idealism).

12. Ng Yu-Kwan (吳汝鈞), "Xiong Shili's Metaphysical Theory about the Non-Separability of Substance and Function," in *New Confucianism: A Critical Examination*, ed. John Makeham (Basingstoke: Palgrave Macmillan, 2003), 219.

13. For a detailed discussion of the debate about *daotong* 道統 (orthodoxy of Confucianism), see John Makeham, "The New *Daotong*," in *New Confucianism: A Critical Examination*, ed. John Makeham (Basingstoke: Palgrave Macmillan, 2003), 55–78; and John Makeham, *Lost Soul: "Confucianism" in Contemporary Chinese Academic Discourse* (Cambridge: Harvard University Asia Center, 2008), chapter 7.

14. See, for example, Tang Junyi [Tang Chun-I] (唐君毅), *Zhongguo renwen jingshen zhi fazhan* 中國人文精神之發展 (The Development of the Chinese Humanistic Spirit), in *Tang Junyi quanji* 唐君毅全集 (Complete Works of Tang Junyi), vol. 6 (Taipei: Xuesheng shuju, 1991); *Renwen jingshen zhi chongjian* 人文精神之重建 (The Reconstruction of the Humanistic Spirit), in *Tang Junyi quanji* 唐君毅全集 (Complete Works of Tang Junyi), vol. 5 (Taipei: Xuesheng shuju, 1991); and *Wenhua yishi yu daode lixing* 文化意識與道德理性 (Cultural Consciousness and Moral Reason), in *Tang Junyi quanji* 唐君毅全集 (Complete Works of Tang Junyi), vol. 20 (Taipei: Xuesheng shuju, 1991).

15. See Xu Fuguan [Hsu Fu-Kuan] (徐復觀), *Rujia zhengzhi sixiang yu minzhu ziyou renquan* 儒家政治思想與民主自由人權 (Confucian Political Thought and Democracy, Liberty, and Human Rights), ed. Xiao Xinyi (蕭欣義) (Taipei: Bashi niandai chuban, 1979), 197–214; and *Xinban xueshu yu zhengzhi zhijian* 新版學術與政治之間 (Between Academia and Politics, New Edition) (Taipei: Xuesheng shuju, 1980), 229–45.

16. Angle, *Contemporary Confucian Political Philosophy*, 82.

17. Feng Youlan [Fung Yu-Lan] (馮友蘭), *Xin lixue* 新理學 (The New Philosophy of Principle) (Chongqing: Commercial Press, 1942), 1.

18. See Stephen L. Carter, *Civility: Manners, Morals, and the Etiquette of Democracy* (New York: Basic Books, 1998).

19. Thomas A. Spragens, "Reconstructing Liberal Theory: Reason and Liberal Culture," in *Liberals on Liberalism*, ed. Alfonso J. Damico (Totowa: Rowan and Littlefield, 1986), 36.

20. Richard Rorty, "Postmodernist Bourgeois Liberalism," in Richard Rorty, *Objectivity, Relativism, and Truth* (Cambridge: Cambridge University Press, 1991), 197–201.

21. Charles Taylor, "Shared and Divergent Values," in *Options for a New Canada*, ed. Ronald Watts and Douglas Brown (Toronto: University of Toronto Press, 1991), 53–76.

22. John Gray, *Two Faces of Liberalism* (Cambridge: Polity, 2000).

23. Alan Ryan, *The Making of Modern Liberalism* (Princeton: Princeton University Press, 2012), 28.

24. In this regard, even the writers such as Edmund Burke can be identified as liberals. See Jennifer Pitts, *A Turn to Empire: The Rise of Imperial Liberalism in Britain and France* (Princeton: Princeton University Press, 2005), 63.

25. Steven Wall, "Introduction," in *The Cambridge Companion to Liberalism*, ed. Steven Wall (Cambridge: Cambridge University Press, 2015), 4.

26. For a critical review of Pocock's attempt to pluralize enlightenments, see Jonathan Israel, "J. G. A. Pocock and the 'Language of Enlightenment' in His Barbarism and Religion," *Journal of the History of Ideas* 77(1) (2016): 107–27.

27. Wall, "Introduction," 9–13.

28. Richard C. Sinopoli, "Liberalism and Contested Conceptions of the Good: The Limits of Neutrality," *The Journal of Politics* 55(3) (1993): 644.

29. Ronald Dworkin, "Rights as Trumps," in *Theories of Rights*, ed. Jeremy Waldron (Oxford: Oxford University Press, 1984), 153; see also *Taking Rights Seriously* (Cambridge: Harvard University Press, 1977).

30. David L. Hall and Roger T. Ames, *The Democracy of the Dead: Dewey, Confucius, and the Hope for Democracy in China* (Chicago and Lasalle: Open Court, 1999), chapter 5.

31. Nicholson, *The Political Philosophy of the British Idealists*, 2; William Sweet, "Introduction: Idealism, Ethics, and Social and Political Thought," in *The Moral, Social and Political Philosophy of the British Idealists*, ed. William Sweet (Exeter: Imprint Academia, 2009), 2.

32. Nicholson, *The Political Philosophy of the British Idealists*, 2–5.

33. Sweet, "Introduction," 17.

34. In L. S. Lockridge's study, the term "self-realization" was coined by Samuel Coleridge, whereas "the OED gives the first use to F. H. Bradley in 1876." See Sweet, "Introduction," 4 note 4.

35. Angle, *Contemporary Confucian Political Philosophy*, 1–2; see also 18, 19.

36. Nicholson, *The Political Philosophy of the British Idealists*, 2.

37. See, for example, Yin Haiguang [Yin Hai-Kuang] (殷海光), *Zhengzhi yu shehui* 政治與社會 (Politics and Society), in *Yin Haiguang quanji* 殷海光全集 (Complete Works of Yin Haiguang), vols. 11–12, ed. Lin Zhenghong (林正弘) (Taipei: Guiguan tushu, 1990); Zhang Foquan [Chang Fo-Chuan] (張佛泉), *Ziyou yu renquan* 自由與人權 (Liberty and Human Rights) (Taipei: Commercial Press, 1993).

38. Indeed, Liang Shuming [Liang Shu-Ming] (梁漱溟 1893–1988) argued long ago that "Chinese thought is [characterized by] accepting and staying within whatever one's role defines (*an fen* 安分), contentment, continence, and maintaining good health. It by no means advocates the pursuit of material enjoyment. The Chinese, no matter under what circumstances, can find satisfaction and demonstrate endurance. He does not necessarily want to change the environment. Eastern cultures seek not conquest of nature but harmony with nature." Quoted in Li Chenyang (李晨陽), *The Tao Encounters the West: Explorations in Comparative Philosophy* (Albany: State University of New York Press, 1999), 173.

39. Jiang Qing (蔣慶), *Zhengzhi Ruxue: dangdai Ruxue de zhuanxiang, tezhi yu fazhan* 政治儒學：當代儒學的轉向、特質與發展 (Political Confucianism: The Changing Direction, Particularities, and Development of Contemporary Confucianism) (Taipei: Yangzhengtang wenhua, 2003). By contrast, Chen Ming (陳

明) is driven to promote a Rousseau-inspired "civil religion." See Chen Ming, *Wenhua Ruxue: sibian yu lunbian* 文化儒學：思辨與論辯 (Cultural Confucianism: Thoughts and Debates) (Chengdu: Sichuan People's Publishing House, 2009); and *Rujiao yu gongming shehui* 儒教與公民社會 (Confucianism and Civil Society) (Beijing: Dongfang chubanshe, 2013).

40. Chen Lai (陳來), *Renxue bentilun* 仁學本體論 (The Ontology of the Learning of Ren) (Beijing: Sanlian shudian, 2014).

41. Chen Lai, *Tradition and Modernity: A Humanist View*, trans. Edmund Ryden (Leiden and Boston: Brill, 2009), 350.

42. The talks of Zeng Yi (曾亦) recorded in *He wei pushi? shei zhi jiazhi? dangdai Rujia lun pushi jiazhi* 何謂普世？誰之價值？當代儒家論普世價值 (What Is Called Universal? Whose Value? Contemporary Confucians Discuss Universal Values), ed. Zeng Yi and Guo Xiaodong (郭曉東) (Shanghai: Huadong Shifan Daxue chubanshe, 2014), 17, 55.

43. Fan Ruiping (范瑞平), *Reconstructing Confucianism: Rethinking Morality after the West* (Dordrecht: Springer, 2010).

44. Kang Xiaoguang (康曉光), *Renzheng: Zhongguo zhengzhi fazhan de disantiaolu* 仁政：中國政治發展的第三條道路 (The Politics of Benevolence: The Third Road for China's Political Development) (Singapore: Global Publishing, 2005).

45. Jiang Qing, *A Confucian Constitutional Order: How China's Ancient Past Can Shape Its Political Future*, ed. Daniel A. Bell and Fan Ruiping, trans. Edward Ryden (Princeton: Princeton University Press, 2012).

46. Daniel A. Bell, *The China Model: Political Meritocracy and the Limits of Democracy* (Princeton: Princeton University Press, 2015); see also *Beyond Liberal Democracy: Political Thinking for an East Asian Context* (Princeton: Princeton University Press, 2006).

47. Bai Tongdong (白彤東), *Jiubang xinming: gujin zhongxi canzhao xia de gudian Rujia zhengzhi zhexue* 舊邦新命：古今中西參照下的古典儒家政治哲學 (New Mission of an Old State: Classical Confucian Political Philosophy in a Contemporary and Comparative Relevance Context) (Beijing: Peking University Press, 2009); and *China: The Political Philosophy of the Middle Kingdom* (New York: Zed Books, 2012).

48. Li Chenyang, "Equality and Inequality in Confucianism," *Dao* 11(3) (2012): 295–313.

49. Joseph Chan (陳祖為), *Confucian Perfectionism: A Political Philosophy for Modern Times* (Princeton: Princeton University Press, 2014).

50. For a comprehensive examination of the different versions of Confucian meritocracy, see *The East Asian Challenge for Democracy: Political Meritocracy in Comparative Perspective*, ed. Daniel A. Bell and Li Chenyang (Cambridge: Cambridge University Press, 2013).

51. The phrases "Confucian democratic perfectionism" and "Confucian meritocratic perfectionism" are used by Sungmoon Kim.

52. Hall and Ames, *The Democracy of the Dead*; and Tan Sor-Hoon (陳素芬), *Confucian Democracy: A Deweyan Reconstruction* (Albany: State University of New York Press, 2004).

53. Angle, *Contemporary Confucian Political Philosophy*.

54. Sungmoon Kim, *Public Reason Confucianism: Democratic Perfectionism and Constitutionalism in East Asia* (Cambridge: Cambridge University Press, 2016); see also *Confucian Democracy in East Asia: Theory and Practice* (Cambridge: Cambridge University Press, 2014), and *Democracy after Virtue: Toward Pragmatic Confucian Democracy* (Oxford: Oxford University Press, 2018).

55. In a critical sense, the difference may have originated in the fact that Dewey had eminently shifted his philosophical position from a Hegelian idealism in search of unification and completeness to a fuller exposition of pragmatic and pluralist social philosophy in *Democracy and Education* (1906) and *Liberalism and Social Action* (1935). See, for example, Burleigh Taylor Wilkins, "James, Dewey, and Hegelian Idealism," *Journal of the History of Ideas* 17(3) (1956): 332–46; Jennifer Welchman, "From Absolute Idealism to Instrumentalism: The Problem of Dewey's Early Philosophy," *Transactions of the Charles S. Peirce Society* 25(4) (1989): 407–19; and Trevor Pearce, "The Dialectical Biologist, circa 1890: John Dewey and the Oxford Hegelians," *Journal of the History of Philosophy* 52(4) (2014): 747–77.

56. Angle, *Contemporary Confucian Political Philosophy*, 17.

57. Ibid., 9, 52, 63, 71.

58. By definition, "public reason Confucianism is a specific mode of Confucian democratic perfectionism that best articulates the complex relationship between Confucian cultural values and Confucian democratic citizenship under the institutional constraints of democratic constitutionalism and within the normative parameters of democratic principles." As a political theory, it is thus intended to "mediate between public reason, commonly affiliated with liberal neutrality, and perfectionism, which endorses the state's non-neutral promotion or prohibition of particular goods or values." Kim, *Public Reason Confucianism*, 19.

59. Ibid., chapter 1.

60. Angle, *Contemporary Confucian Political Philosophy*, 115. As Angle quotes Tu Weiming [Tu Wei-Ming] (杜維明) in remarking: Confucian personal ideals "can be realized more fully in the liberal-democratic society than either in the traditional imperial dictatorship or a modern authoritarian regime." Ibid., 53.

61. See, for example, N. Serina Chan, *The Thought of Mou Zongsan* (Leiden and Boston: Brill, 2011); Sébastien Billioud, *Thinking through Confucian Modernity: A Study of Mou Zongsan's Moral Metaphysics* (Leiden and Boston: Brill, 2012); David Elstein, *Democracy in Contemporary Confucian Philosophy* (London and New York: Routledge, 2015), chapter 3; Zheng Jiadong (鄭家棟), *Mou Zongsan* 牟宗三 (Mou Zongsan) (Taipei: Grand East Book Co., 2000); Tang Zhonggang (湯忠鋼), *Dexing yu zhengzhi: Mou Zongsan's Xinrujia zhengzhi zhexue yanjiu* 德性與政治：牟

宗三新儒家政治哲學研究 (Virtue and Politics: Research on Mou Zongsan's New Confucian Political Philosophy) (Beijing: Zhongguo yanshi chubanshe, 2008); Peng Guoxiang (彭國翔), *Zhizhe de xianshi guanhuai: Mou Zongsan de zhengzhi shehui sixiang* 智者的現世關懷：牟宗三的政治社會思想 (The Practical Concern of a Wiseman: The Political and Social Thought of Mou Zongsan) (Taipei: Linking Publishing Co., 2016); Liu Xiao (劉曉), *Xiandai Xinrujia zhengzhi zhexue* 現代新儒家政治哲學 (The Political Philosophy of Modern New Confucianism) (Beijing: Xianzhuang shuju, 2001); and *Mou Zongsan xiansheng yu Zhongguo zhexue zhi chongjian* 牟宗三先生與中國哲學之重建 (Mou Zongsan and the Reconstruction of Chinese Philosophy), ed. Li Minghui [Lee Ming-Huei] (李明輝) (Taipei: Wenjin chubanshe, 1996).

62. Li Minghui, *Rujia yu Kangde* 儒家與康德 (Confucianism and Kant) (Taipei: Linking Publishing Co., 1990); *Ruxue yu xiandai yishi* 儒學與現代意識 (Confucianism and Modern Consciousness) (Taipei: Wenchin chubanshe, 1991); *Kangde lunlixue yu Mengzi daode sikao zhi zhongjian* 康德倫理學與孟子道德思考之重建 (Kantian Ethics and the Reconstruction of Mencius's Moral Thinking) (Taipei: Academia Sinica, Institute of Chinese Literature and Philosophy, 1994); *Dangdai Ruxue zhi ziwo zhuanhua* 當代儒學之自我轉化 (The Self-Transformation of Contemporary Confucianism) (Taipei: Academia Sinica, Institute of Chinese Literature and Philosophy, 1994); *Mengzi chongtan* 孟子重探 (Mencius Revisited) (Taipei: Linking Publishing Co., 2001); and *Rujia shiye xia de zhengzhi sixiang* 儒家視野下的政治思想 (Political Thought from a Confucian Perspective) (Taipei: National Taiwan University Press, 2005).

63. SM: 234.

64. *DLX*: 12 [CW IX-(1): 15].

65. John Rawls, *Lectures on the History of Moral Philosophy*, ed. Barbara Herman (Cambridge: Harvard University Press, 2000), 330, 352.

66. SYG: 269 [CW XXIII: 295]; WZ: 109 [CW XXXII-(1): 98–99].

67. According to Tang Junyi [Tang Chun-I] (唐君毅 1909–1978), Bradley is "the philosopher of philosophers in the eyes of British Idealists"; in point of fact, as Tang confesses, it is thanks to Bradley's *Appearance and Reality* that he "was led to study the works of great idealists like Kant and Hegel." Tang Junyi, *Yingwen lunzhu huibian* 英文論著彙編 (Essays on Chinese Philosophy and Culture), in *Tang Junyi quanji* 唐君毅全集 (Complete Works of Tang Junyi), vol. 19 (Taipei: Xuesheng shuju, 1991), 419–20.

68. Bernard Bosanquet, *The Philosophical Theory of the State* (London: Macmillan, 1899), 221.

69. *XYW*: preface 3 [CW XXI: preface 5].

70. F. H. Bradley, *Ethical Studies* (Oxford: Clarendon Press, 1988), 78.

71. I am aware that there has been a tendency to challenge the view that Kant was indifferent to cultural difference; see, for example, Sankar Muthu, *Enlightenment against Empire* (Princeton: Princeton University Press, 2003),

chapters 4–5. What concerns me here, however, is the plausibility of applying the rights-based liberalism associated with the Kantian approach to justify rights in the Chinese context.

Notes to Chapter 1

1. *NL*: 457; *SJJ*: 437 [CW XXIX: 437]; see also *YSL*: xiv [CW XXII: 15–16].

2. For a critical introduction to Mou's moral metaphysics, see Sébastien Billioud, *Thinking through Confucian Modernity: A Study of Mou Zongsan's Moral Metaphysics* (Leiden and Boston: Brill, 2012); N. Serina Chan, *The Thought of Mou Zongsan* (Leiden and Boston: Brill, 2011), chapters 4–6.

3. For an insightful discussion of Hegel's influence on Mou, see Chan, *The Thought of Mou Zongsan*, chapter 3; Stephan Schmidt, "Mou Zongsan, Hegel, and Kant: The Quest for Confucian Modernity," *Philosophy East and West* 61(2) (2011): 279–86.

4. Esther C. Su, "Mou Zongsan's Critical Philosophy," in *NL*: xxxv.

5. *XYW*: 3 [CW XXI: 5].

6. *NL*: 67; *SJJ*: 69 [CW XXIX: 69].

7. Mou's Kant-inspired reconstruction of Confucianism has been criticized for "distorting Kant's 'original' philosophy and reading too much Kant into Confucianism." Li Minghui [Lee Ming-Huei] (李明輝), *Confucianism: Its Roots and Global Significance*, ed. David Jones (Honolulu: University of Hawai'i Press, 2017), 17.

8. "Without sensibility," to quote Kant, "no object would be given to us; without understanding no object would be thought. Thoughts without content are empty; intuitions without concepts are blind." Immanuel Kant, *Critique of Pure Reason*, trans. Norman Kemp Smith (London: Macmillan, 1993), 93, A51, B75.

9. In Kant's usage: "We shall entitle the principles whose application is confined entirely within the limits of possible experience, *immanent*, and those on the other hand, which profess to pass beyond these limits, *transcendent*. In the case of these latter, I am not referring to the *transcendental* employment or misemployment of the categories, which is merely an error of the faculty of judgment when it is not duly curbed by criticism, and therefore does not pay sufficient attention to the bounds of the territory within which alone free play is allowed to pure understanding. I mean actual principles which incite us to tear down all those boundary fences and to seize possession of an entirely new domain which recognizes no limits of demarcation. Thus *transcendental* and *transcendent* are not interchangeable terms. The principles of pure understanding . . . allow only of empirical and not of transcendental employment, that is, employment

extended beyond the limits of experience. A principle, on the other hand, which takes away these limits, or even commands us actually to transgress them, is called *transcendent*." Ibid., 298–99, A295–96, B352–53.

10. Ibid., 601, A751, B779.

11. "A transcendental argument or deduction, it will be recalled, proceeds from experience to a discovery of those conditions making this experience possible. It discovers presuppositions or necessary conditions for intelligibility." Similarly, in morality "we see that unless freedom is *presupposed* as a basic value, much of our ordinary moral talk—that which it is the business of the moral philosopher to analyze—would not make sense, would not be intelligible." Jeffrie G. Murphy, *Kant: The Philosophy of Right*, second edition (Macon: Mercer University Press, 1994), 32.

12. Immanuel Kant, *Grounding for the Metaphysics of Morals*, trans. James W. Ellington (Indianapolis: Hackett Publishing Company, 1993), 7.

13. Ibid., 62.

14. Ibid., 9–13.

15. Immanuel Kant, *Critique of Practical Reason*, trans. H. W. Cassirer (Milwaukee: Marquette University Press, 1998), 126–28.

16. Kant, *Critique of Pure Reason*, 657–58, A839–40, B867–68.

17. SSJ: 45f [CW XXX-(1): 45f].

18. NL: 41; SJJ: 45 [CW XXIX: 45].

19. As Charles Taylor puts it, "Kant gives a firm but quite new base to the subjectivization or internationalization of moral sources which Rousseau inaugurates." Charles Taylor, *Sources of the Self: The Making of the Modern Identity* (Cambridge: Cambridge University Press, 1989), 364; see also "Kant's Theory of Freedom," in *Philosophy and the Human Sciences: Philosophical Papers 2* (Cambridge: Cambridge University Press, 1985), 318–37.

20. NL: 16; SJJ: 16 [CW XXIX: 17]. The ancient Chinese also looked upward at Heaven, but, as Mou quotes the *Book of Documents* (*Shangshu* 尚書) in saying, it means "Heaven sees what my people see, and Heaven hears what my people hear"; therefore "looking upward" does not entirely depend on Heaven but also depends on people.

21. NL: 26–27; SJJ: 30 [CW XXIX: 30].

22. NL: 454; SJJ: 434 [CW XXIX: 434].

23. ZZT: 4 [CW XXVIII-(2): 4].

24. NL: 57; SJJ: 62 [CW XXIX: 62].

25. Su, "Mou Zongsan's Critical Philosophy," xli. In this book I am following Su in translating Mencius's *xing* as "*Xing*-nature" because, as Su rightly puts it, "Mou thinks that the expression 'human nature,' normally signifying narrowly the nature of humanity in an anthropological sense, misses the [transcendent] meaning of the Mencian *xing*." Ibid., xxviii note 28.

26. NL: 42; SJJ: 47 [CW XXIX: 47].

27. "The one principle which underlines all moral laws, as well as the duties in conformity with them, is that of the *autonomy* of the will. *Heteronomy* of choice, on the other hand, is not only incapable of serving the basis of any obligation, but, in fact, is opposed to the principle of obligation and to the morality of the will." Kant, *Critique of Practical Reason*, 37.

28. NL: 458; SJJ: 438 [CW XXIX: 438].

29. Nicholas Bunnin, "God's Knowledge and Ours: Kant and Mou Zongsan on Intellectual Intuition," *Journal of Chinese Philosophy* 40(s1) (2013): 53.

30. Ibid., 55.

31. NL: 441, 443; SJJ: 421, 423 [CW XXIX: 421, 423].

32. Kant, *Critique of Pure Reason*, 635, A804, B832.

33. NL: 49–50, 451; SJJ: 54, 431 [CW XXIX: 54, 431].

34. Historically speaking, unlike Daoism, which belittled Zhou rites as constraints on human life, the cardinal virtue of *ren* 仁 (humaneness) was proposed by Confucius to give life to the Zhou rites. "With the principle of *ren*, rites and music were revitalized to become authentic, and their objective validity reestablished." NL: 56; SJJ: 61 [CW XXIX: 61].

35. For a similar account, see Charles Taylor, "Overcoming Epistemology," in Charles Taylor, *Philosophical Arguments* (Cambridge: Harvard University Press, 1995), 1–19.

36. NL: 451; SJJ: 431 [CW XXIX: 431].

37. Chan Wing-Cheuk (陳榮灼), "Mou Zongsan's Transformation of Kant's Philosophy," *Journal of Chinese Philosophy* 33(1) (2006): 130. In this regard, I think Esther Su is correct in translating *liangzhi* 良知 as the "knowing-reality of enlightened awareness" throughout NL.

38. NJ: 451; SJJ: 431–32 [CW XXIX: 431–32].

39. NJ: 451; SJJ: 431–32 [CW XXIX: 431–32].

40. XYX vol. 1: 40–41 [CW V: 44].

41. Kant, *Critique of Practical Reason*, 168.

42. Kant, *Critique of Pure Reason*, 636, A806, B834.

43. Kant, *Critique of Practical Reason*, 164.

44. Kant, *Critique of Pure Reason*, 636, A806, B834.

45. For Mou's discussion of Kant's idea of the *summum bonum*, see YSL: chapters 3–4 [CW XXII: chapters 3–4]; NL: 341–44, 390–95; SJJ: 327–30, 373–78 [CW XXIX: 327–30, 373–78].

46. Kant, *Critique of Pure Reason*, preface to second edition, 29, Bxxx.

47. Kant, *Critique of Practical Reason*, 158.

48. Quoted in NL: 452; SJJ: 432 [CW XXIX: 432].

49. YSL: ii [CW XXII: ii].

50. As Mou puts it: "According to the doctrines of the Song and Ming Confucians, knowledge does not only imply 'hear-and-see knowing' (i.e., empir-

ical knowledge acquired by encountering things, by seeing and hearing), but it also embraces 'virtuous knowing.' Comprehension is not only one that has epistemic meaning, but it is also one that has practical meaning." *XYX* vol. 1: 145 [*CW* V: 151].

51. *SSJ*: 81–82 [*CW* XXX-(1): 82]. Here Mou is following Kant's distinction between "transcendental" and "transcendent" discussed above (see note 9). For a succinct analysis of this distinction offered by Mou, see *SSJ*: 50 [*CW* XXX-(1): 50].

52. *NL*: 74; *SJJ*: 77 [*CW* XXIX: 77].

53. The *Analects* (*Lunyu* 論語), trans. D. C. Lau (London: Penguin Books, 1979), 7: 29; 12: 1. Unless otherwise stated, all translations of the *Analects* are adapted from Lau's.

54. Thus, for example, when Zai Yu (宰予) asked about whether or not a mourning period of three years for the death of parents was too long, Confucius replied: "Would your heart-mind be easy if you ate rice and dressed in brocade" during the very period of mourning? And in response to Zai Yu's thoughtless answer, "Yes, I would be at ease," Confucius was not reluctant to impart the teaching that Zai Yu was away from *ren*. *Analects* 17: 21.

55. *Analects* 5: 11.

56. The *Mencius* (*Mengzi* 孟子), trans. D. C. Lau (London: Penguin Books, 1970), 6A: 6; emphasis mine. Unless otherwise stated, all translations of the *Mencius* are adapted from Lau's.

57. *Mencius* 6A: 6.

58. The *Doctrine of the Mean* (*Zhongyong* 中庸), in *The Chinese Classics*, vol. 1, trans. James Legge (Taipei: SMC Publishing Inc., 2001), I.

59. *Analects* 1: 4.

60. *NL*: 76; *SJJ*: 80 [*CW* XXIX: 80].

61. *NL*: 78–79; *SJJ*: 81–82 [*CW* XXIX: 81–82].

62. Li, *Confucianism*, 16.

63. *XYX* vol. 1: 58–59 [*CW* V: 62–63].

64. *NL*: 431, 458; *SJJ*: 415, 439 [*CW* XXIX: 415, 439].

65. Before studying Heidegger's work, Mou's reception of Kant's first *Critique* was greatly influenced by his teacher Xiong Shili [Hsiung Shih-Li] (熊十力 1885–1968) with the purpose of working out a Neo-Kantian theory of knowledge. See Mou Zongsan, *Renshixin zhi pipan* 認識心之批判 (Critique of the Cognitive Mind) (Taipei: Xuesheng shuju, 1990), 2 vols.; collected in *CW* XVIII, XIX. In brief, instead of understanding the Kantian categories as "conditions of possibility of objects of cognition," Mou in this earlier book attempted to establish them as "conditions of possibility of cognition"; that is to say, for Mou, "the Kantian categories represent the *a priori* structure of our cognition, rather than the *a priori* structure of the world." Chan, "Mou Zongsan's Transformation of Kant's Philosophy," 126.

66. Kant, *Critique of Pure Reason*, 635, A805, B833.

67. Martin Heidegger, *Kant and the Problem of Metaphysics*, fifth edition, trans. Richard Taft (Indianapolis: Indiana University Press, 1990), 152.

68. In brief, according to Kant, insofar as phenomena as appearances required something that appears, the understanding may refer to this something as the "object of sensible intuition." Since "the conditions of the *possibility of experience* in general are likewise conditions of the *possibility of the objects of experience*," "this something, thus conceived, is only the transcendental object; and by that is meant a something=X, of which we know, and with the present constitution of our understanding can know, nothing whatsoever, but which, as a correlate of the unity of apperception, can serve only for the unity of the manifold in sensible intuition." Kant, *Critique of Pure Reason*, 194, A158, B197; 268, A250.

69. Heidegger, *Kant and the Problem of Metaphysics*, 153, 1; emphasis mine.

70. Su, "Mou Zongsan's Critical Philosophy," xxii. More exactly, Mou opposes Heidegger's Dasein-analytic for two main reasons: it remains faithful to the Kantian thesis of the finitude of human beings, and it adopts a "morally-neutral" approach, failing to come to terms with the Kantian concepts of freedom, immortality, and God. See Chan, "Mou Zongsan's Transformation of Kant's Philosophy," 128–29.

71. If it is true that when writing the first *Critique* Kant had second thoughts about beginning "Transcendental Logic" with "Transcendental Dialectic" instead of "Transcendental Analytic," then what Kant really establishes in the first *Critique* is "a sufficient foundation for both a metaphysics of morals and a metaphysics of nature." Henry E. Allison, *Kant's Groundwork for the Metaphysics of Morals*, quoted in Su, "Mou Zongsan's Critical Philosophy," xxxvii note 37.

72. XYW: 22 [CW XXI: 22].

73. XYW: preface 3 [CW XXI: preface 5].

74. Su, "Mou Zongsan's Critical Philosophy," xl; cf. ZDZ: 196–99 [CW XX: 252–57].

75. Tang Refeng (唐熱風), "Mou Zongsan on Intellectual Intuition," in *Contemporary Chinese Philosophy*, ed. Cheng Zhongying [Cheng Chung-Ying] (成中英) and Nicholas Bunnin (Oxford: Blackwell, 2002), 333.

76. ZDZ: 190 [CW XX: 245].

77. To quote Mou: "As the existence of things is concerned, intuition is a principle of cognitive presentation, if the intuition is sensible, (in that case, it is receptive, not creative, and it also requires a unification of thought which is based on concepts); on the other hand, intuition is a principle of ontological [creative] actualization, if the intuition is intellectual." ZDZ: 184 [CW XX: 237].

78. NL: 451; SJJ: 431–32 [CW XXIX: 431–32].

79. NL: 461–66; SJJ: 441–45 [CW XXIX: 441–45].

80. XYW: 99 [CW XXI: 103–4]; the translation of this quotation is Tang Refeng's with modifications, see Tang, "Mou Zongsan on Intellectual Intuition," 335.

81. *NL*: 453; *SJJ*: 433–34 [*CW* XXIX: 433–34].
82. *XYW*: 5, 13, 14 [*CW* XXI: 5, 13, 14].
83. *XYW*: 7 [*CW* XXI: 7].
84. *XYW*: 16 [*CW* XXI: 16].
85. Liu Shuxian [Liu Shu-Hsien] (劉述先), *Essentials of Contemporary Neo-Confucian Philosophy* (Westport: Praeger, 2003), 119.
86. *NL*: 464; *SJJ*: 443 [*CW* XXIX: 443].
87. *NL*: 453; *SJJ*: 433–34 [*CW* XXIX: 433–34].
88. *ZDZ*: 184 [*CW* XX: 237]; *SM*: 43.
89. Mou's "two-level ontology" states: "The heart-mind espoused in the *Awakening of Faith* is the [transcendent] true-permanency heart-mind on which all dharmas ultimately rest (*yizhi*). 'All dharmas' include all contaminated dharmas in the circulation of arising-and-ceasing and all clear-and-pure dharmas in undefiled seeds. The pure heart-mind of *tathāgatagarbha* is where all dharmas of both types ultimately rest. The Chinese word for 'ultimately rest on,' *yizhi*, contains two characters, *yi* and *zhi*: *Yi* is the *yi* in *yikao* of the meaning of 'to rely on'; and *zhi* is the *zhi* in *zhiyu zhishan* of the meaning of 'to rest in the ultimate good.' Since all dharmas ultimately rest on the pure heart-mind of *tathāgatagarbha*, it can open two gates. One is the gate of arising-and-ceasing, connecting to the phenomena of the transmigration of life and death, with arising, ceasing, and changes at every instant, which are reflected in the saying: 'All acts are without permanency, and all dharmas are without substantial-self' (*Samyuktāgama Sūtra*, T02n0099_p0066b14); the other is the gate of suchness, opening directly to the undefiled clear-and-pure dharmas." *NL*: 305; *SJJ*: 291 [*CW* XXIX: 291].
90. *YSL*: 239–40 [*CW* XXII: 234–35].
91. *LW*: 91; *YSL*: preface ii, 306 [*CW* XXII: preface 4, 297–98].
92. *YSL*: 58 [*CW* XXII: 54–55].
93. Mou's explanation of the "perfect teaching" (*yuanjiao* 圓教) consists of an attempt to combine the *Lotus Sūtra* (*Saddharmapuṇḍarīka Sūtra*), which affirms the objective existence of all dharmas, with the *Prajñāpāramitā Sūtras*, which expresses the subjective wisdom revealing *prajñā* realness: "*Prajñā* realness alone, as the intellectual intuition horizontally connecting all dharmas, does not secure the necessity of the objective existence of all dharmas. However, once combined with the vertical core of the ontology of the existence of all dharmas, it provides the necessity for all mundane beings to become Buddha, which is the ultimate 'happiness' in the Buddhist sense." Su, "Mou Zongsan's Critical Philosophy," xli.
94. In the case of Daoism, although Laozi [Lao Tzu] (老子) begins his "vertical system" by remarking that "*Dao* creates it, and *de* 德 (virtue) nurtures it" and that "*wu* 無 (no-thing) names the beginning of Heaven and earth, and *you* 有 (some-thing) names the mother of all things," he nonetheless gives this "vertical system" a horizontal explanation as Laozi's sayings cited above "are all vision-type expressions of the ultimate realm, not substantial-type expressions." In other words, Daoism is originally a vertical system in the sense that "nothing

can exist if it is separated from *Dao*" and that "*Dao* makes a thing become itself." But in the end Laozi's *Dao* is not the "creative generation" of the substantial type; instead, it is the "creation without creating" of the vision-type, carrying a passive meaning. NL: 443–44; SJJ: 423–24 [CW XXIX: 423–24]. On the other hand, Buddhism is even more likely to treat the problem of "transcendental ground" in a negative way as it does not affirm any "Being," be it the Brahman of Brahmanism, or the *Dao*-reality of Confucianism. Yet, for Mou, Buddhism is still a "vertical system," because of "its ultimate pursuit of an ultimate realm." NL: 447; SJJ: 426–27 [CW XXIX: 426–27].

95. YSL: 305 [CW XXII: 296]. For a detailed discussion of the perfect teaching in Confucianism, see YSL: 305–35 [CW XXII: 296–325].

96. YSL: 255 [CW XXII: 248–49]. For a detailed discussion of *ren* in this context, see XYX vol. 2: 219–24 [CW VI: 232–38].

97. *Doctrine of the Mean*, XXII.

98. YSL: 325 [CW XXII: 316]; the translation of this quotation is Serina Chan's with modifications, see Chan, *The Thought of Mou Zongsan*, 211.

99. *Mencius* 6B: 16; 7A: 21. For a detailed analysis of these issues, see YSL: chapter 3 [CW XXII: chapter 3].

100. YSL: 324 [CW XXII: 314–15].

101. Kant, *Critique of Pure Reason*, 526, B662; see also Chan, "Mou Zongsan's Transformation of Kant's Philosophy," 130.

102. NL: 72; SJJ: 76 [CW XXIX: 76]); cf. YSL: 134 [CW XXII: 131–32].

103. Bunnin, "God's Knowledge and Ours," 52.

104. XYX vol. 1: 155 [CW V: 160–61].

105. For an insightful discussion of this issue, see Chan Wing-Cheuk, "Mou Zongsan on Confucian and Kant's Ethics: A Critical Reflection," *Journal of Chinese Philosophy* 38(s1) (2011): 146–64. I shall briefly touch on the topic of moral feeling in relation to that of freedom in chapter 3.

106. Bunnin, "God's Knowledge and Ours," 49–50.

107. NL: 468; SJJ: 447 [CW XXIX: 447].

108. NL: 478; SJJ: 443–44 [CW XXIX: 443–44].

109. XYX vol. 1: 39 [CW V: 42].

110. Billioud, *Thinking through Confucian Modernity*, 21.

111. NL: 31; SJJ: 35 [CW XXIX: 35]; emphasis mine.

112. XYX vol. 1: 38–39 [CW V: 42].

113. Su, "Mou Zongsan's Critical Philosophy," xxxix.

114. Quoted in Chan, *The Thought of Mou Zongsan*, 109; SM: 218.

115. As Mou says in a public lecture: "The harm was not yet apparent in Hegel himself, but with Karl Marx, the arising of dialectic from absolute existence settled upon existence as 'materialist dialectic,' whose emergence was not just the 'source of tremendous chaos' but became actual chaos for the whole world and caused millions of heads to fall." LW: 119 [CW XXVII: 463–64].

116. *NL*: 464; *SJJ*: 443 [*CW* XXIX: 442–43].
117. *XYX* vol. 1: 38–39 [*CW* V: 42].
118. *LSZ*: 371 [*CW* IX-(2): 422–23]; cf. *DLX*: 5 [*CW* IX-(1): 6–7]; *SM*: 237.
119. *DLX*: 204 [*CW* IX-(1): 263].
120. Charles Taylor, *Hegel* (Cambridge: Cambridge University Press, 1975), 571; see also *Hegel and Modern Society* (Cambridge: Cambridge University Press, 1979), 168.
121. Li, *Confucianism*, 15.
122. Schmidt, "Mou Zongsan, Hegel, and Kant," 280–81.
123. *RJL*: 118 [*CW* XXVIII-(1): 140–41].
124. *NL*: 31; *SJJ*: 36 [*CW* XXIX: 35–36].
125. *NL*: 35; *SJJ*: 39 [*CW* XXIX: 38–39].
126. *NL*: 37; *SJJ*: 42 [*CW* XXIX: 41–42].
127. Hegel's revision of Kant signifies "a culmination of the tradition of reflection on freedom and politics that begins with Rousseau and runs through Kant and Fichte" in terms of self-determination. Paul Franco, *Hegel's Philosophy of Freedom* (New Haven: Yale University Press, 1999), 32.
128. William Sweet, "Introduction: Idealism, Ethics, and Social and Political Thought," in *The Moral, Social and Political Philosophy of the British Idealists*, ed. William Sweet (Exeter: Imprint Academia, 2009), 4. For a fuller discussion of this issue, see Avital Simhony, "A Liberal Commitment to the Common Good: T. H. Green's Social and Political Morality," in ibid., 31–64.
129. Peter Nicholson, *The Political Philosophy of the British Idealists* (Cambridge: Cambridge University Press, 1990), 12–13.

Notes to Chapter 2

1. For a particularly notable work on this topic, see Tu Weiming [Tu Wei-Ming] (杜維明), *Centrality and Commonality: An Essay on Confucian Religiousness* (Albany: State University of New York Press, 1989). For a historical review of this topic with philosophical insights, see Li Minghui [Lee Ming-Huei] (李明輝), *Confucianism: Its Roots and Global Significance*, ed. David Jones (Honolulu: University of Hawai'i Press, 2017), chapter 2.

2. Tang Junyi [Tang Chun-I] (唐君毅), *Yingwen lunzhu huibian* 英文論著彙編 (Essays on Chinese Philosophy and Culture), in *Tang Junyi quanji* 唐君毅全集 (Complete Works of Tang Junyi), vol. 19 (Taipei: Xuesheng shuju, 1991), 509. The "Declaration" was largely drafted by Tang Junyi, who presents a comprehensive version of the transcendental meaning of moral religion, by and large, in his masterpiece, *Shengming cunzai yu xinling jingjie* 生命存在與心靈境界 (The Existence of Life and Horizons of the Soul), in *Tang Junyi quanji* 唐君毅全集 (Complete Works of Tang Junyi), vols. 23–24 (Taipei: Xuesheng

shuju, 1991). In this context, the term "transcendental" is used to denote the "transcendental spirit" (*chaoyue jingshen* 超越精神) of the moral agent in Confucianism in general, which does not necessarily refer to the specific distinction between "transcendental metaphysics" and "transcendent metaphysics" made by Mou in the previous chapter.

3. Tu, *Centrality and Commonality*, 116.

4. Through in-depth research into Confucius temples, the celebrated historian Huang Jinxing [Huang Chin-Shing] (黃進興) shows otherwise that Confucianism actually served as an "official religion" in imperial China. See Huang Jinxing, *Confucianism and Sacred Space: The Confucius Temple from Imperial China to Today* (New York: Columbia University Press, 2021).

5. Tu, *Centrality and Commonality*, 102.

6. Tang Junyi, *Xin wu yu rensheng* 心物與人生 (Mind, Body, and Human Life), in *Tang Junyi quanji* 唐君毅全集 (Complete Works of Tang Junyi), vol. 2 (Taipei: Xuesheng shuju, 1991), 212.

7. See esp. Tu Weiming, *Confucian Thought: Selfhood as Creative Transformation* (Albany: State University of New York Press, 1985).

8. While both Mou Zongsan and Tang Junyi [Tang Chun-I] (唐君毅 1909–1978) regard religiousness as the transcendental spirit of Confucian humanism, Xu Fuguan [Hsu Fu-Kuan] (徐復觀 1904–1982) argues that in the Spring and Autumn Period (春秋 *Chunqiu* 770–476 BC) the Zhou (周) people's "consciousness of sorrow and worry" (*youhuan yishi* 憂患意識) rooted in the idea of the "reverence of Heaven" (*jing tian* 敬天) had already been transformed into a sense of responsibility within humanity. See Xu Fuguan, *Zhongguo renxing lun shi: xian Qin pian* 中國人性論史: 先秦篇 (A History of Chinese Theories of Human Nature: The Pre-Qin Period) (Taipei: Commercial Press, 1969), esp. chapters 2–3. In this regard, one of the major contributions that Confucius has made to Chinese culture is to substitute religion for the spirit of humanism in a fuller sense. As Xu puts it, when Confucius says "at fifty I understood the Decree of Heaven" (*Analects* 2: 4), what he really meant is "the Decree of Heaven in the moral sense, not in the religious sense." Ibid., 88. At this junction, it is instructive to note that Mou opposes this kind of "headless humanism" encouraged by Xu. See Li, *Confucianism*, esp. 26, 29, 33–34, 36. In a like manner, Tang Junyi remarks that while religion is surely a part of human activity, "the spirit of religion goes beyond the humanist world at the same time," for the reason that religiousness must imply a sense of transcendence. In the case of Confucianism, what is at issue is an "infinite and transcendental subject." Tang Junyi, *Renwen jingshen zhi chongjian* 人文精神之重建 (The Reconstruction of the Humanistic Spirit), in *Tang Junyi quanji* 唐君毅全集 (Complete Works of Tang Junyi), vol. 5 (Taipei: Xuesheng shuju, 1991), 587; see also *Zhongguo renwen jingshen zhi fazhan* 中國人文精神之發展 (The Development of the Chinese Humanistic Spirit), in *Tang Junyi quanji* 唐君毅全集 (Complete Works of Tang Junyi), vol. 6 (Taipei:

Xuesheng shuju, 1991), 371. From the standpoint I have been taking, the fact that both Mou and Tang are far more concerned with the metaphysical and transcendental aspects of Confucianism than Xu, for the most part, has to do with their philosophical link with idealism. In terms of moral religion, for Mou, as for Tang, Hegelianism is of great importance in making sense of the idea of religiousness in Confucianism.

9. Sébastien Billioud, *Thinking through Confucian Modernity: A Study of Mou Zongsan's Moral Metaphysics* (Leiden and Boston: Brill, 2012), 9–10; see also Stephan Schmidt, "Mou Zongsan, Hegel, and Kant: The Quest for Confucian Modernity," *Philosophy East and West* 61(2) (2011): 278.

10. N. Serina Chan, *The Thought of Mou Zongsan* (Leiden and Boston: Brill, 2011), 95.

11. Schmidt, "Mou Zongsan, Hegel, and Kant," 278.

12. As Tang Junyi singles out: "Now I realize that every person has a mind-substance or a moral self, which is both immanent and transcendental." Tang Junyi, *Zhongguo wenhua zhi jingshen jiazhi* 中國文化之精神價值 (The Spiritual Values of the Chinese Culture), in *Tang Junyi quanji* 唐君毅全集 (Complete Works of Tang Junyi), vol. 4 (Taipei: Xuesheng shuju, 1991), preface 5. Cf. Xu Fuguan, *Xinban xueshu yu zhengzhi* 新版學術與政治之間 (Between Academia and Politics, New Edition) (Taipei: Xuesheng shuju, 1980), 405; and *Rujia zhengzhi sixiang yu minzhu ziyou renquan* 儒家政治思想與民主自由人權 (Confucian Political Thought and Democracy, Liberty, and Human Rights), ed. Xiao Xinyi (蕭欣義) (Taipei: Bashi niandai chuban, 1979), 62. For a more recent discussion of this important issue, see Tu Weiming, *Ruxue disanqi fazhan de qianjing wenti—Dalu jiangxue, wennan, he taolun* 儒學第三期發展的前景問題—大陸講學, 問難, 和討論 (The Prospective Issues concerning the Third Phase of Development for Confucianism: Lectures, Interrogations, and Discussion in Mainland China) (Taipei: Linking Publishing Co., 1989), 165–211; Liu Shuxian [Liu Shu-Hsien] (劉述先), *Rujia zhexue de dianfan chonggou yu quanshi* 儒家哲學的典範重構與詮釋 (Reconstructing and Interpreting the Confucian Philosophical Paradigm) (Taipei: Wanjuanlou tushu, 2010), 19–50.

13. Quoted in Raymond Plant, *Hegel on Religion and Philosophy* (London: Phoenix, 1997), 13–14.

14. To quote Hegel, "[Jesus] was the teacher of a purely moral religion, not a positive one. Miracles and so forth were not intended to be the basis of doctrines, for these cannot rest on observed facts; those striking phenomena were perhaps simply meant to awaken the attention of a people deaf to morality. On this view, many ideas of his contemporaries, e.g., their expectations of a Messiah, their representation of immortality under the symbol of resurrection, their ascription of serious and incurable diseases to the agency of a powerful evil being, etc., were simply *used* by Jesus, partly because they stand in no immediate connection with morality, partly with a view to attaching a nobler meaning to

them; as contemporary ideas they do not belong to the content of a religion, because any such content must be eternal and unalterable." G. W. F. Hegel, *Early Theological Writings*, trans. T. M. Knox and Richard Kroner (Philadelphia: University of Pennsylvania Press, 1971), 71.

15. Put simply, since "the moral principle of the Gospel is charity, or love, and love is the beauty of the heart, a spiritual beauty which combines the Greek Soul and Kant's Moral Reason," it appears to Hegel that the possibility of bringing together God and the world, the divine and human life, may lie in the ultimate truth of "moral beauty" that appears in the Gospel. Richard Kroner, "Introduction: Hegel's Philosophical Development," in Hegel's *Early Theological Writings*, 9. In this regard, the spirit of Jesus can be understood as "a spirit raised above morality," and "the opposition of duty to inclination has found its unification in the modifications of love, i.e., in the virtues." Hegel, *Early Theological Writings*, 212, 225.

16. Ibid., 301.

17. G. W. F. Hegel, *Phenomenology of Spirit*, trans. A. V. Miller (Oxford: Oxford University Press, 1977), 131.

18. Judith N. Shklar, *Freedom and Independence: A Study of the Political Ideas of Hegel's "Phenomenology of Mind"* (Cambridge: Cambridge University Press, 1976), 30, 184.

19. As Charles Taylor (quoting H. S. Harris) points out, Hegel rests his hope of "new religion" on the following three rational goals: that "its doctrine must be grounded in universal reason"; that "fancy, heart and sensibility must not thereby go empty away"; that "it must be so constituted that all the needs of life and the public affairs of the state are tied in with it." Charles Taylor, *Hegel* (Cambridge: Cambridge University Press, 1975), 55.

20. Indeed, there are transitions in some important works such as *The Earliest System-Programme of German Idealism* and *The Difference between Fichte's and Schelling's System of Philosophy*.

21. Taylor, *Hegel*, 102.

22. G. W. F. Hegel, *Lectures on the Philosophy of Religion, One-Volume Edition: The Lectures of 1827*, ed. Peter C. Hodgson, trans. R. F. Brown et al. (Berkeley: University of California Press, 1988), 459.

23. Plant, *Hegel on Religion and Philosophy*, 50.

24. Hegel, *Lectures on the Philosophy of Religion*, 78.

25. The dialectical movement involves what Hegel calls *Aufhebung*, meaning that while the defects and contradictions of the previous modes of knowledge are "annulled" and "cancelled," their partial truths are "preserved" and "enhanced" by being incorporated into a richer mode. Thus, the "reconciliation" (*Versöhnung*) between God and humanity implies that "the two terms remain, but that their opposition is overcome"; for the unity that is achieved in reconciliation does not really "abolish" the dualism between man and God, but just provides for

a richer form of understanding, in which the elements of what preceded it are both "annulled and preserved" (*Aufhebung*). Taylor, *Hegel*, 49–50.

26. Ibid., 104. As Hegel put it, "substance is in itself or implicitly Subject, all content is its own reflection into itself." Hegel, *Phenomenology of Spirit*, 33.

27. Hegel, *Phenomenology of Spirit*, 10.

28. Plant, *Hegel on Religion and Philosophy*, 26.

29. Ibid., 32.

30. G. W. F. Hegel, *Hegel's Philosophy of Nature*, vol. 1, ed. M. J. Petry (London: George Allen and Unwin, 1970), 205.

31. Taylor, *Hegel*, 102.

32. Ibid., 101.

33. Hegel, *Hegel's Philosophy of Nature*, 205.

34. Hegel, *Lectures on the Philosophy of Religion*, 455.

35. Plant, *Hegel on Religion and Philosophy*, 33.

36. Quoted in ibid., 33.

37. Hegel, *Phenomenology of Spirit*, 493.

38. Shklar, *Freedom and Independence*, 185.

39. Charles Taylor, *Sources of the Self: The Making of Modern Identity* (Cambridge: Cambridge University Press, 1989), 367.

40. "Green's metaphysical doctrine of the reproduction of the 'eternal consciousness' within the individual consciousness," as Andrew Vincent rightly argues, is "reliant upon the background of a Hegelian theology" and owes a great deal to German Hegelian theologist Ferdinand Christian Baur. Andrew Vincent, "T. H. Green: Citizenship as Political and Metaphysical," in David Boucher and Andrew Vincent, *British Idealism and Political Theory* (Edinburgh: Edinburgh University Press, 2000), 38.

41. T. H. Green, "Four Lectures on the English Revolution," in T. H. Green, *Collected Works of T. H. Green*, vol. 3, *Miscellanies and Memoir with an Appendix*, ed. Peter Nicholson (Bristol: Thoemmes Press, 1997), 281.

42. Ibid., 279; cf. Vincent, "T. H. Green: Citizenship as Political and Metaphysical," 33, 37.

43. T. H. Green, "Essay on Christian Dogma," in Green, *Collected Works*, vol. 3, 164.

44. Ibid., 182; Green, "Four Lectures on the English Revolution," 280, 282.

45. Green, "Four Lectures on the English Revolution," 279.

46. Green, "Essay on Christian Dogma," 182.

47. Vincent, "T. H. Green: Citizenship as Political and Metaphysical," 34.

48. Bernard M. G. Reardon, "T. H. Green as a Theologian," in *The Philosophy of T. H. Green*, ed. Andrew Vincent (Aldershot: Gower Publishing Co. Ltd., 1986), 41.

49. T. H. Green, "Popular Philosophy in Its Relation to Life," in Green, *Collected Works*, vol. 3, 93.

50. Green, "Essay on Christian Dogma," 182.

51. Quoted in Andrew Vincent and Raymond Plant, *Philosophy, Politics and Citizenship* (Oxford: Basil Blackwell, 1984), 9.

52. T. H. Green, "Review of J. Caird: 'Introduction to the Philosophy of Religion,'" in Green, *Collected Works*, vol. 3, 146.

53. Vincent and Plant, *Philosophy, Politics and Citizenship*, 16.

54. In general, "the Hegelian element of Green's metaphysics is that the 'eternal consciousness,' which is the self-organizing principle at the heart of his system, gradually realizes itself through the 'society' of finite individuals." Jeremy Dunham et al., *Idealism: The History of a Philosophy* (Durham: Acumen, 2011), 167.

55. T. H. Green, "Fragment of an Address on the Text 'The World Is Nigh Thee,'" in Green, *Collected Works*, vol. 3, 221.

56. Green, "Essay on Christian Dogma," 184.

57. T. H. Green, "The Witness of God," in Green, *Collected Works*, vol. 3, 233.

58. Andrew Vincent, "T. H. Green and the Religion of Citizenship," in *The Philosophy of T. H. Green*, 54; Vincent, "T. H. Green: Citizenship as Political and Metaphysical," 38.

59. Green, "Essay on Christian Dogma," 183.

60. The attempt to treat the true self as divine and rational is quite common to many British idealists. For example, A. C. Bradley writes that "the stirring of religion is the feeling that my only true self in the end is God, to be a pulse-beat of his infinite life, to feel and know that I am that and nothing but that, and that this horrible core of selfishness in my heart, that parts me from him, is not there in his eyes at all." A. C. Bradley, *Ideals of Religion, Gifford Lectures Delivered in the University of Glasgow in 1907* (London: Macmillan, 1940), 242. On the other hand, John Stuart Mackenzie argues that the "true self is what is perhaps best described as the *rational* self. It is the universe that we occupy in our moments of deepest wisdom and insight." John S. Mackenzie, *A Manual of Ethics*, fourth edition (London: W. B. Clive, 1901), 148.

61. Green, "Fragment of an Address on the Text 'The World Is Nigh Thee,'" 223.

62. Vincent, "T. H. Green: Citizenship as Political and Metaphysical," 38.

63. Ibid.

64. Ibid., 40.

65. David O. Brink, "Editor's Introduction," in T. H. Green, *Prolegomena to Ethics*, ed. David O. Brink (Oxford: Clarendon Press, 2003), xviii.

66. Andrew Vincent, "Introduction," in *The Philosophy of T. H. Green*, 4.

67. Reardon, "T. H. Green as a Theologian," 41.

68. Immanuel Kant, *Critique of Pure Reason*, trans. N. K. Smith (London: Macmillan, 1993), 9, Axii.

69. T. H. Green, *Prolegomena to Ethics*, ed. David O. Brink (Oxford: Clarendon Press, 2003), 155, §137.

70. Ibid., 85, §74.

71. Ibid., 173, §153.

72. Ibid., 93, §82.

73. Brink, "Editor's Introduction," xxviii.

74. Vincent, "T. H. Green: Citizenship as Political and Metaphysical," 53.

75. Quoted in ibid., 53.

76. Green, *Prolegomena to Ethics*, 336, §283.

77. For example, F. H. Bradley famously articulated that "the 'individual' apart from the community is an abstraction. It is not anything real and hence not anything that we can realize, however much we may wish to do so. We have seen that I am myself by sharing with others, by including in my essence relations to them, the relations of the social state. If I wish to realize my true being, I must therefore realize something beyond my being as a mere this or that; for my true being has in it a life which is not the life of any mere particular, and so must be called a universal life. What is it then that I am to realize? We have said it in 'my station and its duties.'" F. H. Bradley, *Ethical Studies* (Oxford: Clarendon Press, 1988), 173.

78. Green, *Prolegomena to Ethics*, 401, §332.

79. Vincent and Plant, *Philosophy, Politics and Citizenship*, 12.

80. Green, "The Witness of God," 239.

81. Green, *Prolegomena to Ethics*, 120, §107.

82. SM: 82.

83. DLX: 183–85 [CW IX-(1): 237–39].

84. "Mencius said, 'Our body and complexion are given to us by Heaven. Only a sage can give his body complete fulfillment.'" The *Mencius* (*Mengzi* 孟子), trans. D. C. Lau (London: Penguin Books, 1970), 7A: 38.

85. SM: 222.

86. DLX: 159 [CW IX-(1): 206–7].

87. Tu, *Confucian Thought*, 20.

88. DLX: 43 [CW IX-(1): 56].

89. It is interesting to note that influenced by Mou's ethico-spiritual approach to Confucianism, the two prominent scholars from the "third generation" of New Confucianism, namely, Liu Shuxian [Liu Shu-Hsien] (劉述先 1934–2016) and Tu Weiming [Tu Wei-Ming] (杜維明), have tried to re-create an even more comprehensive framework of "universal ethics," aiming to promote Confucianism as a "spiritual resource for living in the contemporary world and for the formulation of a universal spiritual world creed" without discarding Catholicism, Judaism, or Islamism. Chan, *The Thought of Mou Zongsan*, 285.

90. ZZT: 138 [CW XXVIII-(2): 107].

91. SM: 32–33.

92. *DLX*: 125–41 [*CW* IX-(1): 162–83].
93. *DLX*: 259 [*CW* IX-(1): 334].
94. *DLX*: 152 [*CW* IX-(1): 197].
95. *ZZT*: 23 [*CW* XXVIII-(2): 16].
96. *LSZ*: 371 [*CW* IX-(2): 422–23]; cf. *DLX*: 5 [*CW* IX-(1): 6–7]; *SM*: 237.
97. Even in his later work, Mou retains the idealist thesis that "there is no event outside of the mind, and there is nothing outside of the mind." *XYW*: 442 [*CW* XXI:457].
98. *ZZT*: 55 [*CW* XXVIII-(2): 42–43].
99. Chan, *The Thought of Mou Zongsan*, 106–7.
100. Chan Wing-Tsit (陳榮捷), "Chinese and Western Interpretations of Jen (Humanity)," *Journal of Chinese Philosophy* 2(2) (1975): 109.
101. *ZZT*: 43 [*CW* XXVIII-(2): 31–32]; see also *DLX*: 14–15, 24 [*CW* IX-(1): 18–20, 31].
102. The *Analects* (*Lunyu* 論語), trans. D. C. Lau (London: Penguin Books, 1979), 14: 23.
103. *LSZ*: 178 [*CW* IX-(2): 204].
104. *DLX*: 41, 44 [*CW* IX-(1): 54, 57]; see also *NL*: 75; *SJJ*: 80 [*CW* XXIX: 79–80].
105. Quoted in *LSZ*: Appendix 1, 15 [*CW* IX-(2): 448].
106. *LSZ*: 98 [*CW* IX-(2): 113–14].
107. *Mencius* 7A: 1.
108. *XYX* vol. 1: 4–6 [*CW* V: 6–8].
109. *ZZT*: 92 [*CW* XXVIII-(2): 72].
110. *ZZT*: 92 [*CW* XXVIII-(2): 72].
111. *Analects* 7: 30.
112. *Analects* 15: 29.
113. *Mencius* 6A: 6.
114. Cheng Zhongying [Cheng Chung-Ying] (成中英), *New Dimensions of Confucian and Neo-Confucian Philosophy* (Albany: State University of New York Press, 1991), 298.
115. Tu, *Confucian Thought*, 8.
116. *ZZT*: 138 [*CW* XXVIII-(2): 107].
117. *SM*: 43.
118. Charles Taylor, "Conditions of an Unforced Consensus on Human Rights," in *The East Asian Challenge for Human Rights*, ed. Joanne R. Bauer and Daniel A. Bell (Cambridge: Cambridge University Press, 1999), 125.
119. Wm. Theodore de Bary, *The Liberal Tradition in China* (New York: Columbia University Press, 1983), 43.
120. Zhang Hao [Chang Hao] (張灝), *Youan yishi yu minzhu chuantong* 幽暗意識與民主傳統 (The Consciousness of Gloominess and the Tradition of

Democracy) (Taipei: Linking Publishing Co., 1989), 33–34. The translation of this quotation is Li Minghui's, see Li, *Confucianism*, 91.

121. *DLX*: 22 [CW IX-(1): 28]; see also 158–59 [CW IX-(1): 205–6].

Notes to Chapter 3

1. *SYG*: 269 [CW XXIII: 295]; *WZ*: 109 [CW XXXII-(1): 98–99].

2. *XYW*: preface 3 [CW XXI: preface 5].

3. Tang Junyi [Tang Chun-I] (唐君毅), *Yingwen lunzhu huibian* 英文論著彙編 (Essays on Chinese Philosophy and Culture), in *Tang Junyi quanji* 唐君毅全集 (Complete Works of Tang Junyi), vol. 19 (Taipei: Xuesheng Shuju, 1991), 419–20.

4. See Zeng Guoxiang [Roy Tseng] (曾國祥), *The Sceptical Idealist: Michael Oakeshott as a Critic of the Enlightenment* (Exeter: Imprint Academic, 2003), 78–84.

5. Tang Junyi, *Zhexue gailun* 哲學概論 (An Outline of Philosophy), vol. 2, in *Tang Junyi quanji* 唐君毅全集 (Complete Works of Tang Junyi), vol. 22 (Taipei: Xuesheng shuju, 1991), 326. See F. H. Bradley, *Appearance and Reality: A Metaphysical Essay* (Oxford: Clarendon Press, 1969), Book I.

6. Bradley, *Appearance and Reality*, 120.

7. Richard Wollheim, *F. H. Bradley* (London: Penguin, 1969), 208.

8. Far from it, Bradley states: "Reality is one in this sense that it has a positive nature exclusive of discord, a nature which holds throughout everything that is to be real. Its diversity can be diverse only so far as not to clash, and what seems otherwise anywhere cannot be real. And, from the other side, everything which appears must be real. Appearance must belong to reality, and it must therefore be concordant and other than it seems. The bewildering mass of phenomenal diversity must hence somehow be at unity and self-consistent; for it cannot be elsewhere than in reality, and reality excludes discord. Or again we may put it so: the real is the individual. It is one in the sense that its positive character embraces all differences in an inclusive harmony. And this knowledge, poor as it may be, is certainly more than bare negation or simple ignorance. So far as it goes, it gives us positive news about absolute reality." Bradley, *Appearance and Reality*, 123–24.

9. Tang, *Zhexue Gailun*, vol. 2, 326.

10. Bradley, *Appearance and Reality*, 127, 432. In other words, the Absolute in Bradley "signifies a comprehensive unity, or totally, self-subsistent and coherent, implying non-contradiction." David Boucher and Andrew Vincent, *British Idealism: A Guide for the Perplexed* (London: Continuum, 2012), 43.

11. See esp. Bradley, *Appearance and Reality*, chapter 24.

12. Ibid., preface.

13. *NL*: 265; *SJJ*: 257–58 [CW XXIX: 257–58].

14. ZAO vol. 1: 32 [CW XXV: 32].
15. Bradley, *Appearance and Reality*, 320–21.
16. Michael Oakeshott, *Experience and Its Modes* (Cambridge: Cambridge University Press, 1990), 2, 112.
17. Tang, *Zhexue Gailun*, vol. 2, 326.
18. Bradley, *Appearance and Reality*, 488–89.
19. Ibid., 489.
20. G. W. F. Hegel, *Phenomenology of Spirit*, trans. A. V. Miller (Oxford: Oxford University Press, 1977), 11.
21. "The movement towards the solution of [any] contradiction consists in the extension of the lower so as to take in and resolve its conflicting elements in a higher unity." F. H. Bradley, *Ethical Studies* (Oxford: Clarendon Press, 1988), 249.
22. Ibid., 74.
23. Ibid., 89.
24. As Bradley puts it: "All philosophy has to do is 'to understand what is,' and moral philosophy has to understand morals which exist, not to make them or give directions for making them. Such a notion is simply ludicrous. Philosophy in general has not to anticipate the discoveries of the particular sciences nor the evolution of history; the philosophy of religion has not to make a new religion or teach an old one; and aesthetics has not to produce works of fine art, but to theorize the beautiful which it finds; political philosophy has not to play tricks with the state, but to understand it; and ethics has not to make the world moral, but to reduce to theory the morality current in the world." Ibid., 193.
25. Bernard Williams argues likewise that "morality is not an invention of philosophers. It is an outlook, or, incoherently, part of the outlook, of almost all of us." Bernard Williams, *Ethics and the Limits of Philosophy* (London: HarperCollins, 1993), 174.
26. T. H. Green, *Prolegomena to Ethics*, ed. David O. Brink (Oxford: Clarendon Press, 2003), 381. Cf. Bradley, *Ethical Studies*, 225.
27. Tang, *Yingwen lunzhu huibian*, 47.
28. See, for example, *NL*: 264–71; *SJJ*: 257–63 [CW XXIX, 257–63]. Cf. Tang Junyi, *Zhongguo zhexue yuanlun: yuan dao pian* 中國哲學原論原道篇 (On the Sources of Chinese Philosophy: The Sources of Dao), vol. 3, in *Tang Junyi quanji* 唐君毅全集 (Complete Works of Tang Junyi), vol. 16 (Taipei: Xuesheng shuju, 1991), 68–69; and *Shengming cunzai yu xinling jingjie* 生命存在與心靈境界 (The Existence of Life and Horizons of the Soul), vol. 1, in *Tang Junyi quanji* 唐君毅全集 (Complete Works of Tang Junyi), vol. 23 (Taipei: Xuesheng shuju, 1991), 264, 404.
29. ZAO vol. 1: 565–66 [CW XXV: 565–66].
30. SM: 181, 183, 193.
31. SSJ: 9–12 [CW XXX-(1): 8–13].

32. The *Mencius* (*Mengzi* 孟子), trans. D. C. Lau (London: Penguin Books, 1970), 7A: 1.

33. I am going to deal with T. H. Green's criticism of utilitarianism and his endeavor to merge utilitarianism with Kantian deontology into a nondominant theory of the common good in chapter 7.

34. Immanuel Kant, *The Metaphysics of Morals*, trans. Mary Gregor (Cambridge: Cambridge University Press, 1991), 201.

35. Ibid., 201–2.

36. Chan Wing-Cheuk (陳榮灼), "Mou Zongsan on Confucian and Kant's Ethics: A Critical Reflection," *Journal of Chinese Philosophy* 38(s1) (2011): 148.

37. XYX vol. 1: 155 [CW V: 160].

38. XYX vol. 1: 127 [CW V: 131–32]; the translation of this quotation is Chan Wing-Cheuk's with modifications, see Chan, "Mou Zongsan on Confucian and Kant's Ethics," 149.

39. Mou Zongsan, *Kangde de daode zhexue* 康德的道德哲學 (Kant's Moral Philosophy) (Taipei: Xuesheng shuju, 1982), 297; collected in CW XV: 334–35. According to Chan Wing-Cheuk, Mou's identification of "enlightened feeling" (*jueqing* 覺情) with moral reason is not entirely faithful to Confucianism; also, he argues that Mou overlooks the real purpose of Kant's theory of the typic in reconnecting morals with nature by making possible the theses that "ought implies can" and that "should implies ought to be." See Chan, "Mou Zongsan on Confucian and Kant's Ethics," esp. 150–53, 157–60.

40. *Mencius* 6A: 7.

41. *Mencius* 2A: 6.

42. *Mencius* 6A: 6.

43. *Mencius* 7A: 3.

44. XYX vol. 1: 164 [CW V: 170].

45. Tang Junyi, *Zhongguo wenhua zhi jingshen jiazhi* 中國文化之精神價值 (The Spiritual Values of the Chinese Culture), in *Tang Junyi quanji* 唐君毅全集 (Complete Works of Tang Junyi), vol. 4 (Taipei: Xuesheng shuju, 1991), 134–35.

46. Bradley, *Ethical Studies*, 152–53.

47. Ibid., 156–57.

48. R. G. Collingwood, *The New Leviathan, or, Man, Society, Civilization and Barbarism*, ed. David Boucher (Oxford: Clarendon Press, 1992), 104.

49. Bradley, *Ethical Studies*, 199–200.

50. W. J. Mander, *British Idealism: A History* (Oxford: Oxford University Press, 2011), 203.

51. Maria Dimova-Cookson and W. J. Mander, "Introduction," in *T. H. Green: Ethics, Metaphysics, and Political Philosophy*, ed. Maria Dimova-Cookson and W. J. Mander (Oxford: Oxford University Press, 2006), 9.

52. David Boucher, "Introduction," in *The British Idealists*, ed. David Boucher (Cambridge: Cambridge University Press, 1997), xix–xxi.

53. Henry Jones, "The Social Organism," in *The British Idealists*, 4, 9.
54. Ibid., 14, 25, 26.
55. Boucher and Vincent, *British Idealism*, 16.
56. G. W. F. Hegel, *Elements of the Philosophy of Right*, ed. Allen W. Wood, trans. H. B. Nisbet (Cambridge: Cambridge University Press, 1991), 190, §146, 191, §148. Or alternatively, to quote Henry Jones, "Freedom, the unity, the life, differentiates itself; it flows out into the individual in the forms of rights, and returns to itself through its members in the form of services and duties." Jones, "The Social Organism," 24–25.
57. Bradley, *Ethical Studies*, 166, 173.
58. David G. Ritchie, *Philosophical Studies*, ed. Robert Latta (London: Macmillan, 1905), 249.
59. *DLX*: 5 [CW IX-(1): 6–7].
60. *SSJ*: 117 [CW XXX-(1): 117].
61. Bradley, *Ethical Studies*, 71.
62. Ibid., 74.
63. Ibid., 173.
64. Bradley, *Appearance and Reality*, 217.
65. John S. Mackenzie, *A Manual of Ethics*, fourth edition (London: W. B. Clive, 1901), 148.
66. Bernard Bosanquet, *Psychology of the Moral Self* (London: Macmillan, 1897), 95.
67. *ZZT*: 37, 41, 44 [CW XXVIII-(2): 27, 30, 32].
68. Bradley, *Ethical Studies*, 125.
69. Ibid., 188.
70. *SM*: 43.
71. *SM*: 299.
72. Boucher and Vincent, *British Idealism*, 43. See F. H. Bradley, *The Principles of Logic* (Oxford: Clarendon Press, 1922), 656.
73. *SM*: 43.
74. Peter P. Nicholson, *The Political Philosophy of the British Idealists* (Cambridge: Cambridge University Press, 1990), 12–13.
75. Bradley, *Ethical Studies*, 80.
76. Ibid., 225.
77. Ibid., 234.
78. Ibid., 298, 308.
79. Ibid., 234.
80. Ibid., 314.
81. Ibid., 319, 322.
82. Ibid., 334.
83. Ibid., 342.
84. Bradley, *Appearance and Reality*, 150, 140–41.

85. *XYW*: 12 [*CW* XXI: 14].
86. *YSL*: 133 [*CW* XXII: 133].
87. The *I Ching* (*Yi Jing* 易經), in *The Sacred Books of the East*, vol. 16, second edition, trans. James Legge (New York: Dover Publications, 1963), Appendix 4, II-(6): 34.
88. *XYX* vol. 1: 40–41 [*CW* V: 40–41].
89. Cheng Zhongying [Cheng Chung-Ying] (成中英), *New Dimensions of Confucian and Neo-Confucian Philosophy* (Albany: State University of New York Press, 1991), 298.

Notes to Chapter 4

1. As I have already mentioned in the introduction, in the eyes of anti-Confucian or Westernized liberalism, the attempt to combine Confucianism with liberal values not only commits an error of neglecting the cultural incompatibility between the Chinese and Western worlds, but it also falls victim to a categorical confusion between morality and politics and to ill-treatments of positive freedom, a common good, and the authoritative character of the state. In contrast, in the works of antiliberal or anti-Westernized Confucianism, while the error of neglecting the cultural incompatibility is further negatively taken to be Western-centric, the pursuit of liberal politics is bitterly blamed for being unrealistic on the failure of democracy and the political problems confronting China, as well as unauthentic toward the political tradition of Confucianism itself. For a succinct comparison between Confucian values and Democratic values, see Li Chenyang (李晨陽), *The Tao Encounters the West: Explorations in Comparative Philosophy* (Albany: State University of New York Press, 1999), chapter 7.

2. See, for example, Karl Popper, *The Open Society and Its Enemies*, vol. 2, *The High Tide of Prophecy: Hegel, Marx, and the Aftermath* (London: Routledge and Kegan Paul, 1962); and Isaiah Berlin, *Four Essays on Liberty* (Oxford: Oxford University Press, 1969).

3. I shall try to give a critical account of the Kantian approach with regard to rights justification in chapter 8.

4. David L. Hall and Roger T. Ames, *The Democracy of the Dead: Dewey, Confucius, and the Hope for Democracy in China* (Chicago and Lasalle: Open Court, 1999); Tan Sor-Hoon (陳素芬), *Confucian Democracy: A Deweyan Reconstruction* (Albany: State University of New York Press, 2004).

5. Stephen C. Angle, *Contemporary Confucian Political Philosophy* (Cambridge: Polity, 2012).

6. Joseph Chan, *Confucian Perfectionism: A Political Philosophy for Modern Times* (Princeton: Princeton University Press, 2014).

7. Deng Yuren [Norman Yujen Teng] (鄧育仁), *Gongmin Ruxue* 公民儒學 (Civic Confucianism) (Taipei: National Taiwan University Press, 2015).

8. Sungmoon Kim, *Public Reason Confucianism: Democratic Perfectionism and Constitutionalism in East Asia* (Cambridge: Cambridge University Press, 2016); see also Sungmoon Kim, *Confucian Democracy in East Asia: Theory and Practice* (Cambridge: Cambridge University Press, 2014).

9. John Rawls, *Lectures on the History of Moral Philosophy*, ed. Barbara Herman (Cambridge: Harvard University Press, 2000), 330, 352.

10. Charles Taylor, "Hegel's Ambiguous Legacy for Modern Liberalism," in *Hegel and Legal Theory*, ed. Drucilla Cornell, Michel Rosenfeld and David G. Carlson (New York: Routledge, 1991), 76.

11. See Charles Taylor, *Hegel* (Cambridge: Cambridge University Press, 1975), chapter 20.

12. Tom Rockmore, *Before and After Hegel: A Historical Introduction to Hegel's Thought* (Berkeley: University of California Press, 1993), 175.

13. Taylor, *Hegel*, 538, 546, 570.

14. Charles Taylor, *The Ethics of Authenticity* (Cambridge: Harvard University Press, 1991).

15. Taylor, *Hegel*, 76–80.

16. Lucio Cortella, *The Ethics of Democracy: A Contemporary Reading of Hegel's Philosophy of Right*, trans. Giacomo Donis (Albany: State University of New York Press, 2011), 10.

17. Ibid., 390.

18. Ibid., 85–86.

19. For an insightful account of a "democratic ethical life" from a Hegelian perspective, see Cortella, *The Ethics of Democracy*. With the scheme of "social freedom," Axel Honneth has succeeded in showing how a theory of recognition can lay the *ethical* foundation for social justice and democracy. See Axel Honneth, *The Struggle for Recognition: The Moral Grammar of Social Conflicts*, trans. Joel Anderson (Cambridge: Polity, 1995); and *Freedom's Right: The Social Foundations of Democratic Life*, trans. Joseph Ganahl (New York: Columbia University Press, 2015).

20. Zeng Guoxiang [Roy Tseng] (曾國祥), "The Idea of Freedom in Comparative Perspective: Critical Comparisons between Discourses of Liberalism and Neo-Confucianism," *Philosophy East and West* 66(2) (2016): 539–58.

21. SYGX: 280–81 [CW XXIV: 280–81].

22. Peter Singer, *Hegel* (Oxford: Oxford University Press, 1983), 78.

23. DLX: 5 [CW IX-(1): 7].

24. RJL: 118 [CW XXVIII-(1): 141].

25. On this key point, Tang Junyi [Tang Chun-I] (唐君毅 1909–1978), similar to Mou, argues that "the Chinese spirit of [governing] democracy was present only in the 'moral spirit' of Confucianism, and thus in a 'hidden' form

that never amounted to the manifestation of a 'political spirit.' Consequently, the Chinese people were not aware of their status as political subjects and had no conception of any claim to political rights." Thomas Fröhlich, *Tang Junyi: Confucian Philosophy and the Challenge of Modernity* (Leiden and Boston: Brill, 2017), 219.

26. The *Mencius* (*Mengzi* 孟子), trans. D. C. Lau (London: Penguin Books, 1970), 6A: 1–15.

27. Allen W. Wood, "Introduction," in G. W. F. Hegel, *Elements of the Philosophy of Right*, ed. Allen W. Wood, trans. H. B. Nisbet (Cambridge: Cambridge University Press, 1991), xvii. To be sure, as Lucio Cortella correctly puts it: "Ethical life is an objectified freedom that is not opposed to inner freedom: indeed, individuals do not experience it as aliens. The distinctive feature of the ethical world resides in the fact that, in it, the moment of subjective freedom is not lost." Cortella, *The Ethics of Democracy*, 5.

28. ZYZ: 46, 51 [CW X: 51, 57]; cf. SM: 53–67.

29. ZYZ: 52–53 [CW X: 58].

30. The *Great Learning* (*Daxue* 大學), in *The Chinese Classics*, vol. 1, trans. James Legge (Taipei: SMC Publishing Inc., 2001), I: 4.

31. *Great Learning*, I: 5.

32. Judith N. Shklar, *Freedom and Independence: A Study of the Political Ideas of Hegel's 'Phenomenology of Mind'* (Cambridge: Cambridge University Press, 1976), 30; for Hegel's discussion of "unhappy consciousness," see G. W. F. Hegel, *Phenomenology of Spirit*, trans. A. V. Miller (Oxford: Oxford University Press, 1977), esp. 130–32, §216, §217.

33. Stephen Houlgate, *An Introduction to Hegel: Freedom, Truth and History* (Oxford: Blackwell, 2005), 13.

34. G. W. F. Hegel, *Encyclopedia of the Philosophical Sciences in Outline and Critical Writings*, ed. Ernst Behler (New York: Continuum, 1990), 225.

35. Ibid.

36. Ibid., 241–64.

37. G. W. F. Hegel, *Elements of the Philosophy of Right*, ed. Allen W. Wood, trans. H. B. Nisbet (Cambridge: Cambridge University Press, 1991), 151, §124 R.

38. G. W. F. Hegel, *Lectures on the Philosophy of World History: Introduction: Reason in History*, trans. H. B. Nisbet (Cambridge: Cambridge University Press, 1975), 197.

39. LSZ: 68 [CW IX-(2): 78].

40. G. W. F. Hegel, *Lectures on the History of Philosophy*, vol. 1, *Greek Philosophy to Plato*, trans. E. S. Haldane (Lincoln: University of Nebraska Press, 1995), 121.

41. Ibid., 54. Cf. LSZ: 56–82 [CW IX-(2): 65–115].

42. LSZ: 80 [CW IX-(2): 92].

43. LSZ: 81 [CW IX-(2): 92].

44. ZYZ: 157 [CW X: 172].
45. Cf. LSZ: 188, 192, 229 [CW IX-(2): 215, 219, 263]. By the same token, Tang Junyi writes that "Confucian thought contains the highest democratic spirit, because [Chinese thought] believes in the highest sense that every human being can become a sage and join Heaven in virtue. Now people may ask: Why didn't Confucians talk about Western style democratic politics . . . ? . . . My answer is: Originally, Confucians took politics just as a direct extension of morality; politics [was thought of as an] occasion for the direct realization of human moral consciousness." Tang Junyi [Tang Chun-I] (唐君毅), *Renwen jingshen zhi chongjian* 人文精神之重建 (The Reconstruction of the Humanistic Spirit), in *Tang Junyi quanji* 唐君毅全集 (Complete Works of Tang Junyi), vol. 5 (Taipei: Xuesheng shuju, 1991), 419; the translation of this quotation is Thomas Fröhlich's, see Fröhlich, *Tang Junyi*, 219.
46. For another crucial example of the translation of "self-restriction" (*ziwoxianzhi* 自我限制), see Angle, *Contemporary Confucian Political Philosophy*, chapter 2.
47. David Elstein, *Democracy in Contemporary Confucian Philosophy* (London and New York: Routledge, 2015), 50.
48. LSZ: 188 [CW IX-(2): 215]; Elstein, *Democracy in Contemporary Confucian Philosophy*, 46.
49. Elstein, *Democracy in Contemporary Confucian Philosophy*, 51.
50. Ibid., 52.
51. Ibid., 53; see also 54–57.
52. DLX: 19, 29 [CW IX-(1): 24, 37].
53. DLX: 12 [CW IX-(1): 15].
54. LSZ: 172–73; 181–85 [CW IX-(2): 198–99; 208–12].
55. LSZ: 192 [CW IX-(2): 219–20].
56. ZYZ: 56 [CW X: 62].
57. ZYZ: 57 [CW X: 63].
58. ZYZ: 57, 59 [CW X: 63, 65].
59. XYW: 122 [CW XXI: 126].
60. ZYZ: 58 [CW X: 64].
61. SM: 253.
62. ZYZ: 59 [CW X: 65].
63. ZYZ: 59 [CW X: 65]; LSZ: 28 [CW IX-(2): 33].
64. ZYZ: 60 [CW X: 66].
65. Hegel, *Elements of the Philosophy of Right*, 189–90, §144, §145.
66. G. W. F. Hegel, "Heidelberg Lectures of 1817–1818," quoted in Allen W. Wood, "Editorial Notes," in Hegel, *Elements of the Philosophy of Right*, 404.
67. Hegel, *Elements of the Philosophy of Right*, preface 11.
68. Ibid., 279, § 258 *Addition* (G).
69. Rawls, *Lectures on the History of Moral Philosophy*, 331–32.

70. Wood, "Editorial Notes," 404.
71. *SM*: 253–54.
72. *LSZ*: 68 [*CW* IX-(2): 78].
73. *LSZ*: 117–18 [*CW* IX-(2): 136].
74. *SM*: 252.
75. *NL*: 464; *SJJ*: 443 [*CW* XXIX: 443].
76. Huang Junjie [Huang Chun-Chieh] 黃俊傑, "Dangdai Rujia dui Zhongguo wenhua de jieshi ji qi ziwo dingwei—yi Xu Fuguan wei zhongxin 當代儒家對中國文化的解釋及其自我定位—以徐復觀為中心 (The Interpretation and Self-Identity of Chinese Culture in Contemporary Confucianism: Focusing on Xu Fuguan)," in *Dangdai Ruxue lunji: chuantong yu chuangxin* 當代儒學論集: 傳統與創新 (Anthology of Contemporary Confucianism: Tradition and Innovation), ed. Liu Shuxian [Liu Shu-Hsien] (劉述先) (Taipei: Academia Sinica, Institute of Chinese Literature and Philosophy, 1995), 191.
77. See, for example, Michael J. Sandel, *Liberalism and the Limits of Justice*, second edition (Cambridge: Cambridge University Press, 1998).
78. For a profound discussion of Hegel's ethical liberalism, see Xiao Gaoyan [Carl K. Y. Shaw] (蕭高彥), "Toward a Reconstruction of Hegel's Ethical Liberalism," *Journal of Social Sciences and Philosophy* 8(2) (1996): 305–38.

Notes to Chapter 5

1. For the sake of clarity, in this book I have decided to make a distinction between "tradition" and "traditionalism," or between "traditional" and "traditionalistic."
2. The *Xunzi* (荀子): *The Complete Text*, trans. Eric L. Hutton (Princeton: Princeton University Press, 2014), 1: 140–41. Unless otherwise stated, all translations of the *Xunzi* are adapted from Hutton's.
3. Benjamin J. Schwartz, *The World of Thought in Ancient China* (Cambridge: Belknap Press of Harvard University Press, 1985), 67. Hence the "law" only refers to regulations and punishments; laws can only tell people *what not to do* and therefore will remain second order. Beyond them is a higher order: the rituals and proprieties through which people come to know what is *right* to do and lead positively to a virtuous and harmonious society, rather than to a society negatively regulated by punishments. Thus, Confucius says: "When proprieties and music do not flourish, punishments will not be properly awarded. When punishments are not properly awarded, the people do not know how to move hand and foot." The *Analects* (*Lunyu* 論語), trans. D. C. Lau (London: Penguin Books, 1979), 13: 3.
4. "The gentleman's approach to ritual is that he respects and finds comfort in it." *Xunzi* 12: 115–16.

5. *Analects* 13: 2.

6. The *Book of Rites* (*Liji* 禮記), vol. 2, ed. Zhai Chu [Chai Ch'u] (翟楚) and Zhai Wenbo [Winberg Chai] (翟文伯), trans. James Legge (New Hyde Park: University Books, 1967), XIV: 4. "There are five things by means of which the ancient kings secured the good government of the kingdom: the honor which they paid to the virtuous; to the noble; and to the old; the reverence which they showed to the aged; and their kindness to the young." *Book of Rites*, vol. 2, XXI, I: 13. "The ancient kings valued (men's) possession of virtue (*de* 德), honored those who pursued the right course, and employed those who displayed ability. They selected men of talents and virtue, and appointed them. They assembled the whole of them and solemnly addressed them." *Book of Rites*, vol. 1, VIII, II: 11.

7. According to Sungmoon Kim, while Confucius initiates the "paradigm of Confucian virtue politics" in terms of four key constituents: "(a) the primacy of virtue as the wellsprings of human excellence and flourishing, (b) a mode of government relying primarily on the ruler's moral character, (c) moral education of the people, and (d) the material conditions for the people's moral well-being," it is in the works of Mencius and Xunzi that a *systematic* political theory has been truly established in the sense of "extending virtue ethics to virtue politics in both domestic politics and interstate relations." Sungmoon Kim, *Theorizing Confucian Virtue Politics: The Political Philosophy of Mencius and Xunzi* (Cambridge: Cambridge University Press, 2020), 10–11. My general description of "rule by virtue" here is analogous to the first three propositions of the "paradigm of Confucian virtue politics," whereas the material conditions will be touched upon where appropriate in the discussion that follows.

8. As mentioned, there exist two levels of social order: that of the regulation of laws and punishments, and that of the guidance of rituals and proprieties. Although the enforcement of punishments is quite fundamental to the maintenance of social order, it would only forbid people to commit crimes and therefore would not lead to a better society. Only through a plethora of virtues and proprieties will people be transformed from *within*, becoming better people. Here, Confucius said it best: "If the people be led by laws, and uniformity sought to be given them by punishments, they will try to avoid the punishment, but have no sense of shame. If they be led by virtue, and uniformity sought to be given them by the rules of propriety, they will have the sense of shame, and moreover will become good." *Analects* 2: 3.

9. Hence Confucius articulates that "when a prince's personal conduct is correct, his government is effective without the issuing of orders. If his personal conduct is not correct, he may issue orders, but they will not be followed." *Analects* 13: 6.

10. *Analects* 12: 7; cf. 13: 3, 6, 13, and 14: 15. For Confucius, "government is rectification. When the ruler is correct himself, all the people will follow his

government." To this end, the correction of the following three relations is of great importance: "Husband and wife have their separate functions; between father and son there should be affection; between ruler and minister there should be a strict adherence to their several parts." *Book of Rites*, vol. 2, XXIV: 8.

11. By and large, the call for political legitimization began reframing the Chinese mindset largely thanks to Yan Fu's [Yen Fu] (嚴復 1854–1921) ground-breaking translations and interpretations of Western political canons. While Yan asserted that China would become a modern civilized country by treating "liberty as the substance and democracy as the function," Kang Youwei [Kang Yu-Wei] (康有為 1858–1927), the leading Confucian thinker at that time, all at once embarked on a reactionary mission of transforming Confucianism into a sturdy form of "state religion." Put briefly, Kang Youwei and his celebrated disciple, Liang Qichao [Liang Chi-Chao] (梁啟超 1873–1929), set out to embark on a discourse involved in reinterpreting the "theory of Three Ages" depicted in the *Gongyang* commentary of the *Spring and Autumn Annals* (*Chunqiu Gongyang Zhuan* 春秋公羊傳). As a result, in contrast to Yan Fu's anti-Confucian stance, the counter-proposal for the political modernization of China was otherwise set forth with the purpose of establishing a form of "constitutional monarchy" anchored in "Confucian religion."

12. Liu Shuxian [Liu Shu-Hsien] (劉述先), *Essentials of Contemporary Neo-Confucian Philosophy* (Westport: Praeger, 2003), 16.

13. Despite the fact that many of these expressions were first translated from Japanese, it remains the case that they originate essentially from a generalized European context. In an important sense, I thus agree with Michael Oakeshott's comment that "European has become an adjective which refers to something which may be found in any part of the world." Michael Oakeshott, *What Is History? and Other Essays*, ed. Luke O'Sullivan (Exeter: Imprint Academic, 2004), 436.

14. Benjamin I. Schwarz, *In Search of Wealth and Power: Yen Fu and the West* (Cambridge: Harvard University Press, 1964).

15. Shi Yuankang [Shih Yuan-Kang] (石元康), *Cong Zhongguo wenhua dao xiandaixing: dianfan zhuanyi?* 從中國文化到現代性: 典範轉移? (From Chinese Culture to Modernity: A Paradigm Shift?) (Taipei: Sanmin shuju, 1998), 26.

16. Alasdair MacIntyre, *After Virtue: A Study in Moral Theory*, second edition (London: Duckworth, 1980), 2.

17. For a historical account of this issue, see Wang Qingjia [Q. Edward Wang] (王晴佳), "Confucius in the May Fourth Era," in *A Concise Companion to Confucius*, ed. Paul R. Goldin (Oxford: Wiley Blackwell, 2017), 330–51.

18. May Fourth (*Wu Si* 五四) was "a complicated phenomenon, including the 'new thought tide,' the literary revolution, the student movement, the merchant's and workers' strikes, and boycott against Japan, as well as other social and political activities of the new intellectuals, all inspired by the patriotic sentiments

after the Twenty-one Demands and the Shan-tung resolution, and by the spirit of science and democracy in order to build a new China." Zhou Cezong [Chow Tse-Tsung] (周策縱), *The May Fourth Movement: Intellectual Revolution in Modern China* (Cambridge: Harvard University Press, 1960), 5.

19. Lin Yusheng [Lin Yu-Sheng] (林毓生), *The Crisis of Chinese Consciousness: Radical Antitraditionalism in the May Fourth Era* (Madison: University of Wisconsin Press, 1979), 26.

20. Leigh K. Jenco, "Chinese Liberalism," in *Encyclopedia of Political Theory*, ed. Mark Bevir (London: Sage Publications, 2010), 165.

21. For a detailed discussion on this matter, see Joseph R. Levenson, *Confucian China and Its Modern Fate* (Berkeley: University of California Press, 1958–1965), 3 vols.

22. Zhou, *The May Fourth Movement*, 342.

23. In spite of the launching of different solutions for a new China, both Chen Duxiu's [Chen Tu-Hsiu] (陳獨秀 1879–1942) promotion of "Mr. Democracy" and "Mr. Science" over old Chinese thinking and Hu Shi's [Hu Shih] (胡適 1891–1962) mission of "reorganizing the national heritage" with "the new methods of historiography and philology" consisted of similar endeavors to "demolish the Confucian shop" in the name of modernity. Even though the rival traditionalists such as Liang Shuming [Liang Shu-Ming] (梁漱溟 1893–1988) passed judgment on the radicalism of the May Fourth Movement, the real question Liang flagged was not so much about the conflict between Confucianism and modernity but about the superiority of Western values over Confucian civilization. In truth, despite the fact that after 1949 Hu Shi's "liberal wing" of anti-Confucianism and Chen Duxiu's "socialist wing" of anti-Confucianism seemed to have affected the formulation of political cultures in Taiwan and China respectively, what remains unchanged is the "standard viewpoint" hovering over Chinese political discourse in general, namely, that Confucianism is deeply at odds with modernity.

24. Yin Haiguang [Yin Hai-Kuang] (殷海光), *Zhengzhi yu shehui* 政治與社會 (Politics and Society), in *Yin Haiguang quanji* 殷海光全集 (Complete Works of Yin Haiguang), vol. 11, ed. Lin Zhenghong (林正弘) (Taipei: Guiguan tushu, 1990), 360.

25. Zhang Foquan [Chang Fo-Chuan] (張佛泉), *Ziyou yu renquan* 自由與人權 (Liberty and Human Rights) (Taipei: Commercial Press, 1993), 164.

26. Zhang Rulun (張汝倫), "Oakeshott in China," in *Michael Oakeshott's Cold War Liberalism*, ed. Terry Nardin (Basingstoke: Palgrave Macmillan, 2015), 140, 146–47.

27. Virginia Sapiro, "Considering Political Civility Historically: A Case Study of the United States," quoted in Susan Herbst, *Rude Democracy: Civility and Incivility in American Politics* (Philadelphia: Temple University Press, 2010), 12.

28. For a comprehensive account of civility as good manners, see Ernest Barker, *Traditions of Civility* (Cambridge: Cambridge University Press, 1948);

Harold Nicolson, *Good Behaviour: Being a Study of Certain Types of Civility* (London: Constable, 1955).

29. As C. Craig points out, there were seventeen conventional *loci* of invective established in Greek and Roman practice by Cicero's time: "embarrassing family origin; being unworthy of one's family; physical appearance; eccentricity of dress; gluttony and drunkenness, possibly leading to acts of *crudelitas* and *libido*; hypocrisy for appearing virtuous; avarice, possibly linked with prodigality; taking bribes; pretentiousness; sexual misconduct; hostility to family; cowardice in war; squandering of one's patrimony/financial embarrassment; aspiring to *regnum* or tyranny; cruelty to citizens and allies; plunder of private and public property; and oratorical ineptitude." Quoted in Kathleen Hall Jamieson, et al., "The Political Uses and Abuses of Civility and Incivility," in *The Oxford Handbook of Political Communication*, ed. Kate Kenski and Kathleen Hall Jamieson (Oxford: Oxford University Press, 2017), 209.

30. Michael Oakeshott, *On Human Conduct* (Oxford: Clarendon Press, 1975), 55–56.

31. The three main themes of the *Deeds of the Kings*, as Rees Davies summarizes, follow: "first, the making of the English into one people; second, the political unification of England under a single king; third, the cultural and social improvement in manners and civility, learning and governance"; or in the words of Revd. J. Sharp, writing in 1815, the topics that concern William include: "the gradual progress of man toward civilization; his mental improvement; his advance from barbarism to comparative refinement." Quoted in John Gillingham, "Civilizing the English? The English Histories of William of Malmesbury and David Hume," *Historical Research* 74(183) (2001): 17–18. It is notable that the idea of "civilizing the English" as such also had been conveyed to discuss the improvement of Scotland and to justify the invasion of Ireland in the eleven-seventies. For a detailed account of the English version of "Celtic barbarians," which regards the Welsh, Scots, and Irish as people of barbarity, see John Gillingham, *The English in the Twelfth Century: Imperialism, National Identity and Political Values* (Woodbridge: Boydell & Brewer, 2000).

32. Stephen L. Carter, *Civility: Manners, Morals, and the Etiquette of Democracy* (New York: Basic Books, 1998), 14.

33. See Gillingham, "Civilizing the English?" 21 note 23.

34. John Gillingham, "From *Civilitas* to Civility: Codes of Manners in Medieval and Early Modern England," *Transactions of the Royal Historical Society* 12 (2002): 267.

35. Gillingham, "Civilizing the English?" 20.

36. Arnaldo D. Momigliano, *Studies in Historiography* (London: Weidenfeld and Nicolson, 1966), 21. For example, one of the earliest usages of the word "civilization" appears at the very beginning of Ferguson's *An Essay on the History of Civil Society*, in which the author writes: "Natural productions are generally

formed by degree. . . . Not only the individual advances from infancy to manhood, but the species itself from rudeness to civilization." Adam Ferguson, *An Essay on the History of Civil Society*, ed. Fania Oz-Salzberger (Cambridge: Cambridge University Press, 1995), 7.

37. J. G. A. Pocock, *Barbarism and Religion*, vol. 2, *Narratives of Civil Government* (Cambridge: Cambridge University Press, 1999), 20.

38. Quoted in Gillingham, "Civilizing the English?" 25–26. For this reason, Forbes argues that Hume's *History of England* is not so much "a history of the English people, or of English civilization" but "a history of civilization in England." Duncan Forbes, *Hume's Philosophical Politics* (Cambridge: Cambridge University Press, 1985), 297–98.

39. Indeed, seen from the perspective of historical sociology, Norbert Elias has famously singled out that the "civilizing process" means that one of the major tasks of the modern state was to educate its members on how to act civilly by means of the self-control of the body, emotions, and speech. In other words, the development of civility in the seventeenth and eighteenth centuries entered the new era with a brand-new look, because the modern state had tried hard to employ rules of civility in teaching the citizens the importance of gaining control of the impulses and appetites of the body, such as urinating in the street or burping at the dinner table. Norbert Elias, *The Civilizing Process: Sociogenetic and Psychogenetic Investigation* (Oxford: Wiley Blackwell, 2000).

40. Pocock, *Barbarism and Religion*, vol. 2, 20.

41. For a detailed account of "civilization" in respect of the virtue of a commercial society, see J. G. A. Pocock, *Virtue, Commerce, and History* (Cambridge: Cambridge University Press, 1995). At this point, it is interesting to note that Burke, for instance, powerfully writes: "Nothing is more certain than that our manners, our civilizations, and all the good things which are connected with manners and civilizations, have in this European world of ours depended for ages upon two principles, and were indeed the result of both combined; I mean the spirit of a gentlemen, and the spirit of religion." Quoted in Pocock, *Virtue, Commerce, and History*, 198.

42. Jamieson, et al., "The Political Uses and Abuses of Civility and Incivility," 207.

43. Herbst, *Rude Democracy*, 12–13.

44. Quoted in Jamieson, et al., "The Political Uses and Abuses of Civility and Incivility," 211.

45. Alternatively, scholars have argued that the function of civility varies in accordance with the different models of the public spheres in modern democracies, such as representative, participatory, discursive, and constructionist. Myra Marx Ferree et al., "Four Models of the Public Sphere in Modern Democracies," *Theory and Society* 31(3) (2002): 289–324. See also Myra Marx Ferree et al., *Shaping Abortion Discourse: Democracy and the Public Sphere in Germany and the United States* (Cambridge: Cambridge University Press, 2002).

46. Michael Oakeshott, *Morality and Politics in Modern Europe: The Harvard Lectures*, ed. Shirley Robin Letwin (New Haven: Yale University Press, 1993), 58.
47. Ibid., 64.
48. Ibid., 78.
49. To quote Oakeshott: "I believe it to be a virtue in any theory that it avoids calling upon unnecessary *hypotheses* [emphasis mine]. And if this is so we are likely to conclude that many of the versions of the political theory of individualism are capable of improvement in this respect. Writers in this idiom, in order to make their position impregnable, have been accustomed to constructing a foundation far in excess of what is required to carry the superstructure." Oakeshott, *Morality and Politics in Modern Europe*, 83–84.
50. It is basically along this line of thinking that the regulations of Wikipedia, for instance, state: "Civility is part of Wikipedia's code of conduct, . . . Stated simply, editors should always treat each other with consideration and respect."
51. Richard C. Sinopoli, "Thick-Skinned Liberalism: Redefining Civility," *The American Political Science Review* 89(3) (1995): 612–13.
52. In fact, even in political science some scholars have payed attention to the notion of civility as communication and collaboration. For instance, according to Heinz Eulau, the politics of civility "refers to a broad range of potential behavioral patterns that can be expressed by such participles as persuading, soliciting, consulting, advising, bargaining, compromising, coalition-building, and so on—in other words, forms of behavior in which at least two actors stand in a mutually dependent relationship to each other. . . . In a civil relationship, then, the interaction is reciprocal, though not necessarily symmetrical, in that both actors gain from it." Heinz Eulau, "Technology and the Fear of the Politics of Civility," *The Journal of Politics* 35(2) (1973): 369.
53. Herbst, *Rude Democracy*, 19.
54. John Rawls, *Political Liberalism: John Dewey Essays in Philosophy* (New York: Columbia University Press, 1993), 217.
55. Michael Oakeshott, *The Vocabulary of a Modern European State*, ed. Luke O'Sullivan (Exeter: Imprint Academic, 2008), 254; see also Oakeshott, *On Human Conduct*, 201–3, 313–15.
56. Oakeshott, *The Vocabulary of a Modern European State*, 254; see also Oakeshott, *On Human Conduct*, 203–6, 315–17.
57. See, for example, Oakeshott, *Morality and Politics in Modern Europe*.
58. See, for example, Michael Oakeshott, *The Politics of Faith and the Politics of Scepticism*, ed. Timothy Fuller (New Haven: Yale University Press, 1996).
59. See, for example, Michael Oakeshott, *Lectures in the History of Political Thought*, ed. Terry Nardin and Luke O'Sullivan (Exeter: Imprint Academic, 2006).
60. Oakeshott, *On Human Conduct*, 124.
61. Edward Shils, *The Virtue of Civility: Selected Essays on Liberalism, Tradition, and Civil Society*, ed. Steven Grosby (Indianapolis: Liberty Fund, 1997), 335.

62. Ibid., 49 note 24, 68.
63. Ibid., 4, 335, 340.
64. Ibid., 49.
65. In general, Shils is similar to Oakeshott in making distinction between tradition and traditionalism, in reconciling modernity (individuality) with tradition (forms of life), in defending pluralism, and in arguing against "ideological politics" or "rationalistic politics," among other things.
66. Shils, *The Virtue of Civility*, 338.
67. Carter, *Civility*, xii, 74, 50, 98.
68. As a matter of fact, due to the political developments in the British and French empires, the growth of civilizational confidence, economic development and industrialization, as well as the bias of race and human difference, since about 1830 there even appeared a turn to "liberal imperialism" in the writings of Mill and Tocqueville, among other thinkers. Jennifer Pitts, *A Turn to Empire: The Rise of Imperial Liberalism in Britain and France* (Princeton: Princeton University Press, 2005), 11–21.
69. R. G. Collingwood, *The New Leviathan, or, Man, Society, Civilization and Barbarism*, ed. David Boucher (Oxford: Clarendon Press, 1992), 286.
70. David Boucher, *The Social and Political Thought of R. G. Collingwood* (Cambridge: Cambridge University Press, 1989), 147.
71. Collingwood, *The New Leviathan*, 189–90.
72. Boucher, *The Social and Political Thought of R. G. Collingwood*, 158.
73. Collingwood, *The New Leviathan*, 342.
74. Boucher, *The Social and Political Thought of R. G. Collingwood*, 221.
75. Frank H. Knight, *Freedom and Reform: Essays in Economics and Social Philosophy* (Indianapolis: Liberty Fund, 1982), 253–54; see also Shils, *The Virtue of Civility*, 112.
76. See, for example, Peter Gay, *The Enlightenment: An Interpretation* (New York: Alfred A. Knopf, 1966–1969), 2 vols.
77. For a critical review of Pocock's attempt to pluralize enlightenments, see Jonathan Israel, "J. G. A. Pocock and the 'Language of Enlightenment' in His Barbarism and Religion," *Journal of the History of Ideas* 77(1) (2016): 107–27.
78. J. G. A. Pocock, "Conservative Enlightenment and Democratic Revolutions: The American and French Cases in British Perspective," *Government and Opposition* 24(1) (1989): 81–105.
79. Gillingham, "Civilizing the English?" 33 note 92; cf. Forbes, *Hume's Philosophical Politics*, 167–69.
80. Shils, *The Virtue of Civility*, 115.
81. Ibid., 116.
82. Jaroslav Pelikan, *The Vindication of Tradition* (New Haven: Yale University Press, 1984), 65.

83. Shils takes tradition seriously because what he calls macrosociology is aimed at understanding "a variant in a contemporary idiom of the great efforts of the human mind to render judgment on *man's vicissitudes on earth* (emphasis mine.)" Edward Shils, *The Calling of Sociology and Other Essays on the Pursuit of Learning* (Chicago: University of Chicago Press, 1980), 32.

84. Oakeshott, *On Human Conduct*, 79.

85. Michael Oakeshott, *Rationalism in Politics and Other Essays*, new and expanded edition (Indianapolis: Liberty Fund, 1991), 53–54.

86. Timothy Fuller, "Introduction," in Michael Oakeshott, *The Voice of Liberal Learning: Michael Oakeshott on Education*, ed. Timothy Fuller (New Haven: Yale University Press, 1989), 10.

87. Maurice Cranston, "Michael Oakeshott's Politics," *Encounter* 28 (1967): 82–86. Cf. Noel O'Sullivan, "In the Perspective of Western Thought," in *The Achievement of Michael Oakeshott*, ed. Jesse Norman (London: Duckworth, 1993), 101.

88. For Herder's philosophical thinking, see Johann Gottfried von Herder, *Philosophical Writings*, ed. and trans. Michael N. Forster (Cambridge: Cambridge University Press, 2002).

89. See also Zeng Guoxiang [Roy Tseng] (曾國祥), "Conservatism, Romanticism, and the Understanding of Modernity," in *The Meanings of Michael Oakeshott's Conservatism*, ed. Corey Abel (Exeter: Imprint Academic, 2010), 126–42.

90. See Charles Taylor, *Sources of the Self: The Making of the Modern Identity* (Cambridge: Cambridge University Press, 1989), esp. chapter 8.

91. See Michael Sandel, *Liberalism and the Limits of Justice*, second edition (Cambridge: Cambridge University Press, 1998).

92. See MacIntyre, *After Virtue*, chapters 2–3.

93. In the present context, it seems appropriate to add that for the British idealists, "true individualism," to use Boucher's phrase, is "the self-realization of one's capacities in the context of society." David Boucher, "Introduction," in *The British Idealists*, ed. David Boucher (Cambridge: Cambridge University Press, 1997), xxiv. Also quoted in Derrick Darby, *Rights, Race, and Recognition* (Cambridge: Cambridge University Press, 2009), 33.

94. I am aware that for Hegel's absolutist reading of human history, there is only one human civilization, with different societies (and therefore their national cultures) ranked at different stages of its history. As I have explained in chapter 4, however, this book does not accept Hegel's viewpoint about the final terminus of human history. As regards the emergence of the diversity of civilizations, together with the idea of value pluralism, Herder's insight is of greater significance.

95. Andrew Terjesen, "Civility and Magnanimity," in *Civility in Politics and Education*, ed. Deborah S. Mower and Wade L. Robison (New York and

London: Routledge, 2012), 100. According to Terjesen, the third common usage of civility is as "something that facilitates civic harmony."

96. Michael J. Meyer, "Liberal Civility and the Civility of Etiquette: Public Ideals and Personal Lives," *Social Theory and Practice* 26(1) (2000): 69–84.

97. See Howard J. Curzer, "An Aristotelian Account of Civility," in *Civility in Politics and Education*, 80–81.

98. Stephen C. Angle, "Neither Morality nor Law: Ritual Propriety as Confucian Civility," in *Civility in Politics and Education*, 132.

99. Ferguson, *An Essay on the History of Civil Society*, 149.

100. See G. W. F. Hegel, *Elements of the Philosophy of Right*, ed. Allen W. Wood, trans. H. B. Nisbet (Cambridge: Cambridge University Press, 1991), 220–74, §182–§256. Hegel's identification of the system of needs—"a private sphere of trading and socially interacting individuals"—as an essential part of civil society was influenced by the German version of Ferguson's *An Essay on the History of Civil Society*, in which civil society was translated as *"bürgerliche Gesellschaft."* Fania Oz-Salzberger, "Introduction," in *An Essay on the History of Civil Society*, xix.

101. Quoted in Carter, *Civility*, 23, 279.

102. On this broader reading, in spite of Karl Popper's criticisms of Hegel, Popper's own definition of the "open society" wherein we may use "what reason we may have to plan as well as we can for both security *and* freedom" is not counter to the idea of a civilized society discussed here. Karl Popper, *The Open Society and Its Enemies*, vol. 2, *The High Tide of Prophecy: Hegel, Marx, and the Aftermath* (London: Routledge and Kegan Paul, 1962), 201.

103. Shils, *The Virtue of Civility*, 322.

104. Ibid., 87.

105. Ibid., 335.

106. Ibid., 346.

107. Jim Leach, "Foreword," in *Civility in Politics and Education*, ix.

108. For the purposes of this book, it is interesting to note that for Kant to act civilly by showing oneself as "approachable, affable, polite, hospitable, and gentle" to others is not a moral virtue, but a social virtue related to the sensation of an intimacy, or a "feeling for virtue," which inspires us to fulfill moral obligations; in short, the aim of civility is merely to bring "virtue into *vogue*" such that moral obligation becomes attractive and desirable to us. Megan J. Laverty, "Communication and Civility," in *Civility in Politics and Education*, 71–72.

109. By way of contrast, Cheshire Calhoun argues that while civility is an important part of moral discourse, because "the target of civility might reasonably be interpreted as making clear that I recognize some morally considerable fact about her that makes her worth treating with respect," civility names a distinctive virtue, different from simply treating people with respect or tolerance. This

is mainly because civility may be seen as an "essentially *communicative* form of moral conduct" as it helps "display" one's willingness to consider "others' feelings or the fact that they have tastes and views of their own"; in order to make clear such a "display," the moral agent is, therefore, required to "follow whatever the socially established norms are for showing people considerateness, tolerance, or respect." Seen in this light, civility not only aims to "safeguard the possibility of a common social life together," but it also, and for that reason, reflects "how deeply social the enterprise of morality is." Cheshire Calhoun, "The Virtue of Civility," *Philosophy and Public Affairs* 29(3) (2000): 259, 260, 272, 274.

110. Michael Schudson, "Why Conversation Is Not the Soul of Democracy." *Critical Studies in Media Communication* 14(4) (1997): 307.

111. Randall Kennedy, "The Case against 'Civility,'" *American Prospect* 41 (1998): 85.

112. In the analysis of Shils, progressivism in this context includes emancipationism, egalitarianism, populism, scientism, and ecclesiastical abdication, as well as what he calls "collective liberalism" and antipatriotism. See the essays "Observations on some Tribulations of Civility," "Ideology and Civility," "Tradition and Liberty," "The Antinomies of Liberalism," and "Nation, Nationality, Nationalism, and Civil Society," collected in *The Virtue of Civility*.

113. Herbst, *Rude Democracy*, 13.

114. Shils, *The Virtue of Civility*, 341.

115. Alan Tomhave, "Civility as a Condition of Citizenship," in *Civility in Politics and Education*, 154.

116. T. H. Marshall, "Citizenship and Social Class," in *Citizenship and Social Class*, ed. T. H. Marshall and Tom Bottomore (London: Pluto Press, 1992), 3–51.

117. David Miller, "Bounded Citizenship," in *Cosmopolitan Citizenship*, ed. Kimberly Hutchings and Roland Dannreuther (New York: St. Martin's Press, 1999), 62–63.

118. John Gray, *Two Faces of Liberalism* (Cambridge: Polity, 2000).

119. Richard Rorty, "Postmodernist Bourgeois Liberalism," in Richard Rorty, *Objectivity, Relativism, and Truth* (Cambridge: Cambridge University Press, 1991), 197–201.

120. Charles Taylor, "Shared and Divergent Values," in *Options for a New Canada*, ed. Ronald Watts and Douglas Brown (Toronto: University of Toronto Press, 1991).

121. As far as this contrast is concerned, Berlin actually belongs to the category of "practice-based liberalism." Therefore, to incorporate Berlin into the narrow Chinese liberal project that rejects New Confucianism is to commit an error of cultural transmission. For, in making this move, some of the vital features of Berlin's liberalism, such as expressionism, value pluralism, and Humean moderate skepticism are replaced with a prevailing form of political rationalism

fostered by Popper's "methodological individualism" (and indeed, "abstract universalism"). For a further discussion on the error of cultural transmission, see Michael Freeden and Andrew Vincent, "Introduction: The Study of Comparative Political Thought," in *Comparative Political Thought: Theorizing Practices*, ed. Michael Freeden and Andrew Vincent (London: Routledge, 2013), 15–18.

122. Angle, "Neither Morality nor Law," 133.

123. Stephen C. Angle, *Contemporary Confucian Political Philosophy* (Cambridge: Polity, 2012), 82.

124. Robert F. Ladenson, "Civility as Democratic Civic Virtue," in *Civility in Politics and Education*, 210.

125. *Book of Rites*, vol. 2, XVII, I: 19, 20.

126. Stephen C. Angle and Justin Tiwald, *Neo-Confucianism: A Philosophical Introduction* (Cambridge: Polity, 2017), 163.

127. Quoted in ibid.

128. "Humans are born having desires. When they have desires but do not get the objects of their desire, then they cannot but seek some means of satisfaction. If there is no measure or limit to their seeking, then they cannot help but struggle with each other. If they struggle with each other then there will be chaos, and if there is chaos then they will be impoverished. The former hated such chaos, and so they established rituals and *yi* 義 (righteousness) in order to divide things among people, to nurture their desires, and to satisfy their seeking. . . . This is how ritual arose." *Xunzi* 19: 1–11.

129. Cf. *LSZ*: 120 [*CW* IX-(2): 139].

130. "Human nature is the original beginning and the raw material, and deliberate effort (*wei* 偽) is what makes it patterned, ordered, and exalted. If there were no human nature, then there would be nothing for deliberate effort to be applied to. If there were no deliberate effort, then human nature would not be able to beautify itself. Human nature and deliberate effort must unite, and then the reputation of the sage and the work of unifying all under Heaven are thereupon brought to completion." *Xunzi* 19: 359–66.

131. *MYX*: 226 [*CW* II-(1): 196].

132. *Xunzi* 8: 499–500; see also *Xunzi* 23: 284–85.

133. *LSZ*: 124–27 [*CW* IX-(2): 143–47].

134. Mencius surely agrees that "between father and son, there should be affection; between sovereign and minister, righteousness; between husband and wife, attention to their separate functions; between old and young, a proper order; and between friends, fidelity." The *Mencius* (*Mengzi* 孟子), trans. D. C. Lau (London: Penguin Books, 1970), 3A: 4.

135. While these four virtues are agreed upon by the Song and Ming Neo-Confucians of all stripes, most *Daoxue* 道學 Confucians also add a fifth virtue, trustworthiness (*xin* 信). For a general account of virtues in Neo-Confucianism, see Angle and Tiwald, *Neo-Confucianism*, chapter 8.

136. Xu Fuguan [Hsu Fu-Kuan] (徐復觀), *Xinban xueshu yu zhengzhi zhijian* 新版學術與政治之間 (Between Academia and Politics, New Edition) (Taipei: Xuesheng shuju, 1980), 206.
137. *Mencius* 4B: 28; 7A: 21.
138. *Mencius* 1A: 5.
139. Xu, *Xinban xueshu yu zhengzhi zhijian*, 449.
140. *Xunzi* 9: 82–84; 9: 291.
141. *Xunzi* 8: 546–48.
142. Angle, "Neither Morality nor Law," 148.
143. *Book of Rites*, vol. 1, VII, IV: 9, 11.
144. *Book of Rites*, vol. 1, VIII, I: 2. Besides, the practice of *li* must be supported by music (*yue* 樂): "Virtue is the strong stem of (man's nature), and music is the blossoming of virtue." *Book of Rites*, vol. 2, XVII, II: 21.
145. *Book of Rites*, vol. 1, VIII, II: 8. "Therefore the sphere in which music acts is the interior of man, and that of ceremonies is his exterior. The result of music is a perfect harmony, and that of ceremonies is a perfect observance (of propriety). When one's inner man is thus harmonious, and his outer man thus docile, the people behold his countenance and do not strive with him; they look to his demeanor, and no feeling of indifference or rudeness arises in them." *Book of Rites*, vol. 2, XXI, II: 8.
146. Eric L. Hutton, "Introduction," in *Xunzi*, xxvii.
147. *Xunzi* 14: 94–96.
148. *Xunzi* 1: 140–41.
149. *Xunzi* 12: 140–41.
150. *Xunzi* 12: 81–82.
151. *Book of Rites*, vol. 2, XXI, I: 20. "Of all things by which the people live the rites are the greatest. Without them they would have no means of regulating the services paid to the spirits of Heaven and Earth; without them they would have no means of distinguishing the positions proper to father and son, to high and low, to old and young; without them they would have no means of maintaining the separate character of the intimate relations between male and female, father and son, elder brother and younger, and conducting the intercourse between the contracting families in a marriage, and the frequency or infrequency (of the reciprocities between friends). These are the grounds on which superior men have honored and reverenced (the rites) as they did." *Book of Rites*, vol. 2, XXIV: 1.
152. Xu, *Xinban xueshu yu zhengzhi zhijian*, 216.
153. See esp. LSZ: 120 [CW IX-(2): 139]; MYX: 199 [CW II-(1): 171].
154. MYX: 201–4 [CW II-(1): 172–75].
155. LSZ: 128 [CW IX-(2): 147].
156. MYX: 194 [CW II-(1): 166].
157. LSZ: 128 [CW IX-(2): 147].

158. *LSZ*: 127 [*CW* IX-(2): 147].
159. *LSZ*: 127 [*CW* IX-(2): 147].
160. *MYX*: 238 [*CW* II-(1): 206–7].
161. *MYX*: 234 [*CW* II-(1): 203].
162. *MYX*: 237 [*CW* II-(1): 205–6].
163. *Mencius* 3B: 9.
164. Xu, *Xinban xueshu yu zhengzhi zhijian*, 104.
165. Ibid.
166. Ibid., 216. For Xu's interpretation of Xunzi's political thought, see 199–220. In a like manner, Mou contends that unlike the ancient Legalists, Xunzi abides by the Confucian tradition in seeing the king as the holy embodiment of the perfect sagehood in accordance with the *Dao* of Heaven (*tiandao* 天道). On this reading, Mou is also likely to interpret the basic principle of Zunxi's thought as "the fulfillment of Heaven and humanity" (*tiancheng rencheng* 天成人成). *MYX*: 213–28 [*CW* II-(1): 184–98].
167. Xu, *Xinban xueshu yu zhengzhi zhijian*, 104.
168. Ibid., 49.
169. Ibid., 104; see also 280.
170. Ibid., 93, 333; see also 498–500.
171. *Analects* 9: 25.
172. *Analects* 12: 7. For Xu's analysis of "trustworthiness" as a governing virtue, see *Xinban xueshu yu zhengzhi zhijian*, 295–302.
173. *Book of Rites*, vol. 2, XXIV: 13.
174. *Book of Rites*, vol. 2, XXIV: 22.
175. Xu, *Xinban xueshu yu zhengzhi zhijian*, 230.
176. The *Great Learning* (*Daxue* 大學), in *The Chinese Classics*, vol. 1, trans. James Legge (Taipei: SMC Publishing Inc., 2001), X: 3; Xu, *Xinban xueshu yu zhengzhi zhijian*, 235–36.
177. Xu, *Xinban xueshu yu zhengzhi zhijian*, 53, 60, 220, 243, 294, 311.
178. Ibid., 293, 461.
179. Ibid., 461.
180. I shall reexamine the spirit of *ren* with regard to the double meaning of freedom, namely, negative freedom and positive freedom, in chapter 8.
181. Xu, *Xinban xueshu yu zhengzhi zhijian*, 332.
182. Ibid., 41–42.
183. Ibid., 538.
184. Ibid., 59–61.
185. In this book, I am using the term "civic virtue" in a stricter sense, that is, the virtue of the citizen in respect of civil society. Notice that some writers such as Sungmoon Kim refer to civic virtues more broadly as "the virtues that are directly instrumental to ritual order and social harmony." As Kim quotes William Galston in saying, civic virtue is "valued instrumentally, for its contri-

bution to sustaining a political community." In this regard, as Kim continues, while Mencius sees *li* as one of the cardinal moral virtues, in Xunzi's political philosophy, "ritual propriety is featured primarily as a civic virtue composed of civilities that undergird the backbone of the ritual institutions." Kim, *Theorizing Confucian Virtue Politics*, 18, 91, 113.

186. Thomas A. Metzger, *A Cloud across the Pacific: Essays on the Clash between Chinese and Western Political Theories Today* (Hong Kong: Chinese University Press, 2005), 705.

187. *Analects* 12: 1.

Notes to Chapter 6

1. For other important works of political meritocracy, see Li Chenyang (李晨陽), "Equality and Inequality in Confucianism," *Dao* 11(3) (2012): 295–313; Fan Ruiping (范瑞平), "Confucian Meritocracy for Contemporary China," in *The East Asian Challenge for Democracy: Political Meritocracy in Comparative Perspective*, ed. Daniel A. Bell and Li Chenyang (Cambridge: Cambridge University Press, 2013), 88–115; Bai Tongdong (白彤東), *Jiubang xinming: gujin zhongxi canzhao xia de gudian Rujia zhengzhi zhexue* 舊邦新命: 古今中西參照下的古典儒家政治哲學 (New Mission of an Old State: Classical Confucian Political Philosophy in a Contemporary and Comparative Relevance Context) (Beijing: Peking University Press, 2009), *China: The Political Philosophy of the Middle Kingdom* (New York: Zed Books, 2012), and "A Confucian Version of Hybrid Regime: How Does it Work, and Why Is It Superior?" in *The East Asian Challenge for Democracy*, 55–87; Joseph Chan (陳祖為), "Political Meritocracy and Meritorious Rule: A Confucian Perspective," in *The East Asian Challenge for Democracy*, 31–54, and *Confucian Perfectionism: A Political Philosophy for Modern Times* (Princeton: Princeton University Press, 2014).

2. Daniel A. Bell, *Communitarianism and Its Critics* (Oxford: Clarendon Press, 1993).

3. G. W. F. Hegel, *Elements of the Philosophy of Right*, ed. Allen W. Wood, trans. H. B. Nisbet (Cambridge: Cambridge University Press, 1991), 344, §303; see also 346–48, §308.

4. Daniel A. Bell, *East Meets West: Human Rights and Democracy in East Asia* (Princeton: Princeton University Press, 2000), 295; cf. Hegel, *Elements of the Philosophy of Right*, 271–72, §253.

5. Bell, *East Meets West*, 295. Here Bell is clearly following in Charles Taylor's footsteps in explaining Hegel's conception of freedom. See Charles Taylor, *Hegel and Modern Society* (Cambridge: Cambridge University Press, 1979). In his recent work, Bell has somewhat turned to place an emphasis on the spirit of cities.

See Daniel A. Bell and Avner de-Shalit, *The Spirit of Cities: Why the Identity of a City Matters in a Global Age* (Princeton: Princeton University Press, 2011).

6. Xu Fuguan [Hsu Fu-Kuan] (徐復觀), *Xinban xueshu yu zhengzhi zhijian* 新版學術與政治之間 (Between Academia and Politics, New Edition) (Taipei: Xuesheng shuju, 1980), 41–42.

7. See, for example, Bell, *East Meets West*, part 3.

8. Daniel A. Bell, *The China Model: Political Meritocracy and the Limits of Democracy* (Princeton: Princeton University Press, 2015), 9.

9. Ibid., 180, 195.

10. Daniel A. Bell, *Beyond Liberal Democracy: Political Thinking for an East Asian Context* (Princeton: Princeton University Press, 2006), 154; see also, Bell, *East Meets West*, 290.

11. Bell, *The China Model*, 58, 154, 156. Although, to his credit, Bell's goal is to reconcile normative political theory with empirical research on China's political systems, the China model that he proposes, as a number of reviewers point out, is self-contradictory in theory and fails to grasp the reality of Chinese politics.

12. Practically, the recruitment procedures in the Chinese civil services are through written examinations and oral interviews, and the CCP's political leaders are selected through a long-term evaluation of "cadres" within an inner-party process.

13. Although China is confronted with many perplexities at the moment, in Bell's observation, "most citizens perceive China as a harmonious society, and the country is more harmonious than large democratic countries such as India and the United States." Bell, *The China Model*, 60. Here, it is interesting to note that Bell actually thinks of himself as "politically progressive—as a 'man of the left.'" Putting aside Bell's position in the political spectrum of contemporary China, I think he is correct in rejecting the stereotype that Confucians must be "politically conservative"; as a matter of fact, historically speaking, "Confucius, Mencius, and Xunzi were all radical critics of the status quo." Daniel A. Bell, *China's New Confucianism: Politics and Everyday Life in a Changing Society* (Princeton: Princeton University Press, 2008), 157.

14. Bell, *China's New Confucianism*, 175.

15. Jiang Qing (蔣慶), *Zhengzhi Ruxue: dangdai Ruxue de zhuanxiang, tezhi yu fazhan* 政治儒學: 當代儒學的轉向、特質與發展 (Political Confucianism: The Changing Direction, Particularities, and Development of Contemporary Confucianism) (Taipei: Yangzhengtang wenhua, 2003), 44–61, 316. On Jiang's remarkable contributions to the recent appearance of political Confucianism in China, see *The Renaissance of Confucianism in Contemporary China*, ed. Fan Ruiping (Dordrecht: Springer, 2011). Jiang's opening essay "From Mind Confucianism to Political Confucianism" provides a point of reference for the other essays collected in the book.

16. Jiang Qing, *Gongyangxue yinlun* 公羊學引論 (Introduction to Gongyang School) (Shenyang: Liaoning jiaoyu chubanshe, 1995), 1–60; and *Shengming xinyang yu wangdao zhengzhi: Rujia wenhua de xiandai jiazhi* 生命信仰與王道政治: 儒家文化的現代價值 (A Faith in Life and the Kingly Way of Politics: The Modern Value of Confucian Culture) (Taipei: Yangzhengtang wenhua, 2004), 168. More broadly speaking, the origins of political Confucianism can be stretched from the *Spring and Autumn Annals* (*Chunqiu* 春秋) and the *Xunzi* (荀子), via the Gongyang School in the Western Han Dynasty (*Handai Gongyangxue* 漢代公羊學), the New Text Studies in the Western Han Dynasty (*Handai Jinwenjingxue* 漢代今文經學), and the works of Wang Tong (王通) in the Sui Dynasty, to the New Text Studies in the Qing Dynasty (*Qingdai Jinwenjingxue* 清代今文經學).

17. By and large, this means that the harmonious political order embracing the *Dao* of Heaven, the *Dao* of earth, and the *Dao* of humanity altogether.

18. Jiang, *Zhengzhi Ruxue*, 174.

19. Jiang Qing, *A Confucian Constitutional Order: How China's Ancient Past Can Shape Its Political Future*, ed. Daniel A. Bell and Fan Ruiping, trans. Edward Ryden (Princeton: Princeton University Press, 2012). Put briefly, in accordance with the *Dao* of Heaven, there is the sacred source of legitimacy, represented by the House of Confucian Tradition (*Tongru Yuan* 通儒院); in accordance with the *Dao* of earth, there is the historical and cultural source of legitimacy, embodied by the House of Cultural Community (*Guoti Yuan* 國體院); in accordance with the *Dao* of humanity, there is the popular source of legitimacy, signified by the House of the People (*Shumin Yuan* 庶民院). Later on, Jiang adds a symbolic monarch to stabilize the historical and cultural identification of Chinese people and their loyalty and patriotism to the state, as well as a branch of the Academy (*Tai Xue* 太學), which, hopefully, may help guide the governmental body to actualize Confucian values. For a more detailed account of Jiang Qing's Confucian Constitutionalism, see David Elstein, *Democracy in Contemporary Confucian Philosophy* (London and New York: Routledge, 2015), chapter 7.

20. Elstein, *Democracy in Contemporary Confucian Philosophy*, 151.

21. Jiang, *A Confucian Constitutional Order*, 33.

22. Xu Fuguan, *Rujia zhengzhi sixiang yu minzhu ziyou renquan* 儒家政治思想與民主自由人權 (Confucian Political Thought and Democracy, Liberty, and Human Rights), ed. Xiao Xinyi (蕭欣義) (Taipei: Bashi niandai chuban, 1979), 62.

23. On the major differences between these two thinkers, see Chen Ming (陳明), *Rujiao yu gongming shehui* 儒教與公民社會 (Confucianism and Civil Society) (Beijing: Dongfang chubanshe, 2013), 130–32.

24. In an interview, Chen Ming confesses, "I always have a certain affinity with liberalism; this is the original intention that I have never changed." Ibid., 123.

25. Ibid., 127.

26. Chen Ming, *Wenhua Ruxue: sibian yu lunbian* 文化儒學：思辨與論辯 (Cultural Confucianism: Thoughts and Debates) (Chengdu: Sichuan People's Publishing House, 2009), 51.

27. Chen, *Rujiao yu gongming shehui*, 81, 107–17.

28. Kang Xiaoguang (康曉光), *Renzheng: Zhongguo zhengzhi fazhan de disantiaolu* 仁政：中國政治發展的第三條道路 (The Politics of Benevolence: The Third Road for China's Political Development) (Singapore: Global Publishing, 2005), viii. For Kang's further criticisms of liberalism, see xxv–xxviii, 91–96, 126.

29. According to Kang Xiaoguang, the formula of a "cooperative state" consists of four principles: authoritarian politics, free market economy, corporatism (*fatuanzhuyi* 法團主義), and the welfare state. Ibid., 101.

30. For example, Hao Zhaokuan (郝兆寬) argues that "China has its own subjectivity capable of transcending both the Left and the Right in a way that returns to its own traditional thought," and Zeng Yi (曾亦) remarks that "China, as a great country with such a prolonged history of civilization, must have a say about its own universal values." *He wei pushi? shei zhi jiazhi? dangdai Rujia lun pushi jiazhi* 何謂普世？誰之價值？當代儒家論普世價值 (What Is Called Universal? Whose Value? Contemporary Confucians Discuss Universal Values), ed. Zeng Yi and Guo Xiaodong (郭曉東) (Shanghai: Huadong Shifan Daxue chubanshe, 2014), 14, 25.

31. Ibid., 17, 55.

32. ZYZ: chapters 7–8 [CW X: 117–78]; cf. LSZ: 188, 192, 229 [CW IX-(2): 215, 219, 263–64].

33. Cf. Elstein, *Democracy in Contemporary Confucian Philosophy*, 44.

34. LSZ: 188 [CW IX-(2): 215]; Elstein, *Democracy in Contemporary Confucian Philosophy*, 46.

35. Elstein, *Democracy in Contemporary Confucian Philosophy*, 47.

36. ZYZ: chapters 7–8 [CW X: 117–78].

37. Xu Fuguan's reexamination of Confucius's idea of "rule by virtue" bears a striking resemblance to Mou's viewpoint. See Xu, *Rujia zhengzhi sixiang yu minzhu ziyou renquan*, 93–114.

38. The *Mencius* (*Mengzi* 孟子), trans. D. C. Lau (London: Penguin Books, 1970), 5A: 5.

39. ZYZ: 128 [CW X: 140]; *Mencius* 5A: 6.

40. *Mencius* 5A: 6.

41. *Mencius* 5A: 6.

42. ZYZ: 114–15 [CW X: 125–26].

43. Huang Zongxi [Huang Tsung-Hsi] (黃宗羲), *Waiting for the Dawn: A Plan for the Prince, Huang Tsung-Hsi's Ming-I Tai-Fang Lu* 明夷待訪錄, trans. Wm. Theodore de Bary (New York: Columbia University Press, 1993), 92.

44. Ibid., 98. ZYZ: new preface 20 [CW X: new preface 23].

45. ZYZ: new preface 12 [CW X: new preface 14–15].
46. The *Analects* (*Lunyu* 論語), trans. D. C. Lau (London: Penguin Books, 1979), 15: 25.
47. ZYZ: new preface 12 [CW X: new preface 14–15]; see also ZYZ: 10, 117 [CW X: 11, 128].
48. *Analects* 17: 21.
49. When it comes to government, Mencius articulates that "there are two ways and two only: benevolence and cruelty." *Mencius* 4A: 2.
50. ZYZ: new preface 12 [CW X: new preface 14–15].
51. What has been said above is largely based on Mou's discussion of the depraved tyrants (*ba* 霸) as categorically opposed to the kingly way (*wangdao* 王道). I am aware that traditionally the "*ba*" refers to the politically powerful rulers, such as Duke Huan of Qi (*Qihuangong* 齊桓公) and Duke Wen of Jin (*Jinwengong* 晉文公). According to Mencius, "A man who mutilates *ren* 仁 (humaneness) is a mutilator (*zei* 賊), while one who cripples *yi* 義 (righteousness) is a crippler (*can* 殘). He who is both a crippler and a mutilator is an 'outcast.' I have indeed heard of the punishment of the 'outcast Zhou (紂),' but I have not heard of any regicide." *Mencius* 1B: 8. Against this context, Zhou is regarded as a "crippler and mutilator," whose rank is surely lower than the classification of "*ba*" associated with the politically powerful rulers.
52. *Mencius* 1B: 8.
53. Youngmin Kim, *A History of Chinese Political Thought* (Cambridge: Polity, 2018), 64.
54. ZYZ: 117, 118, 126, 129 [CW X: 129, 138, 143, 145].
55. ZYZ: 118, 120 [CW X: 129, 131].
56. ZYZ: 117 [CW X: 129].
57. ZYZ: 117 [CW X: 129].
58. *Mencius* 1B: 4.
59. *Mencius* 1B: 5. In a like manner, the ruler had better take seriously the opinions of the people. Thus, Mencius says: "When your close attendants all say of a man that he is good and wise, that is not enough; when the Counsellors all say the same, that is not enough; when everyone says so, you must have the case investigated. If the man turns out to be good and wise, then and only then should he be given office. When your close attendants all say of a man that he is unsuitable, do not listen to them; when the Counsellors all say the same, do not listen to them; when everyone say says so, then have the case investigated. If the man turns out to be unsuitable, then and only then should he be removed from office." *Mencius* 1B: 7.
60. ZYZ: 120 [CW X: 132].
61. *Analects* 8: 19.
62. *Analects* 15: 5.

63. *Analects* 5: 26. A fuller illustration of the "human relations" (*renlun guanxi* 人倫關係) is provided by Mencius: "Tillers of land were taxed one part in nine; descendants of officials received hereditary emoluments; there was inspection but no levy at border stations and market places; fish-traps were open for all to use; punishment did not extend to the wife and children of an offender. Old men without wives, old women without husbands, old people without children, young children without fathers—these four types of people are the most destitute and have no one to turn to for help. Whenever King Wen (*Wenwang* 文王) put benevolent measures into effect, he always gave them first consideration. *The Book of Odes* (*Shi Jing* 詩經) says, 'Happy are the rich; but have pity on the helpless.'" *Mencius* 1B: 5.

64. ZYZ: 121 [CW X: 133]; *A Source Book in Chinese Philosophy*, trans. Chan Wing-Tsit (陳榮捷) (Princeton: Princeton University Press, 1963), 552.

65. Xu, *Rujia zhengzhi sixiang yu minzhu ziyou renquan*, 105.

66. Xu, *Xinban xueshu yu zhengzhi zhijian*, 335; see also 375.

67. ZYZ: 120 [CW X: 132].

68. ZYZ: 120 [CW X: 132].

69. ZYZ: 112 [CW X: 123].

70. *Mencius* 7B: 14.

71. According to Mou, a "pinnacle of individualism" in association with the spirit of "stepping aside, spreading out, and leaving things as they are" (*rangkai sankai, wu gefu wu* 讓開散開, 物各付物) has, in fact, been made more obvious by Daoism; on this matter, what really distinguishes Confucianism from Daoism is that Confucianism takes political cultivation as a vital means to enable people to "attain accomplishment according to the individual's nature" (*jiu geti er shuncheng* 就個體而順成). ZYZ: 122 [CW X: 134].

72. ZYZ: 126 [CW X: 138].

73. ZYZ: 124 [CW X: 136].

74. *Analects* 2: 1.

75. *Analects* 12: 17.

76. *Analects* 13: 6.

77. *Analects* 12: 19.

78. *Mencius* 4A: 4.

79. At this point, I think Youngmin Kim is correct in remarking that for Mencius the invocation of the four-limb simile clearly implies that "morality is self-generating," that "morality comes from humanity itself," and thus, that "it does not ask for an external legislator who imposes morality outside the human realm." Kim, *A History of Chinese Political Thought*, 66.

80. *Mencius* 7A: 13.

81. *Analects* 2: 3.

82. *Mencius* 7A: 13.

83. *Mencius* 4A: 1.

84. The *Doctrine of the Mean* (*Zhongyong* 中庸), in *The Chinese Classics*, vol. 1, trans. James Legge (Taipei: SMC Publishing Inc., 2001), XX: 3.

85. Xu, *Xinban xueshu yu zhengzhi zhijian*, 299. For Xu Fuguan's further examination of the notion of "making the people wealthy before cultivation" (*xianfu houjiao* 先富後教), see 199–220, 229–45, 295–302.

86. ZYZ: 127 [CW X: 140].

87. ZYZ: 127 [CW X: 140].

88. ZYZ: 61 [CW X: 68]; *A Source Book in Chinese Philosophy*, 698.

89. ZYZ: 132–42 [CW X: 146–57]; see esp. 140 [CW X: 155].

90. ZYZ: 140 [CW X: 155].

91. ZYZ: 157–60 [CW X: 173–77].

92. See, for example, David O. Brink, *Perfectionism and the Common Good: Themes in the Philosophy of T. H. Green* (Oxford: Oxford University Press, 2003).

93. *Doctrine of the Mean*, XX: 4.

94. *Doctrine of the Mean*, XX: 2.

95. Mou himself confesses that there are three main reasons for him to bring attention to the Confucian political ideal: (1) to make people truly realize the functions and representations of reason in human history; (2) to inform the supporters of liberal democracy that the traditions of rationalism and idealism cannot be thrown away, that the "rational grounding of democracy" cannot be cut off, and that the expressions of universal humanity, the essence of reason and the like cannot be abandoned; (3) to give people the firm belief that instead of sliding into communism, the right path to liberating the laborious working class so as to make the world a better place to live consists in a far-reaching appreciation of the two presentations of reason. ZYZ: 160–61 [CW X: 176–77].

Notes to Chapter 7

1. On the contemporary debate between liberal neutralism and liberal perfectionism, see Jonathan Quong, *Liberalism without Perfection* (Oxford: Oxford University Press, 2011); and Matthew H. Kramer, *Liberalism with Excellence* (Oxford: Oxford University Press, 2017). For an important rejoinder to liberal neutralism from a perfectionist standpoint, see Joseph Chan (陳祖為), "Legitimacy, Unanimity, and Perfectionism," *Philosophy and Public Affairs* 29(1) (2000): 5–42. Chan has later developed his perfectionist stance into a political theory of Confucian moderate perfectionism. See Joseph Chan, *Confucian Perfectionism: A Political Philosophy for Modern Times* (Princeton: Princeton University Press, 2014).

2. David O. Brink, "Editor's Introduction," in T. H. Green, *Prolegomena to Ethics*, ed. David O. Brink (Oxford: Clarendon Press, 2003), lxvi–lxxv.

3. SYG: 11 [CW XXIII: 36–37].

4. SYG: 111 [CW XXIII: 135].

5. As Xu Fuguan [Hsu Fu-Kuan] (徐復觀 1904–1982) remarks, inasmuch as democracy is not merely a form of political institution, but also a way of social life, the "inner spirit" of democratic life is consistent with the "way of *zhongshu*" (*zhongshu zhi dao* 忠恕之道). Xu Fuguan, *Xinban xueshu yu zhengzhi zhijian* 新版學術與政治之間 (Between Academia and Politics, New Edition) (Taipei: Xuesheng shuju, 1980), 28–30.

6. For a detailed analysis of the debate about "panmoralism" (*fan daodezhuyi* 泛道德主義) in Confucianism, see Li Minghui [Lee Ming-Huei] (李明輝), *Ruxue yu xiandai yishi* 儒學與現代意識 (Confucianism and Modern Consciousness) (Taipei: Wenchin chubanshe, 1991), 67–133; John Makeham, *Lost Soul: "Confucianism" in Contemporary Chinese Academic Discourse* (Cambridge: Harvard University Asia Center, 2008), 235–36; and Jason Clower, "Introduction," in Mou Zongsan, *Late Works of Mou Zongsan: Selected Essays on Chinese Philosophy*, ed. and trans. Jason Clower (Leiden and Boston: Brill, 2014), 11–12.

7. SYGX: 35, 95 [CW XXIV: 35, 95].

8. SYG: 187 [CW XXIII: 211].

9. SYGX: 103 [CW XXIV: 103]. The *Mencius* (*Mengzi* 孟子), trans. D. C. Lau (London: Penguin Books, 1970), 7A: 24.

10. Hence, Mou once comes to depict the "objective form" of constitutional democracy as a renovated expression of the political ideal of "public rulership" in Confucianism that Wang Fuzhi [Wang Fu-Chih] (王夫之 1619–1692) calls "attaining a millennial, or seemingly timeless height of human [moral] practice" (*li qiannian zhi renji* 立千年之人極). SYG: 390 [CW XXIII: 411].

11. SYGX: 256, 269, 272 [CW XXIV: 256, 269, 272].

12. SYGX: 233 [CW XXIV: 233].

13. SYGX: 36 [CW XXIV: 36].

14. SYG: 75, 108 [CW XXIII: 99, 132].

15. SYG: 390 [CW XXIII: 410–11].

16. SYG: 294, 386 [CW XXIII: 320, 407].

17. SYG: 116 [CW XXIII: 139].

18. SYG: 378–80 [CW XXIII: 400–1]; cf. 383, 386 [CW XXIII: 404–5, 407].

19. SYG: 112–18, 245, 321, 367 [CW XXIII: 135–42, 270, 346, 390–91].

20. SYG: 397 [CW XXIII: 417–18].

21. ZYZ: 140 [CW X: 155].

22. ZYZ: chapter 7 [CW X: 117–41].

23. The *Analects* (*Lunyu* 論語), trans. D. C. Lau (London: Penguin Books, 1979), 5: 26.

24. SYG: 423 [CW XXIII: 441–42].

25. SYG: 373 [CW XXIII: 395]; cf. 386 [CW XXIII: 407].

26. SYGX: 264, 271 [CW XXIV: 264, 271].

27. SYG: 5, 187 [CW XXIII: 31, 211].

28. ZYZ: 120 [CW X: 132].

29. SYG: 92–95, 373–74 [CW XXIII: 116–19, 395–96].
30. SYG: 320, 374 [CW XXIII: 345–46, 396].
31. The *Doctrine of the Mean* (*Zhongyong* 中庸), in *The Chinese Classics*, vol. 1, trans. James Legge (Taipei: SMC Publishing Inc., 2001), I: 5.
32. The *I Ching* (*Yi Jing* 易經), in *The Sacred Books of the East*, vol. 16, second edition, trans. James Legge (New York: Dover Publications, 1963), Appendix 1, I-(1): 4.
33. Huang Zongxi [Huang Tsung-Hsi] (黃宗羲), *Waiting for the Dawn: A Plan for the Prince, Huang Tsung-Hsi's Ming-I Tai-Fang Lu* 明夷待訪錄, trans. Wm. Theodore de Bary (New York: Columbia University Press, 1993), 98. ZYZ: new preface 20 [CW X: new preface 23]; SYG: 318, 355, 369, 373, 374 [CW XXIII: 343, 379, 392, 395, 396].
34. SYG: 113, 321, 358 [CW XXIII: 136–37, 346, 381–82].
35. SYG: 11, 329, 415, 428 [CW XXIII: 36–37, 353–54, 434–35, 446].
36. *Analects* 12: 1.
37. *Mencius* 4A: 4.
38. SYG: 416 [CW XXIII: 434–35].
39. SYG: 3 [CW XXIII: 29].
40. SYG: 13, 117 [CW XXIII: 38–39, 140]; cf. 358 [CW XXIII: 381–82].
41. SYG: 111 [CW XXIII: 134].
42. SYG: 281, 325 [CW XXIII: 307].
43. SYG: 9 [CW XXIII: 34].
44. SYG: 12 [CW XXIII: 37–38].
45. SYG: 183–84 [CW XXIII: 207–8].
46. SYGX: 74–75 [CW XXIV: 74–75].
47. SYGX: 51, 77 [CW XXIV: 51, 77].
48. SYGX: 204 [CW XXIV: 204].
49. ZYZ: 61 [CW X: 68]; *A Source Book in Chinese Philosophy*, trans. Chan Wing-Tsit (陳榮捷) (Princeton: Princeton University Press, 1963), 698.
50. SYG: 371, 392–95 [CW XXIII: 393, 413–15].
51. SYG: 4, 23 [CW XXIII: 30, 46].
52. Immanuel Kant, *Kant: Political Writings*, ed. Hans Reiss, trans. H. B. Nisbet (Cambridge: Cambridge University Press, 1991).
53. Chan, *Confucian Perfectionism*. For a criticism of Joseph Chan's "Confucian meritocratic perfectionism" from the viewpoint of "Confucian democratic perfectionism," see Sungmoon Kim, *Public Reason Confucianism: Democratic Perfectionism and Constitutionalism in East Asia* (Cambridge: Cambridge University Press, 2016).
54. *Analects* 4: 15.
55. *Analects* 5: 15.
56. *Analects* 12: 1.
57. *Doctrine of the Mean* I: 3.

58. The *Great Learning* (*Daxue* 大學), in *The Chinese Classics*, vol. 1, trans. James Legge (Taipei: SMC Publishing Inc., 2001), I: 1.

59. *Mencius* 2A: 6. For a brief discussion of the manners in which *shu* shapes Mencius's views about the "goodness of *Xing*-nature" and "four germs" in Neo-Confucianism, see Stephen C. Angle and Justin Tiwald, *Neo-Confucianism: A Philosophical Introduction* (Cambridge: Polity, 2017), 68, 100–1.

60. SYG: 11. 12, 239, 253 [CW XXIII: 37, 38, 264–65, 279].

61. *Analects* 6: 30.

62. Liu Baonan [Liu Pao-Nan] (劉寶楠), *Lunyu zhengyi* 論語正義 (Exegesis on the Analects of Confucius) (Taipei: Taiwan Chunghwa Book, 1970), 5: 8.

63. Zhu Xi [Chu Hsi] (朱熹), *Lunyu jizhu* 論語集註 (Collected Annotations of the Analects) (Taipei: Zhonghua congshu weiyuanhui, 1958), 153.

64. *Analects* 4: 1.

65. *Analects* 4: 25.

66. *Analects* 15: 10.

67. *Analects* 12: 24.

68. "The Master said, 'Even when walking in the company of two other men, I am bound to be able to learn from them. The good points of the one I copy; the bad points of the other I correct in myself.'" *Analects* 7: 22.

69. ZYZ: 120 [CW X: 132].

70. SYG: 245 [CW XXIII: 270].

71. ZYZ: 131 [CW X: 145–46].

72. *Analects* 12: 2.

73. *Analects* 5: 26.

74. *Analects* 12: 16.

75. *Mencius* 2A: 8.

76. SYG: 10, 14, 117 [CW XXIII: 35–36, 39–40, 140].

77. "Mencius said, 'A gentleman is sparing with things but shows no benevolence toward them; he shows benevolence toward the people but is not attached to them. He is attached to his parents but is merely benevolent toward the people; he is benevolent toward the people but is merely sparing with things.'" *Mencius* 7A: 45.

78. *Mencius* 4B: 29.

79. *Analects* 14: 42.

80. The *Book of Rites* (*Liji* 禮記), vol. 1, ed. Zhai Chu [Chai Ch'u] (翟楚) and Zhai Wenbo [Winberg Chai] (翟文伯), trans. James Legge (New Hyde Park: University Books, 1967), VII: 1.

81. SYG: 93–95 [CW XXIII: 117–19].

82. Jiang Qing (蔣慶), *A Confucian Constitutional Order: How China's Ancient Past Can Shape Its Political Future*, ed. Daniel A. Bell and Fan Ruiping (范瑞平), trans. Edward Ryden (Princeton: Princeton University Press, 2012), 33.

83. David Elstein, *Democracy in Contemporary Confucian Philosophy* (London and New York: Routledge, 2015), 151.

84. Charles Taylor, *Philosophy and the Human Sciences: Philosophical Papers 2* (Cambridge: Cambridge University Press, 1985); and "Hegel's Ambiguous Legacy for Modern Liberalism," in *Hegel and Legal Theory*, ed. Drucilla Cornell, Michel Rosenfeld, and David G. Carlson (New York: Routledge, 1991), 64–77.

85. Green's major work in political philosophy is entitled *Lectures on the Principles of Political Obligation*, first published in the posthumous *Collected Works* of 1885–1888.

86. T. H. Green, *Lectures on the Principles of Political Obligation and Other Writings*, ed. Paul Harris and John Morrow (Cambridge: Cambridge University Press, 1986), 110, §141.

87. William J. Mander, *British Idealism: A History* (Oxford: Oxford University Press, 2011), 229–30.

88. Green, *Lectures*, 103, §132.

89. T. H. Green, *Prolegomena to Ethics*, ed. David O. Brink (Oxford: Clarendon Press, 2003), 401, §332.

90. As Mander correctly comments: "Full knowledge of the common good is beyond the grasp of any one, while partial grasp in so far as it is obtained is *the distributed possession of all* [emphasis mine]. Green champions a collective moral purpose, the common goal of a common good, but there is nothing monolithic about this. The state cannot identify this goal for us, because it—together with all its institutions, laws, duties, freedoms, and rights—is but a device to help us in the great endeavor of collectively identifying our mutual good, a good to which each citizen must both contribute and adjust himself." Mander, *British Idealism*, 231.

91. Douglas B. Rasmussen and Douglas J. Den Uyl, *Norms of Liberty: A Perfectionist Basis for Non-Perfectionist Politics* (University Park: Pennsylvania State University Press, 2005), 49.

92. Green, *Lectures*, 161–62, §209, §210.

93. Rasmussen and Uyl, *Norms of Liberty*, 48.

94. Colin Tyler, "Contesting the Common Good: T. H. Green and Contemporary Republicanism," in *T. H. Green: Ethics, Metaphysics, and Political Philosophy*, ed. Maria Dimova-Cookson and W. J. Mander (Oxford: Oxford University Press, 2006), 291.

95. Green, *Lectures*, 16, §7.

96. Tyler, "Contesting the Common Good," 291.

97. Cf. Mander, *British Idealism*, 230.

98. Michael Oakeshott, *On Human Conduct* (Oxford: Clarendon Press, 1975), 290–97.

99. Rasmussen and Uyl, *Norms of Liberty*, xiv. For a detailed account of "individualistic perfectionism," see *Norms of Liberty*, chapters 6–7.

100. Green, *Lectures*, 79, §98.

101. Thom Brooks, "Introduction," in *Ethical Citizenship: British Idealism and the Politics of Recognition*, ed. Thom Brooks (Basingstoke: Palgrave Macmillan, 2014), 2, 4.

102. Andrew Vincent, "The New Liberalism and Citizenship," in *The New Liberalism: Reconciling Liberty and Community*, ed. Avital Simhony and David Weinstein (Cambridge: Cambridge University Press, 2001), 215.

103. T. H. Green, "The Witness of God," in T. H. Green, *Collected Works of T. H. Green*, vol. 3, *Miscellanies and Memoir with an Appendix*, ed. Peter Nicholson (Bristol: Thoemmes Press, 1997), 251.

104. Avital Simhony, "Beyond Dualistic Constructions of Citizenship: T. H. Green's Idea of Ethical Citizenship as Mutual Membership," in *Ethical Citizenship*, 37.

105. Green, *Prolegomena to Ethics*, 232, §202.

106. F. H. Bradley, *Ethical Studies* (Oxford: Clarendon Press, 1988).

107. Green, *Prolegomena to Ethics*, 246–47, §213.

108. Quoted in ibid., 247, §214.

109. Ibid.

110. Ibid., 248, §214.

111. Ibid.

112. Ibid.

113. Rex Martin, "The Metaphysics and Ethics of T. H. Green's Idea of Persons and Citizens," in *Ethical Citizenship*, 27.

114. Quoted in Matt Hann, "'Who Is My Neighbour?' T. H. Green and the Possibility of Cosmopolitan Ethical Citizenship," in *Ethical Citizenship*, 178.

115. Green, *Prolegomena to Ethics*, 288–89, §245.

116. Immanuel Kant, *Grounding for the Metaphysics of Morals*, trans. James W. Ellington (Indianapolis: Hackett Publishing Company, 1993), 62–63.

117. Mander, *British Idealism*, 203.

118. Green, *Prolegomena to Ethics*, 255, §219.

119. In Green's definition, while "the will is simply the man," "will is equally and indistinguishably desire and thought." Ibid., 172–73, §153. For a detailed account on this issue, see ibid., 130–73, §115–§53.

120. T. H. Green, "Lectures on the Philosophy of Kant," in T. H. Green, *Collected Works of T. H. Green*, vol. 2, *Philosophical Works with an Appendix*, ed. Peter Nicholson (Bristol: Thoemmes Press, 1997), 154.

121. Green, *Prolegomena to Ethics*, 293, §247.

122. R. G. Collingwood, *The New Leviathan, or, Man, Society, Civilization and Barbarism*, ed. David Boucher (Oxford: Clarendon Press, 1992), 104.

123. Cf. Mander, *British Idealism*, 198.
124. Green, *Prolegomena to Ethics*, 210, §183.
125. Ibid., 290, §246.
126. Ibid., 289, §245.
127. Ibid., 267, §207.
128. Ibid., 229, §199. Or alternatively, as Bradley notes, because "the self to be realized is not exclusive of other selves, but on the contrary is determined, characterized, made what it is by relation to others," and because "myself which I aim at is the realization in me of a moral world which is a system of selves, an organism in which I am a member, and in whose life I live," it seems affirmative that "I cannot aim at my own well-being without aiming at that of others," who "are not mere means to me, but are involved in my essence." Bradley, *Ethical Studies*, 116.
129. Green, *Lectures*, 97, §124.
130. Simhony, "Beyond Dualistic Constructions of Citizenship," 38.
131. Avital Simhony, "Beyond Negative and Positive Freedom: T. H. Green's View of Freedom," *Political Theory* 21(1) (1993): 31–32.

Notes to Chapter 8

1. It is interesting to note that before Isaiah Berlin's inaugural lecture on "Two Concepts of Liberty" (1958), Zhang Foquan [Chang Fo-Chuan] (張佛泉 1907–1994) in his *Ziyou yu renquan* 自由與人權 (Liberty and Human Rights 1954) had already touched on a similar issue regarding the two concepts of freedom in the Chinese context. In my view, this is largely because both Berlin and Zhang actually refer to T. H. Green when making their distinctions between negative and positive freedom. As a matter of fact, the bibliography of *Ziyou yu renquan* is full of the major works of the British idealists.
2. Avital Simhony, "Beyond Negative and Positive Freedom: T. H. Green's View of Freedom," *Political Theory* 21(1) (1993): 28–54.
3. Andrew Vincent and Raymond Plant, *Philosophy, Politics and Citizenship* (Oxford: Basil Blackwell, 1984), 42.
4. Isaiah Berlin, *Four Essays on Liberty* (Oxford: Oxford University Press, 1969), xl, 122.
5. Ibid., 131.
6. Ibid., 135–44.
7. Ibid., 150.
8. Ibid., 131 note 1.
9. Gerald MacCallum, for example, argues that Berlin's dual distinction fails because freedom is a triadic concept and always involves an "agent" who

is free "from" something so as "to" do something. Gerald MacCallum, "Negative and Positive Freedom," in *Liberty: Oxford Readings in Politics and Government*, ed. David Miller (Oxford: Oxford University Press, 1991), 100–22.

10. Quentin Skinner and Philip Pettit, for instance, attempt to search for a third possibility under the name of republican freedom, a possibility that is excluded by Berlin's fallible juxtaposition of negative and positive freedom. Quentin Skinner, "The Paradoxes of Political Liberty," in *Liberty*, 183–205; Philip Pettit, *Republicanism: A Theory of Freedom and Government* (Oxford: Claredon Press, 1997), 17–27, and "Republican Political Theory," in *Political Theory: Tradition and Diversity*, ed. Andrew Vincent (Cambridge: Cambridge University Press, 1997), 112–31.

11. Paul Franco argues that Berlin's analysis "crystallizes the prejudices of a certain empiricist and (one might say) English way of thinking about freedom which refuses to consider freedom in any but a negative way." Paul Franco, *Hegel's Philosophy of Freedom* (New Haven: Yale University Press, 1999), 180.

12. Charles Taylor, for example, tries to dissolve negative freedom into a form of "opportunity concept" and reformulate positive freedom as a more plausible form of "exercise concept." Charles Taylor, "What's Wrong with Negative Liberty," in *The Idea of Freedom: Essays in Honour of Isaiah Berlin*, ed. Alan Ryan (Oxford: Oxford University Press, 1979), 175–93.

13. In reference to Harold Laski's *Reflections on the Revolution of Our Own Time* (1943), Zhang remarks that "in Britain, the United States and other countries there is merely negative freedom; only Russia alone is concerned with real freedom. What is most urgent in 'planned democracy' is positive freedom." Zhang Foquan [Chang Fo-Chuan] (張佛泉), *Ziyou yu renquan* 自由與人權 (Liberty and Human Rights) (Taipei: Commercial Press, 1993), 5.

14. Ibid., 12.

15. Ibid., 15–16. Cf. A. D. Lindsay, *The Modern Democratic State*, vol. 1 (Oxford: Oxford University Press, 1943), 87, 247; John C. Murray, "The Natural Law," in *Great Expressions of Human Rights*, ed. R. M. MacIver (New York: Institute for Religious and Social Studies, 1950), 88; Edward S. Corwin, *The Constitution and What It Means Today* (Princeton: Princeton University Press, 1938).

16. Zhang, *Ziyou yu renquan*, 23–24. Cf. The *Analects* (*Lunyu* 論語), trans. D. C. Lau (London: Penguin Books, 1979), 2: 4.

17. Zhang, *Ziyou yu renquan*, 21–22; see also 172–73, 189–96.

18. T. H. Green, "On the Different Senses of 'Freedom' as Applied to Will and the Moral Progress of Man" (hereafter cited as "Freedom"), in T. H. Green, *Lectures on the Principles of Political Obligation and Other Writings*, ed. Paul Harris and John Morrow (Cambridge: Cambridge University Press, 1986), 228–49.

19. Zhang, *Ziyou yu renquan*, 31 note 21.

20. Ibid., 239–40.

21. Ibid., 128, 244, 294.

22. Ibid., 130, 142, 150.

23. See, for example, Liu Xiao (劉曉), *Xiandai Xinrujia zhengzhi zhexue* 現代新儒家政治哲學 (The Political Philosophy of Modern New Confucianism) (Beijing: Xianzhuang shuju, 2001); and Tang Zhonggang (湯忠鋼), *Dexing yu zhengzhi: Mou Zongsan's Xinrujia zhengzhi zhexue yanjiu* 德性與政治: 牟宗三新儒家政治哲學研究 (Virtue and Politics: Research on Mou Zongsan's New Confucian Political Philosophy) (Beijing: Zhongguo yanshi chubanshe, 2008). For a defense of New Confucianism on this issue, see Li Minghui [Lee Ming-Huei] (李明輝), *Rujia shiye xia de zhengzhi sixiang* 儒家視野下的政治思想 (Political Thought from a Confucian Perspective) (Taipei: National Taiwan University Press, 2005), chapters 2 and 10.

24. Zhang, *Ziyou yu renquan*, 164.

25. Ibid., 300. Cf. Yin Haiguang [Yin Hai-Kuang] (殷海光), *Zhengzhi yu shehui* 政治與社會 (Politics and Society), in *Yin Haiguang quanji* 殷海光全集 (Complete Works of Yin Haiguang), vol. 11, ed. Lin Zhenghong (林正弘) (Taipei: Guiguan tushu, 1990), 360.

26. Zhang, *Ziyou yu renquan*, 183–84.

27. T. H. Green, "Lectures on Liberal Legislation and Freedom of Contract" (hereafter cited as "Liberal Legislation"), in Green, *Lectures*, 194–212.

28. Some interpreters argue that there are three meanings of freedom used in "Freedom," namely juristic freedom, formal freedom, and "true" freedom. See, for example, Colin Tyler, *The Metaphysics of Self-Realization and Freedom, Part 1 of the Liberal Socialism of Thomas Hill Green* (Exeter: Imprint Academic, 2010), 110.

29. Maria Dimova-Cookson, "A New Scheme of Positive and Negative Freedom: Reconstructing T. H. Green on Freedom," *Political Theory* 31(4) (2003): 509.

30. Ibid., 511.

31. Some scholars are likely to see Green's moral theory as a mixture of Aristotle's eudaimonism and a Fichtean form of Kant's ethics. See, for example, Tyler, *The Metaphysics of Self-Realization and Freedom, Part 1 of the Liberal Socialism of Thomas Hill Green*.

32. T. H. Green, *Prolegomena to Ethics*, ed. David O. Brink (Oxford: Clarendon Press, 2003), 336, §283.

33. To quote Hegel, while the will is "a particular way of thinking—thinking translating itself into existence, thinking as the drive to give itself existence"; "the freedom of the will can be best explained by reference to physical nature. For freedom is just as much a basic determination of the will as weight is a basic determination of bodies." G. W. F. Hegel, *Elements of the Philosophy of Right*, ed. Allen W. Wood, trans. H. B. Nisbet (Cambridge: Cambridge University Press, 1991), 35, §4A.

34. Charles Taylor, *Philosophy and the Human Sciences: Philosophical Papers 2* (Cambridge: Cambridge University Press, 1985), 219.

35. As Green puts it, "since in all willing a man is his own object to himself, the object by which the act is determined, the will is always free—or

more properly that a man in willing is necessarily free, since willing constitutes freedom, and 'free will' is a pleonasm='free freedom.'" Green, "Freedom," 228.

36. Ibid., 242.
37. Hegel, *Elements of the Philosophy of Right*, 54, § 23.
38. Quoted in Simhony, "Beyond Negative and Positive Freedom," 42.
39. Green, "Freedom," 241.
40. Hegel, *Elements of the Philosophy of Right*, 64, §33A.
41. Ibid., 186, §141A.
42. Green, "Freedom," 232.
43. Simhony, "Beyond Negative and Positive Freedom," 39.
44. Green, "Freedom," 231. Cf. Hegel, *Elements of the Philosophy of Right*, 49, 63, 162, §15, §33, §135.
45. Cf. Hegel, *Elements of the Philosophy of Right*, 275–79, §258.
46. Simhony, "Beyond Negative and Positive Freedom," 35.
47. For a conventional liberal picture of Hegel, see Z. A. Pelczynski, "The Hegelian Conception of the State," in *Hegel's Political Philosophy: Problems and Perspectives*, ed. Z. A. Pelczyński (Cambridge: Cambridge University Press, 1971), chapter 1; and Shlomo Avineri, *Hegel's Theory of the Modern State* (Cambridge: Cambridge University Press, 1972).
48. Green, "Liberal Legislation," 200.
49. Ibid., 199.
50. Simhony, "Beyond Negative and Positive Freedom," 31–32.
51. Franco, *Hegel's Philosophy of Freedom*, 32.
52. Green, *Prolegomena to Ethics*, 401, §323.
53. Tyler, *The Metaphysics of Self-Realization and Freedom, Part 1 of the Liberal Socialism of Thomas Hill Green*, 115.
54. T. H. Green, *Lectures on the Principles of Political Obligation and Other Writings*, ed. Paul Harris and John Morrow (Cambridge: Cambridge University Press, 1986), 26.
55. The recent development of Hegel's political philosophy actually reaffirms Green's insights in many significant ways. For example, according to Lucio Cortella, "As the ground on which the autonomy of the individual is built, it creates the conditions for him to find the way to self-realization." He further cites Axel Honneth in remarking: "Subjects are equally in a position to determine their life-goals without external influence only to the extent to which the establishment of civil law gives them all, in principle, individual [negative] freedom to make decisions. In short, self-realization is dependent on social prerequisite of legally guaranteed autonomy, because only with its help can subjects come to conceive of themselves as persons who can deliberate about their desires." Thus seen, as Cortella continues, "self-realization is not in conflict with autonomy but is its further development." Lucio Cortella, *The Ethics of*

Democracy: A Contemporary Reading of Hegel's Philosophy of Right, trans. Giacomo Donis (Albany: State University of New York Press, 2011), 168.

56. Berlin, *Four Essays on Liberty*, 133 note 1.
57. Green, "Liberal Legislation," 212.
58. Berlin, *Four Essays on Liberty*, lviii.
59. Green, "Liberal Legislation," 202.
60. Ibid., 194.
61. Ibid., 203.
62. Xu Fuguan [Hsu Fu-Kuan] (徐復觀), *Xinban xueshu yu zhengzhi zhijian* 新版學術與政治之間 (Between Academia and Politics, New Edition) (Taipei: Xuesheng shuju, 1980), 459–60.
63. Ibid., 503.
64. As He Xinquan [Ho Hsin-Chuan] (何信全) puts it, "Mou Zongsan's idea of freedom is basically related to the convention of Hegel's philosophy of freedom." He Xinquan, *Ruxue yu xiandai minzhu: dangdai Xinrujia zhengzhi zhexue yanjiu* 儒學與現代民主: 當代新儒家政治哲學研究 (Confucianism and Modern Democracy: A Study of Contemporary New Confucian Political Philosophy) (Taipei: Academia Sinica, Institute of Chinese Literature and Philosophy, 1996), 186.
65. ZYZ: 60 [CW X: 66].
66. ZYZ: 155 [CW X: 170–71].
67. Berlin, *Four Essays on Liberty*, chapter 3.
68. SM: 234.
69. *DLX*: 13 [CW IX-(1): 17].
70. *DLX*: 12 [CW IX-(1): 15].
71. The *Mencius* (*Mengzi* 孟子), trans. D. C. Lau (London: Penguin Books, 1970), 7B: 16.
72. Tang Junyi [Tang Chun-I] (唐君毅), *Zhongguo renwen jingshen zhi fazhan* 中國人文精神之發展 (The Development of the Chinese Humanistic Spirit), in *Tang Junyi quanji* 唐君毅全集 (Complete Works of Tang Junyi), vol. 6 (Taipei: Xuesheng shuju, 1991), 10. For a detailed analysis of Tang's idea of freedom, see He, *Ruxue yu xiandai minzhu*, chapter 5.
73. *Analects* 12: 1. Tang Junyi, *Renwen jingshen zhi chongjian* 人文精神之重建 (The Reconstruction of the Humanistic Spirit), in *Tang Junyi quanji* 唐君毅全集 (Complete Works of Tang Junyi), vol. 5 (Taipei: Xuesheng shuju, 1991), 346.
74. As Thomas Fröhlich puts it, "Although the modern Chinese term for freedom (*ziyou* 自由), was unknown to pre-modern Confucianism, Tang listed expressions like 'pursuing the perfection of one's personality' (*qui renge de wanman* 求人格的完滿), 'self-fulfillment' (*zi cheng* 自成), or 'self-pursuit' (*zi qiu* 自求) as identical in meaning." Thomas Fröhlich, *Tang Junyi: Confucian Philosophy and the Challenge of Modernity* (Leiden and Boston: Brill, 2017), 190.
75. Tang, *Renwen jingshen zhi chongjian*, esp. 232–41.

76. Ibid., 357–62.
77. Ibid., 354–57.
78. SM: 102.
79. ZYZ: 120 [CW X: 132].
80. Xu, *Xinban xueshu yu zhengzhi zhijian*, 37.
81. Zhang Junmai [Carsun Chang] (張君勱), *Liguo zhi dao* 立國之道 (The Way of the Country) (Taipei: Commercial Press, 1971), 145.
82. SYGX: 264 [CW XXIV: 264].
83. As Green puts it: Hegel "thinks of the 'state' in a way not familiar to Englishmen, a way not unlike that in which Greek philosophers thought of the *polis*, as a society governed by laws and institutions and established customs which secure the common good of the members of the society—enable them to make the best of themselves—and are recognized as doing so. Such a state is 'objective freedom'—freedom is realized in it—because in it the reason, the self-determining principle operating in man as his will, was found a perfect expression for itself as an artist may be considered to express himself in a perfect work of art." Green, "Freedom," 231. Cf. Hegel, *Elements of the Philosophy of Right*, 275–82, §257–§59.
84. SYGX: 270 [CW XXIV: 270].
85. SYGX: 52, 79 [CW XXIV: 52, 79].
86. SYGX: 52 [CW XXIV: 52].
87. SYGX: 35–36 [CW XXIV: 35–36].
88. SYGX: 59 [CW XXIV: 59].
89. Roger Scruton, "Liberalism Versus Conservatism," in Roger Scruton, *The Meaning of Conservatism*, second edition (London: Macmillan, 1990), 192–203.
90. Hans Reiss, "Introduction," in Immanuel Kant, *Kant: Political Writings*, ed. Hans Reiss, trans. H. B. Nisbet (Cambridge: Cambridge University Press, 1991), 21.
91. Immanuel Kant, *Kant: Political Writings*, ed. Hans Reiss, trans. H. B. Nisbet (Cambridge: Cambridge University Press, 1991), 133.
92. Roger Scruton, *The Meaning of Conservatism*, second edition (London: Macmillan, 1990), 197.
93. Taylor, *Philosophy and the Human Sciences*, 188.
94. For an insightful introduction to this topic, see Li Minghui, *Dangdai Ruxue zhi ziwo zhuanhua* 當代儒學之自我轉化 (The Self-Transformation of Contemporary Confucianism) (Taipei: Academia Sinica, Institute of Chinese Literature and Philosophy, 1994), 53–87. As a follower of Mou, in some critical senses Li has delved deeper into the similarities and dissimilarities between Confucianism and Kant. See, for example, Li Minghui, *Rujia yu Kangde* 儒家與康德 (Confucianism and Kant) (Taipei: Linking Publishing Co., 1990); *Kangde lunlixue yu Mengzi daode sikao zhi zhongjian* 康德倫理學與孟子道德思考之重建 (Kantian Ethics and the Reconstruction of Mencius's Moral Thinking) (Taipei: Academia Sinica,

Institute of Chinese Literature and Philosophy, 1994); and *Mengzi chongtan* 孟子重探 (Mencius Revisited) (Taipei: Linking Publishing Co., 2001).

95. Onora O'Neill, "Kantian Ethics," in *A Companion to Ethics*, ed. Peter Singer (Oxford: Blackwell, 1993), 184.

96. Kant, *Kant: Political Writings*, 54–55.

97. Taylor, *Philosophy and the Human Sciences*, 241. As Kant puts it: "Everything in nature works according to laws. Only a rational being has the power to act according to his conception of laws, i.e., according to principles, and thereby has he a will." Immanuel Kant, *Grounding for the Metaphysics of Morals*, trans. James W. Ellington (Indianapolis: Hackett Publishing Company, 1993), 23.

98. Jiang Nianfeng [Chiang Nien-Feng] (蔣年豐), "Fazheng zhuti yu xiandai shehui: dangqian Rujia yinggai sikao de wenti 法政主體與現代社會：當前儒家應該思考的問題 (The Legal-Political Subject and Modern Society: The Issue that Confucianism Should Take into Account at Present)," *Zhongguo wenhua yuekan* 中國文化月刊 (Chinese Cultural Monthly) 111 (1989): 283.

99. Ibid.

100. Li Minghui, *Ruxue yu xiandai yishi* 儒學與現代意識 (Confucianism and Modern Consciousness) (Taipei: Wenchin chubanshe, 1991), 20, 140–42.

101. Li, *Rujia shiye xia de zhengzhi sixiang*, 60–61, 124.

102. David L. Hall and Roger T. Ames, *The Democracy of the Dead: Dewey, Confucius, and the Hope for Democracy in China* (Chicago and Lasalle: Open Court, 1999), 109.

103. Ibid., 234.

104. At this point, it is interesting to note that Li Minghui [Lee Ming-Huei] (李明輝) actually grants that while Kant's ethics offers a groundbreaking justification of moral autonomy, post-Kantian philosophers, including Schiller, Fichte, and Hegel, all take autonomy seriously, in spite of picking holes in Kant's specific frame of moral subjectivity. Li, *Rujia yu Kangde*, 35, 48–49.

105. David Boucher, "The Recognition Theory of Rights, Customary International Law and Human Rights," *Political Studies* 59(3) (2011): 756.

106. Derrick Darby, *Rights, Race, and Recognition* (Cambridge: Cambridge University Press, 2009), 16.

107. Boucher, "The Recognition Theory of Rights," 756.

108. Green, *Lectures*, 25, §25.

109. Ronald Dworkin, "Liberalism," in *Public and Private Morality*, ed. Stuart Hampshire (Cambridge: Cambridge University Press, 1978), 136.

110. Boucher, "The Recognition Theory of Rights," 756.

111. Green, *Lectures*, 23, §20.

112. Ibid., 28, §30. To quote Green: "Morality and political subjection thus have a common source—political subjection being distinguished from that of a slave, as a subjection which secures rights to the subject. That common source is the rational recognition by certain human beings—it may be merely by

children of the same parent—of a common well-being which *is* their well-being, and which they conceive as their well-being whether at any moment any one of them is inclined to it or no, and the embodiment of that recognition in rules by which the inclinations of the individuals are restrained, and a corresponding freedom of action for the attainment of well-being on the whole is secured." Ibid., 92, §117.

113. Ibid., 108, §139.

114. For a further account of recognition and rights in Green's thought, see Ann R. Cacoullos, *Thomas Hill Green: Philosopher of Rights* (New York: Twayne, 1974), 88–104; Gerald F. Gaus, "The Rights Recognition Thesis: Defending and Extending Green," in *T. H. Green: Ethics, Metaphysics, and Political Philosophy*, ed. Maria Dimova-Cookson and W. J. Mander (Oxford: Oxford University Press, 2006), 209–35; L. T. Hobhouse, *The Metaphysical Theory of the State* (London: George Allen and Unwin, 1918), 120; Rex Martin, "Natural Rights: Human Rights and the Role of Social Recognition," *Collingwood and British Idealism Studies* 17(1) (2011): 91–115; Darin R. Nesbitt, "Recognizing Rights: Social Recognition in T. H. Green's System of Rights," *Polity* 33(3) (2001): 423–37; W. D. Ross, *The Right and the Good*, ed. Philip Stratton-Lake (Oxford: Clarendon Press, 2002), 50–51; and Matt Hann, *Egalitarian Rights Recognition: A Political Theory of Human Rights* (Basingstoke: Palgrave Macmillan, 2016), chapter. 2.

115. Hall and Ames, *The Democracy of the Dead*, 109.

116. Ibid., 238.

117. Brian Barry, *Culture and Equality: An Equalitarian Critique of Multiculturalism* (Cambridge: Harvard University Press, 2001), 282.

Notes to Conclusion

1. Considering the purposes of this book, it is instructive to note that in his recent English work, Li Minghui [Lee Ming-Huei] (李明輝), one of most prominent Kant authorities and Mou-inspired Confucian thinkers in East Asia, writes: "The learning of inner sagehood in traditional Confucianism essentially belongs to the realm of *Moralität* [in the Kantian sense]. As for *Sittlichkeit* in the Hegelian sense, it is not limited to the realm of politics, but covers the household, civil society, the state, and even world history. In this sense, the areas touched on by Confucianism's outer kingliness are principally the same as those found in *Sittlichkeit*. For Hegel, *Moralität* cannot stop at the self, but must necessarily extend to *Sittlichkeit*. In response to Kant's more abstract moral philosophy, Hegel wishes to synthesize the best of *Moralität* and *Sittlichkeit*, that is, to embed *Moralität* into the concrete forms of what Confucians refer to as *li*—the rites, customs, and ritual proprieties of cultural traditions that manifest in the feelings, moods, emotions, behaviors, and mental states of individual

human beings. In other words, this way of thinking resonates with Confucianism's extension of inner sagehood to outer kingliness." Li Minghui, *Confucianism: Its Roots and Global Significance*, ed. David Jones (Honolulu: University of Hawai'i Press, 2017), 7; see also 93.

2. Feng Youlan [Fung Yu-Lan] (馮友蘭), *Xin lixue* 新理學 (The New Philosophy of Principle) (Chongqing: Commercial Press, 1942), 1.

3. Quoted in Li, *Confucianism*, 1–2.

4. This is a famous statement articulated by Zhang Zai [Chang Tsai] (張載 1020–1077). Quoted in Xu Fuguan [Hsu Fu-Kuan] (徐復觀), *Rujia zhengzhi sixiang yu minzhu ziyou renquan* 儒家政治思想與民主自由人權 (Confucian Political Thought and Democracy, Liberty, and Human Rights), ed. Xiao Xinyi (蕭欣義) (Taipei: Bashi niandai chuban, 1979), 183.

Bibliography

Angle, Stephen C. 2009. *Sagehood: The Contemporary Significance of Neo-Confucian Philosophy*. Oxford: Oxford University Press.
———. 2012a. *Contemporary Confucian Political Philosophy*. Cambridge: Polity.
———. 2012b. "Neither Morality nor Law: Ritual Propriety as Confucian Civility." In *Civility in Politics and Education*, edited by Deborah S. Mower and Wade L. Robison, 132–53. New York and London: Routledge.
Angle, Stephen C., and Justin Tiwald. 2017. *Neo-Confucianism: A Philosophical Introduction*. Cambridge: Polity.
Avineri, Shlomo. 1972. *Hegel's Theory of the Modern State*. Cambridge: Cambridge University Press.
Bai Tongdong 白彤東. 2009. *Jiubang xinming: gujin zhongxi canzhao xia de gudian Rujia zhengzhi zhexue* 舊邦新命: 古今中西參照下的古典儒家政治哲學 (New Mission of an Old State: Classical Confucian Political Philosophy in a Contemporary and Comparative Relevance Context). Beijing: Peking University Press.
———. 2012. *China: The Political Philosophy of the Middle Kingdom*. New York: Zed Books.
———. 2013. "A Confucian Version of Hybrid Regime: How Does It Work, and Why Is It Superior?" In *The East Asian Challenge for Democracy: Political Meritocracy in Comparative Perspective*, edited by Daniel A. Bell and Li Chenyang 李晨陽, 55–87. Cambridge: Cambridge University Press.
Barker, Ernest. 1948. *Traditions of Civility*. Cambridge: Cambridge University Press.
Barry, Brian. 2001. *Culture and Equality: An Equalitarian Critique of Multiculturalism*. Cambridge: Harvard University Press.
Bauer, Joanne R., and Daniel A. Bell, eds. 1999. *The East Asian Challenge for Human Rights*. Cambridge: Cambridge University Press.
Bell, Daniel A. 1993. *Communitarianism and Its Critics*. Oxford: Clarendon Press.
———. 2000. *East Meets West: Human Rights and Democracy in East Asia*. Princeton: Princeton University Press.

———. 2006. *Beyond Liberal Democracy: Political Thinking for an East Asian Context*. Princeton: Princeton University Press.

———. 2008. *China's New Confucianism: Politics and Everyday Life in a Changing Society*. Princeton: Princeton University Press.

———. 2015. *The China Model: Political Meritocracy and the Limits of Democracy*. Princeton: Princeton University Press.

Bell, Daniel A., and Avner de-Shalit. 2011. *The Spirit of Cities: Why the Identity of a City Matters in a Global Age*. Princeton: Princeton University Press.

Bell, Daniel A., and Li Chenyang 李晨陽, eds. 2013. *The East Asian Challenge for Democracy: Political Meritocracy in Comparative Perspective*. Cambridge: Cambridge University Press.

Berlin, Isaiah. 1969. *Four Essays on Liberty*. Oxford: Oxford University Press.

Billioud, Sébastien. 2012. *Thinking through Confucian Modernity: A Study of Mou Zongsan's Moral Metaphysics*. Leiden and Boston: Brill.

Bosanquet, Bernard. 1897. *Psychology of the Moral Self*. London: Macmillan.

———. 1899. *The Philosophical Theory of the State*. London: Macmillan.

Boucher, David. 1989. *The Social and Political Thought of R. G. Collingwood*. Cambridge: Cambridge University Press.

———. 1997. "Introduction." In *The British Idealists*, edited by David Boucher, viii–xxxiii. Cambridge: Cambridge University Press.

———. 2001. "The Recognition Theory of Rights, Customary International Law and Human Rights." *Political Studies* 59(3): 753–71.

Boucher, David, and Andrew Vincent. 2000. *British Idealism and Political Theory*. Edinburgh: Edinburgh University Press.

———. 2012. *British Idealism: A Guide for the Perplexed*. London: Continuum.

Bradley, A. C. 1940. *Ideals of Religion, Gifford Lectures Delivered in the University of Glasgow in 1907*. London: Macmillan.

Bradley, F. H. 1922. *The Principles of Logic*. Oxford: Clarendon Press.

———. 1969. *Appearance and Reality: A Metaphysical Essay*. Oxford: Clarendon Press.

———. 1988. *Ethical Studies*. Oxford: Clarendon Press.

Brink, David O. 2003a. "Introduction." In T. H. Green, *Prolegomena to Ethics*, edited by David O. Brink, xiii–cx. Oxford: Clarendon Press.

———. 2003b. *Perfectionism and the Common Good: Themes in the Philosophy of T. H. Green*. Oxford: Oxford University Press.

Brooks, Thom, ed. 2014. *Ethical Citizenship: British Idealism and the Politics of Recognition*. Basingstoke: Palgrave Macmillan.

Bunnin, Nicholas. 2013. "God's Knowledge and Ours: Kant and Mou Zongsan on Intellectual Intuition." *Journal of Chinese Philosophy* 40(s1): 47–58.

Cacoullos, Ann R. 1974. *Thomas Hill Green: Philosopher of Rights*. New York: Twayne.

Calhoun, Cheshire. 2000. "The Virtue of Civility." *Philosophy and Public Affairs* 29(3): 251–75.

Carter, Stephen L. 1998. *Civility: Manners, Morals, and the Etiquette of Democracy*. New York: Basic Books.
Chan, Joseph 陳祖為. 2000. "Legitimacy, Unanimity, and Perfectionism." *Philosophy and Public Affairs* 29(1): 5–42.
———. 2013. "Political Meritocracy and Meritorious Rule: A Confucian Perspective." In *The East Asian Challenge for Democracy: Political Meritocracy in Comparative Perspective*, edited by Daniel A. Bell and Li Chenyang 李晨陽, 31–54. Cambridge: Cambridge University Press.
———. 2014. *Confucian Perfectionism: A Political Philosophy for Modern Times*. Princeton: Princeton University Press.
Chan, N. Serina. 2011. *The Thought of Mou Zongsan*. Leiden and Boston: Brill.
Chan Wing-Cheuk 陳榮灼. 2006. "Mou Zongsan's Transformation of Kant's Philosophy." *Journal of Chinese Philosophy* 33(1): 125–39.
———. 2011. "Mou Zongsan on Confucian and Kant's Ethics: A Critical Reflection." *Journal of Chinese Philosophy* 38(s1): 146–64.
Chan Wing-Tsit 陳榮捷, 1975. "Chinese and Western Interpretations of Jen (Humanity)." *Journal of Chinese Philosophy* 2(2): 107–29.
———, trans. 1963. *A Source Book in Chinese Philosophy*. Princeton: Princeton University Press.
Chen Lai 陳來. 2009. *Tradition and Modernity: A Humanist View*, translated by Edmund Ryden. Leiden and Boston: Brill.
———. 2014. *Renxue bentilun* 仁學本體論 (The Ontology of the Learning of Ren). Beijing: Sanlian shudian.
Chen Ming 陳明. 2009. *Wenhua Ruxue: sibian yu lunbian* 文化儒學: 思辨與論辯 (Cultural Confucianism: Thoughts and Debates). Chengdu: Sichuan People's Publishing House.
———. 2013. *Rujiao yu gongming shehui* 儒教與公民社會 (Confucianism and Civil Society). Beijing: Dongfang chubanshe.
Cheng Zhongying [Cheng Chung-Ying] 成中英. 1991. *New Dimensions of Confucian and Neo-Confucian Philosophy*. Albany: State University of New York Press.
Clower, Jason. 2014. "Introduction." In *Late Works of Mou Zongsan: Selected Essays on Chinese Philosophy*, edited and translated by Jason Clower, 1–27. Leiden and Boston: Brill.
Collingwood, R. G. 1992. *The New Leviathan, or, Man, Society, Civilization and Barbarism*, edited by David Boucher. Oxford: Clarendon Press.
Confucius. 1979. *The Analects* 論語, translated by D. C. Lau. London: Penguin Books.
Cortella, Lucio. 2011. *The Ethics of Democracy: A Contemporary Reading of Hegel's Philosophy of Right*, translated by Giacomo Donis. Albany: State University of New York Press.
Corwin, Edward S. 1938. *The Constitution and What It Means Today*. Princeton: Princeton University Press.
Cranston, Maurice. 1967. "Michael Oakeshott's Politics." *Encounter* 28: 82–86.

Curzer, Howard J. 2012. "An Aristotelian Account of Civility." In *Civility in Politics and Education*, edited by Deborah S. Mower and Wade L. Robison, 80–98. New York and London: Routledge.
Darby, Derrick. 2009. *Rights, Race, and Recognition*. Cambridge: Cambridge University Press.
De Bary, Wm. Theodore. 1983. *The Liberal Tradition in China*. New York: Columbia University Press.
Deng Yuren [Norman Yujen Teng] 鄧育仁. 2015. *Gongmin Ruxue* 公民儒學 (Civic Confucianism). Taipei: National Taiwan University Press.
Dimova-Cookson, Maria. 2003. "A New Scheme of Positive and Negative Freedom: Reconstructing T. H. Green on Freedom." *Political Theory* 31(4): 508–32.
Dimova-Cookson, Maria, and W. J. Mander, eds. 2006. *T. H. Green: Ethics, Metaphysics, and Political Philosophy*. Oxford: Oxford University Press.
Dunham, Jeremy, Iain Hamilton Grant, and Sean Watson. 2011. *Idealism: The History of a Philosophy*. Durham: Acumen.
Dworkin, Ronald. 1977. *Taking Rights Seriously*. Cambridge: Harvard University Press.
———. 1978. "Liberalism." In *Public and Private Morality*, edited by Stuart Hampshire, 113–43. Cambridge: Cambridge University Press.
———. 1984. "Rights as Trumps." In *Theories of Rights*, edited by Jeremy Waldron, 153–67. Oxford: Oxford University Press.
Elias, Norbert. 2000. *The Civilizing Process: Sociogenetic and Psychogenetic Investigation*. Oxford: Wiley Blackwell.
Elstein, David. 2015. *Democracy in Contemporary Confucian Philosophy*. London and New York: Routledge.
Eulau, Heinz. 1973. "Technology and the Fear of the Politics of Civility." *The Journal of Politics* 35(2): 367–85.
Fan Ruiping 范瑞平. 2010. *Reconstructing Confucianism: Rethinking Morality after the West*. Dordrecht: Springer.
———. 2013. "Confucian Meritocracy for Contemporary China." In *The East Asian Challenge for Democracy: Political Meritocracy in Comparative Perspective*, edited by Daniel A. Bell and Li Chenyang 李晨陽, 88–115. Cambridge: Cambridge University Press.
———, ed. 2011. *The Renaissance of Confucianism in Contemporary China*. Dordrecht: Springer.
Feng Youlan [Fung Yu-Lan] 馮友蘭. 1942. *Xin lixue* 新理學 (The New Philosophy of Principle). Chongqing: Commercial Press.
Ferguson, Adam. 1995. *An Essay on the History of Civil Society*, edited by Fania Oz-Salzberger. Cambridge: Cambridge University Press.
Ferree, Myra Marx, William A. Gamson, Jürgen Gerhards, and Dieter Rucht. 2002a. "Four Models of the Public Sphere in Modern Democracies." *Theory and Society* 31(3): 289–324.

———. 2002b. *Shaping Abortion Discourse: Democracy and the Public Sphere in Germany and the United States*. Cambridge: Cambridge University Press.
Forbes, Duncan. 1985. *Hume's Philosophical Politics*. Cambridge: Cambridge University Press.
Franco, Paul. 1999. *Hegel's Philosophy of Freedom*. New Haven: Yale University Press.
Freeden, Michael, and Andrew Vincent. 2013. "Introduction: The Study of Comparative Political Thought." In *Comparative Political Thought: Theorizing Practices*, edited by Michael Freeden and Andrew Vincent, 1–23. London: Routledge.
Fröhlich, Thomas. 2017. *Tang Junyi: Confucian Philosophy and the Challenge of Modernity*. Leiden and Boston: Brill.
Fuller, Timothy. 1989. "Introduction." In Michael Oakeshott, *The Voice of Liberal Learning: Michael Oakeshott on Education*, edited by Timothy Fuller, 1–16. New Haven: Yale University Press.
Gaus, Gerald F. 2006. "The Rights Recognition Thesis: Defending and Extending Green." In *T. H. Green: Ethics, Metaphysics, and Political Philosophy*, edited by Maria Dimova-Cookson and W. J. Mander, 209–35. Oxford: Oxford University Press.
Gay, Peter. 1966. *The Enlightenment: An Interpretation*, vol. 1, *The Rise of Modern Paganism*. New York: Alfred A. Knopf.
———. 1969. *The Enlightenment: An Interpretation*, vol. 2, *The Science of Freedom*. New York: Alfred A. Knopf.
Gillingham, John. 2000. *The English in the Twelfth Century: Imperialism, National Identity and Political Values*. Woodbridge: Boydell and Brewer.
———. 2001. "Civilizing the English? The English Histories of William of Malmesbury and David Hume." *Historical Research* 74(183): 17–43.
———. 2002. "From *Civilitas* to Civility: Codes of Manners in Medieval and Early Modern England." *Transactions of the Royal Historical Society* 12: 267–89.
Gray, John. 2000. *Two Faces of Liberalism*. Cambridge: Polity.
Green, T. H. 1986. *Lectures on the Principles of Political Obligation and Other Writings*, edited by Paul Harris and John Morrow. Cambridge: Cambridge University Press.
———. 1997a. *Collected Works of T. H. Green*, vol. 1, *Philosophical Works*, edited by Peter Nicholson. Bristol: Thoemmes Press.
———. 1997b. *Collected Works of T. H. Green*, vol. 2, *Philosophical Works with an Appendix*, edited by Peter Nicholson. Bristol: Thoemmes Press.
———. 1997c. *Collected Works of T. H. Green*, vol. 3, *Miscellanies and Memoir with an Appendix*, edited by Peter Nicholson. Bristol: Thoemmes Press.
———. 2003. *Prolegomena to Ethics*, edited by David O. Brink. Oxford: Clarendon Press.
Hall, David, and Roger T. Ames. 1987. *Thinking through Confucius*. Albany: State University of New York Press.

———. 1995. *Anticipating China: Thinking through the Narratives of Chinese and Western Culture*. Albany: State University of New York Press.

———. 1998. *Thinking through the Han: Self, Truth, and Transcendence in Chinese and Western Culture*. Albany: State University of New York Press.

———. 1999. *The Democracy of the Dead: Dewey, Confucius, and the Hope for Democracy in China*. Chicago and Lasalle: Open Court.

Hann, Matt. 2014. "'Who Is My Neighbour?' T. H. Green and the Possibility of Cosmopolitan Ethical Citizenship." In *Ethical Citizenship: British Idealism and the Politics of Recognition*, edited by Thom Brooks, 177–99. Basingstoke: Palgrave Macmillan.

———. 2016. *Egalitarian Rights Recognition: A Political Theory of Human Rights*. Basingstoke: Palgrave Macmillan.

He Xinquan [Ho Hsin-Chuan] 何信全. 1996. *Ruxue yu xiandai minzhu: dangdai Xinrujia zhengzhi zhexue yanjiu* 儒學與現代民主：當代新儒家政治哲學研究 (Confucianism and Modern Democracy: A Study of Contemporary New Confucian Political Philosophy). Taipei: Academia Sinica, Institute of Chinese Literature and Philosophy.

Hegel, G. W. F. 1970. *Hegel's Philosophy of Nature*, vol. 1, edited by M. J. Petry. London: George Allen and Unwin.

———. 1971. *Early Theological Writings*, translated by T. M. Knox and Richard Kroner. Philadelphia: University of Pennsylvania Press.

———. 1975. *Lectures on the Philosophy of World History: Introduction: Reason in History*, translated by H. B. Nisbet. Cambridge: Cambridge University Press.

———. 1977. *Phenomenology of Spirit*, translated by A. V. Miller. Oxford: Oxford University Press.

———. 1988. *Lectures on the Philosophy of Religion, One Volume Edition: The Lectures of 1827*, edited by Peter C. Hodgson, translated by R. F. Brown, P. C. Hodgson, and J. M. Stewart. Berkeley: University of California Press.

———. 1990. *Encyclopedia of the Philosophical Sciences in Outline and Critical Writings*, edited by Ernst Behler. New York: Continuum.

———. 1991. *Elements of the Philosophy of Right*, edited by Allen W. Wood, translated by H. B. Nisbet. Cambridge: Cambridge University Press.

———. 1995. *Lectures on the History of Philosophy*, vol. 1, *Greek Philosophy to Plato*, translated by E. S. Haldane. Lincoln: University of Nebraska Press.

Heidegger, Martin. 1990. *Kant and the Problem of Metaphysics*, fifth edition, translated by Richard Taft. Indianapolis: Indiana University Press.

Herbst, Susan. 2010. *Rude Democracy: Civility and Incivility in American Politics*. Philadelphia: Temple University Press.

Herder, J. G. 2002. *Philosophical Writings*, edited and translated by Michael N. Forster. Cambridge: Cambridge University Press.

Hobhouse, L. T. 1918. *The Metaphysical Theory of the State*. London: George Allen and Unwin.

Honneth, Axel. 1995. *The Struggle for Recognition: The Moral Grammar of Social Conflicts*, translated by Joel Anderson. Cambridge: Polity.

———. 2015. *Freedom's Right: The Social Foundations of Democratic Life*, translated by Joseph Ganahl. New York: Columbia University Press.

Houlgate, Stephen. 2005. *An Introduction to Hegel: Freedom, Truth and History*. Oxford: Blackwell.

Huang Jinxing [Huang Chin-Shing] 黃進興. 2021. *Confucianism and Sacred Space: The Confucius Temple from Imperial China to Today*. New York: Columbia University Press.

Huang Junjie [Huang Chun-Chieh] 黃俊傑. 1995. "Dangdai Rujia dui Zhongguo wenhua de jieshi ji qi ziwo dingwei—yi Xu Fuguan wei zhongxin 當代儒家對中國文化的解釋及其自我定位—以徐復觀為中心 (The Interpretation and Self-Identity of Chinese Culture in Contemporary Confucianism: Focusing on Xu Fuguan)." In *Dangdai Ruxue lunji: chuantong yu chuangxin* 當代儒學論集: 傳統與創新 (Anthology of Contemporary Confucianism: Tradition and Innovation), edited by Liu Shuxian [Liu Shu-Hsien] 劉述先, 119–204. Taipei: Academia Sinica, Institute of Chinese Literature and Philosophy.

Huang Yong 黃勇. 2017. "New Confucianism." In *A Concise Companion to Confucius*, edited by Paul R. Goldin, 352–74. Oxford: Wiley Blackwell.

Huang Zongxi [Huang Tsung-Hsi] 黃宗羲. 1993. *Waiting for the Dawn: A Plan for the Prince*, Huang Tsung-Hsi's Ming-I Tai-Fang Lu 明夷待訪錄, translated by Wm. Theodore de Bary. New York: Columbia University Press.

Hutton, Eric L., trans. 2014. *Xunzi: The Complete Text*. Princeton: Princeton University Press.

Israel, Jonathan. 2016. "J. G. A. Pocock and the 'Language of Enlightenment' in His Barbarism and Religion." *Journal of the History of Ideas* 77(1): 107–27.

Jenco, Leigh K. 2010a. "Chinese Liberalism." In *Encyclopedia of Political Theory*, edited by Mark Bevir, 164–66. London: Sage Publications.

———. 2010b. *Making the Political: Founding and Action in the Political Theory of Zhang Shizhao*. Cambridge: Cambridge University Press.

Jian Nianfeng [Chiang Nien-Feng] 蔣年豐. 1989. "Fazheng zhuti yu xiandai shehui: dangqian Rujia yinggai sikao de wenti 法政主體與現代社會: 當前儒家應該思考的問題 (The Legal-Political Subject and Modern Society: The Issue that Confucianism Should Take into Account at Present)." *Zhongguo wenhua yuekan* 中國文化月刊 (Chinese Cultural Monthly) 111: 283.

Jian Qing 蔣慶. 1995. *Gongyangxue yinlun* 公羊學引論 (Introduction to Gongyang School). Shenyang: Liaoning jiaoyu chubanshe.

———. 2003. *Zhengzhi Ruxue: dangdai Ruxue de zhuanxiang, tezhi yu fazhan* 政治儒學: 當代儒學的轉向、特質與發展 (Political Confucianism: The Changing Direction, Particularities, and Development of Contemporary Confucianism). Taipei: Yangzhengtang wenhua.

———. 2004. *Shengming xinyang yu wangdao zhengzhi: Rujia wenhua de xiandai jiazhi* 生命信仰與王道政治: 儒家文化的現代價值 (A Faith in Life and the Kingly Way of Politics: The Modern Value of Confucian Culture). Taipei: Yangzhengtang wenhua.

———. 2012. *A Confucian Constitutional Order: How China's Ancient Past Can Shape Its Political Future*, edited by Daniel A. Bell and Fan Ruiping 范瑞平, translated by Edward Ryden. Princeton: Princeton University Press.

Kang, Xiaoguang 康曉光. 2005. *Renzheng: Zhongguo zhengzhi fazhan de disantiaolu* 仁政: 中國政治發展的第三條道路 (The Politics of Benevolence: The Third Road for China's Political Development). Singapore: Global Publishing.

Kant, Immanuel.1991a. *Kant: Political Writings*, translated by H. B. Nisbet. Cambridge: Cambridge University Press.

———. 1991b. *The Metaphysics of Morals*, translated by Mary Gregor. Cambridge: Cambridge University Press.

———. 1993a. *Critique of Pure Reason*, translated by Norman Kemp Smith. London: Macmillan.

———. 1993b. *Grounding for the Metaphysics of Morals*, translated by James W. Ellington. Indianapolis: Hackett Publishing Company.

———. 1998. *Critique of Practical Reason*, translated by H. W. Cassirer. Milwaukee: Marquette University Press.

Kennedy, Randall. 1998. "The Case against 'Civility.'" *American Prospect* 41: 84–90.

Kim, Sungmoon. 2014. *Confucian Democracy in East Asia: Theory and Practice*. Cambridge: Cambridge University Press.

———. 2016. *Public Reason Confucianism: Democratic Perfectionism and Constitutionalism in East Asia*. Cambridge: Cambridge University Press.

———. 2018. *Democracy after Virtue: Toward Pragmatic Confucian Democracy*. Oxford: Oxford University Press.

———. 2020. *Theorizing Confucian Virtue Politics: The Political Philosophy of Mencius and Xunzi*. Cambridge: Cambridge University Press.

Kim, Youngmin. 2018. *A History of Chinese Political Thought*. Cambridge: Polity.

Knight, Frank H. 1982. *Freedom and Reform: Essays in Economics and Social Philosophy*. Indianapolis: Liberty Fund.

Kramer, Matthew H. 2017. *Liberalism with Excellence*. Oxford: Oxford University Press.

Ladenson, Robert F. 2012. "Civility as Democratic Civic Virtue." In *Civility in Politics and Education*, edited by Deborah S. Mower and Wade L. Robison, 207–20. New York and London: Routledge.

Laski, Harold J. 1943. *Reflections on the Revolution of Our Own Time*. New York: Viking Press.

Laverty, Megan J. 2012. "Communication and Civility." In *Civility in Politics and Education*, edited by Deborah S. Mower and Wade L. Robison, 65–79. New York and London: Routledge.

Leach, Jim. 2012. "Foreword." In *Civility in Politics and Education*, edited by Deborah S. Mower and Wade L. Robison, ix–xiv. New York and London: Routledge.
Legge, James, trans. 1963. *The I Ching* 易經. In *The Sacred Books of the East*, vol. 16, second edition. New York: Dover Publications.
———, trans. 1967. *The Book of Rites* 禮記, edited by Zhai Chu [Chai Ch'u] 翟楚 and Zhai Wenbo [Winberg Chai] 翟文伯, 2 volumes. New Hyde Park: University Books.
———, trans. 2001a. *The Doctrine of the Mean* 中庸. In *The Chinese Classics*, vol. 1. Taipei: SMC Publishing Inc.
———, trans. 2001b. *The Great Learning* 大學. In *The Chinese Classics*, vol. 1. Taipei: SMC Publishing Inc.
Levenson, Joseph R. 1958. *Confucian China and Its Modern Fate*, vol. 1, *The Problem of Intellectual Continuity*. Berkeley: University of California Press.
———. 1964. *Confucian China and Its Modern Fate*, vol. 2, *The Problem of Monarchial Decay*. Berkeley: University of California Press.
———. 1965. *Confucian China and Its Modern Fate*, vol. 3, *The Problem of Historical Significance*. Berkeley: University of California Press.
Li Chenyang 李晨陽. 1999. *The Tao Encounters the West: Explorations in Comparative Philosophy*. Albany: State University of New York Press.
———. 2012. "Equality and Inequality in Confucianism." *Dao* 11(3): 295–313.
Li Minghui [Lee Ming-Huei] 李明輝. 1990. *Rujia yu Kangde* 儒家與康德 (Confucianism and Kant). Taipei: Linking Publishing Co.
———. 1991. *Ruxue yu xiandai yishi* 儒學與現代意識 (Confucianism and Modern Consciousness). Taipei: Wenjin chubanshe.
———. 1994a. *Dangdai Ruxue zhi ziwo zhuanhua* 當代儒學之自我轉化 (The Self-Transformation of Contemporary Confucianism). Taipei: Academia Sinica, Institute of Chinese Literature and Philosophy.
———. 1994b. *Kangde lunlixue yu Mengzi daode sikao zhi zhongjian* 康德倫理學與孟子道德思考之重建 (Kantian Ethics and the Reconstruction of Mencius's Moral Thinking). Taipei: Academia Sinica, Institute of Chinese Literature and Philosophy.
———. 2001. *Mengzi chongtan* 孟子重探 (Mencius Revisited). Taipei: Linking Publishing Co.
———. 2005. *Rujia shiye xia de zhengzhi sixiang* 儒家視野下的政治思想 (Political Thought from a Confucian Perspective). Taipei: National Taiwan University Press.
———. 2017. *Confucianism: Its Roots and Global Significance*, edited by David Jones. Honolulu: University of Hawai'i Press.
———, ed. 1996. *Mou Zongsan xiansheng yu Zhongguo zhexue zhi chongjian* 牟宗三先生與中國哲學之重建 (Mou Zongsan and the Reconstruction of Chinese Philosophy). Taipei: Wenjin chubanshe.

Lin Yusheng [Lin Yu-Sheng] 林毓生. 1979. *The Crisis of Chinese Consciousness: Radical Antitraditionalism in the May Fourth Era*. Madison: University of Wisconsin Press.

Lindsay, A. D. 1943. *The Modern Democratic State*, vol. 1. Oxford: Oxford University Press.

Liu Bonan [Liu Pao-Nan] 劉寶楠. 1970. *Lunyu zhengyi* 論語正義 (Exegesis on the Analects of Confucius). Taipei: Taiwan Chunghwa Book.

Liu Shuxian [Liu Shu-Hsien] 劉述先. 2003. *Essentials of Contemporary Neo-Confucian Philosophy*. Westport: Praeger.

———. 2007. *Ruxue de fuxing* 儒學的復興 (The Confucian Renaissance). Hong Kong: Tiandi tushu.

———. 2010. *Rujia zhexue de dianfan chonggou yu quanshi* 儒家哲學的典範重構與詮釋 (Reconstructing and Interpreting the Confucian Philosophical Paradigm). Taipei: Wanjuanlou tushu.

Liu Xiao 劉曉. 2001. *Xiandai Xinrujia zhengzhi zhexue* 現代新儒家政治哲學 (The Political Philosophy of Modern New Confucianism). Beijing: Xianzhuang shuju.

MacCallum, Gerald. 1991. "Negative and Positive Freedom." In *Liberty: Oxford Readings in Politics and Government*, edited by David Miller, 100–22. Oxford: Oxford University Press.

MacIntyre, Alasdair. 1980. *After Virtue: A Study in Moral Theory*, second edition. London: Duckworth.

Mackenzie, John S. 1901. *A Manual of Ethics*, fourth edition. London: W. B. Clive.

Makeham, John. 2003. "The Retrospective Creation of New Confucianism." In *New Confucianism: A Critical Examination*, edited by John Makeham, 25–53. Basingstoke: Palgrave Macmillan.

———. 2008. *Lost Soul: "Confucianism" in Contemporary Chinese Academic Discourse*. Cambridge: Harvard University Asia Center.

———, ed. 2003. *New Confucianism: A Critical Examination*. Basingstoke: Palgrave Macmillan.

Mander, W. J. 2011. *British Idealism: A History*. Oxford: Oxford University Press.

Marshall, T. H. 1992. "Citizenship and Social Class." In *Citizenship and Social Class*, edited by T. H. Marshall and Tom Bottomore, 1–52. London: Pluto Press.

Martin, Rex. 2011."Natural Rights: Human Rights and the Role of Social Recognition." *Collingwood and British Idealism Studies* 17(1): 91–115.

———. 2014. "The Metaphysics and Ethics of T. H. Green's Idea of Persons and Citizens." In *Ethical Citizenship: British Idealism and the Politics of Recognition*, edited by Thom Brooks, 13–34. Basingstoke: Palgrave Macmillan.

Mencius. 1970. *The Mencius* 孟子, translated by D. C. Lau. London: Penguin Books.

Metzger, Thomas A. 2005. *A Cloud across the Pacific: Essays on the Clash between Chinese and Western Political Theories Today*. Hong Kong: Chinese University Press.

Meyer, Michael J. 2000. "Liberal Civility and the Civility of Etiquette: Public Ideals and Personal Lives." *Social Theory and Practice* 26(1): 69–84.
Miller, David. 1999. "Bounded Citizenship." In *Cosmopolitan Citizenship*, edited by Kimberly Hutchings and Roland Dannreuther, 60–82. New York: St. Martin's Press.
Momigliano, Arnaldo D. 1966. *Studies in Historiography*. London: Weidenfeld and Nicolson.
Mou Zongsan [Mou Tsung-San] 牟宗三. 1959. *Daode de lixiangzhuyi* 道德的理想主義 (Moral Idealism). Taipei: Xuesheng shuju.
———. 1961. *Zhengdao yu zhidao* 政道與治道 (The Way of Politics and the Way of Governance). Taipei: Xuesheng shuju.
———. 1963. *Zhongguo zhexue de tezhi* 中國哲學的特質 (The Features of Chinese Philosophy). Taipei: Xuesheng shuju.
———. 1968a. *Xinti yu xingti* 心體與性體 (Mind-Reality and Xing-Reality), vol. 1. Taipei: Zhengzhong shuju.
———. 1968b. *Xinti yu xingti* 心體與性體 (Mind-Reality and Xing-Reality), vol. 2. Taipei: Zhengzhong shuju.
———. 1969 *Xinti yu xingti* 心體與性體 (Mind-Reality and Xing-Reality), vol. 3. Taipei: Zhengzhong shuju.
———. 1970. *Shengming de xuewen* 生命的學問 (The Learning of Life). Taipei: Sanmin shuju.
———. 1971. *Zhi de zhijue yu Zhongguo zhexue* 智的直覺與中國哲學 (Intellectual Intuition and Chinese Philosophy). Taipei: Commercial Press.
———. 1975. *Xianxiang yu wuzishen* 現象與物自身 (Phenomena and Noumena). Taipei: Xuesheng shuju.
———. 1979. *Mingjia yu Xunzi* 名家與荀子 (School of Names and Xunzi). Taipei: Xuesheng shuju.
———. 1982. *Kangde de daode zhexue* 康德的道德哲學 (Kant's Moral Philosophy). Taipei: Xuesheng shuju.
———. 1983. *Zhongguo zhexue shijiu jiang* 中國哲學十九講 (Nineteen Lectures on Chinese Philosophy). Taipei: Xuesheng shuju.
———. 1985. *Yuanshan lun* 圓善論 (On the Summum Bonum). Taipei: Xuesheng shuju.
———. 1988. *Lishi zhexue* 歷史哲學 (Philosophy of History). Taipei: Xuesheng shuju.
———. 1989. *Wushi zishu* 五十自述 (Autobiography at the Age of Fifty). Taipei: Ehu chubanshe.
———. 1990a. *Renshixin zhi pipan* 認識心之批判 (Critique of the Cognitive Mind), 2 volumes. Taipei: Xuesheng shuju.
———. 1990b. *Zhongxi zhexue zhi huitong shisi jiang* 中西哲學之會通十四講 (Fourteen Lectures on the Merging of Chinese and Western Philosophy). Taipei: Xuesheng shuju.
———. 1995. *Shidai yu ganshou* 時代與感受 (Impression of the Times). Taipei: Ehu chubanshe.

———. 1996. *Renwen jiangxi lu* 人文講習錄 (Lectures on Humanity). Taipei: Xuesheng shuju.

———. 2003a. *Mou Zongsan xiansheng quanji* 牟宗三先生全集 (Complete Works of Mou Zongsan), 33 volumes. Taipei: Linking Publishing Co.

———. 2003b. *Shidai yu ganshou xupian* 時代與感受續篇 (The Sequel to Impression of the Times), collected in *Mou Zongsan xiansheng quanji* 牟宗三先生全集 (Complete Works of Mou Zongsan), vol. 24. Taipei: Linking Publishing Co.

———. 2003c. *Zaoqi wenji* 早期文集 (Early Writings), collected in *Mou Zongsan xiansheng quanji* 牟宗三先生全集 (Complete Works of Mou Zongsan), vols. 25–26. Taipei: Linking Publishing Co.

———. 2014. *Late Works of Mou Zongsan: Selected Essays on Chinese Philosophy*, edited and translated by Jason Clower. Leiden and Boston: Brill.

———. 2015. *Nineteen Lectures on Chinese Philosophy: A Brief Outline of Chinese Philosophy and the Issues It Entails*, translated by Esther C. Su. San Jose: The Foundation for the Study of Chinese Philosophy and Culture.

Mower, Deborah S., and Wade L. Robison, eds. 2012. *Civility in Politics and Education*. New York and London: Routledge.

Murphy, Jeffrie G. 1994. *Kant: The Philosophy of Right*, second edition. Macon: Mercer University Press.

Murray, John C. 1950. "The Natural Law." In *Great Expressions of Human Rights*, edited by R. M. MacIver, 69–104. New York: The Institute for Religious and Social Studies.

Muthu, Sankar. 2003. *Enlightenment against Empire*. Princeton: Princeton University Press.

Nesbitt, Darin R. 2001. "Recognizing Rights: Social Recognition in T. H. Green's System of Rights." *Polity* 33(3): 423–37.

Ng Yu-Kwan 吳汝鈞. 2003. "Xiong Shili's Metaphysical Theory about the Non-Separability of Substance and Function." In *New Confucianism: A Critical Examination*, edited by John Makeham, 219–51. Basingstoke: Palgrave Macmillan.

Nicholson, Peter P. 1990. *The Political Philosophy of the British Idealists*. Cambridge: Cambridge University Press.

Nicolson, Harold. 1955. *Good Behaviour: Being a Study of Certain Types of Civility*. London: Constable.

Oakeshott, Michael. 1975. *On Human Conduct*. Oxford: Clarendon Press.

———. 1989. *The Voice of Liberal Learning: Michael Oakeshott on Education*, edited by Timothy Fuller. New Haven: Yale University Press.

———. 1990. *Experience and Its Modes*. Cambridge: Cambridge University Press.

———. 1991. *Rationalism in Politics and Other Essays*, new and expanded edition. Indianapolis: Liberty Fund.

———. 1993. *Morality and Politics in Modern Europe: The Harvard Lectures*, edited by Shirley Robin Letwin. New Haven: Yale University Press.

———. 1996. *The Politics of Faith and the Politics of Scepticism*, edited by Timothy Fuller. New Haven: Yale University Press.

———. 2004. *What Is History? and Other Essays*, edited by Luke O'Sullivan. Exeter: Imprint Academic.

———. 2006. *Lectures in the History of Political Thought*, edited by Terry Nardin and Luke O'Sullivan. Exeter: Imprint Academic.

———. 2008. *The Vocabulary of a Modern European State*, edited by Luke O'Sullivan. Exeter: Imprint Academic.

O'Neill, Onora. 1993. "Kantian Ethics." In *A Companion to Ethics*, edited by Peter Singer, 175–85. Oxford: Blackwell.

O'Sullivan, Noel. 1993. "In the Perspective of Western Thought." In *The Achievement of Michael Oakeshott*, edited by Jesse Norman, 101–6. London: Duckworth.

Pearce, Trevor. 2014. "The Dialectical Biologist, circa 1890: John Dewey and the Oxford Hegelians." *Journal of the History of Philosophy* 52(4): 747–77.

Pelczyński, Z. A. 1971. "The Hegelian Conception of the State." In *Hegel's Political Philosophy: Problems and Perspectives*, edited by Z. A. Pelczyński, 1–29. Cambridge: Cambridge University Press.

Pelikan, Jaroslav. 1984. *The Vindication of Tradition*. New Haven: Yale University Press.

Peng Guoxiang 彭國翔. 2016. *Zhizhe de xianshi guanhuai: Mou Zongsan de zhengzhi shehui sixiang* 智者的現世關懷: 牟宗三的政治社會思想 (The Practical Concern of a Wiseman: The Political and Social Thought of Mou Zongsan). Taipei: Linking Publishing Co.

Pettit, Philip. 1997a. *Republicanism: A Theory of Freedom and Government*. Oxford: Clarendon Press.

———. 1997b. "Republican Political Theory." In *Political Theory: Tradition and Diversity*, edited by Andrew Vincent, 112–31. Cambridge: Cambridge University Press.

Pitts, Jennifer. 2005. *A Turn to Empire: The Rise of Imperial Liberalism in Britain and France*. Princeton: Princeton University Press.

Plant, Raymond. 1997. *Hegel on Religion and Philosophy*. London: Phoenix.

Pocock, J. G. A. 1989. "Conservative Enlightenment and Democratic Revolutions: The American and French Cases in British Perspective." *Government and Opposition* 24(1): 81–105.

———. 1995. *Virtue, Commerce, and History*. Cambridge: Cambridge University Press.

———. 1999. *Barbarism and Religion*, vol. 2, *Narratives of Civil Government*. Cambridge: Cambridge University Press.

Popper, Karl. 1962. *The Open Society and Its Enemies*, vol. 2, *The High Tide of Prophecy: Hegel, Marx, and the Aftermath*. London: Routledge and Kegan Paul.

Quong, Jonathan. 2011. *Liberalism without Perfection*. Oxford: Oxford University Press.
Rasmussen, Douglas B., and Douglas J. Den Uyl. 2005. *Norms of Liberty: A Perfectionist Basis for Non-Perfectionist Politics*. University Park: Pennsylvania State University Press.
Rawls, John. 1993. *Political Liberalism: John Dewey Essays in Philosophy*. New York: Columbia University Press.
———. 2000. *Lectures on the History of Moral Philosophy*, edited by Barbara Herman. Cambridge: Harvard University Press.
Reardon, Bernard M. G. 1986. "T. H. Green as a Theologian." In *The Philosophy of T. H. Green*, edited by Andrew Vincent, 36–47. Aldershot: Gower Publishing Co. Ltd.
Reiss, Hans. 1991. "Introduction." In Immanuel Kant, *Kant: Political Writings*, translated by H. B. Nisbet, 1–40. Cambridge: Cambridge University Press.
Ritchie, David G. 1905. *Philosophical Studies*, edited by Robert Latta. London: Macmillan.
Rockmore, Tom. 1993. *Before and after Hegel: A Historical Introduction to Hegel's Thought*. Berkeley: University of California Press.
Rorty, Richard. 1991. *Objectivity, Relativism, and Truth*. Cambridge: Cambridge University Press.
Ryan, Alan. 2012. *The Making of Modern Liberalism*. Princeton: Princeton University Press.
Sandel, Michael J. 1998. *Liberalism and the Limits of Justice*, second edition. Cambridge: Cambridge University Press.
Schmidt, Stephan. 2011. "Mou Zongsan, Hegel, and Kant: The Quest for Confucian Modernity." *Philosophy East and West* 61(2): 279–86.
Schudson, Michael. 1997. "Why Conversation Is Not the Soul of Democracy." *Critical Studies in Media Communication* 14(4): 297–309.
Schwartz, Benjamin I. 1964. *In Search of Wealth and Power: Yen Fu and the West*. Cambridge: Harvard University Press.
———. 1985. *The World of Thought in Ancient China*. Cambridge: Belknap Press of Harvard University Press.
Scruton, Roger. 1990a. "Liberalism versus Conservatism." In Roger Scruton, *The Meaning of Conservatism*, second edition, 192–203. London: Macmillan.
———. 1990b. *The Meaning of Conservatism*, second edition. London: Macmillan.
Shi Yuankang [Shi Yuan-Kang] 石元康. 1998. *Cong Zhongguo wenhua dao xiandaixing: dianfan zhuanyi?* 從中國文化到現代性: 典範轉移? (From Chinese Culture to Modernity: A Paradigm Shift?) Taipei: Sanmin shuju.
Shils, Edward. 1980. *The Calling of Sociology and Other Essays on the Pursuit of Learning*. Chicago: University of Chicago Press.
———. 1997. *The Virtue of Civility: Selected Essays on Liberalism, Tradition, and Civil Society*, edited by Steven Grosby. Indianapolis: Liberty Fund.

Shklar, Judith N. 1976. *Freedom and Independence: A Study of the Political Ideas of Hegel's "Phenomenology of Mind."* Cambridge: Cambridge University Press.

Simhony, Avital. 1993. "Beyond Negative and Positive Freedom: T. H. Green's View of Freedom." *Political Theory* 21(1): 28–54.

———. 2009. "A Liberal Commitment to the Common Good: T. H. Green's Social and Political Morality." In *The Moral, Social and Political Philosophy of the British Idealists*, edited by William Sweet, 31–64. Exeter: Imprint Academia.

———. 2014. "Beyond Dualistic Constructions of Citizenship: T. H. Green's Idea of Ethical Citizenship as Mutual Membership." In *Ethical Citizenship: British Idealism and the Politics of Recognition*, edited by Thom Brooks, 35–56. Basingstoke: Palgrave Macmillan.

Simhony, Avital, and David Weinstein, eds. 2001. *The New Liberalism: Reconciling Liberty and Community*. Cambridge: Cambridge University Press.

Singer, Peter. 1983. *Hegel*. Oxford: Oxford University Press.

Sinopoli, Richard C. 1993. "Liberalism and Contested Conceptions of the Good: The Limits of Neutrality." *The Journal of Politics* 55(3): 644–63.

———. 1995. "Thick-Skinned Liberalism: Redefining Civility." *The American Political Science Review* 89(3): 612–20.

Skinner, Quentin. 1991. "The Paradoxes of Political Liberty." In *Liberty: Oxford Readings in Politics and Government*, edited by David Miller, 183–205. Oxford: Oxford University Press.

Spragens, Thomas A. 1986. "Reconstructing Liberal Theory: Reason and Liberal Culture." In *Liberals on Liberalism*, edited by Alfonso J. Damico, 34–53. Totowa: Rowan and Littlefield.

Su, Esther C. 2015. "Mou Zongsan's Critical Philosophy." In Mou Zongsan, *Nineteen Lectures on Chinese Philosophy: A Brief Outline of Chinese Philosophy and the Issues It Entails*, translated by Esther C. Su, xvii–xliv. San Jose: The Foundation for the Study of Chinese Philosophy and Culture.

Sweet, William, ed. 2009. *The Moral, Social and Political Philosophy of the British Idealists*. Exeter: Imprint Academia.

Tan Sor-Hoon 陳素芬. 2004. *Confucian Democracy: A Deweyan Reconstruction*. Albany: State University of New York Press.

Tang Junyi [Tang Chun-I] 唐君毅. 1991a. *Renwen jingshen zhi chongjian* 人文精神之重建 (The Reconstruction of the Humanistic Spirit), collected in *Tang Junyi quanji* 唐君毅全集 (Complete Works of Tang Junyi), vol. 5. Taipei: Xuesheng shuju.

———. 1991b. *Shengming cunzai yu xinling jingjie* 生命存在與心靈境界 (The Existence of Life and Horizons of the Soul), collected in *Tang Junyi quanji* 唐君毅全集 (Complete Works of Tang Junyi), vols. 23–24. Taipei: Xuesheng shuju.

———. 1991c. *Wenhua yishi yu daode lixing* 文化意識與道德理性 (Cultural Consciousness and Moral Reason), collected in *Tang Junyi quanji* 唐君毅全集 (Complete Works of Tang Junyi), vol. 20. Taipei: Xuesheng shuju.

———. 1991d. *Yingwen lunzhu huibian* 英文論著彙編 (Essays on Chinese Philosophy and Culture), collected in *Tang Junyi quanji* 唐君毅全集 (Complete Works of Tang Junyi), vol. 19. Taipei: Xuesheng shuju.

———.1991e. *Zhexue gailun* 哲學概論 (An Outline of Philosophy), vol. 2, collected in *Tang Junyi quanji* 唐君毅全集 (Complete Works of Tang Junyi), vol. 22. Taipei: Xuesheng shuju.

———. 1991f. *Zhongguo renwen jingshen zhi fazhan* 中國人文精神之發展 (The Development of the Chinese Humanistic Spirit), collected in *Tang Junyi quanji* 唐君毅全集 (Complete Works of Tang Junyi), vol. 6. Taipei: Xuesheng shuju.

———. 1991g. *Zhongguo wenhua zhi jingshen jiazhi* 中國文化之精神價值 (The Spiritual Values of the Chinese Culture), collected in *Tang Junyi quanji* 唐君毅全集 (Complete Works of Tang Junyi), vol. 4. Taipei: Xuesheng shuju.

———. 1991h. *Zhongguo zhexue yuanlun: yuan dao pian* 中國哲學原論原道篇 (On The Sources of Chinese Philosophy: The Sources of Dao), vol. 3, collected in *Tang Junyi quanji* 唐君毅全集 (Complete Works of Tang Junyi), vol. 16. Taipei: Xuesheng shuju.

Tang Refeng 唐熱風. 2002. "Mou Zongsan on Intellectual Intuition." In *Contemporary Chinese Philosophy*, edited by Cheng Zhongying [Cheng Chung-Ying] 成中英 and Nicholas Bunnin, 327–46. Oxford: Blackwell.

Tang Zhonggang 湯忠鋼. 2008. *Dexing yu zhengzhi: Mou Zongsan's Xinrujia zhengzhi zhexue yanjiu* 德性與政治: 牟宗三新儒家政治哲學研究 (Virtue and Politics: Research on Mou Zongsan's New Confucian Political Philosophy). Beijing: Zhongguo yanshi chubanshe.

Taylor, Charles. 1975. *Hegel*. Cambridge: Cambridge University Press.

———. 1979a. *Hegel and Modern Society*. Cambridge: Cambridge University Press.

———. 1979b. "What's Wrong with Negative Liberty." In *The Idea of Freedom: Essays in Honour of Isaiah Berlin*, edited by Alan Ryan, 175–93. Oxford: Oxford University Press.

———. 1985. *Philosophy and the Human Sciences: Philosophical Papers 2*. Cambridge: Cambridge University Press.

———. 1989. *Sources of the Self: The Making of the Modern Identity*. Cambridge: Cambridge University Press.

———. 1991a. *The Ethics of Authenticity*. Cambridge: Harvard University Press.

———. 1991b. "Hegel's Ambiguous Legacy for Modern Liberalism." In *Hegel and Legal Theory*, edited by Drucilla Cornell, Michel Rosenfeld, and David G. Carlson, 64–77. New York: Routledge.

———. 1991c. "Shared and Divergent Values." In *Options for a New Canada*, edited by Ronald Watts and Douglas Brown, 53–76. Toronto: University of Toronto Press.

———. 1995. *Philosophical Arguments*. Cambridge: Harvard University Press.

———. 1999. "Conditions of an Unforced Consensus on Human Rights." In *The East Asian Challenge for Human Rights*, edited by Joanne R. Bauer and Daniel A. Bell, 124–44. Cambridge: Cambridge University Press.

Terjesen, Andrew. 2012. "Civility and Magnanimity." In *Civility in Politics and Education*, edited by Deborah S. Mower and Wade L. Robison, 99–116. New York and London: Routledge.

Tomhave, Alan. 2012. "Civility as a Condition of Citizenship." In *Civility in Politics and Education*, edited by Deborah S. Mower and Wade L. Robison, 154–70. New York and London: Routledge.

Tu Weiming [Tu Wei-Ming] 杜維明. 1985. *Confucian Thought: Selfhood as Creative Transformation*. Albany: State University of New York Press.

———. 1989a. *Centrality and Commonality: An Essay on Confucian Religiousness*. Albany: State University of New York Press.

———. 1989b. *Ruxue disanqi fazhan de qianjing wenti—Dalu jiangxue, wennan, he taolun* 儒學第三期發展的前景問題—大陸講學, 問難, 和討論 (The Prospective Issues Concerning the Third Phase of Development for Confucianism: Lectures, Interrogations, and Discussion in Mainland China). Taipei: Linking Publishing Co.

Tyler, Colin. 2006."Contesting the Common Good: T. H. Green and Contemporary Republicanism." In *T. H. Green: Ethics, Metaphysics, and Political Philosophy*, edited by Maria Dimova-Cookson and W. J. Mander, 262–91. Oxford: Oxford University Press.

———. 2010. *The Metaphysics of Self-Realization and Freedom, Part 1 of the Liberal Socialism of Thomas Hill Green*. Exeter: Imprint Academic.

———. 2017. *Common Good Politics: British Idealism and Social Justice in the Contemporary World*. Basingstoke: Palgrave Macmillan.

Vincent, Andrew. 1986. "Introduction." In *The Philosophy of T. H. Green*, edited by Andrew Vincent, 1–20. Aldershot: Gower Publishing Co. Ltd.

———. 2001. "The New Liberalism and Citizenship." In *The New Liberalism: Reconciling Liberty and Community*, edited by Avital Simhony and David Weinstein, 205–77. Cambridge: Cambridge University Press.

———, ed. 1986. *The Philosophy of T. H. Green*. Aldershot: Gower Publishing Co. Ltd.

Vincent, Andrew, and Raymond Plant. 1984. *Philosophy, Politics and Citizenship*. Oxford: Basil Blackwell.

Wall, Steven. 2015. "Introduction." In *The Cambridge Companion to Liberalism*, edited by Steven Wall, 1–18. Cambridge: Cambridge University Press.

Wang Qingjia [Q. Edward Wang] 王晴佳. 2017. "Confucius in the May Fourth Era." In *A Concise Companion to Confucius*, edited by Paul R. Goldin, 330–51. Oxford: Wiley Blackwell.

Welchman, Jennifer. 1989. "From Absolute Idealism to Instrumentalism: The Problem of Dewey's Early Philosophy." *Transactions of the Charles S. Peirce Society* 25(4): 407–19.

Wilkins, Burleigh Taylor. 1956. "James, Dewey, and Hegelian Idealism." *Journal of the History of Ideas* 17(3): 332–46.

Williams, Bernard. 1993. *Ethics and the Limits of Philosophy*. London: HarperCollins.

Wollheim, Richard. 1969. *F. H. Bradley*. London: Penguin.

Wood, Allen W. 1991. "Introduction." In G. W. F. Hegel, *Elements of the Philosophy of Right*, edited by Allen W. Wood, translated by H. B. Nisbet, vii–xxxii. Cambridge: Cambridge University Press.

Xiao Gaoyan [Carl K. Y. Shaw] 蕭高彥. 1996. "Toward a Reconstruction of Hegel's Ethical Liberalism." *Journal of Social Sciences and Philosophy* 8(2): 305–38.

Xu Fuguan [Hsu Fu-Kuan] 徐復觀. 1969. *Zhongguo renxing lun shi: xian Qin pian* 中國人性論史：先秦篇 (A History of Chinese Theories of Human Nature: The Pre-Qin Period). Taipei: Commercial Press.

———. 1979. *Rujia zhengzhi sixiang yu minzhu ziyou renquan* 儒家政治思想與民主自由人權 (Confucian Political Thought and Democracy, Liberty, and Human Rights), edited by Xiao Xinyi 蕭欣義. Taipei: Bashi niandai chuban.

———. 1980. *Xinban xueshu yu zhengzhi zhijian* 新版學術與政治之間 (Between Academia and Politics, New Edition). Taipei: Xuesheng shuju.

Xunzi. 2014. *The Xunzi: The Complete Text*, translated by Eric L. Hutton. Princeton: Princeton University Press.

Yin Haiguang [Yin Hai-Kuang] 殷海光. 1990. *Zhengzhi yu shehui* 政治與社會 (Politics and Society), collected in Yin Haiguang quanji 殷海光全集 (Complete Works of Yin Haiguang), vols. 11–12, edited by Lin Zhenghong 林正弘. Taipei: Guiguan tushu.

Zeng Guoxiang [Roy Tseng] 曾國祥. 2003. *The Sceptical Idealist: Michael Oakeshott as a Critic of the Enlightenment*. Exeter: Imprint Academic.

———. 2010. "Conservatism, Romanticism, and the Understanding of Modernity." In *The Meanings of Michael Oakeshott's Conservatism*, edited by Corey Abel, 126–42. Exeter: Imprint Academic.

———. 2016. "The Idea of Freedom in Comparative Perspective: Critical Comparisons between Discourses of Liberalism and Neo-Confucianism." *Philosophy East and West* 66(2): 539–58.

Zeng Yi 曾亦, and Guo Xiaodong 郭曉東, eds. 2014. *He wei pushi? shei zhi jiazhi? dangdai Rujia lun pushi jiazhi* 何謂普世？誰之價值？當代儒家論普世價值 (What Is Called Universal? Whose Value? Contemporary Confucians Discuss Universal Values). Shanghai: Huadong Shifan Daxue chubanshe.

Zhang Foquan [Chang Fo-Chuan] 張佛泉. 1993. *Ziyou yu renquan* 自由與人權 (Liberty and Human Rights). Taipei: Commercial Press.

Zhang Junmai [Carsun Chang] 張君邁. 1971. *Liguo zhi dao* 立國之道 (The Way of the Country). Taipei: Commercial Press.

Zhang Rulun 張汝倫. 2015. "Oakeshott in China." In *Michael Oakeshott's Cold War Liberalism*, edited by Terry Nardin, 137–51. Basingstoke: Palgrave Macmillan.

Zheng Jiadong 鄭家棟. 2000. *Mou Zongsan* 牟宗三 (Mou Zongsan). Taipei: Grand East Book Co.

Zhou Cezong [Chow Tse-tsung] 周策縱. 1960. *The May Fourth Movement: Intellectual Revolution in Modern China*. Cambridge: Cambridge University Press.

Zhu Xi [Chu Hsi] 朱熹. 1958. *Lunyu jizhu* 論語集註 (Collected Annotations of the Analects). Taipei: Zhonghua congshu weiyuanhui.

Index

Absolute
  as a "bare concept" without moral import, 18, 53, 58, 87, 90, 92, 95
  Bradley on, 91–94, 104, 107–8, 303n10
  completeness, 94, 220
  and *Dao*-reality, 94
  Green on, 73, 75
  Hegel on, 65, 67, 75, 79–80, 95, 123, 139
  ren as, 80, 94–95
Ackerman, Bruce, 10
Ames, Roger, 15, 269
Analects (*Lunyu*), 38, 82, 171, 197, 200, 202, 223, 225, 249, 291n54, 296n8, 311n3, 312n9
Angle, Stephen C., 1, 15
anti-individualism, 23, 213, 218. See also individualism
Aristotle, 11, 119
"attaining sagehood" (*chengsheng*), 33, 61, 86, 90, 125, 139, 177, 198, 200, 226
"attaining virtue" (*chengde*), 81, 90, 220, 260
autonomy. See also self-determination
  as condition of human conduct, 84
  and liberal values, 22, 217–20, 222
  moral, 95, 150, 249, 343n104

  Green on, 74, 232, 242, 246, 249, 256, 258
  Kant on, 27, 30–33, 35, 49, 57, 61, 63, 95, 220, 246–47, 252–53, 256, 269–70, 290n27
  in Mencius, 192, 201, 220
  of moral subject, 55, 220
  personal, 269
  and personalism, 86
  and positive freedom, 150, 248–49
  and self-realization, 340n55, 343n104
  universal right to, 266

Bai Tongdong 白彤東, 14
Barry, Brian, 274
Baur, F. C., 75
Bell, Daniel A.
  China Model, 14, 185–86, 326n11, 326n13, 326n14
  and Confucian meritocracy, 14, 188
  on Hegel, 185
  and Jiang Qing, 14, 185–87, 192, 205
  and Taylor, 185, 325n5
Bentham, Jeremy, 236–37, 248
Berlin, Isaiah
  as cold war liberal, 4, 115
  and Green, 246, 248, 253, 337n1

Berlin, Isaiah (*continued*)
  on freedom, two concepts of,
    247–48, 253
    criticism of, 248, 337n9, 338n10,
      338n11, 338n12
    negative, 119, 150, 247–48
    positive, 248, 253, 261
"blossoming of democracy" (*minzhu kaichu*). *See also* Confucian democracy
  criticism of, 3, 115
  dialectical movement, 123–24,
    132–33
  divorce between political subject
    and moral subject, 121
  and Hegelian scheme, 3, 116–26,
    133, 139, 143, 270
  and Kantian framework, 4, 115,
    266–67
  objectification of subjectivity, 140
  political consequences of, 22, 168–
    69, 177–79, 216
  and "politics of innovation,"168,
    214
  and "self-negation," process of, 55,
    123–24, 131–36, 217, 276
  and "way of politics," 141, 180,
    276
body politic, 12, 159
Book of History (*Shang Shu*), 203
Book of Odes (*Shi Jing*), 201, 330n63
Book of Rites (*Liji*), 146, 169, 172,
  176, 194, 312n6, 312n10,
  323n144, 323n145, 323n151
Bosanquet, Bernard
  as British idealist, 11, 261
  and critical individualism, 262
  on ideal self, 262
  Philosophical Theory of the State,
    250
  Zhang Foquan's criticism of, 250

Bradley, F. H.
  Appearance and Reality, 91–92, 109,
    287n67
  as British idealist, 11, 87, 261
  "duty for duty's sake," 20, 93, 96,
    236, 238, 239, 241. *See also*
    deontology
  Ethical Studies, 93
  and Green, 71, 90–91, 100
  and Hegel, 87, 91–94, 103–5
  on ideal morality and religion, 107–8
  on individuality, 301n77
  "my station and its duties," 20, 89,
    90–91, 93, 96, 102–7, 236, 241,
    245, 254, 301n77. *See also* ethics
    of self-realization
  "pleasure for pleasure's sake,"
    20, 93, 96, 236, 241. *See also*
    utilitarianism
  on reality, 90, 93–94, 303n8,
    303n10
  reconciliation of Kant and Hegel,
    89–91, 104
  "reconciliatory dialectic," 18, 58,
    89–93, 106
    coherence, 91–92, 108
    comprehensiveness, 92–93, 108
  on self-realization, 20, 58, 95–96,
    284n34, 337n128
Brink, David, 73
Buddhism, 17, 27, 32, 42, 47, 53, 94,
  294n94

"caring about others," 224, 227–28
Carter, Stephen, 8, 157
Chan Wing-Tsit 陳榮捷, 79
Chan, Joseph 陳祖為, 14, 222
Chen Lai 陳來, 14
Chen Ming 陳明, 188, 284n39
Cheng Mingdao 程明道, 84
Cheng Yichuan 程伊川, 40, 198

Cheng Zhongying 成中英, 5, 82, 110
Christianity. *See also* God
  Green's criticism of, 68–75
  Hegel's criticism of, 53, 63–67, 75–76, 79, 118, 297n14, 298n15, 298n19
  as "distant religion" (*lijiao*), 76–77
  Mou's criticism of, 75–78
Chuang Tzu 莊子, 60
Cicero, 315n29
  De Officiis, 130
citizen (-ship), 3, 22–23, 62, 115, 122, 125, 231, 274
  Christian, in Green, 71
  and civil society, 166–67
  in Confucianism, lack of, 147, 169, 178, 183
  cruelty to, 315n29
  definition of, 166
  democratic, 16, 163, 165, 178–79, 212, 286n58
  ethical, 163, 165, 216, 263
    in British idealism, 13, 126, 235, 241
    Confucian, 169, 179, 220, 224, 205–6, 213–18
    Green on, 13, 23, 74, 214, 235–43, 263, 335n90
  good, 179, 263
  of heaven, in Hegel, 63
  Hegel on, 137
  moral power of, 255, 257–58, 272
  and nonselfishness and nonexploitation, 242–43
  and obligations, 166
  and political subject, 20, 128, 169, 178, 183, 206
  and rights, 166, 178, 257
  and state, 11, 206, 215–18, 231–35, 242, 258–59, 278, 316n39

  virtue of, 151, 156, 165, 169, 178, 217, 324n185. *See also* civic virtue
civic virtue, 263, 277
  and "blossoming of democracy," 22, 168
  and civil society, 144, 151, 157, 165–66, 169, 185, 324
  and common good, 144, 156
  and moral grounding of democracy, 151, 180
  and public spirit, in Montesquieu, 156
  Shils on, 165
civil society, 154, 163–64, 168
  in ancient China, lack of, 123, 147
  and citizen, 166–67
  and civic virtue, 144, 151, 157, 165–66, 169, 185, 324
  Collingwood on, 158
  and common good, 144, 163–65, 238
  and Confucian *res publica*, 8
  and democratic political culture, 16
  emergence of, 153–54, 157, 164
  Ferguson on, 164, 315n36, 320n100
  Green on, 74, 246
  Hegel on, 124, 137–38, 164, 320n100, 344n1
  in Locke, 164
  moral grounding of, 151, 163–64
  Rawls on, 155
  Shils on, 165
  in utilitarianism, 238
civility, 118, 143, 149, 151–57
  basic values of, 157, 164–65, 169, 180
  and citizen, 21, 154–57, 166–67
  and civic virtue, 21, 144, 156, 165–66

370 | Index

civility (continued)
  and civil society, 21, 154, 163–64
  as civilization, 10, 144, 151–52, 157–63, 180
  Collingwood on, 12, 158–60, 181
  and common good, 156–57, 163, 165–66
  communication and collaboration, 317n52
  and democracy, 144, 155, 164–65, 316n45
  democratic, 165, 180
  and dignity, 155–57
  duty of, 157
  in Rawls, 155, 165
  as good manners, 144, 151–54
  and *li*, 167–68
  liberal, 164–65, 180
  as a moral virtue, in Calhoun, 320n109
  as non-instrumental rule, in Oakeshott, 155–56
  polite, 163–64
  political, 163–65
  and politics, 1, 2, 11, 19, 21, 121, 141, 212
  as public good, 144, 163–67
  as public norms, 144, 154–56
  and rights discourse, 268
  and "self-restriction," principle of, 141, 270
  Shils on, 156–57, 165–66
  as a social virtue, in Kant, 320n108
  and "way of governance," 143
civilization, 84, 122, 163
  and barbarism, 21, 144, 149, 152, 158–60
  Chinese, 76, 144, 147, 160, 179–80, 328n30
  and commercial society, 153, 316n41
  Confucian, 7, 9, 147, 168, 180, 276, 314n23
  crisis of, 9, 147–49
  East Asian, 83
  and Enlightenment, 152–53
  Ferguson on, 315n36
  in Hegel, 319n94, 319n314
  and history of historiography, 152–53
  Hume on, 153, 161, 316n38
  and *li*, 144, 168
  and modern state, 153, 316n39
  as progress of man, 315n31
  and understanding of politics, 12, 117, 181
  Western, 76, 149–50, 158–59, 282n4
civilized society, 158, 160, 164, 173, 278, 320n120
civilizing process, 9, 152–53, 158–59, 316n39
Collingwood, R. G.
  as British idealist, 11–12, 101
  on civilization and barbarism, 158–60
  "misfit between yourself and your situation," 101, 239
  New Leviathan, 160
  and Oakeshott, 12, 145
common good, 19, 23, 58, 111, 121–22, 144, 156–57, 166, 185, 199, 207
  and civic virtue, 144, 156
  and civil society, 144, 163–65, 238
  Confucian conception of, 8, 10–11, 22, 140, 168, 179, 188, 203, 207, 216, 222. See also Confucian *res publica*
  and ethics of self-realization, 222
  as "good for each and all," in Green, 228, 235–40

in Hegel, 121–22, 342n83
liberal conception of, 13, 125–26, 166, 212, 222, 227
nondominant theory of, 16, 62, 199, 205–6, 213, 270, 276, 279, 335n90
  noncentralization, 241
  nonexploitation, 242–43
  nonselfishness, 242–43
and positive freedom, 23, 251, 255–58, 261–62
and rights
  justification, 24, 205, 234
  recognition, 270–74, 279
and state interference, 258–59
communitarianism, philosophical, 23, 163, 277
concrete universal
  Bradley on, 90–91, 93, 104, 108
  Hegel on, 18, 20, 28, 52, 56–57, 85, 90–91, 93, 116–17, 270
  ren as, 51, 54, 56, 104, 139
"conformity of Heaven and man in union" (*tianren heyi*), 19, 45–46, 48, 60, 79, 109, 125. See also Heaven
Confucian civic virtue, 179, 183, 202. See also "way of *zhongshu*"
  "caring about the worst-off," 23, 214, 217–18, 222, 229–31, 235, 240, 243
  "ethical mutuality," 23, 214, 217, 222, 224–27, 235, 243
  "helping others do good," 23, 214, 217, 222, 227–29, 235, 243
  "tolerance, patience, and self-restraint," 169
  and "way of *zhongshu*," 169, 179, 217, 222–31
Confucian civility, 8, 10–11, 16–17, 21–22, 121, 168, 180–81, 183, 229, 270, 276

Confucian democracy, 4, 6, 87, 115, 123. See also "blossoming of democracy"
and Confucian meritocracy, 3, 15–16, 279
definition of, 121, 124, 213, 270
ethical version of, 133, 139, 141, 189–92, 204. See also democracy: ethical
and flourishing of human good, 205, 207
moral basis of, 125, 133
and moral weakness of liberal democracy, 118, 204–5, 207
as "new outer kingliness," 6, 135, 204
and objective spirit, 117
and political crisis of modern China, 118, 139
subtlest model of, 8, 20–21, 116, 136–41, 168, 179, 189, 191, 204, 207, 213, 270, 278
synthesis of "way of politics" and "way of governance," 126, 143, 168, 178–79, 183, 191, 207, 211, 217, 242, 278
three questions of, 116, 122, 124, 126
Confucian democratic civility, 8, 10, 121, 140, 143, 145, 157, 167–81, 268, 275. See also Confucian public virtue
and Confucian governing and civic virtues, 16, 21, 145, 169, 183
and Confucian public virtue, 8, 168, 268
definition of, 179
liberal features of, 183
Mou's reconstruction of, 16, 22, 121, 146, 169, 180, 276

Confucian forms of life, 2, 21, 115, 121, 125, 133, 140, 160, 168, 181, 205, 276, 279
Confucian governing virtue, 179, 183–84. *See also* "self-restriction," principle of
"cultivation and its limitation," 200–3
"convenience of life" (*liyong*), 203, 216, 230
"making the people wealthy before cultivation" (*xianfu houjiao*), 203, 216, 230, 242
"rectification of the people's virtue" (*zhengde*), 203, 216, 230
"securing abundant means of sustenance" (*housheng*), 203, 216, 230
"minimal and universal humanity" (*qima er pupian de rendao*), 204
"the people as fundamental" (*minben*), 192–96, 199, 216, 280
"Heaven conferring, people conferring" (*tianyu renyu*), 193
political order, three levels of, 195, 329n51
"public rulership," 192–94, 206, 332n10
"rule by virtue" (*dezhi*), 6, 123, 144–47, 168
"according to their nature, with what is proper to them" (*yiren zhiren*), 197, 218
"direction of the people's hearts" (*minxin suoxiang*), 196–97
"individual life in existence" (*cunzai de shengming geti*), 196, 203
"to love what the people love, and to hate what the people hate" (*minzhisuohao haozhi, minzhisuowu wuzhi*), 176, 197
ren-centered model of, in Confucius, 180
"stepping aside exhaustively" (*quanfu rangkai*), 196, 200
values of, 175
transformed into Confucian civic virtue, 22, 168–69, 179, 217
and virtuous ruler, 22, 146, 171, 175, 177, 179–80, 183–84, 186, 193, 196–200, 202, 206, 212, 217
and "way of *zhongshu*," 169, 200–3, 217
Confucian meritocracy, 3, 14–16, 21, 179, 183, 184–89, 192, 199, 204–7, 279
Confucian moral metaphysics, 15, 27–28, 35, 57, 81, 86, 127, 145, 217, 220. *See also* "intellectual intuition"
contrasted with "metaphysics of morals," in Kant, 28, 42, 48–51, 96
"infinite heart-mind" (*wuxianxin*), 28, 42–43, 45–49, 53, 77, 86, 91, 108
"one heart-mind opening two gates" (*yixin kai liangmen*), 46
"ontology of nonattachment" (*wuzhi de cunyoulun*), 28, 44–46, 77
"perfect teaching" (*yuanjiao*), 28, 42, 46–48, 76–77, 91, 109–10, 125, 175, 217, 293n93
as "transcendent metaphysics" (*chaojue de xingshangxue*), 37, 42, 296n2
Confucian political theory, contemporary, 3–4, 13–19, 215, 279

Confucian pragmatism, 15, 115
Confucian public virtue, 8. *See also* Confucian *res publica*
　and "attaining accomplishment according to the individual's nature" (*jiu geti er shuncheng*), 139, 177, 180, 196–97, 201, 205
　and "attaining self-accomplishment," 191, 199
　categories of, 192
　　legitimacy of authority, 192–96
　　limits on the abuse of power, 200–4
　　purpose of government, 196–200
　and Confucian democratic civility, 8, 168, 268
　and Confucian governing and civic virtues, 119, 140
　Mou's restatement of, 169
Confucian religiousness, 75–84
Confucian *res publica*, 16, 24, 125, 231. *See also* Confucian public virtue
　and "all being provided for" (*jie you suo yan*), 229–30
　as "attaining accomplishment according to the individual's nature" (*jiu geti er shuncheng*), 10, 22, 203, 211, 216, 218, 220–21, 230, 242–43, 330n71
　as "attaining self-accomplishment," 216
　and common good, nondominant theory of, 213, 241–43, 276, 279
　and Confucian democratic civility, 8, 179, 279
　and Confucian governing and civic virtues, 8, 11, 276, 279
　and Confucian public virtue, 8, 22
　and "humane government," 8–9, 212, 230, 279
　liberal aspects of, 11, 13, 212, 217–19
　and moderate perfectionism, 222
　as moral foundation of democracy, 8
　and rights, justification of, 24, 261, 270, 273
　and "self-restriction," principle of, 217, 270, 276
　as ultimate end of politics, 211
Confucianism. *See also* Neo-Confucianism; New Confucianism
　antiliberal, 2–3, 6, 8, 13–14, 20–21, 23–24, 115, 126, 141, 143–44, 149, 183–84, 190, 213, 222, 230–31, 245, 247, 265, 270, 273, 275
　anti-Westernized, 10, 307n1
　authentic, 5, 176, 192
　civic, 115
　as concrete philosophy, 51–58
　intrinsic character of
　　"inner morality" (*neizai daodexing*), 27, 31–33, 35, 37–38, 78, 81, 85, 99, 170, 188, 223, 266, 278
　　"perfect good" (*yuanshan*), 27–28, 35–38, 85, 90, 266, 278
　　"vertical expression of the vertical system" (*zongguan zongjiang*), 27, 33–35, 47, 85, 170, 266, 278
　as Kantian liberalism, 264–67
　modern transformation of, 115, 173, 204, 273, 277
　orthodox, 27, 38–40, 70
　political (*zhengzhi Ruxue*), 14, 186–88, 326n15, 327n16
　progressive, 15, 115
　public reason, 15–16, 115
　spiritual (*xinxing Ruxue*), 13, 187–88

Confucius. See also *Analects*
  and Confucian civic virtue, 225, 227, 229–30
  and free society, 177
  on governance, 146, 171, 192, 194–95, 200–1, 203, 312n8, 312n9, 312n10
  on Heaven, 48, 83, 286n8
  Hegel on, 130
  legacy of, 173
  on *li*, 145, 172
  on *ren*, 32–34, 38, 42–43, 48, 78–79, 81–83, 98, 103, 106, 145, 220, 260, 290n34, 291n54
  Schwartz on, 145
  Tang Junyi on, 80, 261
  temples, 296n4
  on "way of *zhongshu*," 223–24, 227
  on *xin* (trustworthiness), 175
conservatism, 21, 143, 149, 181, 277
  contrasted with radicalism, 10, 147
  tradition vs. traditionalism, 161, 181, 311n1, 318n65
considerateness, 164–65, 321n109
Constant, Benjamin, 43, 99, 127, 215, 248, 273
constitutionalism, 9, 14, 147, 161, 186, 190–91, 206, 208, 286n58, 327n19
Corwin, Edward, 249
cross-cultural dialogue, 1, 56, 84, 205, 273, 276–77
"cultivating oneself" (*xiuji*)
  contrasted with "governing the people," 6–7, 21, 139, 169, 175–77, 191, 196, 221
  as moral achievement, 139, 175–77

Daoism, 17, 27, 32, 41–42, 53, 94, 175, 290n34, 293n94, 330n71
Dao-reality (*daoti*), 43–45, 51, 54, 86, 94
De Bary, William Theodore, 85, 104

"Declaration on Behalf of Chinese Culture Respectively Announced to the People of the World" (*Wei Zhongguo wenhua jinggao shijie renshi xuanyan*), 5, 59, 260
democracy. See also Confucian democracy
  basic values of, 17, 178, 264
  constitutional, 7, 213–15, 224, 228, 230, 263, 268
  criticized by antiliberal Confucianism, 13–15, 184–89, 192, 247
  ethical, 122–26, 183–84, 189–92, 199, 205, 207
  and incivility, 158–60
  liberal, 6–7, 13–14, 17, 21–22, 24, 61, 118, 143–44, 149–50, 157–58, 160, 166, 177–78, 180–81, 183–87, 189–92, 204, 207–8, 214, 231, 247, 264, 270, 275–76, 331n95
  moral grounding of, 6, 8, 21, 61, 123, 133, 151, 177, 180–81, 184, 186, 189, 191, 331n95
  moral weakness of, 24, 190–91, 204–5, 207–8, 270
  stability of, 160, 166
  and "way of politics," 7, 17, 21, 143, 184, 190, 214
deontology, 58, 90–91, 93, 96, 126, 236, 238, 271, 305n33. See also Bradley: "duty for duty's sake"
Dewey, John, 15
dignity
  as character of Confucianism, 6
  and civility, 155–57
  as highest good of modernity, 137
  human, 2, 22, 78, 84, 99, 177, 179, 199, 213, 222–27, 237–38, 241, 243, 250–51, 256, 273, 277
  as liberal moral ideal, 222–27

Index | 375

ren as, 119, 177
Dimova-Cookson, Maria, 252
Doctrine of the Mean (*Zhongyong*), 38–40, 47, 78, 84, 197, 202, 218
Duke of Zhou 周公, 193
duty
  "act from," 30, 54, 96, 100, 290n27
  of civility, 157
    in Rawls, 155, 165
  conflicts of, 100–1
  and Confucianism, 2, 143
  and cosmopolitanism, 107
  of humankind, 188
  of right, 265, 268
  of treating all men equally, 236–37
  of treating humanity as an end, 230
Dworkin, Ronald, 10, 157, 180, 266

Elstein, David, 132–33
embodiment
  Bradley on, 104
  of God, 76, 83
  Green on, 73, 344n112
  of Heaven, 130, 324n166
  principle of, in Hegel, 18, 57, 61, 66–67, 70, 76, 99–100, 163, 254, 270, 274
  of *ren*, 140
Enlightenment, 9, 149, 152–53
  conservative, 161, 179, 181
  family of, 10, 160
equal respect. *See* respect
Erasmus of Rotterdam, 151–52
  De Civilitate Morum Puerilium, 151
ethical life, 15, 77, 80, 138, 239, 262, 309n27. *See also Sittlichkeit*
  democratic, 308n19
  Hegel on, 23, 119, 124, 133, 136–39, 164, 181, 212, 231, 239, 254, 256, 308n19, 309n27

ethical personality, 69, 71, 75, 77, 130, 261
ethics of self-realization, 2, 4, 10, 12–13, 15, 19–20, 22, 58, 61–62, 84–87, 89–91, 95–96, 102, 110, 122, 125, 140, 198–99, 201, 205, 231–32, 236, 240–42, 246, 249, 252, 254, 257, 261, 263, 272, 277
"exact correspondence of morality and happiness" (*defu yixhi*), 36, 46, 48
extensional truth, 32, 56, 95

Fan Ruiping 范瑞平, 14
Feng Youlan 馮友蘭, 5, 8
Ferguson, Adam, 153, 164
Fichte, Johann Gottlieb, 19, 50, 52, 100, 256, 261, 291n65, 292n70
freedom, 19, 256, 270, 295n127. *See also* Hegel: on freedom
  juristic
    first form of enjoyment, 253
    Green on, 249, 252–53
    related to ordinary action, 252
    and true freedom, 252, 255, 257, 261, 339n28
  negative
    Berlin on, 119, 150, 247–48
    Green on, 232, 252–53, 255, 257, 271
    of the individual, 245, 264
    as an opportunity concept, 338n12
    and positive freedom, 3, 11, 23, 205, 245, 247, 249, 252, 255, 261, 271, 279, 324n180, 337n1
    as rights, 246, 250–51, 260, 271
    and Westernized liberals, 150
    Zhang Foquan on, 150, 245, 248–50

freedom *(continued)*
  positive
    Berlin on, 248, 253, 261
    in Confucianism, 249
    criticized by Westernized liberals, 13, 126, 150, 250, 307n1
    as an exercise concept, 338n12
    Green on, 232, 246, 255–58
    in relation to oppressive society, 23, 245, 251
    and self-realization, 246, 251–55
    and state interference, 122, 258–59
    Zhang Foquan on, 248–50, 337n1, 338n13
  subjective, 119, 122, 124, 129–30, 138, 173, 264, 270
    in Confucianism, lack of, 20, 123, 128–31, 263
    contrasted with substantial freedom, 129
    developing toward ethical life, 136–40, 309n27
    and Kant's morality, 124, 137
    and political subject, 123–24, 131, 134
    and "way of politics," 178
    and Xunzi, 173
  true
    actualization of, 58, 158, 261
    in Confucianism, 245–46, 264
    and democracy, 258
    as "exercise of humaneness," 262
    Green on, 248–49, 251–55
    and positive freedom, 251, 256, 261
    as rational reflection, 253
    related to moral action, 252
    ren as, 120, 259–62
French Revolution, 120, 129
Fuller, Timothy, 162

Giannone, Pietro, 153
Gibbon, Edward
  History of the Decline and Fall of Roman Empire, 153
God
  creation, 46, 53
  and *Dao*-reality, 45, 86, 109
  existence of, 30, 36, 45–46, 51, 54, 73–74
  external, 19, 64, 75
  and Heaven, 59, 77–79, 109
  as highest good, 36
  and history, 19, 75
  as ideal self, 73
  immanent, 62, 71, 80, 86
  "immortal love," 108
  inaccessibility of, 104
  incarnation of, 66, 80
  infinite, 44–45
  and "intellectual intuition," 29, 42, 45, 49, 51
  internalization of, 19, 66, 75
  invocation of, 47
  and Kant's three postulates, 29–30, 45, 73
  knowledge of, 29, 36
  and man (humanity)
    division between, 19, 51, 63, 72, 76, 118
    Green's reconciliation of, 68–75
    Hegel's reconciliation of, 63–67, 79, 298n15, 298n25
  rational faith in, 36, 86
Gongyang commentary of the *Spring and Autumn Annals* (*Chunqiu Gongyang Zhuan*), 187, 313n11
"governing the people" (*zhiren*). *See also* "humane government"
"laying down rule for conduct," 176
liberal treatment of, 199

Index | 377

political value of, 203
and public virtue, 6, 139, 175, 191
"rectifying the hearts of men" (*zheng ren xin*), 174
and "self-restriction," principle of, 169, 175, 200
and "virtue-competence" (*de liang*), 175
Grand Union (*Datong*), 193–95
Gray, John, 9, 167
Great Learning (*Daxue*), 38–39, 197
Great Void (*taixu*), 45
Green, T. H.
  as British idealist, 11, 205, 212, 246, 251, 261, 275
  on common good, 23, 230–43, 255–59, 271–73, 335n90
  eternal consciousness, 69–71, 73–74, 249, 299n40, 300n54
  on freedom, 23, 232, 246, 248–49, 251–62, 264, 271, 339n28, 339n35, 336n119. See also freedom
  and Hegel, 13, 19, 57, 65, 68–72, 74–75, 77–78, 91, 100, 213, 219, 231–32, 253–56, 270, 342n83, 340n55
  and "individualist perfectionism," 234–35
  and Kant, 71–75, 91, 100–2, 219, 232, 236, 238–39, 259, 339n31
  Lectures on the Principles of Political Obligations, 251, 257, 335n85
  and perfectionist liberalism, 74, 205, 231–35, 246, 251, 262–63
  on political obligation, 231, 234
  Prolegomena to Ethics, 72, 74, 251–52, 254, 256
  reconciliation of Kant and Hegel, 57, 246, 254–56
  "removing obstacles to self-realization," 232–34, 242, 262
  rights recognition thesis, 24, 270–74, 343n112
  and Rousseau, 219
  on selfhood, 71–75, 81
  on self-realization, 71, 74, 79, 90, 101–2, 232, 235, 241–43, 249, 252–56, 263, 272, 340n55
  on self-satisfaction, 97, 101, 239–40, 252–53, 256
  on state and state interference, 213–14, 231–34, 258–59
  synthesis of Kantianism and utilitarianism, 235, 240–41, 305n33
  on tradition, 94
  on virtue, conditions of, 240
Gu Yanwu 顧炎武, 194

Hall, David, 15, 269
He Lin 賀麟, 5
Heaven (*Tian*)
  and *benxin* (authentic heart-mind), 39, 110
  Cheng Mingdao on, 84
  concept of, in ancient China, 59–60, 218–19, 289n20
  creation, 109
  Dao of, 38, 40, 43, 78–80, 83, 109–10, 324n166, 327n17, 327n19
  in Daoism, 293n94
  and earth
    coexists with me, 103, 109
    and myriad things, 45, 77, 84, 106, 109, 139
  internationalization of, 60, 78–81
  and man (humanity), 61, 76–77, 79–80, 85–86, 324n166. See also "conformity of Heaven and man in union"

Heaven (continued)
  and *ren*, 42–43, 83
  Wang Yangming on, 45, 83–84, 106
  and *Xing*-nature, 39, 83, 109
  Xu Fuguan on, 296n8
Hegel, Georg Wilhelm Friedrich
  on abstract right, 124, 129, 137, 254
  Aufheben/Aufhebung, 138, 298n25
  beyond, 3, 57–58
  and concrete philosophy, 18, 27–28, 52–53, 116, 270
  dialectic, 17, 53, 58, 61, 87, 90, 92, 105, 120
  Early Theological Writings, 118
  Elements of the Philosophy of Right, 124, 129, 137, 253
  Encyclopedia of the Philosophical Sciences in Outline, 129
  and Fichte, 19, 50, 52, 100, 261
  on freedom, 18–19, 119, 133, 137, 185, 254, 259–60
    abstract, 120, 129
    concrete, 119
    objective, 264, 270, 342n83
    radical, 118–19
    situated, 119
    subjective, 18, 119, 128–31, 136–39, 173, 263, 270
    substantial, 129–30, 173
  immanent theology, 19, 62, 70–71
  and Kant, 2, 4, 11, 17, 19, 50–51, 57–58, 61, 71, 85–86, 90–91, 99–100, 104, 124, 133, 187, 219, 261, 277–78, 287n67, 344n1
  Lectures on the Philosophy of World History, 130
  method of political theorization, 121–22
  on objective spirit, 18, 173
  Phenomenology of Spirit, 64, 67, 118, 124, 128
  Philosophy of History, 76, 120, 122, 124
  philosophy of history, 20, 51, 55, 61, 117, 319n91
  on reality, 51, 55–56, 270
  and Rousseau, 19, 219, 256, 270
  and Schelling, 50, 52
  on self-knowledge, 66–67
  on self-positing God, 65–67, 86
  state, theory of, 53, 122, 232
  on subjectivity, 53–55, 270
  on "unhappy consciousness," 64, 68, 128, 130
Heidegger, Martin
  and Kant, 41, 44
  Kant and the Problems of Metaphysics, 41
Herder, Johann Gottfried, 155, 162–63
highest good, 17, 33, 35–39, 44, 46–47, 53–54, 83, 90, 108–9, 137, 145, 220. See also *summum bonum*
Hobbes, Thomas, 248, 271
  Leviathan, 160
Holland, Scott, 74
Hong Kong, 1, 211, 279
Hu Shi 胡適, 149
Hu Wufeng 胡五峰, 40, 48
Huang Zongxi 黃宗羲, 194, 219
"human relations" (*renlun guanxi*), 80, 145, 171–72, 198, 200, 226, 235, 260, 330n63. See also ethical life
"humane government" (*renzheng*). See also "way of governance"
  basic principles of, 191–204
  and Confucian civic virtue, 22, 183, 230

and Confucian democratic civility, 279
and Confucian governing virtue, 22, 183
as Confucian political ideal, 3, 7, 121, 131, 139, 146, 183, 189, 245, 276
criticized by anti-Confucian liberalism, 245–46
and democratic society, 120, 139, 140, 173, 177, 189, 217
and ethical democracy, 183
and "governing the people," 177, 191
liberal rebuilding of, 184, 213, 279
Mencius on, 146, 171, 180
as moral grounding of democracy, 21, 191
moral merits of, 184, 204–5
political pitfalls of, 184, 204–5
and *ren*-centered reading of *li*, 180
and "self-restriction," principle of, 22, 139, 141, 187, 276
and "way of governance," 7, 10, 121, 141, 180, 184, 211–12, 279
Hume, David
and conservative Enlightenment, 161
History of England, 153
and Kant, 255

I Ching (*Yi Jing*), 218
idealism
absolute
of Bradley, 91–94
of Green, 74
of Hegel, 55, 74, 86
British
and common good, 241, 249
and communitarianism, philosophical, 163, 231, 277
and ethical citizenship, 235, 241
and ethical liberalism, 58, 87
and ethics of self-realization, 12–13, 19, 57, 87, 89, 96, 101, 122, 125, 235, 249, 254, 277
and Hegel, 2–4, 11–12, 18–19, 51, 57–58, 85–86, 89, 91, 102, 104, 122, 254, 277
as Hegelian liberalism, 2, 11, 18, 275
and Kant, 19, 57–58, 85–86, 89, 101, 277
New Liberalism of, 16
and perfectionist liberalism, 12, 122, 126, 205, 212, 241
as post-Kantian philosophical school, 12, 57, 100–2, 275
religious thought of, 68
representatives of, 11, 261
and republicanism, 277, 231
and selfhood, 57, 102–4, 300n60, 319n93
and *Sittlichkeit*, 163, 254
and true freedom, 249, 251
humanist, 213
rational, 78–79
subjective, 74
"immanent transcendence" (*neizai chaoyue*), 33, 81, 95
individual (-ity), 165, 197. *See also* individualism
abstract, 103, 136, 185
atomistic, 118
autonomous, 269
and community, 3, 21, 90, 96, 102–3, 105, 118, 120, 144, 150, 158, 161–63, 187, 247, 254, 278, 300n54, 301n77
and freedom, 9, 120, 128–31, 138, 162, 167, 185, 199, 262, 264
and history, 264

individual (-ity) (*continued*)
and human dignity, 223–27, 250
isolated, 85
as liberal moral ideal, 22, 115, 154, 213, 222, 277
principle of, in Hegel, 55, 62
and public institutions, Greek harmony between, 119
respect for, 104, 213, 264
rights, 146, 148, 273
and *sittlichkeit*, 67, 105, 309n27
and sociability, 11, 86, 320n100
and social norms, 272
and state, 205, 250
and tradition, 12, 24
value of, 2, 74, 143, 163, 174, 196, 199, 226, 233, 248, 250, 256, 262, 264
individualism
abstract, 14, 54, 155, 162, 187, 199, 205, 262
asocial, 85
atomistic, 24, 85, 162, 187–88, 199, 226, 256, 270
and collectivism, 86
concrete, 162
in Confucianism. *See also* personalism
"accomplishing humaneness by cultivation" (*renwen huacheng*), 264
"existence of personality" (*renge de cunzai*), 198
full-blown, 104
pinnacle of, 199, 226, 262, 330n71
"self-awareness of the individual" (*geti de zijue*), 18, 264
critical, 262–63
embodied, 50, 62, 89, 96, 97, 102, 111, 155, 162, 199, 205, 226, 231, 246, 254, 256, 262–64, 274. *See also* subjectivity: embodied

and liberalism, 85, 246–47, 251, 263
methodological, 321n121
organic, in Spencer, 102
plural forms of, 251, 256, 259, 279
rationalistic, 148
realistic, 263
true, 319n93
uncritical, 148, 262–63
utilitarian, 162
"inner sagehood" (*neisheng*)
"learning" of (*neisheng zhi xue*), 81, 173, 344n1
as a moral feature of Confucianism, 2, 19, 38, 62, 79, 85, 120, 134–36, 140, 143
and "outer kingliness" (*waiwang*), 6, 120, 125, 127–28, 131, 134–36, 173, 175, 214, 251, 344n1
"intellectual intuition" (*zhi de zhijue*)
affirmation of
in Chinese philosophy, 17, 41–44
in Confucianism, 34, 38, 47–49, 90–91, 97, 108–10, 128, 130
in British idealists, 91, 101, 108
and "enlightened feeling" (*jueqing*), 97, 99, 110
in Fichte, Hegel, and Schelling, 52–53
as God's knowledge, 29, 45, 51
Kant's denial of, 17, 28–30, 41, 43–44, 50
and "perfect teaching" (*yuanjiao*), 109, 393n93
intensional truth, 32, 56, 95

Jamieson, K. H., 154
Jenco, Leigh K., 148
Ji Kang Zi 季康子, 200–1
Jiang Nianfeng 蔣年豐, 267
Jiang Qing 蔣慶, 14, 185–88, 192, 205, 231, 327n19

Jie 桀, 193, 195
Jin Yaoji 金耀基, 5
Jones, Henry, 102

Kang Xiaoguang 康曉光, 14, 188–89
Kant, Immanuel
  bifurcated world, 17, 30, 44, 49, 50, 62, 72, 74, 98, 239
    "empirical self" and "moral self," 30, 49, 74, 107, 239
    "finite essence of human being" and "infinite mind of God," 17, 28, 41, 44
    nature and freedom (morality), 17, 29–31, 72, 98, 254–55
    phenomena and noumena, 17, 30, 43–44, 46, 49, 72, 254
    "sensible intuition" and "intellectual intuition," 17, 29–30, 35, 38, 41, 128
    sensibly dependent feeling and moral feeling, 96–97
  Bradley's criticism of, 20, 87, 90–91, 97, 100–2
  on categorical imperative (moral law), 30, 42, 47, 49, 96–97, 101–2, 236, 238, 253–54, 266
  on "causality of the will," 35, 43
  Christian background, 17, 36, 44
  "Copernican revolution," 29
  Critique of Practical Reason, 36
  Critique of Pure Reason, 28, 31, 41, 62, 72, 291n65, 292n71
  "the end in itself," formula of, 230, 238–39, 241, 243
  on existence of God, 46, 54, 86
  on freedom (free will) as a postulate, 17, 20, 30, 33–34, 50, 54, 86, 96–99, 100, 239, 252, 270
  Green's criticism of, 71, 238–40, 253–56
  Hegelian critique of, 18, 28, 50, 53, 55, 62, 87, 99, 191, 253–54, 256, 275, 295n127
  and Heidegger, 41, 44, 97
  on immortality of soul, 45, 54, 74
  on "kingdom of ends," 30
  metaphysics of morals, 17, 28, 35, 42, 48–49, 51, 85, 96, 97, 110, 267, 270, 278
  on moral feeling, 96–97, 101
  moral theology, 28, 36, 48, 51
  Mou's criticism of, 17–18, 31, 40–51, 54–55, 61, 87, 96–99
  Religion within the Limits of Reason Alone, 36
  right, universal principle of, 133, 265–66
  rights, theory of, 247, 254, 266–69
  and Rousseau, 19, 219, 256, 259, 270, 289n19, 295n127
  "unity of apperception," 49, 72, 292n68
  on "worthiness of being happy," 36
Kim, Sungmoon, 15–16, 285n51, 286n58, 312n7, 324n185, 333n53
King Wen 文王, 195
King Wu 武王, 195
"kingly way" (*wangdao*), 190, 194–96, 202, 212, 215, 218–21, 228
"knowing subject" (*zhixing zhuti*), 28, 46, 49, 72, 74, 118, 127–28, 131, 135, 173, 252, 256
Kymlicka, Will, 10

Lao Siguang 勞思光, 221
Lao Tzu 老子, 60, 293n94
Larmore, Charles, 10
Legal School (*Fajia*), 174–75
Levenson, Joseph, 148
Li (rites, ritual propriety). See also *ren*
  and civilization (*wenming*), 168

Li (continued)
  as *de* (virtue), 169–71, 324n185
  as "decrees and regulations" (*dianxian*), 123
  as "deliberate effort" (*wei*), in Xunzi, 170
  as good manners, 144–45, 151, 167–68
  inclusive version of, 145, 168–69, 172, 180
  and music (*liyue*), 33, 187, 195, 323n11
  as objective spirit, 172–74
  as "outer guidance," in Xunzi, 170–71
  as "patterning" (*wen*), 168
  ren-centered reading of, 169–72, 174, 180
  and *Sittlichkeit*, 344n1
  as social norms, 145, 167, 170
Li Chenyang 李晨陽, 14, 284n38, 307n1
Li Minghui 李明輝, 17, 267–68, 288n7, 343n104, 344n1
Liang Shuming 梁漱溟, 5, 284n38, 314n23
Liangzhi (original knowing), 31, 41–42, 47, 61, 106, 133, 136, 290n37
  "original knowing in morality" (*daode liangzhi*), 124
liberal
  expressions, 1, 4, 22, 122, 167, 212–13
  ideas, 126, 258
  imperialism, 158, 318n68
  language, 125, 150, 213, 275, 278
  neutralism, 212
  perfectionism, 212
  values, 2, 4, 8–14, 22–23, 121, 132, 143, 155, 157, 163, 165, 168, 184–85, 188, 207, 213, 217–18, 222, 231, 251, 276, 279, 307n1
  vocabulary, 2, 20
liberalism
  anti-Confucian, 2–3, 6, 8, 13, 20–21, 23, 115, 126, 141, 143, 149, 190, 211, 213, 231, 245, 275
  autonomy-based, 264, 266
  Chinese, 133, 147–48, 248, 250
  civil, 10–11, 20–21, 113, 115, 122, 126, 141, 144–45, 151, 154, 157, 160, 165–66, 168, 178, 180–81, 183, 275–76, 278–80
  cold war, 53
  definition of, 9–11
  diversity of, 4, 9, 157, 167, 212, 247, 251, 259, 273, 279
  ethical, 2, 9, 11, 13, 58, 87, 132, 141, 163, 166–67, 279, 231
  Hegelian, 1–2, 4, 9, 11, 18, 24, 122, 145, 167, 255, 262, 275, 277–78
  hypothesis-based, 167
  Kantian, 4, 24, 167, 262, 264–69
  Mou's examination of
    "moral ideals," 212–13, 222–31
    "objective form," 212–18, 224, 228, 230
    "social version," 212–13, 218–22, 224, 228, 230
  perfectionist, 11–12, 22–23, 74, 122, 126, 141, 166, 205, 209, 212, 214, 230–31, 241, 245–46, 251, 254, 261, 263–64, 270, 276, 278–80
  practice-based, 167, 321n121
  procedural, 9, 167
  radical, 148
  republican, 9, 167
  rights-based, 9–11, 60, 141, 155, 165, 180, 264, 268
  Westernized, 143–44, 149–50, 153, 157, 160, 167, 181, 265, 307n1

Index | 383

Lin Yusheng 林毓生, 148
Lindsay, A. D., 249
Liu Baonan 劉寶楠, 225
Liu Jishan 劉蕺山, 40
Liu Shuxian 劉述先, 5, 301n89
Locke, John, 160, 164, 248, 261, 271
Lu Xiangshan 陸象山, 40

MacIntyre, Alasdair, 147, 162
Mackenzie, John Stuart, 104
Makeham, John, 4
Marshall, T. H., 166
Marx, Karl, 248
May Fourth Movement (Wu Si Yundong), 123, 144, 148–49, 313n18, 314n23
Mencius. See also *Mencius*
  benxin (authentic heart-mind), 39, 47, 99, 104, 106, 108–10, 127
  and Confucian civic virtue, 224, 227, 229
  and Confucius, 5, 38, 48, 59, 61, 81, 83, 86, 146, 170–73, 192, 194, 195, 203, 326n13
  on "enlightened feeling" (*jueqing*), 97–99, 101, 110, 305n39
  four cardinal virtues, 39, 78, 82, 99, 171
  "four germs" (*si duan*), 39, 43, 79, 98–99, 334n59
    "heart-mind of compassion" (*ceyin zhi xin*), 39, 224, 229
    "heart-mind of courtesy and modesty" (*cirang zhi xin*), 39, 171
    "heart-mind of right and wrong" (*shifei zhi xin*), 39
    "heart-mind of shame" (*xiuwu zhi xin*), 39
  "goodness of Xing-nature" (*xingshan*), 34, 39, 82, 98, 132, 170
  on Heaven and humanity
    "giving full realization to heart-mind" (*jinxin*), 48, 80, 89, 95, 104
    "knowing Heaven" (*zhitian*), 48, 80, 95
    "knowing Xing-nature" (*zhixing*), 48, 80, 95
  on "humane government," 146, 171, 180
  on "inner morality" (*neizai daodexing*), 82, 84, 99, 266, 330n79
  "innerness of humaneness and righteousness" (*renyi neizai*), 266
  and Kant, 37, 39, 82–83, 99
  and moral autonomy, 192, 201, 220
  on "origin of power" (*quan yuan*), 174–75
  on political subjectivity of the people, 171, 175, 199
  on rebellion, 195
  ren-centered reading of *li*, 168–74, 180
  "subjective freedom of morality" (*daode de zhuti ziyou*), 173
  "unity of the heart-mind and Xing-nature" (*xin ji xing*), 170
  on virtuous leader, 171, 193, 197, 202–3, 329n59
  Xing-nature, 32, 34, 39, 42, 48, 81, 83, 95, 98, 106, 109, 171, 289n25, 334n59
  and Xunzi, 146, 169–77, 312n7, 325n185, 326n13
Mencius (*Mengzi*), 38, 80, 98, 193, 214, 301n84, 322n134, 329n49, 329n51, 329n59, 330n63, 334n77
Metzger, Thomas, 178–79
Mill, John Stuart, 248, 261

384 | Index

Miller, David, 166
Ming dynasty, 38, 194, 290n50, 322n125
modernity
  basic values of, 99, 137
  and Confucianism, 10, 138, 148, 279, 314n23
  crisis of, 18, 118, 120, 139, 270
  free subjectivity of, 130, 219
  Hegel's assessment of, 116–22
  multiple facets of, 21, 273, 276
  political, 6, 18, 144–51, 184, 206–7, 211, 215, 219, 273
  and tradition, 11–12, 21, 141, 143–44, 150, 158, 160–61, 318n65
  Western, 2, 32, 50, 118, 120, 143, 147–48, 152, 160–61, 276
Momigliano, Arnaldo, 153
Montesquieu, 156, 164
moral
  ability, 9, 35, 72, 77–78, 82, 89, 101, 104, 108, 171, 226, 241, 246, 252–53, 271
  capability, 106, 235
  consciousness, development of, 96–102
  creativity, principle of, 34–35, 42–44, 47, 49, 53, 86, 91, 109
  development, 15–16, 33, 44, 50, 106, 206
  potentiality, 33, 79, 99, 170, 226, 232–33, 236, 242, 260
  religion, 14, 19, 44, 57, 59–65, 67–69, 71, 73, 75, 77–79, 81, 83, 85, 87, 187, 223, 275, 295n2, 296n8, 297n14
  sentiments, 97
  spontaneity, 35, 89
Moralität, 67, 75, 137, 140, 254
Mou Zongsan 牟宗三
  and Bosanquet, 162
  and Bradley, 18–19, 87, 89–93, 95–96, 105–10
  and British idealism, 4, 11, 13, 18–19, 51, 57, 89, 91, 96–97, 122, 125–26, 179, 275
  and Collingwood, 12, 181
  and Green, 13, 81, 23–24, 57, 62, 77–78, 82–83, 91, 125, 205, 212, 219, 236, 240, 246, 260–61, 263, 272, 275
  and Hegel, 3–4, 11, 17–19, 27–28, 50–57, 61–62, 81, 85–87, 91–92, 95, 99, 115–26, 130–33, 136–39, 164, 187, 212, 259, 263–64, 269–70, 275, 278, 288n3, 341n64
  and Heidegger, 28, 97, 291n65, 292n70
  and Kant, 4, 11–12, 17, 19, 27–28, 31–38, 51–53, 79, 83–85, 96, 187, 191, 230, 278, 291n51, 291n65, 292n70, 305n39
  Lishi zhexue (Philosophy of History), 134, 282n11
  and Oakeshott, 12, 181
  Xianxiang yu wuzishen (Phenomena and Noumena), 135
  Zhengdao yu zhidao (The Way of Politics and the Way of Governance), 135, 282n11
Murray, John C., 249
mutual
  recognition, 235, 255, 271–72, 274
  respect. *See* respect
  understanding, 2, 84, 277

Neo-Confucianism, Song-Ming, 5, 37–38, 40, 48, 61, 95, 322n135, 334n59
"establishing the reality of morality and erecting the ultimate ideal" (*jianti liji*), 95

"hear-and-see knowing" (*jian wen zhi zhi*) and "virtuous knowing" (*dexing zhi zhi*), 37, 46, 290n50
"illuminating the heart-mind and finding the Xing-nature" (*mingxin jianxing*), 61, 95
"learning of the principles of Xing-nature" (*xingli zhi xue*), 81
New Confucianism (*Xinrujia*)
  and "blossoming of democracy," 267
  and British idealism, 2, 11–13, 22, 58, 62, 86, 89, 90, 101, 110, 122, 124–25, 176–77, 214, 241, 259
  and contemporary Confucian political theory, 3, 13–19, 21
  and Hegelian liberalism, 2, 4–13, 145, 275
  and "learning of the heart-mind and Xing-nature" (*xin xing zhi xue*), 81, 178
  legacy of, 3, 273
  and practice-based approach, 156, 321n121
  on religious aspect of Chinese culture, 59, 80
  significance of, 4–7
  and humanism, 59, 61, 178, 198, 260, 280, 296n8
  of Taiwan and Hong Kong, 1, 211, 279
  three generations of, 4–5
  "three unities" (*santong*)
    "knowledge of science" (*xuetong*), 5, 135
    "orthodoxy of Confucianism" (*daotong*), 5
    "politics of democracy" (*zhengtong*), 5, 148, 168, 180
"new outer kingliness" (*xin waiwang*), 6–8, 15, 168, 204, 207, 279

Oakeshott, Michael
  and Bradley, 93
  as British idealist, 11–12
  civitas cupiditatis, 234
  and Collingwood, 12, 145
  on freedom and individuality, 162, 167
  hypothesis-based approach, 154–56, 162, 317n49
  practice-based approach, 154–56, 181
  "*nomocracy*" and "*telocracy*," 156
  on *practice*, 152, 162–63
  on Rationalism, 151
  and Shils, 145, 318n65
  societas and *universitas*, 155–57
open society, 3, 8–9, 13, 22, 115, 122, 125, 141, 178, 186, 212–14, 217–22, 224, 228, 230–31, 242, 275, 278, 320n102
openness, 12, 22, 43, 217–19, 221–22, 232, 242

pan-liberalism, 213, 222, 228, 263
"panmoralism" (*fan daodezhuyi*), 23, 204, 213, 218, 222, 250
"pan-politicism" (*fan zhengzhizhuyi*), 150, 250
Pelikan, Jaroslav, 161
perfectionism. *See also* liberalism: perfectionist; state: perfectionist
  Confucian, 115, 217
  Confucian democratic, 15–16, 285n51, 286n58, 333n53
  Confucian meritocratic, 15, 285n51
  Confucian political, 14, 222
  individualist, 234–35
  liberal, 212, 331n1
  political, 212
personalism, 85, 104, 120, 199, 263
Plant, Raymond, 64

Plato, 11, 41
plurality, 22, 157, 167, 217–21, 242
Pocock, J. G. A., 10, 153, 160–61, 316n41
political meritocracy. *See* Confucian meritocracy
politics
 of civilization, 116–18
 of common good, 11, 243
 of individualism, 156
 of "innovation," 2, 8–9, 115–17, 119, 121, 123, 125, 127, 129, 131, 133, 135, 137, 139, 141, 168
 and morality, 15, 116, 139, 147, 211
  Hegelian reunification of, 121, 124, 132, 137–38, 190, 278
  indirect and specific relationship between, 21, 87, 125, 131, 134–35, 203–4, 218–19, 228
  Kant's view of, 266–67, 269
  liberal divorce of, 13, 86, 144, 150, 163, 180, 187, 190, 212, 248, 250, 307n1
  rigorous bond between, in Confucianism, 123, 175, 203
  transient separation between, in Mou's view, 21, 121, 124, 131–32, 137
 nonmoral concept of, 144, 157
 of rights, 11, 117, 268
 secular form of, 187
 of "virtue and talent" (*xianneng zhengzhi*), 146, 180, 312n7, 328n37. *See also* Confucian governing virtue: "rule by virtue"
Popper, Karl, 4, 115, 218, 320n102
post-Kantian, 12, 18, 50, 52–53, 57, 61, 84, 90–91, 96, 100–1, 111, 212, 275, 343n104
Pre-Qin Period, 5, 38

progressivism, 12, 21, 143, 166, 181, 321n112
public. *See also* common good
 good, 10, 20, 144, 163–64, 168, 180, 207, 275, 278
 norms, 10, 144, 151, 154, 157
 spirit, 21, 144, 156, 160, 168, 188, 268
 virtue, 8, 119, 125, 139–40, 144, 164, 168–69, 178–79, 181, 191–92, 268

Qi 啟, 193–94

Rawls, John
 on democratic political culture, 16
 on duty of civility, 157, 165
 on Hegel and liberal tradition, 18, 116, 270
 Political Liberalism, 132
 and priority of the right over the good, 266, 268
 and rights-based liberalism, 10, 155, 180, 266–67
Reformation, 68, 120
ren (humaneness, benevolence). *See also* Confucius
 as Absolute Spirit, 80, 94–95
 actualization of, in a democratic society, 122, 124–25, 133, 173, 177, 187–88, 214
 Chan Wing-Tsit on, 79
 Cheng Zhongying on, 82, 110
 and Confucian forms of life, 21, 189
 heart-mind of, 43, 47, 89, 171–72, 177, 188, 197, 200, 260
 as highest virtue, 78–79, 171
 and humanity and dignity, 77–78, 119, 145, 177, 260
 and *li*, 38, 172
 as moral grounding of democracy, 133, 207

as moral ideal of liberalism, 213, 223–31
Mou's Hegelian reading of, 79–81, 83–84, 94–95, 104–5, 119–20, 137–38, 260
objectification of, 83–84, 103, 105
as "perfect good," 90
political presentation of
"treating a human being as a human" (*ba ren dang ren*), 178
"rooted global philosophy" of, 13, 188
spirit of, 2, 22, 115–16, 121–22, 131, 145, 177, 189, 197, 200–1, 203, 205, 207, 213, 260
as true freedom, 120, 259–61
as "way of *zhongshu*," 22, 213
ren-reality (*renti*), 80
republicanism, 23, 164, 166, 188, 277
respect, 6, 10, 22, 30, 96–97, 100, 104, 155–57, 163–65, 169–70, 174–75, 178–80, 196, 198, 201, 213, 222, 224, 228–30, 236, 238, 241, 243, 254, 264, 266, 277, 317n50, 320n109
rights
and citizen, 166, 178, 257
and Confucian forms of life, 205
Confucian theory of, 261, 270
in Confucianism, lack of, 123, 177, 202, 221, 247, 261, 268, 273
criticized by antiliberal Confucianism, 24, 247, 270
and culture, 247, 267–70
and duties, 214–16, 220, 232, 234–35, 241–42, 263–64, 306n56, 335n90
equal, 166, 178
Green's view of, 232–34, 257
having, 24, 219, 232, 271
human, 9, 213, 219, 228, 245, 250, 272–74

individual, 146, 148
justification of, 23, 24, 245, 267–74
in the Chinese context, 245, 247, 270, 273–74
and law, 138, 261
Mou on, 259–61
natural, 10, 24, 126, 231, 237, 268–73
and negative freedom, 23, 150–51, 246, 249, 257, 260–61, 264, 271
and office of state, 23, 74, 232–34, 242
of others, 166, 266, 269
political, 147, 166, 202, 271–72, 274, 309n25
and political subject, 20, 343n112
as powers, 257, 271–72
recognition, 24, 58, 62, 126, 261–62, 270–74, 279, 343n112. *See also* Green: rights recognition thesis
social, 166
and society, 237, 268, 271
as trumps, 10, 266, 272
Ritchie, D. G., 103
Robertson, William, 153
Rorty, Richard, 9, 167
Rousseau, Jean-Jacques, 19, 160, 188, 219, 256, 259, 270, 289n19, 295n127
rule of law, 9, 123, 144, 146–47, 156, 174, 184, 186, 191, 206–8, 215, 242, 269
Russell, Bertrand, 32
Ryan, Alan, 9

Sandel, Michael, 162
Schelling, Friedrich Wilhelm Joseph, 50, 52
Schwartz, Benjamin, 145

388 | Index

self. *See also* subject
  alienation of, 118
  atomistic, 103, 227
  authentic, 61, 81–85
  Christian, in Green, 68
  and community, 74–75, 104, 111, 252, 268–69
  disembodied, 269
  disencumbered, 162
  disengaged, 30, 269
  embodied, 227, 235, 239
  emotivist, 162
  empirical, 49, 107, 239
  expressionist, 162
  ideal, 17, 33, 57, 73–74, 79, 83–84, 104, 107–8
  and the infinite whole, 20, 58, 90, 105–7
  isolated, 239
  Kantian, 62, 97
  moral, 20, 30, 49, 57, 74, 102, 104, 107, 239, 297n12
  and other selves, 105–6, 202, 226, 243, 337n128
  private, 106
  real, 80–81, 104–5, 107
  social, 11, 20, 102–4, 105–6
  true, 55, 70–75, 77, 89, 104, 239, 241, 248, 300n60
self-cultivation, 83, 104, 106, 111, 229
self-determination, 67, 84, 137, 248, 250–52, 256, 258–59, 295n127. *See also* autonomy
"self-negation" (*ziwo kanxian*). *See also ziwo kanxian*
  and "blossoming of democracy," 55, 123, 131–36, 217, 276
  contrasted with "self-restriction," principle of, 139–40, 217, 276
  disparity between moral metaphysics and political philosophy, 125
  of "goodness of *Xing*-nature," 173
  as Hegelian terminology, 18, 20, 28, 46, 51–52, 122, 132–33, 173, 270, 276
  of *liangzhi*, 61
  of moral subject, 131
  process of, 134–36
  separation between subjectivity and objectivity, 130
  of "universal subjectivity," 130
self-perfection, 87, 102, 108, 127, 198, 233–34, 239–40
self-realization. *See* ethics of self-realization
"self-restriction" (*ziwoxianzhi*), principle of
  "capacity of the subject" (*zhuti zhi neng*), 180, 200
  and Confucian *res publica*, 217, 270, 276
  definition of, 139–40, 169
  and "heart-mind of morality" (*daode de xin*), 171, 177, 180
  and "humane government," 22, 139, 141, 187, 276
  limits on the abuse of power, 200–3, 206–7, 216–17
  "stepping aside, spreading out, and leaving things as they are" (*rangkai sankai, wu gefu wu*), 140, 180, 192, 196–98, 200, 203, 221, 330n71
  and "way of *zhongshu*," 169, 176, 192, 200–3, 224
Shang dynasty, 38, 194
Shen 參, 223
Shils, Edward
  on civic virtue, 165, 181
  on civil politics, 156–57
  and Oakeshott, 145, 318n65
  on radical "progressivism," 166, 321n112

on tradition and traditionalism, 161–62, 319n83
Virtue of Civility, 156
Shklar, Judith, 64
Shun 舜, 193–95, 197, 225
Simhony, Avital, 235, 255–56
Sinopoli, Richard C., 155
Sittlichkeit, 83, 94–95, 103, 105, 119, 155, 163, 344n1. *See also* ethical life
  contrasted with *Moralität*, 67, 75, 137, 140, 254
skepticism, 64, 156, 321n121
Smith, Adam, 153
Socrates, 120
Song dynasty, 38, 40, 198, 290n50, 322n135
sovereignty, 56, 123, 129, 190–91, 195, 269
Spencer, Herbert, 102
Spring and Autumn Annals (Chunqiu), 80, 203, 327n16
Spring and Autumn Period, 195, 296
St. Paul, 64
"standard viewpoint," 2–3, 6, 149, 203, 250, 276
state
  double meaning of, 214, 231–32, 242
  interference, 122, 126, 258–59
  office of, 74, 233–34, 242, 258
  perfectionist, 213, 215–18, 220, 230, 242, 263
  power, 213, 241–42
Stoicism, 64
subject (-ivity). *See also* self
  disengaged
    Taylor on, 67, 162
  embodied
    in British idealists, 102, 104, 163
    in Hegel, 55–57, 116, 119, 121, 163, 275, 277

and personalism, 85
Taylor on, 55, 85, 119
moral, 18, 20, 27–28, 30, 32, 38–39, 46, 50, 53, 55, 62, 73, 76, 81–82, 89, 95–96, 102, 110, 121, 123–25, 127–28, 131, 134–35, 170, 173, 223, 228, 267–69, 275, 343n104
political, 20, 22, 28, 46, 121, 123–25, 127–28, 131–35, 140, 169, 173, 175, 177–78, 183, 206, 216, 260–61, 267
summum bonum, 33, 35–37, 46–47. *See also* highest good

Taiwan, 1, 149, 157, 211, 279, 314n23
Tan Sor-Hoon 陳素芬, 15
Tang Junyi 唐君毅
  and Bradley, 18, 89–94, 287n67
  on British idealism, 11, 87, 89, 91, 261–62, 287n67
  on Confucian democracy, 308n25, 310n45
  on Confucian religiousness, 61, 80, 296n8
  and ethics of self-realization, 110
  on freedom, 260–61, 341n74
  and Hegel, 11, 18, 91, 100, 287n67, 296n8
  on highest principle of liberalism, 263
  on "immanent transcendence," 297n12
  influenced by Xiong Shili, 5
  and Kant, 91, 287n67
  as New Confucian, 5–6, 260, 280
  on "reconciliatory dialectic," 18, 89–95
Tang 湯, 195
Taylor, Charles
  and communitarianism, philosophical, 74, 231

Taylor, Charles (*continued*)
  on formalist theory, 267
  and forms of liberalism, 9, 167
  and Green, 74, 253, 255
  on Hegel, 65–66, 116–17, 185, 253, 298n19, 298n25, 325n5
  on human constants, 281n2
  on Kant, 67, 162, 289n19
  as liberal republican, 23, 231
  on primacy-of-right theories, 266, 268
thing-in-itself (things-in-themselves), 14, 29, 44, 54, 73, 82, 90
Tocqueville, Alexis de, 149, 164, 185, 248, 318n68
tolerance, 9, 22, 164–65, 169, 180, 213, 222, 224, 227–29, 320n109
totalitarianism, 23, 53, 140, 150, 214–15, 231, 246, 248–49, 251, 254, 257, 259, 262
Toynbee, Arnold, 69
Tu Weiming 杜維明, 5, 83, 286n60, 301n89

utilitarianism. *See also* Bradley:
    "pleasure for pleasure's sake"
  Benthamite, 236, 238
  Bradley on, 58, 90, 93, 96–97
  "greatest happiness for the greatest members," 234, 236–37
  Green's criticism of, 236–38, 305n33
  hedonism, 103, 234
  and Kantianism, synthesis of, 97, 102, 235, 240–41, 305n33
  as liberal theory, 84, 126, 231
  "oppression of the weaker by the stronger," 237–38, 241, 243

Vincent, Andrew, 68
Voltaire, 153

Wang Fuzhi 王夫之, 195, 204, 221–22

Wang Yangming 王陽明, 5, 34, 40, 45, 83, 106
Warring States Period, 146, 195
"way of governance" (*zhidao*). *See also* "humane government"
  and Confucian democratic civility, 8, 10, 21, 121, 143, 180, 276, 279
  and Confucian forms of life, 121, 125, 133, 178, 184
  and Confucian governing and civic virtues, 11, 21, 121, 140, 179, 212
  and Confucian public virtue, 8, 140, 178
  and Confucian *res publica*, 8, 11, 203, 217, 279
  core principles of, 177, 179, 191–92, 212, 217
  definition of, 7–8, 140
  and "functional presentation of reason" (*lixing zhi yunyong biaoxian*), 7, 123, 127, 133, 189, 221
  as "governing democracy" (*zhigquan de minzhu*), 191–92, 194–95, 207
  and "governing the people," 139, 174
  as "governing power" (*zhiquan*), 8, 190, 206, 278
  and "humane government," 7, 10, 121, 141, 180, 184, 211–12, 279
  and "inaction" (*wuwei*), 133, 175, 198
  as "intensional meaning of democracy" (*minzhu zhi neirong de yiyi*), 8, 191, 204–5, 207
  and "kingly way," 190
  liberal aspects of, 140, 217
  and "moral achievement," 195
  political failure of, 191
  and *ren*-centered standpoint, 180

and "self-restriction," principle of, 133, 139, 141
and "Sub-Ordination" (*lishu guanxi*), 7, 127, 215
and "synthetic spirit of the fulfillment of reason" (*zonghe de jinli zhi jingshen*), 131
tradition of, 121
"way of politics" (*zhengdao*)
as "aloof form" (*chaoran de xingshi*), 120
and "analytic spirit of the fulfillment of reason" (*fenjie de jinli zhi jingshen*), 131
and "blossoming of democracy," 141, 180, 276
in Confucianism, lack of, 218
and "constructive presentation of reason" (*lixing zhi jiagou biaoxian*), 7, 123, 127, 131–35, 138, 189, 195, 217, 221
and "Co-Ordination" (*duilie guanxi*), 7, 127, 215
definition of, 7–8, 190
as "extensional meaning of democracy" (*minzhu zhi waiyan de yiyi*), 7–8, 191, 195, 205–6
as "formal concept" (*xingshi gainian*), 190, 193
and legitimacy of political authority, 120, 190
and liberal institutions and values, 7, 9, 14, 21, 140, 143, 184, 190, 211, 214–17
modernity of, 121
moral weakness of, 191
and "new outer kingliness," 135
novelty of, 8, 168, 180, 214, 276
as "political democracy" (*zhengquan de minzhu*), 140–41, 191–92, 195–96, 199, 203–5, 207, 278
as "political power" (*zhengquan*), 8, 190, 206

and "political subject," 140
"providing the people's life with an entrustment" (*wei shengmin li ming*), 280
as "sphere of treatment" (*duidai lingyu*), 215
and "spirit of seeking political achievement" (*shigong jingshen*), 195
and "subjective freedom," rise of, 178
and "way of governance"
Hegelian synthesis of, 9, 17, 21, 124, 168, 179, 184, 211, 213, 242
separation between, 7–8, 124–26, 190–91
"way of *zhongshu*" (*zhongshu zhi dao*). See also *ren*
as Confucian civic virtue, 169, 179, 217, 222–31
as Confucian governing virtue, 169, 200–3, 217
Confucius on, 223–24, 227
and "the end in itself," formula of, 239, 243
as highest principle of politics, 230
and human dignity, 273
as "inner life" of democratic life, 322n5
as a liberal theory of common good, 222
as *ren*, spirit of, 22, 213
and "self-restriction," principle of, 169, 176, 192, 200–3, 224
shu as an other-regarding virtue, 223
"being lenient toward others" (*kuan yi dairen*), 140, 176, 179–80, 192, 200, 202–3, 223
"doing unto others as you would have them do unto you" (*tuiji*), 225
"putting oneself in another person's place" (*tuiji jiren*), 225

"way of *zhongshu*" (*continued*)
   zhong as a self-regarding virtue, 225
      "being strict with oneself" (*yan yi luji*), 140, 176, 179–80, 192, 200, 203, 223
      "making the most out of oneself" (*jinji*), 225
Western-centric, 1, 118, 144, 149, 151, 157, 184, 188, 208, 247, 268, 307n1
Westernization, 144, 148–49, 163, 276
William of Malmesbury
   Deeds of the Kings of the English, 152

Xia dynasty, 38, 194
Xing-reality (*xingti*), 35, 43–44, 51, 54, 86, 136, 170
Xiong Shili 熊十力, 4–6
Xu Fuguan 徐復觀
   on Confucian democracy, 6, 187–88, 280, 332n5
   on "cultivating oneself" and "governing the people," 6, 21, 174, 177, 191, 221
   on "cultivation of civility" (*li de taoye*), 178
   on "cultural cultivation," 216
   on duality of subjectivity, 174–77
   on Heaven, 296n8, 324n166
   on *li*, 171–72, 174, 176
   on liberalism, 177, 259, 263
   as New Confucian, 5, 259, 280
   on "principle of the people as fundamental" (*minben zhuyi*), 174–77
   on rights, 259
   on "rule by virtue," 328n37
Xunzi. See also *Xunzi*
   and authentic Confucianism, 170–71
   and Confucius, 146, 170, 173, 326n13
   on "deliberate effort" (*wei*), 170, 322n130
   on "depravity of man's sociality," 170–71, 322n128
   "entire body is ritual propriety and righteousness" (*tongti shi li yi*), 172
   "heart-mind of intelligence" (*lizhi de xin*), 171
   "heart-mind of knowing" (*renshi de xin*), 171
   "inclusive" understanding of *li*, 145, 168–69, 172, 180
   and Legal School, 175, 324n166
   and Mencius, 146, 169–77, 312n7, 325n185, 326n13
   "modifying humanity through the heart-mind (*yi xin zhi xing*), 170
   and objective spirit, 123, 172–74
   on "origin of power" (*quan yuan*), 174–75
   and political Confucianism, 327n16
   on "rule by *li*" (*lizhi*), 146, 174
Xunzi, 327n16

Yao 堯, 193–95, 197, 225
Yi 益, 193
Yi Commentaries (*Yi Zhuan*), 38–40
Yi Yin 伊尹, 193
Yin Haiguang 殷海光, 13, 85, 149–50, 167, 250
Yu 禹, 193, 195
Yu Yingshi 余英時, 5, 280

Zengzi 曾子, 39, 223, 226–27
Zhang Foquan 張佛泉
   as anti-Confucian liberal, 13, 149
   and Berlin, 150, 245–50, 260, 337n1
   and Bosanquet, 250

Index | 393

and British idealists, 249–50,
    337n1, 338n21
on dignity, 150–51, 250
and Green, 246, 249, 337n1
on freedom
    negative, 150, 245, 248–50
    positive, 248–50, 337n1, 338n13
on rights, 249–50
and Yin Haiguang, 13, 149–50,
    167, 250
Ziyou yu renquan (Liberty and
    Human Rights), 145, 245, 248–49
Zhang Hao 張灝, 85, 104
Zhang Junmai 張君勱, 5, 59, 263
Zhang Zai 張載, 45, 229, 345n4
Zhou Cezong 周策縱, 148

Zhou dynasty, 38, 194, 296n8
Zhou 紂, 193, 195, 329n51
Zhu Xi 朱熹
    Collected Annotations of the Analects
        (*Lunyu jizhu*), 334n63
    on *de* (virtue), 170
    "secondary son installed as clan
        master" (*biezi weizong*), 40
    on "way of *zhongshu*," 225
Zigong 子貢, 225
Zilu 子路, 48, 227
ziwo kanxian
    translated as "self-negation," in
        Mou's gloss, 123, 132, 135
    translated as "self-restriction,"
        132–34, 310n46

www.ingramcontent.com/pod-product-compliance
Lightning Source LLC
Chambersburg PA
CBHW020120240426
43673CB00038B/539